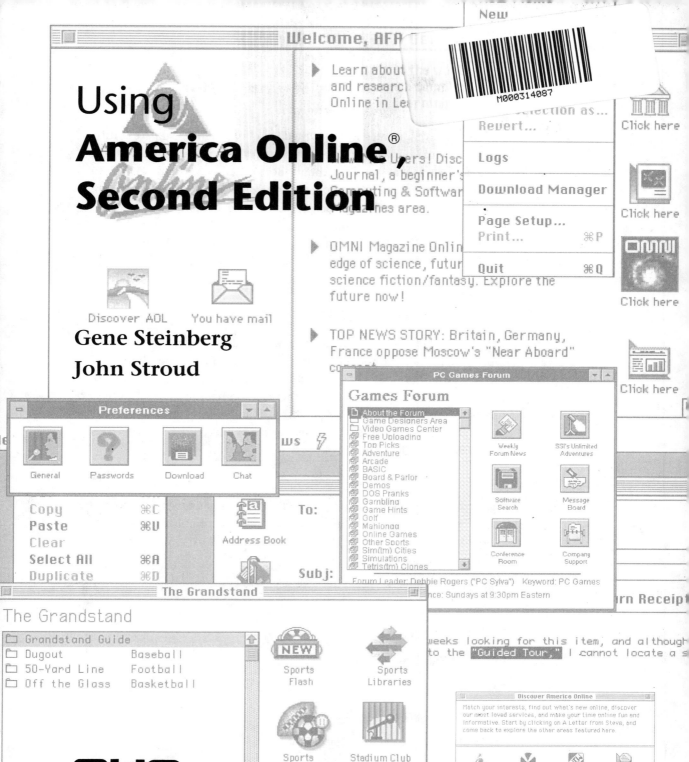

Using America Online, Second Edition

Copyright© 1994 by Que® Corporation

Library of Congress Catalog No.: 94-69590

ISBN: 1-7897-0078-6

97   96   95   94   6   5   4   3   2   1

Interpretation of the printing code: the rightmost double-digit number is the year of the book's printing; the rightmost single-digit number, the number of the book's printing. For example, a printing code of 94-1 shows that the first printing of the book occurred in 1994.

Using America Online is based on Version 2.5 for Macintosh and Version 1 for Windows.

Publisher: David P. Ewing

Associate Publisher: Stacy Hiquet

Associate Publisher—Operations: Corinne Walls

Publishing Director: Brad R. Koch

Managing Editor: Michael Cunningham

Associate Product Marketing Manager: Stacy Collins

Credits

Publishing Manager
Thomas H. Bennett

Acquisitions Editor
Cheryl D. Willoughby

Product Director
Stephanie Gould

Production Editor
Judy J. Brunetti

Technical Editor
Kim Tedrow

Figure Specialist
Cari Ohm

Book Designer
Amy Peppler-Adams

Cover Designer
Dan Armstrong

Acquisitions Assistant
Ruth Slates

Production Team
Stephen Adams
Don Brown
Stephen Carlin
DiMonique Ford
Karen Gregor
Aren Howell
Daryl Kessler
Bob LaRoche
Beth Lewis
Malinda Lowder
Erika Millen
G. Alan Palmore
Kaylene Riemen
Michael Thomas
Jody York

Indexer
Rebecca Mayfield

Operations Coordinator
Patricia J. Brooks

Editorial Assistant
Andrea Duvall

Composed in *Stone Serif* and *MCPdigital* by Que Corporation

About the Authors

Gene Steinberg is an inveterate desktop computer user who first joined America Online in 1989. He quickly became addicted to the new online service and finally earned positions on its computing forum staff. At present, he is Forum Leader of the service's Macintosh Multimedia Forum and Curator of The Gallery, a portrait library for America Online members.

In his regular life, Gene has worked at several occupations. He first studied broadcasting in school and then worked for a number of years as a disc jockey and newscaster. Gene is now a full-time writer and Macintosh software and systems consultant. His published work includes *Using the Macintosh, Special Edition* from Que Publishing and feature articles and product reviews for *Macworld*.

John Stroud has been involved with online services since 1978 and with America Online since 1989. Realizing that he found a place he could call his home away from home, John quickly was inducted into the staff ranks of America Online as a Forum Assistant in the Macintosh Communications Forum. In 1990, he became Forum Leader for the Macintosh Utilities Forum and, after joining Apple Computer's System 7 Answerline, moved to the Macintosh Operating Systems Forum in November 1991.

John lives with his family in the San Francisco area and has been working in the computer industry in one fashion or another for 15 years, including such employers as Eastman Kodak, Ziff-Davis, and Apple Computer. His current "day job" is with Oracle Corporation, where he works as a systems administrator. His published work includes primarily ghost-written material about Macintosh and cross-platform networking.

Acknowledgments

Writing a book is something necessarily done in isolation, one person at a time at a single keyboard. But behind a book is often the work of many individuals, without whose efforts the words would never be written.

Foremost among these individuals is David Liberman, Producer for Computing & Software at America Online. David has not only become a good friend, but he has appointed me to positions as a Remote Staff member for America Online, affording me a huge virtual playground in which to travel and have fun. I also give thanks to America Online's Betsy Davison, Ken Huntsman, Matt Korn, Ann Kort, and Pam McGraw for giving me special insights into the history of the service and its state-of-the-art system architecture. America Online's Jeff Langley was instrumental in helping to provide information and illustrations on the service's updated Windows software. I'd also like to thank America Online remote staffers Jennifer Watson and George Louie for their assistance in compiling this book's glossary and Daniel Fishbach for helping to maintain an up-to-date list of the service's keyword shortcuts.

I am also grateful to America Online's Tim Barwick and my friend and co-writer John Stroud for getting me involved in America Online's forums to begin with.

I must give special praise to the team at Que Corporation for putting up with my many eccentricities and for allowing me a great deal of latitude in outlining and writing this book. They include (in alphabetical order) Tom Bennett, Judy Brunetti, Stephanie Gould, Ruth Slates, and Cheryl Willoughby. Que's dedicated, fearless technical editor, Kim Tedrow, deserves to be singled out for pouring through every written word and every illustration to verify that it was absolutely correct to the last, minute detail.

And last, I wish to offer a heartfelt, loving thank you to my wonderful, beautiful wife Barbara and my extraordinary son Grayson for putting up with the long hours I spent chained to the front of my computer so that my work could be done on schedule.

Gene Steinberg

Trademark Acknowledgments

We'd Like to Hear from You!

As part of our continuing effort to produce books of the highest possible quality, Que would like to hear your comments. To stay competitive, we *really* want you, as a computer book reader and user, to let us know what you like or dislike most about this book or other Que products.

You can mail comments, ideas, or suggestions for improving future editions to the address below, or send us a fax at (317) 581-4663.

Thanks in advance—your comments will help us to continue publishing the best books available on computer topics in today's market.

Thomas H. Bennett
Publishing Manager
Que Corporation
201 W. 103rd Street
Indianapolis, IN 46290

Contents at a Glance

Setting Up

Getting Your Feet Wet

Having Fun

Info at Your Fingertips

Information Superhighway

Online Productivity

Appendixes

Contents

3 Using Your America Online Windows Software   59

6 Meeting People Online   117

7 Communicating with Others   137

III Having Fun   167

8 The Entertainment Chapter   169

9 Lifestyles & Interests   193

12 How to Find Software — 261

13 Learning & Reference — 273

VI Online Productivity   369

19 Saving Time and Money   371

20 Getting Help   379

VII Appendixes   397

A America Online Keywords   399

B Glossary   429

Index   445

Introduction

When a devastating earthquake struck southern California in early 1994, many residents found themselves cut off from relatives and friends. Telephone lines were clogged as callers worldwide tried to learn of the health and welfare of those they knew in the affected area.

Amidst all the chaos and tragedy, the dream of Vice President Albert Gore for a nationwide information superhighway showed the beginnings of becoming a reality. While the major television networks interspersed information about the earthquake between soap operas and titillating talk shows, one of America's fastest growing online services, America Online, provided up-to-the-minute status reports on how California residents were impacted by this major tragedy.

America Online's electronic mail service was also an information conduit for people to get in touch with their loved ones when all other methods of communication failed. With just a computer and a modem at hand, the clogged telephone lines somehow didn't make quite as much of a difference—especially when those messages brought a response.

Reviewing the History of America Online

The dream of an information superhighway wasn't even a glimmer in the Vice President's eye in 1985, when America Online was founded as Quantum Computer Services. In that year, the Apple Macintosh was just a low-powered niche computer, and Microsoft Windows didn't exist. But the Commodore computer was king, and a new, easy-to-use, and affordable telecommunications service was established. It was called *Q-Link*.

Q-Link might best be compared to a national Bulletin Board Service (or BBS), where computer owners can communicate with one another. Members with a specific interest, such as a special type of software, can congregate in a single meeting place called a *forum*. Members can meet for interactive conversations called *chats*.

From this humble beginning, support was added for other computer platforms, such as Apple II and Tandy's DeskMate. The Apple Macintosh and IBM PCs and compatibles soon followed.

Today America Online is a publicly owned company that offers an online community for well over a million members. The service offers online shopping, information services such as daily newspapers and magazines, and even virtual reference books such as encyclopedias.

But just as important, if not more so, America Online is like a huge city, with many people hanging out and communicating with one another on a host of subjects, from the time of day and the weather to the state of the nation and the world. The online experience is unlike any you've ever seen. After you have been introduced to America Online, you'll undoubtedly want to stick around.

Understanding What America Online Is

Take that description of a huge city a bit further to its logical conclusion. In addition to all those people, you can find neighborhoods, highways, byways, stores, markets, libraries, and schools. You interact with that community from your own computer and modem, using America Online's unique graphical interface, which transports you from one place to another when you click on an icon or type a simple keyboard command.

But behind that easy-to-use technology is a huge network of micro- and mini-computers storing many gigabytes of data, linked to the outside world by advanced fiber-optic telephone cables.

Looking at Not Just a Pretty Face

Bear with me for a moment as I give you a few insights into the state-of-the-art equipment that resides in two rooms at America Online's headquarters in Vienna, Virginia. It is a truly advanced setup.

America Online's computers are built on the client-server model with a peer-to-peer application architecture. Their systems consist of Stratus RISC processors running the VOS operating system, Hewlett-Packard RISC processors running the UNIX operating system, and PCs running DOS or OS/2. All these computers are interconnected by high-speed networks. Using a technique called *distributed processing,* they can share information-handling tasks, resulting in extremely fast data processing, enabling thousands of simultaneous transactions. This capability means that thousands of America Online members can log on to the network at the same time without any loss in system performance.

America Online's computer rooms are each cooled to a constant 70 degrees with low humidity. If a power outage occurs (which has happened occasionally), America Online has a battery backup system that provides full power to the system for a short time, until a diesel generator kicks on and continues to supply juice to keep the computers running. The generator can run up to 72 hours between fill-ups, which is more than enough time to replenish fuel or for power to be restored.

Each day, all the files on America Online's huge rigid drives are backed up. Backups are moved off site, so America Online's huge store of data is always protected in case of an emergency.

Understanding How Your Computer Links with America Online

Connecting with America Online is something you can do with a single click of the mouse, but behind that simple action is a complex process of data transfers and computer processing.

You hook up with America Online with two electronic boxes: your computer and a little device called a *modem*. The modem is itself a small computer that converts a stream of digital ones and zeros into audible tones that are fed through telephone lines and received by another modem at a remote location.

When you first dial up America Online (see fig. 1), your software dials a local telephone number that connects your computer to a modem on what is called a PAD (packet assembler/disassembler) in the public data network. This PAD, owned and operated by a packet carrier company such as SprintNet or Tymnet, is called a *node*.

A *node* can be described as a collection of modems that can handle many connections from computers like yours at one time. These local nodes ensure that users who live far away from America Online's host computers don't have to pay long distance phone charges for access to the America Online network.

Requesting Network Attention

When your modem dials the local access number, the modem negotiates a connection with the node. Those blips, burps, and squeals that emanate from your modem (if the sound is turned on, of course) describe a process called *handshaking*. Your modem is adjusting its speed and method of communication to the remote modem.

After the connection is established, you receive a message on your computer about it, as shown in figure 2.

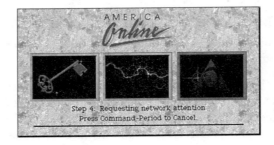

Talking to the Network

The next step is to tell the node who you are and whom you want to call. At this point, your software sends the address to the America Online host computer (see fig. 3), saying something like, "Hey, I'm an America Online member. Can you connect me?"

Fig. 3
The third stage
of hooking up
to America Online
is identifying
yourself.

Connecting to America Online

After the carrier service knows the host computer to which you want to connect, the service dials up America Online's host computers by the fastest method possible (see fig. 4). This setup might change periodically depending on line conditions. But it all happens behind the scenes and takes mere seconds to accomplish.

Fig. 4
"Hey, there,
anybody home?"

When connection with America Online's host computers has been achieved, the next step is to knock on the front door.

Using Your Password

Before they admit you inside, America Online's host computers have to know who you are and whether you have an active account. Then the magic begins. In seconds, the host computers examine the records of over a million America Online members to confirm who you are and to check whether anybody else inside the online community is presently using the same account (see fig. 5).

Then the front door is opened, and you're welcomed into the sprawling but friendly online universe.

Fig. 5
"Hey, there, who
are you?"

Who Can Use This Book?

This book has been written for both the beginning America Online user and the seasoned traveler of the online community. If you've never logged on to a service like America Online before, you need to read the chapters in Parts I and II of this book before you make your first online connection. After you've begun to travel the sprawling online city, you can use the rest of this book as a reference for places to visit and things to do.

If you are already a member of America Online, this book helps you discover many parts of the service you've never visited before and resources you probably did not know were available. This book also provides special coverage of the newest versions of America Online's Macintosh and Windows software, and plans for expanding the network's Internet Center.

Getting Started

You can't become a member of the America Online community until you join America Online. In Chapter 1, "Getting Started on America Online," you learn how to begin. First, you learn how to order your America Online software (if you don't already have a copy), and then you learn how to set up your online mailing address and take a brief tour of the service.

Chapter 2, "Using Your America Online Macintosh Software," and Chapter 3, "Using Your America Online Windows Software," dissect both the Macintosh and Windows versions of America Online software and tell you how to use each of their features. Within a couple of hours, you'll become a first-class traveler in the online community.

Learning the Ropes

After you know how to install and use your America Online software, this book teaches you how to travel the online pathways more effectively.

In Chapter 4, "America Online on the Road," you learn how to stay in touch with America Online no matter where you travel in the U.S.A. In Chapter 5, "Finding Your Way around America Online," you take a brief tour of the service and discover many places you might want to revisit and explore at your leisure.

Because America Online's People Connection is an important part of the service, Chapter 6, "Meeting People Online," and Chapter 7, "Communicating with Others," are devoted to the techniques you need to know to write your own electronic mail, participate in real-time chats, and enjoy all the other communications services offered by America Online.

Chapter 8, "The Entertainment Chapter," covers sources for entertainment-related information, ranging from the world of show business to online game information.

The next seven chapters describe how you can locate the information you want on America Online. Chapter 9, "Lifestyles & Interests," covers everything from hobbies to special information areas you might want to visit often. Chapter 10, "Finding Information on America Online," covers the convenient online search features that are available. You learn how to find what you want to know when you don't know where to look.

Chapter 11, "Computing & Software," describes one of the most popular areas of America Online. You find out where you can learn to use your computer most effectively and how you can contact many of the major hardware and software manufacturers, online, to receive free technical support.

With tens of thousands of software files available to download on America Online, you need to read Chapter 12, "How to Find Software," so that you can learn how to find files in the categories that interest you, how to transfer those files to your computer, and how you can send files to America Online so that other members can share them, too.

Interactive education is described in Chapter 13, "Learning & Reference." You even learn how students can page an online teacher for help with homework and other problems.

In Chapter 14, "News, Magazines, and Business Information," you tour America Online's own newsstand and seek out sources of information that range from real estate listings to help at tax time.

You take a breather in Chapter 15, "The Shopping Chapter," where you learn how you can obtain information to help you with your next product purchase and how you can order many products from the comfort of your own computer, right on America Online.

Because shopping goes hand in hand with travel, Chapter 16, "The Travel Chapter," covers America Online's resources for travel information and shows you how you can easily make your own airline, hotel, and car rental reservations during your online visits.

This introduction has briefly covered the plans for the information superhighway, and Chapter 17, "The Internet Connection," explores it in more detail. You learn how to tap a global resource for information and discussion areas right from America Online.

In Chapter 18, "The Low-Down on Internet Newsgroups," you learn how to access thousands upon thousands of lively Internet discussion groups directly from America Online. This chapter tells you how to find these discussion groups, how to join them, and explains what "netiquette," the ground rules you need to know to participate in these groups, is all about.

Not only does this book deal with ways for you to save money by using America Online's resources the next time you buy a product, but Chapter 19, "Saving Time and Money," tells you how you can reduce your online charges as well.

After you've learned how to navigate the service and find the features you want to explore further, you might want to read Chapter 20, "Getting Help," in case something goes wrong. In that chapter, you learn how to solve common problems you might encounter, and discover where to seek free support on America Online in case you need additional help using the service.

Appendix A provides handy lists of America Online keywords you can use to access the myriad screens, forums, and services available, and Appendix B offers a glossary of terms with which you might not be familiar.

Shooting at a Moving Target

You should know at the outset that America Online, like a large city, is growing and changing constantly. You will find that the service's look and feel will develop and improve over time. Some of the places pictured in this book might look a little different on your screen, too. But the information in these pages will be useful for a long time as a guide to learning about America Online.

As you begin to explore the online community, keep this book at hand. When you have a question or want to learn more about a particular place, you can move directly to that chapter for the information you want.

We began writing this book as experienced America Online visitors. But as the writing progressed, we explored many of the nooks and crannies in the online city that we'd never visited before. The process has been a tremendous, rewarding learning experience.

The online community has, over the years, become our second home. Here we meet and interact with our friends and even conduct our business affairs. We have made deals and begun work projects with people whom we know only by E-mail.

Indeed, the dream of the information superhighway has, to us, become an up-close and personal reality, and we want you to share that dream, too. Let the pages that follow be your starting point on the road to a learning experience that might be unlike any other you've ever had.

Notes on the Second Edition

In the months since the first edition of *Using America Online* was published, the service has undergone huge changes. You've probably read an article about America Online in your local newspaper, or heard one of the many broadcast news stories about the service.

Hundreds of thousands of new members have joined America Online. Between the summer of 1993 and the summer of 1994, the service more than tripled in size. As of July 1994, America Online had over a million active accounts (many of which include two or more employees or family members, which means that the service has a potential audience of several million). Scores of new services were introduced, including a major expansion of America Online's Internet capability. Major alliances were announced with such major media centers as NBC, Simon & Schuster Publishing, *The New York Times,* Time-Warner, and others. Major new revisions of America Online's software have been released to members who use the Apple Macintosh or PCs running Microsoft Windows.

As a result of these changes, you'll find lots of new material in this book, including a complete guide to using America Online's latest software, and detailed coverage of many of the new features that have been added to the service.

The changes to America Online will continue unabated, but you'll see many of the outlines for these changes in the pages of this book. So join with us as we continue to explore the rapidly growing America Online superhighway.

Gene Steinberg

Scottsdale, Arizona

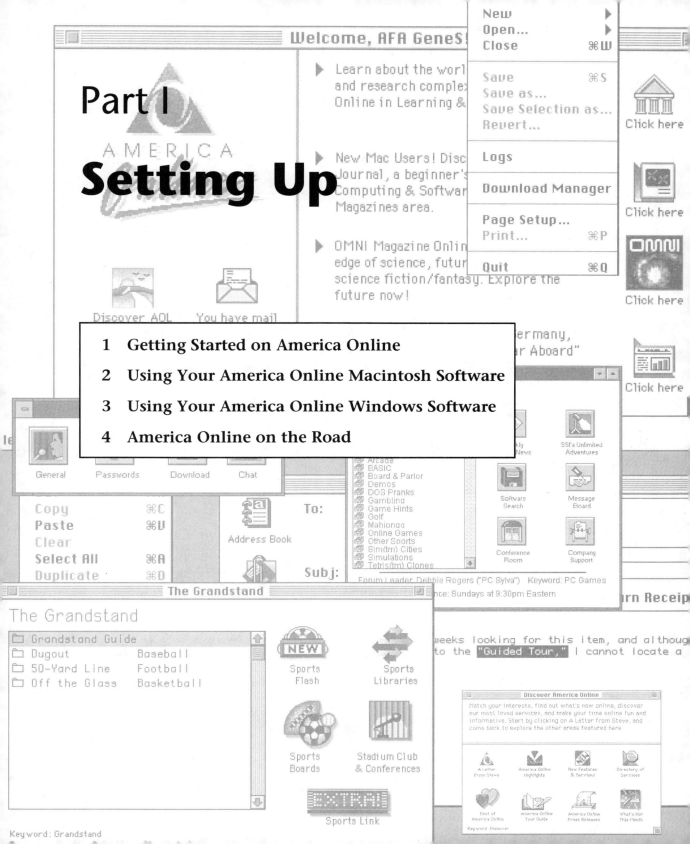

Part I

Setting Up

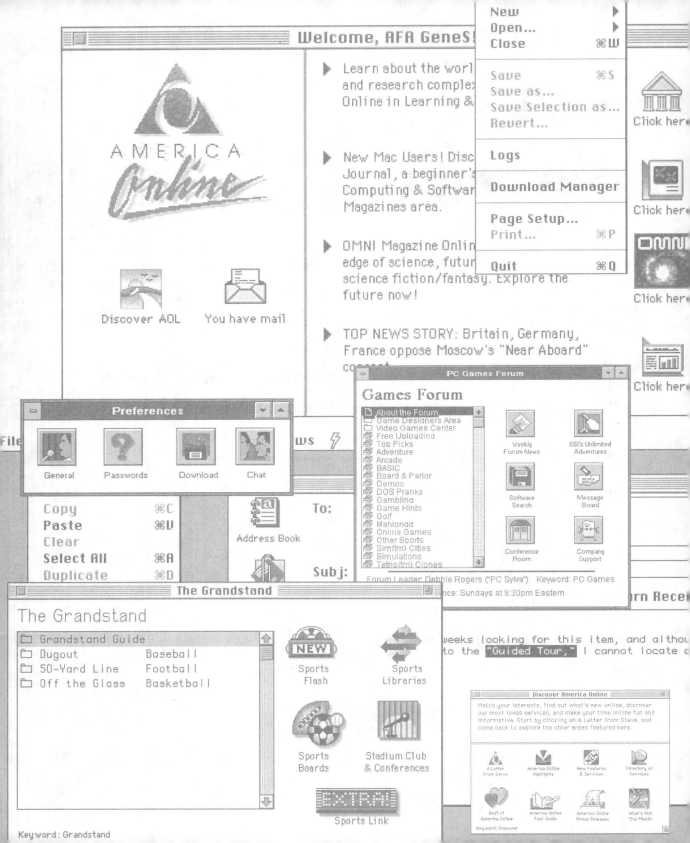

Welcome, AFA GeneS!

New ▶
Open... ▶
Close   ⌘W

Save   ⌘S
Save as...
Save Selection as...
Revert...

Logs

Download Manager

Page Setup...
Print...   ⌘P

Quit   ⌘Q

▶ Learn about the worl
and research comple
Online in Learning &

▶ New Mac Users! Disc
Journal, a beginner's
Computing & Softwar
Magazines area.

▶ OMNI Magazine Onlin
edge of science, futur
science fiction/fantasy. Explore the
future now!

▶ TOP NEWS STORY: Britain, Germany,
France oppose Moscow's "Near Aboard"

AMERICA Online

Discover AOL   You have mail

Click her
Click her
Click her
Click her

Preferences

General   Passwords   Download   Chat

Copy   ⌘C
Paste   ⌘V
Clear
Select All   ⌘A
Duplicate   ⌘D

ws

File

To:
Address Book
Subj:

PC Games Forum

Games Forum

About the Forum
Game Designers Area
Video Games Center
Free Uploading
Top Picks
Adventure
Arcade
BASIC
Board & Parlor
Demos
DOS Pranks
Gambling
Game Hints
Golf
Mahjongg
Online Games
Other Sports
Sim(tm) Cities
Simulations
Tetris(tm) Clones

Weekly Forum News   SSI's Unlimited Adventures

Software Search   Message Board

Conference Room   Company Support

Forum Leader Debbie Rogers ("PC Sylva")   Keyword: PC Games
nce: Sundays at 9:30pm Eastern

rn Rece

The Grandstand

The Grandstand

Grandstand Guide
Dugout   Baseball
50-Yard Line   Football
Off the Glass   Basketball

NEW
Sports Flash   Sports Libraries

Sports Boards   Stadium Club & Conferences

EXTRA!
Sports Link

Keyword: Grandstand

weeks looking for this item, and althou
to the "Guided Tour," I cannot locate

Discover America Online

Match your interests, find out what's new online, discover
our most loved services, and make your time online fun and
informative. Start by clicking an A Letter from Steve, and
come back to explore the other areas featured here.

A Letter From Steve   America Online Highlights   New Features & Services   Directory of Services

Best of America Online   America Online Tour Guide   America Online Press Releases   What's Hot This Month

Keyword: Discover

Chapter 1

Getting Started on America Online

Whether you are using an Apple Macintosh or a PC equipped with Windows, America Online software is easy to install and use. But despite the simplicity of these programs, they provide an extraordinary set of tools to make your online visits more productive and more fun.

In this chapter, you learn how to do the following:

- Order your America Online software

- Install the software

- Set up your online account

- Select your personal online mailing address

- Get acquainted quickly with the huge array of services

Before we tell you how to install your America Online software, we want to give you a couple of quick shortcuts to take you around the online community quickly and enable you to get direct online help if you need it.

The first shortcut we're going to describe is how to use a *keyword*. This is a keyboard command that you can specify *only* while you're connected to America Online. It will take you just about anywhere on America Online, even if you don't know the exact route.

To use keywords, press ⌘-K if you're using a Macintosh or Ctrl+K for Windows; then enter the keyword in the entry field of the Keyword dialog box displayed on your screen. Now press Return or Enter, and in just a few seconds, you'll be transported to the place you want to visit. (Of course, if the keyword is wrong, you'll get a message to that effect.) You'll learn more about keywords in Chapters 2 and 3.

Whenever you're logged on to America Online, you can visit an online support area to get direct assistance with any problem you might have, and it's free of charge. To get there, open the Members menu and select Member Services, or just type the keyword **Help**. A window will appear, asking whether you want to enter this free area.

Okay, now let's get ready to join the online community.

Ordering Your America Online Software

America Online disks are often given free with your new software or computer purchase. Some of your favorite computing magazines also include the software disks from time to time.

If you don't have a disk on hand, you can order one now by calling 1-800-827-6364. Please tell the operator the kind of computer you have so that you receive the correct software. You will get your disk in a couple of weeks. In the meantime, you can review this chapter and the next two about installing your software, establishing your personal online account, and mastering all aspects of the America Online program.

Even if you already have telecommunications software installed on your computer, America Online uses its own proprietary software to provide its unique graphic environment and efficient performance. You need America Online's special software to use the service. It does not work with a general-purpose terminal program.

Installing Your America Online Software

Installing both the Macintosh and Windows versions of America Online software are similar enough procedures that this section describes the steps in roughly the same way and provides illustrations to show the differences. The system requirements are similar, too.

Knowing What You Need

For a Macintosh, you need a Mac Plus or better, running System 6 or later, with 2M or more of installed RAM and at least 2M of free hard drive space.

Any IBM PC or compatible running Windows 3.0 or later should be able to use America Online for Windows software efficiently. You want to have several megabytes of free space on your hard drive to store your new software.

This book also assumes that you are comfortable performing the basic functions of using your computer, such as installing new software from a floppy disk onto your hard drive, performing basic file management chores, opening applications, and using your mouse. If you need a quick refresher course, review the instruction manuals that came with your computer or operating system disks.

Before you install the software, though, make a backup of your original floppy disk. (You should do this sort of thing with all your software and valuable disks.) Then lock the originals in a safe place, in case your copies are damaged.

Yes, you need one more thing, of course, and that is a Hayes-compatible modem with a speed of 2400 bps (bits per second) or greater. If you don't have a modem, you'll want to buy one at your favorite dealer. If you've never used a modem before, let me just briefly explain that a modem is a device that converts the digital information from your computer into analog tones that can be transferred through your telephone lines.

Because America Online has been rolling out its 14,400 bps service—and prices for high-speed modems have dropped—you'll want to buy the fastest model you can afford. You can expect even higher speeds to be supported by America Online in the future.

Installing the Macintosh Version

The Macintosh version of America Online's software is compressed—a technique used to make files smaller so that they take up less room. That way, the software can be supplied on a single 800K floppy disk.

After you've made a backup of your original software disk, you're ready to get the software up and running. Follow these steps:

1. Insert the floppy disk into your Macintosh's floppy drive.

2. Double-click on the America Online icon.

3. Click on the Continue button (see fig. 1.1).

Tip

Before proceeding with your software installation, have your software's registration certificate and your credit card or checkbook handy. Also be sure that your modem has been turned on and is hooked up to your computer and to your phone lines.

Setting Up

4. The program then asks you to select a destination on your hard drive for installation of your software. Your America Online software gets its own special folder. You can either accept the folder name it suggests or pick one of your own.

   After you've decided on the location for the new folder, the installation process continues. America Online keeps you informed of its progress, as shown in figure 1.2.

In a minute or two, you receive a message that the software has been successfully installed. If you have any problems at this point, read Chapter 20, "Getting Help," which contains helpful troubleshooting hints to get you started.

5. Now you can double-click on the AOL application icon to display the screen shown in figure 1.3. You then are guided through the steps needed to adjust the computer to your modem.

For the next few moments, you see several information windows (see fig. 1.4). As America Online software versions are upgraded, the displays might be different from the ones shown here. Just read the instructions carefully before proceeding. If you have any questions or problems, you can choose Cancel to cancel the installation, and resume it at a later time.

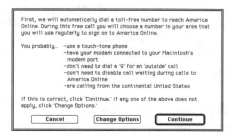

Fig. 1.4
This screen helps you get ready to make your first online connection.

If you've opted for the standard configuration profile, you are connected to America Online's host computer right away (see fig. 1.5).

Fig. 1.5
America Online software probes your modem for information about what it can do.

If you want to check or revise your modem profile, select the Change Options button and continue. If you have decided to change your options, you have a few more things to select:

1. Although the software has made a choice for you as to modem speed and the kind of modem profile it's using, you can change these setups to something you feel might provide better performance (see fig. 1.6). For most users, however, the default selection should work best.

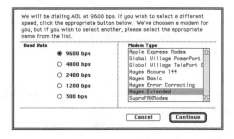

Fig. 1.6
You can change your modem setup on this screen.

2. When you decide to change your setup options, you are asked whether you want to install the option to disable Call Waiting service when you are online. If you have Call Waiting and someone tries to telephone you while you're online, the tones you hear in your telephone quickly terminate your online connection. You might have to check with your local telephone company, however, before choosing this option. Not all services give you the option of turning off Call Waiting for a single call.

3. If your online connections are being made from an office, you might have to dial a special number, usually 9, to get an outside line. So be sure to select this option if you need it; otherwise, you can't make your first online connection.

Installing the Windows Version

The Windows version of America Online software, like its Macintosh counterpart, is compressed—a technique used to make files smaller so that they take up less room. That way, the software can be supplied on a single floppy disk.

After you've made a backup of your original software disk, you're ready to get the software up and running. Follow these steps:

1. Insert the America Online floppy disk into your PC's floppy drive (A or B).

2. Using your Windows Program Manager, select Run from the File menu.

3. Depending on which floppy drive you inserted the disk in, type either **a:\install** or **b:\install**. Then press Enter (see figs. 1.7 and 1.8).

Fig. 1.7
America Online's software installation and setup is easy to follow.

Fig. 1.8
A progress bar shows the status of America Online for Windows' installation process.

4. When your installation is complete, you are returned to your Windows Program Manager. The AOL icon appears among your list of installed Windows applications. Double-click on this icon to open your America Online for Windows software.

5. As soon as the program opens, you're guided step-by-step through the process of setting up your America Online software to work with your modem and telephone. Before making a selection, read the instructions carefully. As America Online software is updated, the information you will read is likely to change.

6. If you decide to opt for a custom installation, you can select Other Options in your first setup window. If you have Call Waiting on the line to which your modem is hooked up, you need to use the option to disable that service so that you aren't knocked offline when a call comes in. Check with your local phone company about this option, though, because dial codes might differ. Some areas might not provide a way to disable Call Waiting.

7. When you are calling America Online from your office, you also might need to have your modem dial 9 or another access number to reach an outside line.

8. You also have the chance to choose the modem profile that best fits your needs—that is, if you decide not to accept the choices made by your software (see fig. 1.9). But if your modem isn't listed, your best bet is to stick with the profile the software chooses for you.

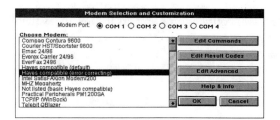

Fig. 1.9
Modem selections appear when you choose Other Options.

The steps for getting a local connection are similar enough in both the Mac and Windows installation, so they are described together in the next section.

Getting a Local Connection

Now you want to have America Online's host computer find a local connection number for you (see fig. 1.10). As soon as your modem setup has been completed, you are asked to enter your area code so that America Online can hook you up to the closest (and thus the cheapest) connection to your area.

Fig. 1.10
This screen appears when you're making your first connection.

The host computer searches its directory of access numbers for ones that match the area code you entered (see fig. 1.11). If you cannot locate a number that's in that area code, you have the option to choose another number from a nearby area code. Because America Online is always adding new connection numbers, you can always to change that number later. (See Chapter 5, "Finding Your Way around America Online," for more information about locating and changing your America Online access numbers.)

Fig. 1.11
Pick your first local access number.

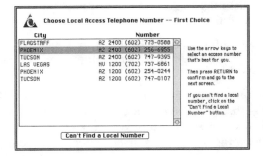

You should select two connection numbers if they are available. That way, if your modem cannot make a connection with the first number—perhaps because it's busy or because of line noise—you have a second chance to connect to America Online.

Establishing Your Online Account

From here on, until you log on to the service for the first time, you are guided through several steps that enable you to establish your own exclusive America Online account and set your billing options. (Now you find out why I suggested that you have handy the certificate that came with your software disks, and your credit card or checkbook.)

The choices you make now are not etched in stone. If you decide to change your password or billing information later, you can easily do so in the free Online Support area.

To establish your online account, follow these steps:

1. First, examine the registration numbers entered on the folder in which your America Online software was packaged. Enter the certificate number and certificate passwords in the blank Certificate Number and Certificate Passwords boxes (see fig. 1.12). You can use the Tab key on your computer's keyboard to move from one entry field to the next.

2. Choose the Continue button.

3. Enter your name, mailing address, and telephone number.

4. Choose the Continue button.

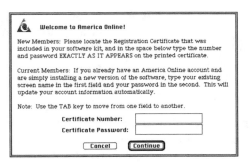

Fig. 1.12
Use this screen to
set up your online
account.

5. Indicate how you want to pay for your America Online service. You can
choose Modify Billing Information and then choose from American
Express, Discover Card, Mastercard, or Visa (see fig. 1.13). Or, if you
prefer, you can have your online charges deducted regularly from your
checking account (see fig. 1.14).

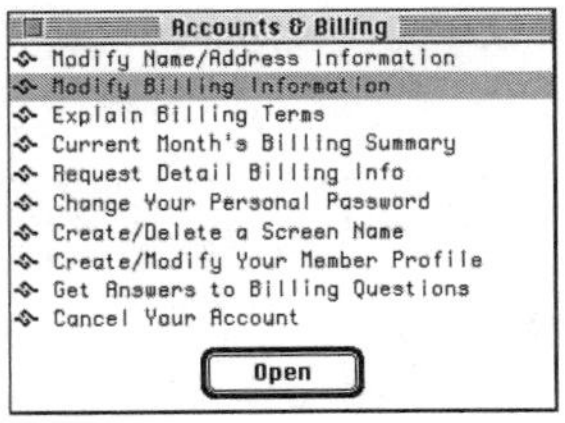

Fig. 1.13
You can easily
change your credit
card billing infor-
mation whenever
you want; just
type the keyword
Billing to reach
AOLs billing area.

To protect you, America Online verifies all your billing information. If the
program encounters a problem in establishing your account, the account is
suspended until you are able to update your billing information. But this
precaution is done solely for your protection. After all, you wouldn't want to
pay for someone else's online charges.

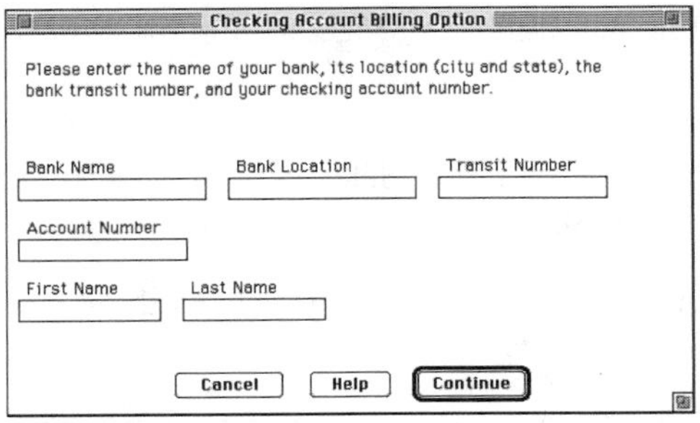

Fig. 1.14
You can opt to
have your online
charges deducted
automatically from
your checking
account.

Creating Your Online Mailing Address

Next you need to enter your online mailing address, or *screen name*. Here's
your golden opportunity to be creative. Your online address can contain from

three to ten characters (letters and numbers). You can identify yourself on America Online by your first name, an abbreviation of your name, or even a descriptive word or two that expresses your own unique personality traits, such as "TheBear."

Tip
To check your usage bill on AOL, type the keyword **Billing**. You are then taken to a free support area where you can view your current bill and make changes to your billing information.

The online name you choose for yourself is used by your master account, and the host computer checks that name (along with the password you select) every time you log on to America Online. You can add up to four additional names to your online account, for use by other members of your family, or for yourself if you decide to try on a change of clothing for size. Remember that you can use only one screen name attached to your account at any one time. If you want to log on simultaneously with more than one screen name, you need to establish separate accounts.

If someone already has the name you selected, you are given the option of using that name plus a number—and the number reflects how many others are using that same name. You may, for example, be offered the choice of using "GeneS12345" if a number of people online are already using a "GeneS."

> **Caution**
>
> Because you cannot delete your master account name without deleting your account, take as much time as you need to select an appropriate screen name.

As you try to locate an available online address (or screen name), America Online searches its database to determine whether someone else already has selected that name. Because America Online is a family-oriented service, names using vulgar language or with a vulgar connotation are not accepted.

Tip
When you select a screen name and password, write it down and place that information in a safe place. That way, if you forget your password, you can find it again quickly when you need it.

After America Online has accepted your screen name, your next step is to select a password. A password is your ounce of protection against someone using your account without your permission, so don't use anything obvious, such as a contraction of your name. Select a unique word or phrase that someone wouldn't stumble on at random.

After you've chosen your online address, you're ready to make your introduction to the online community.

Oh yes, before you are welcomed to the America Online family, you are asked whether you accept the Terms of Service. Carefully read the information displayed. You also can check the text of it in the Online Support area, but basically it requests that you be a good citizen during your online visits and avoid using vulgar language—that sort of thing.

Exploring America Online in Your First Online Session

The first time you log on to America Online (and assuming that your sound is working), you hear a friendly voice intone "Welcome," and a few seconds later, you hear another phrase by that same person, saying, "You've Got Mail." Yes, when you sign onto America Online for the first time, you indeed find a letter in your mailbox. Just click on the You Have Mail icon, and you see your first letter listed in the directory. Just double-click on that directory listing, and the text appears in a new open document window on your computer's screen. The letter is from Steve Case, the president of America Online. He welcomes you to the service and briefly outlines the special features you may want to examine during your beginning travels through the network.

The first screen you see on your computer, the Welcome screen, is your gateway to all the features offered by America Online (see fig. 1.15). Along the right side of the Welcome screen is a list of special announcements, places to visit, and the Top News headline. Just click on the icon to the right of the message you want to investigate (or to the left of the Top News headline), and you are instantaneously transported to that area on America Online. The list you see here changes several times per day as different services are featured and the top news stories change.

Fig. 1.15
Read your first welcome message from America Online.

At the bottom of the Welcome screen (also known as In The Spotlight) is a rectangular box labeled GO TO MAIN MENU. When you click on this box, you'll be taken to the window that lies beneath the Welcome screen (see fig. 1.16), which is your gateway to all the major services on America Online. At the left of the main menu screen are three icons. Clicking on In The Spotlight returns you the original Welcome screen. Beneath it is the icon for America Online's electronic mail center, the Post Office. At the bottom is the Discover AOL icon, which we'll explore further later in this chapter.

Fig. 1.16
Consider America
Online's Main
Menu as its table
of contents to all
the major features
of the service.

To the right of those icons are two rows of colorful rectangular buttons, each of which takes you to a different department. They are clearly labeled, and you can click on any one of them now to explore the service further. These departments are discussed in detail in Chapter 5, "Finding Your Way around America Online."

For now, just take a brief tour of the service.

Beginning a Guided Online Tour

To explore America Online, click on the Discover AOL icon. The Discover America Online screen appears, as shown in figure 1.17.

Fig. 1.17
You can "dis-
cover" America
Online on your
first visit.

You can visit eight different locations, each identified by its own unique icon. Clicking on an icon takes you to the corresponding area on the network.

Before going further, you probably want to click on the A Letter From Steve icon. Every month or two, America Online's president writes a status report on the services, telling about America Online's growth and the new features that are now available, and giving a brief preview of the features you can expect in the near future.

Now you're ready to take that little tour.

Examining America Online Highlights

Using the America Online Highlights icon is a quick way to familiarize yourself with some of the major features of America Online (see figs. 1.18 and 1.19). The services highlighted there change from time to time, so you may want to take this little tour every so often.

Fig. 1.18
This screen appears at the beginning of your guided tour of America Online.

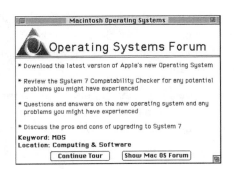

Fig. 1.19
One of the many featured America Online services during the tour is the Macintosh Operating Systems Forum.

The contents of the tour change from time to time, but each window brings up a display providing information about a specific area on America Online.

These areas, called *forums*, are discussed in more detail beginning in Chapter 5, "Finding Your Way around America Online." For now, you can either select the Continue Tour button to go on with the tour, or the Show button, which transports you directly to the area that you are reading about. If you decide to visit one of these forums, you can take the tour again later.

When you have gone through all the area forum windows, the screen shown in figure 1.20 appears, letting you know that you have completed the tour. You then are returned to the Discover AOL area.

Fig. 1.20
Your tour is over, but the fun is just beginning.

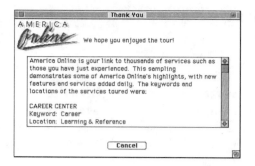

Tip
If you're watching your budget, type the keyword **Clock**. You then see an online clock that displays the amount of time you've spent on the service.

After you've completed your tour, go ahead and poke around the service for yourself. When you move to a new location, you can check it out or move on. Literally thousands of services are available to you, covering many areas of interest. This book lists only some of the highlights because new services are being added almost daily. You will find every online visit an adventure in discovery and enjoyment.

From Here...

Now you've officially joined the online community as a member of America Online. You probably want to take a little time to go off on your own to explore your new home and to get an idea of the vast array of information services that are now available to you.

After you've become a little more accustomed to navigating through America Online, you'll want to begin to master your America Online software. For a description of all the features, refer to the following chapters:

■ Chapter 2, "Using Your America Online Macintosh Software"

■ Chapter 3, "Using Your America Online Windows Software"

Chapter 2

Using Your America Online Macintosh Software

After you've made your introductions on America Online, set up your account, and logged on for the first time, you want to get down to the business of learning your new software.

The Macintosh version of your America Online software doesn't come with a manual, although an extensive Help menu is provided. But so long as you know how to do your everyday tasks on your Macintosh, such as moving and clicking your mouse and selecting menus, you shouldn't have any trouble at all picking up all the ins and outs of using America Online. And with this brief guide in your hands, you can become an expert in just a short time.

In this chapter, you learn just how easily you can master your America Online software. You learn how to:

- Customize your modem settings
- Customize America Online to your personal taste
- Save and print any America Online text window
- Begin to use E-mail and instant messages
- Go to your favorite spots with just two keystrokes
- Adjust window size and position for the best display

Accessing Your America Online Software

If you're a System 7 user, follow these steps to instantly access your America Online software, even at start-up:

1. Make an alias of your America Online application icon (highlight the AOL icon, and select Make Alias from the File menu at your Finder desktop).

2. Take the alias and place it inside the Startup Items folder (it's in the System folder).

America Online launches whenever you boot your Mac. Another alternative is to place the alias in the Apple Menu Items folder for quick access from the Apple menu.

Tip

If you have a problem using your AOL software, and you need an immediate answer, press ⌘-/ or select Help from the Apple menu.

In the pages that follow, you look at all the features of your new software. The text describes how all the menus work and the special features that are offered. And you get some helpful hints to make your online visits more enjoyable.

Changing the Modem Settings

When you first install your America Online software, the software examines your modem and sets a default modem profile for it. If you buy a new modem, you're going to want to change these settings. Or you might want to change your connection numbers to the America Online network.

To change your connection settings, follow these steps:

1. Click on the Setup button on the main America Online window to display the screen shown in figure 2.1. (Keep in mind that you can change these settings only when you're not logged on to the America Online network.)

   You can set up two connection profiles. Your America Online software uses the one on the left, First Try, when trying to make your initial connection to the network. If the connection doesn't succeed for any reason—usually due to a busy connection port or noise on the line—America Online attempts the Second Try.

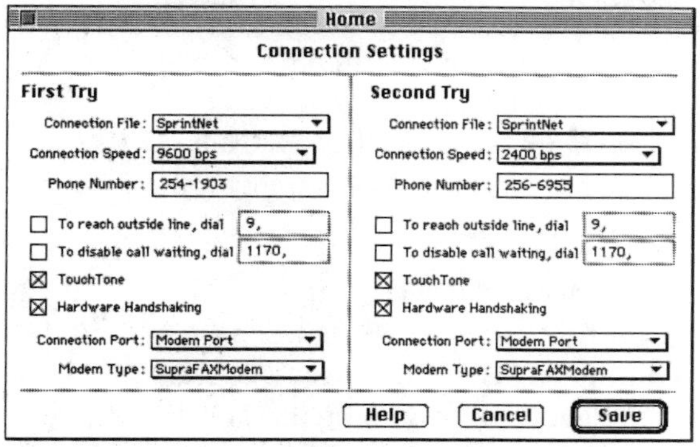

Fig. 2.1
You can quickly
and easily make
changes to your
connection setup.

> **Note**
>
> If you want to change the phone number you are using for any reason—if you've moved to a different location, for example—just log on to America Online. Then type the keyword **Access**. You are asked whether you want to enter the free area. Press Return, or click on Yes. You then see a window with a list of options for finding an access number. For now, just double-click on Search. You see a window with a space to enter the area code you want to check. When you enter that number, America Online checks its online phone directory and produces a list of phone numbers for the selected area. For more information on selecting a new connection number, see Chapter 5, "Finding Your Way around America Online."

2. Changing online numbers is easy. Just type the new number in the Phone Number box. When you change the number, you also might need to change the Connection File, which is the service that America Online uses to connect to its network. When you get a list of phone numbers from America Online for your area, you see such names as SprintNet or BT/Tymnet attached to the phone numbers. In the Connection Settings window, simply pull down the menu at the right of the Connection File label, and select the correct name of the service provider.

3. America Online's phone directory also lists the connection speed supported by each phone number. You need to enter the correct speed in the Connection Speed entry box in the Connection Settings window; otherwise, you cannot connect to the network.

4. The next four check boxes control how the software uses your modem to dial the service. Some businesses have special phone lines that require a dial-out code. Usually, it's 9, but you can change that number if necessary; some hotels we've visited, for example, use 9 as their dial-out prefix. If you need to dial a special number to reach an outside line, check the To Reach Outside Line box.

5. If you have Call Waiting service, you want to disable it when you make your online connection, because the tones that sound in your telephone when someone is trying to reach you can interrupt your online connection and end your session prematurely. The number listed in the To Disable Call Waiting check box, 1170, is for rotary telephones. If you have touch-tone service, the number is usually *70. But to be certain of which number to use, call your local telephone company. Sometimes the ability to disable Call Waiting for a single phone call is an optional service.

6. If you have a touch-tone phone, check the TouchTone check box (it's set that way by default).

7. The fourth check box, Hardware Handshaking, is needed for a high-speed modem, a 9600 or 14,400 bps (or even faster) model. If you're using one of these models, you want to check this box. If not, leave it off.

8. The Connection Port option simply enables you to tell the software which jack your modem is hooked up to. The default setting is Modem Port. If you're using the Printer Port instead (perhaps for a network modem), select that option from its pull-down menu.

9. The final option enables you to choose the make and model of your modem. If a modem profile isn't listed there for the model you have, stick with the one your America Online software picks for you when you first install it. If you are experienced in the arcane science of modem connection strings, you can even set up your own custom profile. For more information, see the "Using the New Option" section in this chapter.

Note

A selection of updated modem drivers is available for download from America Online's Member Services area (keyword: *Help*), by first clicking on the Members' Online Support icon in the main Member Services window and then clicking on Technical Help.

Setting Preferences

The next thing you want to do is set up your America Online software's preferences so that the software looks and feels the way you want it to. Even if everything looks okay to you, trying out a few settings just to see whether you can adjust things a bit better is worth the effort.

To set up preferences, choose Set Preferences from the Members menu, or press ⌘- = . The Preferences dialog box appears, with a list of Preference Categories on the left side. When you choose one of these categories, a list of options appears on the right side of the dialog box.

Setting most of your preferences involves the same steps. You click on an option to select it, and you see a check mark appear next to it. You click again to turn off the item, at which time the check mark disappears (see fig. 2.2).

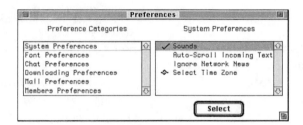

Fig. 2.2
You can toggle Sounds—and other Preferences settings—off and on.

The following sections describe the settings you can change in the Preferences dialog box.

Setting System Preferences

When you first see your Preferences dialog box, you have the option of changing your regular system preferences. Those options are described in the paragraphs that follow.

Sounds

One of the most attractive features of America Online is its voice messages. When you begin your session, you hear a friendly "Welcome" voice. And when you log off, you hear the same voice bid you "Good-bye." But if you work in a busy environment, maybe you just want to turn those sounds off.

Just click on the word Sounds in the Preferences dialog box to toggle off the sounds. You see the check mark vanish. If you want to restore the sounds, click on the word again.

Auto-Scroll Incoming Text

Turn on this feature, and you see text items scroll on your computer's screen as they are received. The normal setting (with this feature off) just shows the beginning of the text, as many lines as can fill a single text window. But you can still scroll through this text by using your computer's scroll bars at the right side of the text window.

Ignore Network News

Normally, when America Online wants to send you a special announcement, you see it appear in a small window at the top of your screen. Such announcements might alert you to an upcoming event, such as a special conference that you wouldn't want to miss, or a special service announcement that you need to know. But if you'd rather not be disturbed by these notices, simply check the Ignore Network News option, and the network announcements are shut off.

Ask To Reset Serial Port

This is an option you only need to disable if you are using a program like Apple Remote Access or fax software and intend to run FlashSessions on America Online (which we'll describe in more detail shortly). If another program is using your Mac's serial port, America Online's software will give you the option to reset the port, so you are able to log on. Otherwise the other communications program takes over the serial port to do its stuff.

Confirm SignOff

Disabling this option also disables the message you get asking if you really want to sign off from America Online when you log off.

Select Time Zone

All the messages you post and all the messages you read are time-stamped—that is, the time they were sent is listed on your screen. The same is true for those special network announcements you see from time to time. But because America Online's home office is located on the East Coast of the U.S., times listed are displayed as Eastern Time (standard or daylight, depending on the season). If you live in a different time zone, you can change the time those network announcements display to show your local time zone. (The time-stamping in the message area isn't changed, though.)

When you choose the Select Time Zone option, you see the window shown in figure 2.3.

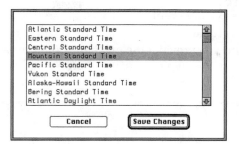

Fig. 2.3
Use this screen to
select the time
zone in which
you live.

Setting Font Preferences

When you choose Font Preferences from the Preferences dialog box, you see
five options on the right side of that window. You can select a separate font,
and you can select the size and color for system messages, chats, E-mail, and
instant messages. Simply double-click on the option you want to change, and
you see a display with two pop-up menus (see fig. 2.4). The pop-up menu on
the left lists all your installed fonts. The one on the right displays your size
options. You also see a sample display showing just how your chosen font
will look. After you've made your decision, click on the Change Font button.
To select the final option, to ignore text colors, simply double click in that
choice, and you'll see a check mark appear to the left of this option.

```
Select a font and size for use in America Online's
windows. This font will be used wherever possible.

Note: Some windows require a specific font and size;
these windows will not use the font you have selected.


                    Text Sample
┌─────────────────────────────────────────────────┐
│ This is a sample of a monospaced font, which is particularly │
│ good for displaying tabular data.                │
└─────────────────────────────────────────────────┘

        Font:  [ Monaco    ▼]    Size:  [ 9  ▼]


            [ Cancel ]      [ Change Font ]
```

Fig. 2.4
Select your
America Online
fonts.

America Online uses the same fonts that are automatically installed on your
Macintosh when you load your System software. The normal selections are
Geneva and Monaco because they're easy to read on your computer's screen.
If you're not happy with these selections or want the display to be a little
larger or a little smaller, make your selections here. Although you might want
to stick with your standard system fonts, feel free to experiment with any
other font you've installed on your Mac, too, in case you like something else
better.

Tip
Choose a
monospaced font,
such as Monaco or
Courier, to display
your messages
online. That way,
material that is
formatted with
tabs lines up
clearly on-screen.

My personal preference is 9-point Monaco—for everything. A monospaced font (a font that has equal spacing for each character) is more readable on your screen, and this size provides the maximum amount of material in a text window, while still keeping it readable. But that's just one person's opinion.

Caution

America Online software uses your standard Macintosh system fonts by default, such as Chicago for menu bar titles, Geneva and Monaco for text display, and New York for the sign-off screen. These fonts are automatically installed when you load system software onto your Mac, so don't remove them.

If you turn on the Ignore Text Colors feature, custom colors used in E-mail messages that you receive won't be shown. If you don't have a color screen, or you want to speed up screen display of long messages, it's a good idea to activate this choice.

Setting Chat Preferences

Chats and conferences are often the most enjoyable experiences on America Online. You can have your chat window display text double-spaced so that it's easier to read (the normal mode is single-spaced). You also can decide whether you want to hear sounds that other members might send.

Bear in mind that you can't hear a chat sound on your computer unless you have installed the same sound. But America Online's sound libraries are huge, so you're bound to find just about any sound that any other member might send. See Chapter 10, "Finding Information on America Online," for more information on locating a file in America Online's computing and software libraries.

When you click on Chat Preferences, your options appear at the right of the Preferences dialog box.

Setting Downloading Preferences

Many files you download from America Online are compressed to make them smaller and thus reduce the time needed to get the files to your computer (and reduce your online charges). America Online software includes a tool to automatically decompress files you've just downloaded. The supported formats include StuffIt, AppleLink Package, and several PC compression formats.

By default, as soon as you end your America Online session, all files that you have just downloaded (if they're in a format that's supported, of course) are decompressed automatically. You should keep this compression option checked. It makes the process of using your downloaded files much easier. If you don't have enough disk space to store all those files, or you want to decide later whether you want to use these files, just turn this option off.

The second option is Delete Compressed Files, which enables you to delete the original file automatically after it's been expanded. This option is one you ought to use with caution, as a protection against the rare occasion when an expanded file might become damaged somehow.

Your final download option is "Confirm Download Later," which produces a reminder window whenever you choose the option to add a file to your download queue. If you don't want to be reminded about it, turn this option off. We'll describe the features of the Download Manager in more detail later in this chapter and in Chapter 12, "How to Find Software."

Setting Graphics Viewing Preferences

America Online's software will not just open text documents, or stuffed documents. You can also open, view, and print files created in several graphics formats, such as GIF, JPEG, and PICT. This is a special advantage, because there are literally thousands of graphic files available for you to download in America Online's huge software libraries. You can download photos of fellow AOL members, weather maps, your favorite movie and TV stars, and much, much more.

The Auto-View Graphics option allows graphic files to appear on your Mac's screen as you are downloading them. You'll see the image draw on your screen and a progress bar showing the progress of your image file download. The neat thing about this feature: If you decide you don't want the file after all, you can just cancel the download before it finishes. This is one option we suggest you leave on.

Note

If a graphic file is very large, America Online's software may not have sufficient memory to view it and you'll receive a message to this effect. You can usually get around this by closing all open document windows and then trying to open the graphic file again. If that doesn't work, give America Online's software additional RAM with the Finder's Get Info command. An additional 500K or so is often enough.

The last option, Use Mac System Colors, just defaults the color rendering of the image file to the standard Macintosh color palette. There's no need to switch off this option, unless you've done some serious customizing of your Mac's color settings.

Setting Mail Preferences

Because electronic mail, or E-mail for short, is such an important feature of your America Online software, several options appear when you select Mail Preferences in the Preferences dialog box.

■ If your mailbox is filled when you log on to America Online, or E-mail is sent during your online session, you hear that same friendly fellow who says "Welcome" tell you that "You've Got Mail." If you don't want to hear his voice (and he seems like such a nice guy), turn off the "Male Voice Announcement" option.

■ Whether you've turned the voice announcement on or off, you probably want to keep the second option active. It's a Mail Waiting Notice that puts up a little flashing mailbox at the upper-right side of your Mac's menu bar. If you don't want to be disturbed, just turn it off.

■ When you send E-mail, your America Online software automatically closes the E-mail document window at the moment the E-mail is sent (transferred to the host computer). If you want to keep your E-mail message on-screen, turn off the preference to Close Mail after Sending.

■ The next mail preference is designed to keep your screen from getting cluttered, especially if you get a lot of E-mail. As you click on the arrow to go to the next or to a previous message, the message you have open is automatically closed. If you prefer to have all those windows stay open despite the clutter, just turn off the Close Mail On Next/Previous option.

■ The option to Save Flashmail as Text (also see Chapter 7, "Communicating with Others," for more information about FlashSessions), is usually turned off. It converts your Flashmail from a regular mail window to a text window. You then can read mail saved to Flashmail in any text processing program.

■ When you choose to send your E-mail while offline, or at a later time, you normally click on the "Send Later" icon at the left of your E-mail message form. You normally receive a confirmation that you've set your

E-mail for later shipment (and the choice to activate a FlashMail session). Turning off this final option keeps this message from appearing.

Setting Members Preferences

You can think of an instant message (IM for short) as "real-time" E-mail. You can send it only to someone who's online, and that person can respond to you only when you're online. Chapters 6 and 7 give you the ins and outs of instant messaging. For now, you just need to know the whys and wherefores of the instant message options in your Preferences dialog box.

One of the most exciting experiences you can have online is getting an instant message. And the usual preference is for America Online to display a little flashing IM notice at the upper-right side of the menu bar on your screen when you get an instant message. If you have E-mail waiting, the IM display alternates with the Mailbox icon. If you don't want to receive this notice, turn off the Instant Message Notice option.

The second preference is just for convenience. By default, whenever you get an instant message, the message window is brought right to the front. But this choice might be a bit disturbing if you're doing something else online. In that case, just turn off this option. If you've left your IM notice options on, you won't miss a message.

And, finally, your IM's arrival is punctuated by a cute little musical sound. I like it myself, and I'm happy to hear this kind of sound. But maybe you don't, so here's your chance to become a music critic and turn it off.

You can also set options with your America Online software, and that's the Personal Choices command in the Members menu. We'll discuss that option later in this chapter.

Using the File Menu

The File menu is much like the one you find in any other Macintosh application (see fig. 2.5). Most of the commands are familiar to you, but America Online has added a few features to its software that are worth some explanation.

The following paragraphs take you step by step through the options on the File menu.

Fig. 2.5
Display the File
menu to access
many file manage-
ment options.

Using the New Memo Option

When you press ⌘-N, you see a blank document window, much like the one
you would find in a text processing program.

America Online comes with a basic text editor, kind of a simple word processor, so that you can write little memos or even a simple letter, or just paste
text you might have grabbed from other memos or message windows online.
You can even format your document by using the Font, Size, Style, and Color
commands from the Edit menu. These topics are discussed later in this chapter, in "Using the Edit Menu."

The Memo feature is not quite as full-featured as your word processing program. It's limited, for example, to 27,000 characters (a little more than 4,000
words), not quite large enough for your new novel, but enough for a long
letter. As in any other America Online text window, you can save and print
your memo. These features are discussed later in this chapter.

Tip
After you write
a memo, if you
decide that you
want to E-mail
it to another
America Online
member, select
Address Memo
from the Mail
menu. Your memo
is magically trans-
formed to an
E-mail window.

Using the New Option

The arrow that follows the New option name indicates that selecting the New
option produces a submenu from which you can select other options.

The New submenu includes two options:

- The first option is Locality, which enables you to configure your
  America Online software for a new location (see fig. 2.6). You can add
  new connection phone numbers and choose from new modem profiles.
  You can save this file and use it whenever you want to pick an alternate
  connection profile. The standard Locality module is labeled *Home*, so
  maybe you want to label a new one *Work* or *Travel* or *Mother-in-Law's
  House*.

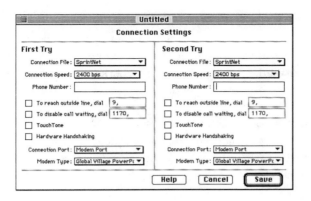

Fig. 2.6
Create a new connection profile using America Online's Locality feature.

- The second option, Modem File, enables you to create a new modem profile (see fig. 2.7). This option is strictly for advanced users, and it enables you to create custom setup information for a modem that may not be part of America Online's standard modem settings. Before you delve into this option, though, check your modem's manual carefully, or even call the manufacturer's technical support people for assistance.

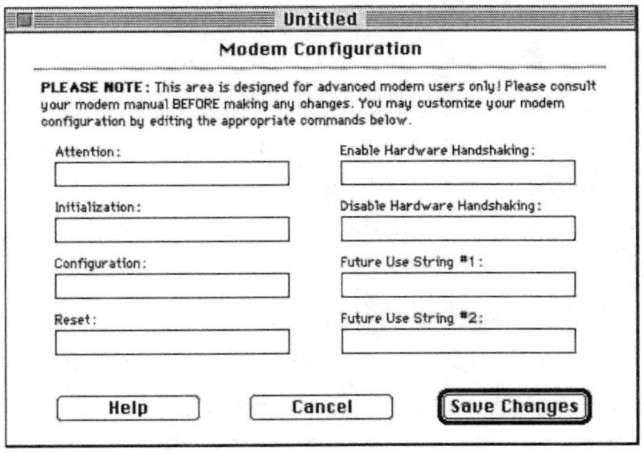

Fig. 2.7
If you know your stuff about modems, you can create a custom modem profile.

Using the Open Option (⌘-O)

This command brings up your standard Macintosh Open dialog box. It enables you to open documents in formats recognized by America Online.

If you click on the pull-down menu next to the Show label at the bottom of the dialog box, you see a list of all the formats your software can read. The default is All Available, and I suggest you leave it that way, unless you need to find a file saved in a specific format but don't know the file's name. Supported formats include documents required by your AOL software, simple text documents, E-mail, compressed files in several formats, and image formats such as GIF, JPEG, and PICT.

Using the Close Option (⌘-W)

This command closes the active file window on your screen. If you have made any changes in the contents of the file before you last saved it—or if you've never saved the file—you are asked whether you want to save the changes before the window is closed.

Using the Save Option (⌘-S)

This command saves the contents of your window to a file that's written to disk. If you haven't saved the file yet, you see a dialog box, enabling you to give the file a name.

Using the Save As Option

Tip

If you want a paper copy of America Online's Help menu, simply select that section, using the Copy command on the Edit menu, and paste it into a new document. You can then save and print that document.

This option enables you to save your document under a new name. You have the choice of saving your document in straight text format or in other formats, depending on the kind of document you have open. For example, if you are reading an E-mail letter, it can be saved in America Online's standard mail format or as a simple text file that can be opened in any text editing or word processing program.

Using the Save Selection As Option

This option is a handy feature you can use to save selected text. During your online visit, all you have to do is highlight an item of text. This item can be an article, a news story, or something in a message area, even the contents of a chat window. After the text is highlighted, choose the Save Selection As... option, and you can save that text in its own document.

Using the Revert Option

Did you make a mistake in updating a saved document, such as a memo? No problem. Choose the Revert... option, and America Online restores the document to the last saved version. When you select this option, you are asked whether you want to discard the changes you just made to your document.

Using the Logs Option

During your visits to America Online, you might sometimes want to save the contents of a message area or an online conference so that you can view and print it later. You have three logging options in your AOL software:

- The first is a System Log. This log enables you to record all the text that you read while you're on America Online. It doesn't record the mail you send or the messages you post, but you can save those anyway, using the Save command described previously.

■ The second is the Chat Log. During your online travels, you might attend a chat in America Online's People Connection or an online conference. This feature enables you to record the entire conversation.

■ And finally, you have the Instant Message Log, which enables you to store all the instant messages you get while online. If you're exchanging instant messages with more than one member at a time, however, the log records all those messages in one log, logging the messages in the order in which they are sent and received.

To use your online tape recorder, follow these steps:

1. Open the Logs window by choosing Logs from the File menu.

2. Select the kind of log you want (see fig. 2.8).

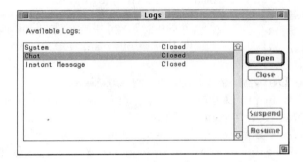

Fig. 2.8
Turn on America Online's virtual tape recorder to log an online session.

3. Click on the Open button. You then see a dialog box much like the Save As... prompt, and you are asked to name your file and indicate where it is to be saved (see fig. 2.9). The software gives the file a default name, based on the kind of log it is, but you can change that if you want.

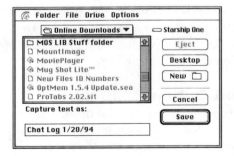

Fig. 2.9
Name your online log in this dialog box.

If you want to pause the online recording process, just return to the File menu, select Logs, and select the Suspend button at the bottom of the Logs window. When you decide to resume the logging process, you need to click on the Resume button. When you are finished logging, choose the Close option.

The logging process is flexible. You can open all three logs at once if you want. What's more, you can suspend and resume and even close each log separately, depending on which one you've highlighted when you make your choice.

America Online software can capture only about 27,000 characters in a single file.

If the log gets bigger than that size, America Online closes the first log and opens a second one automatically. The second log has the same name as the first log file, with a number added to it, such as 2 or 3. This feature helps you view all your logs just as you can any memo file, from within the America Online software.

Using the Download Manager Option

Downloading is the process of transferring a file from America Online's huge software libraries right to your computer. The Download Manager enables you to choose one or more files to download during your online visit. The files are placed in a download queue or sequence. You can begin the download process at any time during your online session, when you log off, or even during a scheduled FlashSession. You learn how to configure the Download Manager to work best for you in Chapter 5, "Finding Your Way around America Online."

Using the Page Setup Option

Tip

Please be sure to select your printer in the Chooser before you open your America Online software. Otherwise you might not be able to print a document after the software is open.

Choosing the Page Setup option displays your standard Page Setup dialog box. In this dialog box, you can change your page size and orientation (portrait or landscape) and select various printer options. These options vary depending on the kind of printer you have and the version of the printer driver you have installed on your Macintosh.

Using the Print Option (⌘-P)

Choosing Print... displays the regular Print dialog box. It enables you to print from any open text window. You can print a memo, your E-mail, a conference window, a message, or any other displayed text on America Online. If a window has more than one text window, say the opening window of an online department, you should move the cursor to the text file you want to print. You can move the cursor either by clicking with the mouse or by pressing Tab.

Using the Quit Option (⌘-Q)

If you are still online when you choose Quit from the File menu, you see a dialog box asking whether you want to Quit (the button that's highlighted) or Sign Off. The first selection ends your online session and quits the application. The second option simply logs you off but keeps the application open. The latter feature is useful if you want to continue some of your work in the program offline, such as writing E-mail or memos. You also want to keep the application running if you decide to schedule a FlashSession (see the instructions on using the Go To menu later in this chapter).

Using the Edit Menu

The first six selections on the Edit menu are very much what you'd find on any Macintosh application (see fig. 2.10). They are Undo (⌘-Z), Cut (⌘-X), Copy (⌘-C), Paste (⌘-V), Clear, and Select All (⌘-A). Because they work the same as in your other Mac software, they aren't discussed further here.

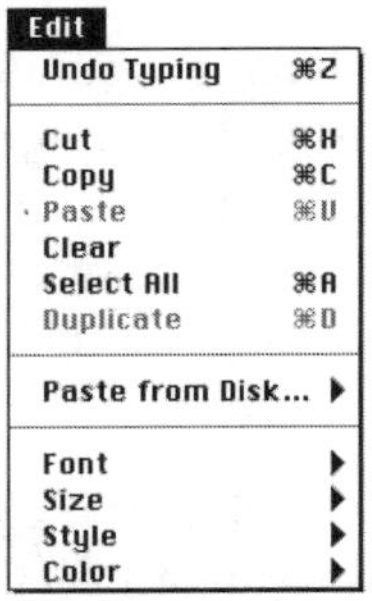

Fig. 2.10
The Edit menu contains several familiar Macintosh commands.

Using the Duplicate Option (⌘-D)

This function is presently inactive. The menu item is designed to support new features that may be added to your America Online software from time to time.

Using the Paste from Disk Option

This feature might better be referred to as an Insert Text command. It works in much the same way a desktop publishing program imports or places text from another document. If you are writing E-mail, a memo, or a message, you can paste text directly from a file. If you compose the document in your word processing software, you must save the document in text format, such as Text Only in Microsoft Word (or in your America Online software).

When you choose Paste from Disk..., you bring up a standard Open dialog box in which you select the file from which you want to paste your text. After you select that file's name, the text in the file is placed right at the insertion point in your open memo or E-mail document.

Tip
Another way to spell check your America Online E-mail or memos is an interactive spell checking program, such as Coach Professional from Deneba Software or Thunder 7 from Baseline Publishing.

You have the added advantage, with this feature, of letting your word processing software spell check a document before you E-mail or post it somewhere online.

Using the Font, Size, Style, and Color Options

Using these options is where you can exercise your online creativity. The options here are similar to the ones you have in your word processing program. You can select from any font that's installed on your Mac. You can use any font size from 1 point to 127 points, but you should restrict your choices to 9 points and larger so that you and the person who receives your message can read the messages easily on-screen.

Your style choices range from Plain text to Bold and Italic (which can be combined as Bold Italic), to Underline, Outline, and Shadow.

To provide greater emphasis and flair to your documents, you can also change the color of your text, using, for example, red or green for text you wish to emphasize. This choice, though, won't do very much good if the recipient of your E-mail doesn't have a color-capable Mac with a color screen. Text with different color styles will appear in drab shades of gray on a grayscale screen.

To alter the text format, you can highlight the text in the memo or E-mail document that you want to change, select each menu (Font, Size, Style, or Color) in turn, and make your changes. Or you can make your formatting changes with nothing selected, as long as you have opened an active memo or the Compose Mail window. All the text you enter after the insertion point will include those changes.

Try to show a bit of restraint, however, in styling your document. See figure 2.11 for a rather extreme example.

All these styles work fine and dandy for your memos and E-mail. But the messages that you post online (chats and instant messages, too) are limited to your basic 128-character ASCII set. That means, for example, that you cannot use "curly quotes," special characters such as ª, ¤, or ¥, or foreign accents for these kinds of messages.

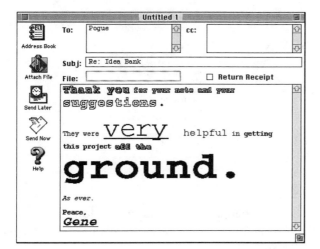

Fig. 2.11
When you compose your E-mail, try not to get carried away with all the sizes and styles at your disposal.

Caution

Be careful what fonts you use when you send E-mail to another America Online member. Even though you might love to use some of those fancy fonts, the person who gets the message isn't able to read the letter in the same typeface unless that person has the font, too. If that person doesn't have the font, it just defaults to the standard E-mail font. You might be better off using the Size and Style selections to create different point sizes and such fancy effects as outlines and shadows to make your E-mail stand out. Choosing a color for emphasis is useful so long as the recipient of your message has a color monitor.

Using the Go To Menu

The Go To menu, shown in figure 2.12, is your launching pad in America Online. It's your gateway to loads of undiscovered treasures that you can find during your travels online.

Fig. 2.12
Discover America
Online by using
the Go To menu.

Go To
Sign Off
Main Menu
In The Spotlight
Keyword ⌘K
Lobby ⌘L
Search Directory of Services
Search Software Libraries
Search Today's News
Network News
Online Clock
Edit Favorite Places...
Computing & Software ⌘1
Online Clock ⌘2
New Services ⌘3
Sign on a Friend ⌘4
File Search ⌘5
Kim Komando's Forum ⌘6
Macworld ⌘7
Mac Operating Systems ⌘8
Mac Utilities ⌘9
Mac Multimedia ⌘0

Setting Up and Signing On

The window shown in figure 2.13 appears automatically when you open your
America Online program. It's the window you use to begin your online session or to change your modem setup.

Fig. 2.13
When you launch
your America
Online software,
you see this
window.

Clicking on the Sign On button at the left of the window (or pressing Return
or Enter) begins the log-on process. You use the button in the middle, Setup,
to change your connection phone numbers or your modem settings; and the
button on the right, Help, brings up the online Help menu to get you
through the rough spots.

Using the Welcome to America Online Option

When you first log on to America Online, the window shown in figure 2.14
serves as your introduction to the service. You can display this window later
by choosing the In The Spotlight option from the Go To menu. At the right

you see information about the latest news, and special features and services you might want to check out further.

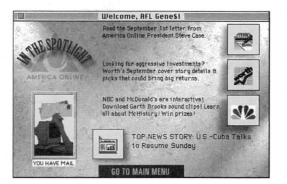

Fig. 2.14
This welcome window is your America Online gateway.

At the bottom left of the Welcome window, you see an icon showing whether you've received any E-mail. If you have America Online's default sounds activated, your sign-on is punctuated with a "Welcome" greeting, followed in a few seconds by a "You've Got Mail" announcement. Clicking on the You Have Mail icon brings up a directory of the mail you've received since you last logged on. If no mail is waiting for you, the icon is labeled *No Mail*.

Beneath the In The Spotlight window when you log on is AOL's Main Menu (which can also be selected, when the window has been closed, from the Go To menu). This window is shown in figure 2.15. The large, colorful graphical icons in two rows on the right side of the Main Menu takes you on to stage two, the gateway to America Online's 14 departments, shown by graphical icons. We'll be discussing those departments in detail throughout this book; after your initial log-on to America Online, you'll want to explore them briefly to get a good feel for the service.

Fig. 2.15
The Main Menu is your jumping-off point to the far-flung reaches of America Online's virtual city.

Using the Keyword Option (⌘-K)

Using the Keyword option (see fig. 2.16) is the fast and easy way to get any-where online. Just select this command from the Go To menu or press the keyboard shortcut (⌘-K). Then enter the keyword, click on the Go button, and you are transported to that location in just seconds.

Fig. 2.16

America Online's keyword feature lets you go right to your favorite online spot, or seek out points of interest.

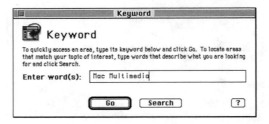

Many of the keywords on America Online are intuitive. If you want to learn more about computers, you type the keyword **Computing**. If you want to read the latest issue of *Time* magazine online, type the keyword **Time**. The Keyword Help button on your Keyword box brings up a list of current America Online keywords. If you want to find sources of information about a particular topic, but you don't know the name of the area you want to visit, you also have a search option (the button at the right shown in fig. 2.16), which brings up a list of probable matches. See Chapter 10, "Finding Infor-mation on America Online," for more details on finding information on America Online.

Using the Directory of Services Option

The Directory of Services option is another shortcut to finding the area you want to visit on America Online. When you choose this option while online, the Directory of Services window appears on your screen in a few seconds. This directory is America Online's database, which enables you to search the entire network for the area or topic you want to know about.

Select Search the Directory from this window, and enter the name of the area or the subject you want to explore. If locations that match your description can be found—and they usually are—you see a list of those areas, along with a summary of what each area deals with and the keywords that enable you to navigate to that area quickly. See Chapter 10, "Finding Information on America Online," for more details.

Using the Lobby Option (⌘-L)

This command takes you to the lobby of America Online's People Connection. For more information on People Connection, see Chapter 6, "Meeting People Online."

Using the Network News Option

Whenever America Online needs to send a message to everyone that's online at that moment, it's done through the Network News feature. The Network News option enables you to review all the items that have been sent to you during your online session. This option is useful if you've closed the Network News window to get more screen space with which to travel online.

Using the Online Clock Option

How long have you been online? If you're on a budget, you'll want to check this option occasionally, just to be sure.

Using the Edit Favorite Places... Option

When you install your America Online software, you have a list in your Go To menu of five regular spots to which you can travel simply by pressing two keys (⌘ plus a number from 0 to 9). You can change these destinations by choosing the Edit Go To Menu option to display the Goto Menu Editor dialog box, shown in figure 2.17. (We've added a few of our favorite online areas to the list we're displaying here; you can add or remove whatever you want.)

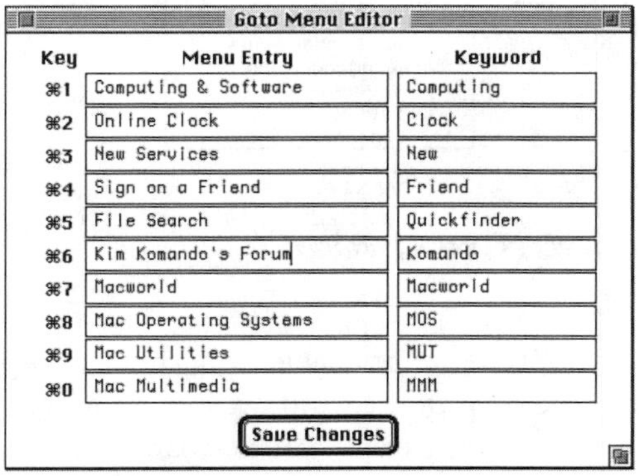

Key	Menu Entry	Keyword
⌘1	Computing & Software	Computing
⌘2	Online Clock	Clock
⌘3	New Services	New
⌘4	Sign on a Friend	Friend
⌘5	File Search	Quickfinder
⌘6	Kim Komando's Forum	Komando
⌘7	Macworld	Macworld
⌘8	Mac Operating Systems	MOS
⌘9	Mac Utilities	MUT
⌘0	Mac Multimedia	MMM

Goto Menu Editor

Save Changes

Fig. 2.17
You can customize your regular stop-off areas on America Online.

Editing the Favorite Places menu is a simple procedure. You can do it whether you're logged on or not. Follow these steps:

1. Open the Go To menu and choose the Edit Favorite Places... option. The Goto Menu Editor dialog box appears.

2. In the left column, type the name of the area you want to visit, and type the online keyword on the right. To move quickly from one entry to the next, just press Tab. The field you go to is highlighted automatically so that whatever information you type replaces what's there already.

3. After you've made your changes and additions to the Go To menu, just click on the Save Changes button. The changes you've made appear immediately in the Go To menu or through your keyboard shortcuts.

Using the Mail Menu

Perhaps the most rewarding part of your online experience is the ability to send and receive electronic mail. The major features for creating and reading E-mail are found in the Mail menu (see fig. 2.18). As mentioned earlier, you can compose your E-mail online, or do it offline and send it with a FlashSession.

Fig. 2.18
The Mail menu contains options for working with E-mail.

Using the Post Office Option
Keyword: Post Office

Most of your mailing options are available from the Post Office window, as a directory listing at the right of the window, shown in figure 2.19, or as a special icon. We'll be discussing each feature separately, though, as it appears on the Mail menu.

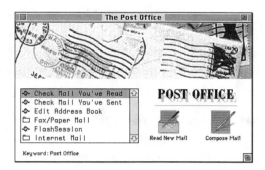

Fig. 2.19
America Online's
virtual post office,
your handy E-mail
center.

Using the Compose Mail Option (⌘-M)

This command brings up the regular America Online E-mail window. It consists of a blank mail form that you can fill in and send while online, or later during a FlashSession.

Please read Chapter 7, "Communicating with Others," for the ins and outs of composing your America Online E-mail.

Using the Read New Mail Option (⌘-R)

When you receive an announcement online that mail is in your mailbox, just select this option, press ⌘-R, or click on the You Have Mail icon at the bottom left of your AOL Welcome screen.

Using the Check Mail You've Read Option

If you want to recheck mail you've previously read, you can use the Check Mail You've Read option while you are online. You also can use this option to see whether other recipients of this mail have seen it too. Your previously read mail is stored in this list for one week after you've read it.

Using the Check Mail You've Sent Option

If you're not sure whether you've sent a letter to another America Online member or you want to find out when it was received, just check the Check Mail You've Sent item while you're online. You see a window listing all the mail you've sent. You can reread the message yourself, or click on the Status button to find out who read it and when. Unread mail is stored here for 30 days; otherwise, it's removed within two weeks.

Using the Address Memo Option

Suppose that you've written a memo, and you want to send it to another America Online member. Simply select the Address Memo option, and your document window is changed to a mail form. Now all you have to do is address the memo and send it.

Using the Edit Address Book Option

As you develop a list of regular online friends, you'll want to put their names in your personal Address Book. This list is your own Rolodex that you can use to send mass mailings to a number of recipients or merely to look up the name of a single individual. To learn more about creating and updating your Address Book, see Chapter 7, "Communicating with Others."

Using the FlashSessions Option

You can use this option to automate your America Online sessions. You can compose a message offline and then schedule a FlashSession to send your message. During that FlashSession, any mail that's been received since your last online visit is saved to your mailbox (choose Read Incoming Mail from the Mail menu to view the mail). In addition, you can opt to download files that have been attached to E-mail during a FlashSession.

See Chapter 7, "Communicating with Others," for the full story on how to schedule your FlashSessions.

Using the Read Incoming Mail Option

This option enables you to view letters that have been saved to your FlashSession mailbox. Letters are stored in your FlashSession mailbox until you delete them. This mail is also available to you offline. You can save mail that you've read online to this file by clicking on the Save to Flashmail icon in the Open Mail window. Please check Chapter 7, "Communicating with Others," for more information on how to run a FlashSession.

Using the Read Outgoing Mail Option

E-mail is stored in your FlashSession mailbox before it's sent during a FlashSession or while you're online. You can edit or delete your E-mail before it's sent, or even attach a file to your message.

Using the Mail Gateway Option

In addition to sending mail to well over a million America Online members, you can also send E-mail to members of other online services and users of the

Internet through AOL's Mail Gateway. We'll discuss the ins and outs of the Internet E-mail in Chapter 17, "The Internet Connection."

Using the FAX/Paper Mail Option

America Online has a service that enables you to send mail to someone who isn't an online member. You can have your letter sent as a FAX or via U.S. mail. When you select the FAX/Paper Mail option while online, you bring up a window that contains full instructions on how to use this service, along with the prices for this extra-cost service. Or just read Chapter 5, "Finding Your Way around America Online."

Using the Members Menu

You learned about one option in the Members menu earlier in this chapter, that of setting your America Online application preferences. The following sections discuss the rest of the options you can select from this menu (see fig. 2.20).

Fig. 2.20
Use the Members menu to keep in touch with other members.

Using the Members Member Services Option

If you want to check your America Online bill, solve a problem with your software, or just learn more about the features available to you online, here's the option to use: Member Services. What's more, this area is free, meaning that you aren't charged for the time you spend in the Online Support section.

Before you enter this area, a window pops up asking whether you're sure that you want to enter the free area, because chat areas and gateways are not available there.

Using the Member Directory Option

If you're not sure whether someone is a member of America Online, you can use this option to search the member directory and find out. You can look for a member by his or her real name or "screen" name. You also can examine members' online profiles, if they're posted, and update your own profile at the same time. Read Chapter 6, "Meeting People Online," for more information on this subject.

Using the Send Instant Message Option (⌘-I)

This option is America Online's way of holding an interactive "conversation" with another member, in private. Simply select this option, type the online address of the person to whom you want to send the message, and then enter your message. Click on Send or press Enter, and your message is sent almost instantaneously.

Using the Get a Members Profile Option (⌘-G)

If you want to learn more about an online member, you use this option. If the member has created an online profile, you can view it by selecting Get a Member's Profile. You can find more information on these and other special features for America Online members in Chapter 6, "Meeting People Online."

Using the Locate a Member Online Option (⌘-F)

Not sure whether your online friend is going to "meet" you at the appointed hour? You can select this option, Locate a Member Online, to find out whether your friend is online. If the member is attending a chat or an online conference, you receive a message announcing where the person is. Otherwise, you are just notified that the person is online. If the person you're looking for is not online, you are notified that the member is not signed on.

Using the Edit Stored Passwords Option

You should use this option with care. It enables you to store one or more of the passwords you use to get online. When you select this option, you bring up a window in which you can enter the password for each of your screen names. The text is reflected on-screen with an asterisk, so someone looking over your shoulder can't see what you type. Your sign-on process is automatic, but if anyone else has access to your computer, storing a password enables that person to use your account without your permission. So think about it carefully before you take this step.

Using the Edit Your Online Profile Option

Your online profile is your chance to write a little bit about yourself, your hobbies, and special interests so that other members can learn more about you. You can even make it humorous if you want, but try to be as accurate about yourself as possible. You don't have to post an online profile, of course, but it helps other members get to know you better if you do. Online profiles are discussed in more detail in Chapter 6, "Meeting People Online."

Using the Edit Screen Names Option

Once you establish your online account, your master account name cannot be changed (unless you leave the service, of course, or start a new account). But you can create up to four additional screen names using this feature. This is useful if you want to give members of your family access to your personal account or employees access to an account used for business purposes. You also have the option of deleting active screen names as your needs require. Before making any changes or additions to your screen names, be sure to review the text files included in the Screen Names window, shown in figure 2.21, which appears when you choose this option.

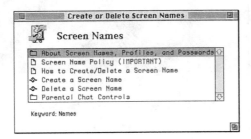

Fig. 2.21
Before you consider adding or removing an AOL screen name, be sure to review the information files shown in the Screen Names directory list.

Using the Windows Menu

After you've visited online for a while, you will no doubt have opened up many forum and text windows. The time will come when you want to tidy up your desktop a little. For this clean-up, use the Windows menu (see fig. 2.22).

Fig. 2.22
Use the Windows menu to straighten up your screen.

Using the Clean Up Windows Option

As you travel online, you begin to open window after window, and finally your desktop starts getting awfully cluttered. This little Clean Up Windows feature stacks all your open windows in a neat row, from left to right (see fig. 2.23).

Fig. 2.23
You can do spring cleaning with Clean Up Windows, cleaning up your cluttered desktop.

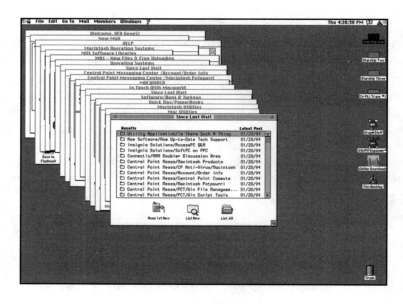

Tip
You also see a list of your open America Online windows when you pull down the Windows menu, and you can activate the one you want simply by highlighting it in the window. The titles are displayed at the top of each open window so that you can select the one you want quickly and easily.

Tip
If you hold down the Option key when you select Remember Size, the option name changes to Remember Size (Not Placement). When you choose this option, only the size of the window is recalled by the application.

Using the Close All Except Front Option

Everything has its limits, and your America Online software cannot just open an unlimited amount of windows before the application runs out of memory. After you've opened a couple of dozen or so windows, you get a warning that the application is running out of memory. At this point, you can choose the Close All Except Front option to close all the windows except the one that's active. This action cleans up your workspace fast.

Using the Remember Size Option

You might decide that the default size of an America Online message window is too small or too large for your screen. You can use the Remember Size option to enable the program to recall the size and position of that type of window (E-mail, message, or whatever) so that America Online always opens that window in the same location and with the same window size.

First, change the size of a window to your taste; then, with that window active, choose Remember Size from the Windows menu.

The Remember Size feature doesn't work for all America Online windows. If it doesn't work in an active window, this option is grayed out in the Windows menu.

Using the Forget Size Option

If you decide to change the window to its default size and location, choose this option.

> **Note**
>
> If you keep getting messages that your America Online software is running out of memory when you have many windows open, you can allow it to open more of them by giving the software more memory. With the application closed, just high-light the AOL application icon, and select Get Info from the File menu at your Finder desktop. All you have to do now is increase the amount of memory the application uses—with a watchful eye to the amount of RAM you've installed on your Mac. I suggest you use between 2000K and 2500K. The next time you log on to America Online, you can open more message windows before you get that annoying message.

From Here...

This chapter covered the basics on using your America Online software. As you read further through Using America Online, you'll find additional infor-mation and helpful hints to make your online sessions even more reward-ing—and fun, too! You can find additional details on some of the subjects discussed so far in these chapters:

- Chapter 4, "America Online on the Road"
- Chapter 5, "Finding Your Way around America Online"
- Chapter 6, "Meeting People Online"
- Chapter 7, "Communicating with Others"
- Chapter 10, "Finding Information on America Online"
- Chapter 17, "The Internet Connection"

Chapter 3

Using Your America Online Windows Software

After you've made your introductions on America Online, set up your account, and logged on for the first time, you want to get down to the business of learning about your new software.

The Windows version of your America Online software doesn't come with a manual, although an extensive Help menu is provided. But as long as you know how to use Microsoft Windows to do your everyday tasks, such as moving and clicking your mouse and selecting from menus, you shouldn't have any trouble at all picking up all the ins and outs of using the software. With this brief guide in your hands, you can become an expert in just a short time.

In this chapter, you learn just how easily you can master your America Online software. You learn how to:

- Customize your modem settings

- Customize your software

- Save and print any text window

- Begin to use E-mail and instant messages

- Go to your favorite areas with two keystrokes or a single click

- Adjust window size and position for the best display

Tip
If you have a problem using your AOL software and need a quick answer, press Alt+H or select Help from the AOL application menu bar. You can even print a topic for later review.

Changing the Network and Modem Settings

When you first install your America Online software, it examines your modem and sets a default modem profile for it. If you buy a new modem, however, you're going to want to change these settings, or you might want to change your connection numbers to the America Online network.

To change your connection settings, follow these steps:

1. Click on the Setup button on your main America Online window. The Network & Modem Setup dialog box appears, as shown in figure 3.1.

Fig. 3.1
Making changes to your network setup is quick and easy.

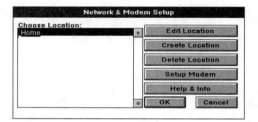

2. Click on the Edit Location option. (Keep in mind that you can make these settings only when you're not logged on to the America Online network.)

You can set up two connection profiles (see fig. 3.2). Your America Online software uses the one on the left when trying to make your initial connection to the network. If the connection doesn't succeed for any reason—usually due to a busy connection port or noise on the line—the program dials the number on the right.

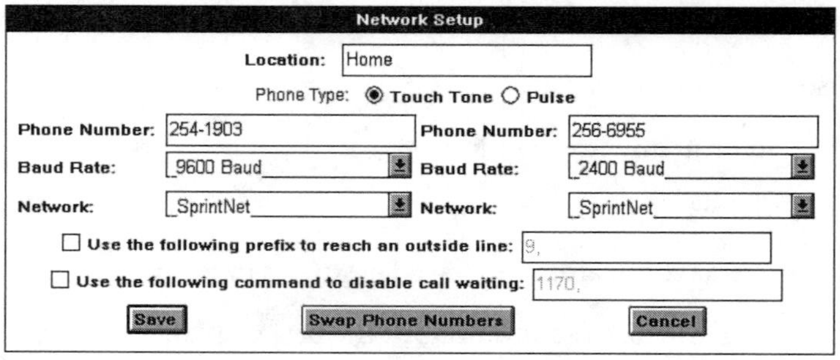

Fig. 3.2
You can change your connection numbers on this screen.

3. The first option, Phone Type, enables you to choose between a standard Touch Tone telephone and a Pulse telephone.

> **Note**
>
> If you want to change the phone number you are using for any reason, such as you've moved to a different location, just log on to America Online. Then type the keyword **Access**. You see a window with a space to enter the area code you want to search. When you enter that number, America Online checks its online phone directory and produces a list of phone numbers for the selected area. For more information on selecting a new connection number, see Chapter 4, "America Online on the Road."

Tip
A quick way to navigate from one data entry point (field) to another is to press Tab. To return to the previous field, press Shift+Tab.

I

Setting Up

4. Changing online numbers is easy. Just type the new number in the Phone Number box. When you change the number, you also might need to change the Network setting as well. The Network setting is the service that America Online uses to connect to its network. When you get a list of phone numbers from America Online for your area, you see such names as SprintNet or BT/Tymnet attached to the phone numbers. Simply pull down the menu at the right of the Network label, and select the correct name of the service provider.

5. America Online's phone directory also lists the baud rate supported by that phone number. You need to select the correct speed in the Baud Rate box of the Network Setup dialog box, or you can't connect to the network.

6. The next two check boxes control how the software uses your modem to dial the service. Some businesses have special phone lines that require a dial out code. Usually it's 9, but you can change that setting if necessary (we've been at some hotels where 8 is used instead). If you need to dial a special number to reach an outside line, check this box.

7. If you have Call Waiting service, you need to disable it when you make your online connection, because the tones that sound in your telephone when someone is trying to reach you can interrupt your online connection and end your session prematurely. The number listed in this entry box, 1170, is for rotary telephones. If you have touch-tone service, the number is usually *70. But to be certain which number to use, call your local telephone company. Sometimes the ability to disable Call Waiting for a single phone call is an optional service.

8. The final option you have is to Swap Phone Numbers. Clicking on that button transfers the information from the left to the right side of the dialog box, and vice versa. This feature is useful if you find that you are getting better online performance with your second connection number.

You used the Edit Location option to change your modem settings. The following paragraphs explain the rest of the options in the Network & Modem Setup dialog box.

- *Create Location.* If you want to log on to America Online from different locations, you can create additional location or network setups. The button for Create Location enables you to create separate profiles for each of these locations. The standard Location module is labeled *Home,* so maybe you want to label a second one *Work, Travel,* or *Mother-in-Law's House.*

- *Delete Location.* If you decide you no longer need a Location profile, use this option to remove it.

- *Setup Modem.* This option enables you to change the modem setting and the port to which it is connected. When you choose Setup Modem, the dialog box shown in figure 3.3 appears.

Fig. 3.3
If you've installed a new modem, you can change your modem selection here.

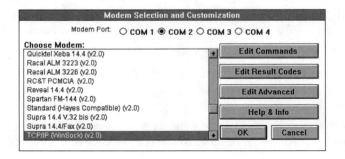

Under most circumstances, you can pick from one of the standard modem profiles and get satisfactory results. The profile highlighted in figure 3.3 supports most high-speed modems. Hayes Compatible (the default) supports your standard 2400 baud modem. If the exact make and model of your new modem is included in the list, choose that one instead.

The three options on the right side of the box—Edit Commands, Edit Result Codes, and Edit Advanced—enable you to tweak a modem profile if you feel that you can make it perform more efficiently. These options are strictly for advanced users, so proceed with caution. Before you delve into this area, check your modem's manual carefully, or even call the manufacturer's technical support people for assistance.

Setting Preferences

The next thing you want to do is set up your America Online software's preferences so that the software looks and feels the way you want it to. Even if everything looks okay to you, trying out a few settings, just to see whether you can adjust things a little better, is worth the effort.

To set up preferences, choose Preferences from the Members menu, or press Ctrl+=. The Preferences dialog box shown in figure 3.4 appears.

Fig. 3.4
You can choose from five Preferences categories.

Setting most of your preferences involves the same steps. You click on the check box next to an item to select it, and you see an *x* appear in that box. You click on the box again to turn the feature off, at which time the *x* disappears. Figure 3.5 shows an example of several options checked in the General Preferences dialog box.

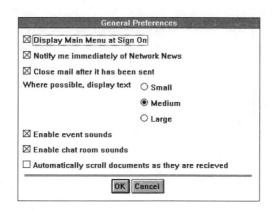

Fig. 3.5
Checking a box is all that's necessary to change your America Online preferences.

Setting General Preferences

The following paragraphs describe the options you find in the General Preferences dialog box, which appears when you select General Preferences from the Preferences dialog box.

- *Display Main Menu at Sign On.* When you first log onto America Online, you see two windows. The top window, In The Spotlight, informs you whether or not you have E-mail awaiting you, the services being highlighted at that time, and the top news headline. Beneath that window is the Main Menu, which allows you to jump directly to America Online's 14 departments or other services. To keep your small screen from being cluttered, you may opt to keep the Main Menu off at sign on. You can bring it up at any time by choosing Main Menu from the Go To menu or typing Ctrl+D.

- *Notify Me Immediately of Network News.* Normally, when America Online wants to send you a special announcement, you see it appear in a small window at the top of your screen. Such announcements might alert you to an upcoming event, such as a special conference that you wouldn't want to miss, or a special service announcement that you need to know. But if you would rather not be disturbed by these notices, simply turn off this option, and the network announcements are shut off.

- *Close Mail after It Has Been Sent.* This feature keeps your screen from being cluttered, so the best thing to do is to leave it on. That way, as soon as E-mail has been sent, the Compose Mail window automatically closes.

- *Where Possible, Display Text As.* This feature gives you three options: Small, Medium, and Large. Choose the option that provides the clearest text display on your computer's screen. The setting takes effect with the window open after you've made that setting. The Medium setting gives you the best all-around display of text, but you might prefer something different.

- *Enable Event Sounds.* One of the most attractive features of America Online is its voice messages. When you begin your session, you hear a friendly "Welcome" voice. And when you log off, you hear the same voice bid you "Good-bye." But if you work in a busy environment, maybe you just want to turn those sounds off. If so, turn off this option.

- *Enable Chat Room Sounds.* This feature enables you to hear sounds sent by other America Online members during a chat. For you to be able to hear the sound, though, you have to have the exact same sound installed on your computer.

- *Automatically Scroll Documents as They Are Received.* Turn on this feature, and you see text items scroll on your computer's screen as they are received. The normal setting (with this feature off) just shows the beginning of the text, as many lines as can fill a single text window. But you can still scroll through this text by using your computer's scroll bars at the right side of the text window.

Setting Passwords Preferences

This feature is one that you should use with caution. It enables the program to store the passwords you select for each of your screen names. That means you can call up America Online and have the program automatically log on for you. But if others are using your computer, and you would prefer not to risk the possibility of someone else using your account without your permission, you should not store your passwords in this manner. If no passwords are stored, you are asked to enter your password at the beginning of your online visit.

If, after reading my warnings, you want to store your online passwords, simply select this option, which brings up a list of your screen names. Enter the correct password in the text entry field next to the appropriate screen name.

Setting Download Preferences

The ability to download files from America Online's vast software libraries and transfer them through the telephone lines right to your computer might become one of your favorite features. You learn some helpful hints on downloading files in Chapter 5, "Finding Your Way around America Online." In the meantime, you want to set your download preferences for the best performance (or just leave them alone as most members do).

Figure 3.6 shows the Download Preferences dialog box that appears when you choose the Download icon from the Preferences dialog box. The following paragraphs describe the options you find in Download Preferences.

Fig. 3.6
You can fine-tune
the software
download process
on America
Online.

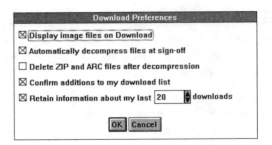

- *Display Image Files on Download.* This option enables you to actually see some picture files appear on your screen as they are being transferred to your computer. Depending on how fast your PC is, this choice could slow down your computer's performance somewhat. If you don't have at least a 486 at hand, you may choose to click this option off.

- *Automatically Decompress Files at Sign-off.* Many files you download from America Online are compressed, to make them smaller and reduce the time needed to get the files to your computer (and reduce your online charges). America Online software includes a tool to automatically decompress files you've just downloaded. The supported formats include ZIP and ARC. By default, as soon as you end your America Online session, all files that you have just downloaded (if they're in a format that's supported, of course) are decompressed automatically. I suggest that you keep this option checked. It makes the process of using your download files much easier.

  If you don't have enough disk space to store all those files, or you want to decide later on whether you want to use these files, just turn this option off.

- *Delete ZIP and ARC files after Decompression.* This option enables you to automatically delete the original file after it's been expanded. This option is one you ought to use with caution, as a protection against the rare occasion when an expanded file might become damaged somehow. But it's useful if space on your hard drive is tight.

- *Confirm Additions to My Download List.* This option produces a message that a file you've decided to download has been added to the queue.

- *Retain Information about My Last __ Downloads.* The Download Manager enables you to review a list of files you've downloaded to your computer. With this option, you can determine how many entries appear in your download log.

Setting Chat Preferences

Figure 3.7 shows the Chat Preferences dialog box that appears when you choose Chat from the Preferences dialog box. The following paragraphs explain the options you find in Chat preferences.

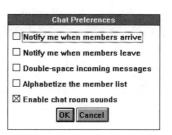

Fig. 3.7
You can have an online chat your way.

- *Notify Me When Members Arrive.* Chats and conferences are often the most enjoyable experiences on America Online. This first check box is turned off by default. But if you want to be notified when another member arrives at the chat, turn on the option.

- *Notify Me When Members Leave.* As soon as another member leaves the chat, you know about it if you select this option.

- *Double-space Incoming Messages.* You can have your chat window display text double-spaced so that it's easier to read (the normal mode is single-spaced).

- *Enable Chat Room Sounds.* You also can decide whether you want to hear sounds that other members might send. This preference is identical to the one provided for General Preferences.

Setting Graphics Preferences

America Online's Windows software allows you to open and print documents created in some graphic formats, such as GIF or JPEG. You can also observe the download of a picture file while it's in progress. Your graphics preferences are shown in figure 3.8 and described here:

- *Display Image Files on Download.* This choice is the same as the one you can set as part of your Download Preferences (see fig. 3.6).

- *JPEG Compression Quality.* This option allows you to choose the optimum quality versus compression of JPEG images. For most purposes, the default setting is just fine.

■ *Set Color Mode.* This button brings up several color preference options. The first, Detect Automatically, will do fine for most monitors. But some video drivers may have performance problems with the standard setting. If graphics do not display properly on your monitor, you may prefer to choose another color display option.

Fig. 3.8
Setting graphics preferences in your AOL Software.

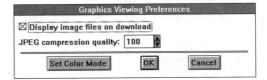

Using the FlashBar

America Online's software gives you a quick way to go directly to an online department or take advantage of the most popular features of your software. This feature is called the FlashBar, and it contains 20 icons, as shown in figure 3.9, each of which represents an online area or command.

Fig. 3.9
The FlashBar and your mouse are a great combination for activating the most-used features of your America Online software.

When you first open your America Online application, most of these icons are grayed out. But when you log on, the icons become bright and colorful. Clicking on the appropriate icon with your mouse takes you directly to the listed online area or activates the listed function.

Tip
If clicking on a mouse isn't your favorite way to travel along the America Online road, check the end of this chapter for a complete list of keyboard shortcuts.

Table 3.1 lists the special functions and destinations attached to each icon. The areas shown correspond, from left to right, to the icons displayed on the FlashBar. All these areas and features are discussed in more detail throughout the remainder of this book.

Table 3.1 Using the FlashBar	
Icon	**Destination or Function**
	Check Mail
	Compose Mail
	Go to Main Menu

Icon	Destination or Function
	Go to Welcome Screen
	Online Help
	Directory of Services
	Lobby in People Connection
	Stock Link
	Top News
	Go to Center Stage
	Internet Connection
	New Features and Services
	Discover America Online
	Go to Keyword
	Download Manager
	File Search
	Online Clock
	Personal Choices
	Print
	Save As

Setting Up

Using the File Menu

America Online's File menu, shown in figure 3.10, is much like the one you find in any other Windows application.

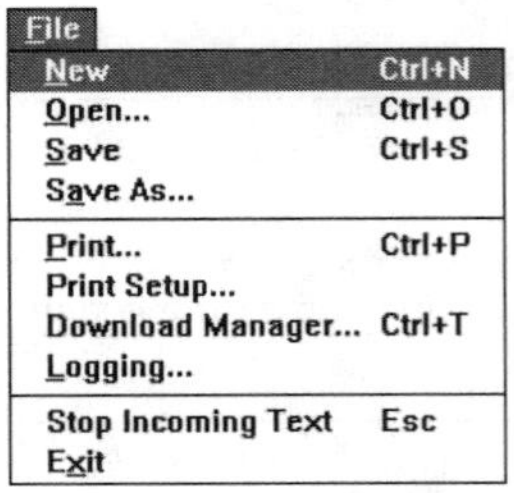

Fig. 3.10
America Online's File menu is similar to the File menus found in other Windows applications.

File	
New	Ctrl+N
Open...	Ctrl+O
Save	Ctrl+S
Save As...	
Print...	Ctrl+P
Print Setup...	
Download Manager...	Ctrl+T
Logging...	
Stop Incoming Text	Esc
Exit	

Most of the commands are familiar to you, but America Online has added a few features to its software that are worth some explanation. The following paragraphs explain the File menu's options.

Using the New Option (Ctrl+N)

America Online comes with a basic text editor, kind of a simple word processor, so you can write little memos, even a simple letter, or just paste text you might have grabbed from other memos or message windows online.

The Memo feature is not quite as full-featured as your word processing program. For example, it's limited to 32,000 characters (less than 5,000 words), not quite large enough for your new novel, but enough for a long letter. As with any other America Online text window, you can save and print your memo.

Using the Open... Option (Ctrl+O)

Choosing the Open... command brings up your standard Windows Open dialog box. It enables you to open text documents. You are limited to 32,000 characters in an open file window; if the file is longer, you can view it in separate pieces, each of which can be up to 32,000 characters in length. Just choose the More button to view the next piece of the file.

Using the Save Option (Ctrl+S)

This command saves the contents of your document window to a file that's written to disk. If you haven't saved the file before, you see a dialog box that enables you to give the file a name.

Using the Save As... Option

This option enables you to save your document under a new name. When you select this option, you see a standard Windows dialog box in which you can specify the new name of your file.

Using the Print... Option (Ctrl+P)

Choosing the Print... option produces your regular Print dialog box (see fig. 3.11). It enables you to print from any open text window. You can print a memo, your E-mail, a conference window, a message, or any other displayed text on America Online. If a window has more than one text window, such as the opening window of an online department, you should move the cursor to the text file you want to print. You can move the cursor either by clicking with the mouse or pressing the Tab key.

Fig. 3.11
Printing the latest news from America Online is a snap.

Using the Print Setup... Option

Choosing Print Setup... displays your standard Print Setup dialog box, in which you can change your page size and orientation (portrait or landscape) and select various printer options. These options vary depending on the kind of printer you have.

Using the Download Manager Option (Ctrl+T)

Downloading is the process of transferring a file from America Online's huge software libraries right to your computer. The Download Manager enables you to choose one or more files to download during your online visit. The files are placed in a download queue or sequence. You can begin the download process at any time during your online session or when you log off.

You learn how to configure the Download Manager to work best for you in Chapter 5, "Finding Your Way around America Online." Figure 3.12 shows the Download Preferences that are available to you in your America Online software.

Fig. 3.12
Configure your
download
preferences here.

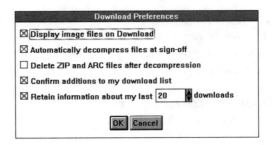

Using the Logging... Option

During your visits to America Online, you sometimes might want to save the
contents of a message area or an online conference so that you can view and
print them later. You have two main logging options in your America Online
software, as shown in figure 3.13.

Fig. 3.13
Recording your
America Online
visit is easy with
the program's
Logging feature.

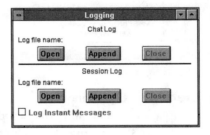

- The first option is the *Chat Log*. During your online travels, you might
  attend a chat in America Online's People Connection or an online conference. The Chat Log enables you to record the entire conversation.

- The second option is a *Session Log*. With this log, you can record all the
  text that you read during your visit to America Online. The log doesn't
  record the mail you send or the messages you post, but you can save
  those anyway, using the Save command described previously. (You also
  can log instant messages if you check that option at the bottom of the
  Logging dialog box.)

To use your online tape recorder, follow these steps:

1. Choose the Logging... option from the File menu, which opens the
   Logging dialog box.

2. Select the kind of log you want to record.

3. Click on the Open button. You then see a dialog box much like the Save As... dialog box, where you are asked to name your file and indicate where it is to be saved (see fig. 3.14). The log is given a default name, such as *session.log*, but you can give the file any name you want, so long as it contains no more than eight characters.

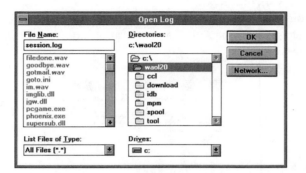

Fig. 3.14
Name your open log.

4. If you want to end the online recording process, just return to the File menu, select Logging..., and choose the Close button in the Logging dialog box.

5. When you decide to resume the logging process or add to a previously created log, you need to click on the Append button in the Logging dialog box.

6. When you are finished logging, choose the Close button in the Logging dialog box.

The logging process is flexible. You can open both logs at once if you prefer. What's more, you can append or close each log separately, depending on which one you've highlighted when you make your choice.

> **Note**
>
> Remember, America Online software can read only 32,000 characters in a single text window. When you want to read additional segments of a long file, you need to select the More option in your Open dialog box.

Using the Stop Incoming Text Option (Esc)

When you open a text window, the text begins to display in the window as it is received from America Online. If you want to stop this incoming text, select the Stop Incoming Text option, or press the Esc key.

Using the Exit Option (Alt+F4).

If you are still online when you choose Exit from the File menu, you see a dialog box asking whether you are sure that you want to sign off (log off) from America Online (see fig. 3.15). You can select Yes to be signed off within a few seconds, but the America Online application remains open for you to continue your work offline. Or you can select No and continue your online session. If you select the Exit Application option at the right side of the dialog box, you are logged off, the America Online application is closed, and you return to Windows.

Fig. 3.15
You log off by using the File menu's Exit option.

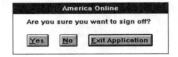

Using the Edit Menu

Five of the first six selections on the Edit menu, as shown in figure 3.16, are much like what you'd find in any Windows application. They are Undo (Ctrl+Z), Cut (Ctrl+X), Copy (Ctrl+C), Paste (Ctrl+V), and Select All (Ctrl+A).

Fig. 3.16
The Edit menu is typical of what you see in many Windows pro-grams.

The Crop option enables you to crop a portion of an image file you are view-ing with the software, and to copy the portion into another document.

The Show tools option only does something if you open a picture file. Then the tools will appear in a movable window, providing a basic set of graphic editing tools. These tools are similar to what you find in an image editing program.

Choose Fit Image to View to resize an image file to fit on your screen. This choice works best when the image file is too large for your monitor. If you use this feature to enlarge a smaller image, you expand the bitmaps that make up the image too, and you're apt to end up with a poor quality display (depending on how small the image was before you used this command).

If you need to refresh your skills on these and other standard Windows commands, please check the manuals that came with your Microsoft Windows software.

Using the Go To Menu

The Go To menu, as shown in figure 3.17, is your launching pad on America Online. It's your gateway to loads of undiscovered treasures that you can find during your travels online.

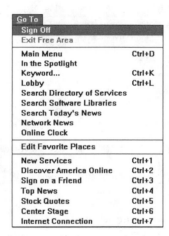

Fig. 3.17
The Go To menu is America Online's launching pad.

Setting Up and Signing On

The window shown in figure 3.18 appears automatically when you open your America Online software. You use this window to begin your online session or to change your modem setup.

Fig. 3.18
This screen is the Sign On screen for America Online.

Click on the Sign On button at the left of the window (or press Return or Enter) to begin the log-on process. You use the Setup button in the middle of the window to change your connection phone numbers or your modem settings, and the Help button on the right to bring up the online Help menu to get you through the rough spots.

Welcome to America Online

When you first log on to America Online, the In The Spotlight window shown in figure 3.19 serves as your introduction to the service.

Fig. 3.19
This screen is your introduction to America Online.

At the bottom left of the welcome window, you see an icon showing whether you've received any E-mail. If you have America Online's default sounds activated, your sign-on is punctuated with a "Welcome" greeting, followed in a few seconds by a "You've Got Mail" announcement. Clicking on the You Have Mail icon brings up a directory of the mail you've received since you last logged on. If no mail is waiting for you, the icon is labeled *No Mail*.

Beneath the In The Spotlight window when you log on is AOL's Main Menu (which can also be selected, when the window has been closed, from the Go To menu). This window is shown in figure 3.20. The large, colorful graphical icons in two rows on the right side of the Main Menu takes you on to stage two, the gateway to America Online's fourteen departments, shown by graphical icons. We'll be discussing those departments in detail throughout this book; after your initial log-on to America Online, you'll want to explore them briefly to get a good feel for the service.

If you want to bring up the In The Spotlight screen after closing it, simply select that command from the Go To menu.

Setting Up

Fig. 3.20
The Main Menu is
your jumping off
point to the far-
flung reaches of
America Online's
virtual city.

Using the Keyword Option (Ctrl+K)

Using the Keyword option (see fig. 3.21) is the fast and easy way to get anywhere online. Just select this command from the Go To menu or press the
keyboard shortcut (Ctrl+K). Then enter the keyword, click on the Go button,
and you are transported to that location in just seconds.

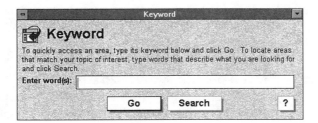

Fig. 3.21
America Online's
keyword feature
lets you go right
to your favorite
online spot, or
seek out points
of interest.

Many of the keywords on America Online are intuitive. If you want to learn
more about computers, you type the keyword **Computing**. If you want to
read the latest issue of *Time* magazine online, type the keyword **Time**. The
Keyword Help button on your Keyword box brings up a list of current
America Online keywords. If you want to find sources of information about a
particular topic, but you don't know the name of the area you want to visit,
you also have a Search option (the button at the right shown in fig. 3.21),
which brings up a list of probable matches. See Chapter 10, "Finding Information on America Online," for more details on finding information on
America Online.

Using the Lobby Option (Ctrl+L)

This command takes you to the Lobby of America Online's People Connection. For more information on People Connection, see Chapter 6, "Meeting People Online."

Using the Search Directory of Services Option

This option is another shortcut to finding the area you want to visit on America Online. When you choose Directory of Services while online, the Directory of Services window appears on-screen in a few seconds. This window accesses America Online's database, which enables you to search the entire network for the area or topic you want to know about.

Select Search the Directory from this window, and enter the name of the area or the subject you want to know about. If locations that match your description can be found—and they usually are—you see a list of those areas, along with a summary of what the area deals with and the keywords with which you can navigate to that area quickly. See Chapter 10, "Finding Information on America Online," for more details.

Using the Search Software Libraries Option

This option allows you to search America Online's vast software repository for thousands of software gems. We'll discuss this feature in more detail in Chapter 12, "How to Find Software."

Using the Search Today's News Option

When you first log onto America Online, the In The Spotlight window shops the top news. But the option to Search Today's News helps you locate news items on a particular topic that interests you. As with other database search features on America Online, simply bringing up the Search Today's News window, and entering the subject of your search will bring a fast result.

Using the Network News Option

Whenever America Online needs to send a message to everyone who's online at that moment, the program handles it through the Network News feature. With the Network News option, you can review all the items that have been sent to you during your online session. This option is useful if you've closed the Network News window to get more screen space with which to travel online.

Using the Edit Favorite Places Option

When you install your America Online software, you have a list of ten regular spots to which you can travel simply by pressing two keys (Ctrl plus a number from 0 to 9).

Editing the Edit Favorite Places menu is a simple task. Just follow these steps if you want to change the default destinations shown in figure 3.22, which are set by the software:

1. In the Favorite Places dialog box, type the name of the area you want to visit on the left, and the online keyword on the right. To move quickly from one entry to the next in the dialog box, just press Tab.

2. After you've made your changes and additions to the Go To menu, click on the Save Changes button. Your changes appear immediately in the Go To menu and are available immediately through your keyboard shortcuts.

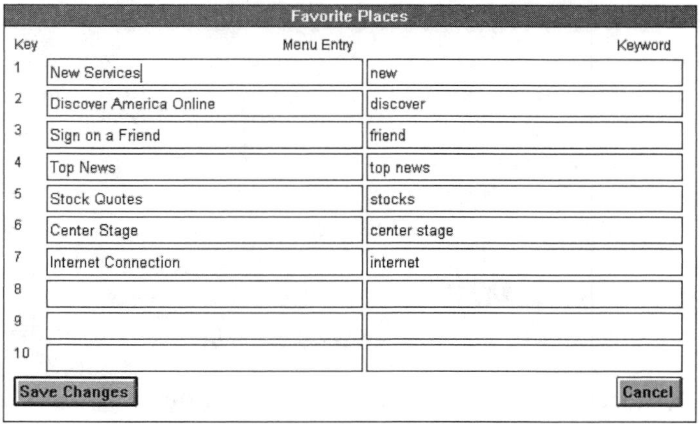

Key	Menu Entry	Keyword
1	New Services	new
2	Discover America Online	discover
3	Sign on a Friend	friend
4	Top News	top news
5	Stock Quotes	stocks
6	Center Stage	center stage
7	Internet Connection	internet
8		
9		
10		

Fig. 3.22
You can list your favorite places on this window for fast access.

Using the Mail Menu

Perhaps the most rewarding part of your online experience is the ability to send and receive electronic mail. The major features for creating and reading E-mail are found in the Mail menu, shown in figure 3.23.

As was mentioned earlier, you can compose your E-mail online, or do it offline and send it with a FlashSession. The following paragraphs describe the options you find on the Mail menu.

Tip
To save time and money during your online session, compose your E-mail *before* you sign on.

Setting Up

Fig. 3.23
Use the Mail menu
for sending and
receiving E-mail.

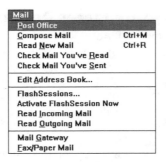

Using the Compose Mail Option (Ctrl+M)

This command brings up the regular America Online E-mail window. It consists of a blank mail form that you can fill in and send while online.

See Chapter 7, "Communicating with Others," for the ins and outs of composing your America Online E-mail.

Using the Read New Mail Option (Ctrl+R)

When you receive an announcement online that mail is in your mailbox (or when you see the icon change on your Welcome screen), just select this option, press Ctrl+R, or click on the You Have Mail icon at the bottom left of your AOL Welcome screen. If you haven't received any new mail, the label *No Mail* appears beneath the icon. Read Chapters 5 and 7 for more information about America Online's E-mail feature.

Using the Check Mail You've Read Option

If you want to recheck mail you've previously read, this option is the way to do it, while you are online. You can use this feature to find out whether other recipients of this mail have seen it too. Your previously read mail is stored in this list for one week after you've read it.

Using the Check Mail You've Sent Option

If you're not sure whether you've sent a letter to another America Online member or you want to find out when it was received, just check this item while you're online. You then see a window listing all the mail you've sent. You can reread the message yourself, or click on the Status button to find out who read it and when. Unread mail is stored here for 30 days; otherwise, it's removed in less than two weeks.

Using the Address Book Option

As you develop a list of regular online friends, you'll want to put their names in your personal Address Book. This list is your own Rolodex that you can use to send mass mailings to a number of recipients or merely to look up the name of a single individual. To learn more about creating and updating your Address Book, see Chapter 7, "Communicating with Others."

Using the FlashSessions Option

You can use this option to automate your America Online sessions. You can compose a message offline and then schedule a FlashSession to send your message. During that FlashSession, any mail that's been received since your last online visit is saved to your mailbox (choose Read Incoming Mail from the Mail menu to view the mail). In addition, you can opt to download files that have been attached to E-mail during a FlashSession.

See Chapter 7, "Communicating with Others," for the full story on how to schedule your FlashSessions.

Using the Read Incoming Mail Option

This option enables you to view letters that have been saved to your FlashSession mailbox. Letters are stored in your FlashSession mailbox until you delete them. This mail is also available to you offline. You can save mail that you've read online to this file by clicking on the Save to Flashmail icon in the Open Mail window. Please check Chapter 7, "Communicating with Others," for more information on how to run a FlashSession.

Using the Read Outgoing Mail Option

E-mail is stored in your FlashSession mailbox before it's sent during a FlashSession or while you're online. You can edit or delete your E-mail before it's sent, or even attach a file to your message.

Using the Mail Gateway Option

This option takes you to America Online's Internet connection, your gateway to sending and receiving E-mail throughout the world on vast Internet networks. You learn more about what Internet is and how to use this feature in Chapter 17, "The Internet Connection."

Using the Fax/Paper Mail Option

America Online has a service that enables you to send mail to someone who isn't an online member. You can have your letter sent as a fax or via U.S. mail. When you select this option while online, a window appears containing full instructions on how to use this service, along with the prices for this extra-cost service. Or just read Chapter 5, "Finding Your Way around America Online."

Setting Up

Using the Members Menu

You learned about one option in the Members menu earlier in this chapter, the option of setting your America Online application preferences. Now you find out about the rest of the options you can select from this menu, as shown in figure 3.24.

Fig. 3.24
The Members menu gives you options for finding out more about other members.

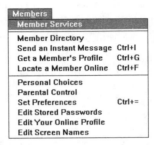

Using the Member Services Option

If you want to check your America Online bill, solve a problem with your software, or just learn more about the features available to you online, this option is the one to use. What's more, this area is free, meaning that you aren't charged for the time you spend in the Member Services section. A dialog box appears, asking you to confirm that you want to go into the free area, because other chat or gateway windows are closed in this area.

Using the Member Directory Option

If you're not sure whether someone is a member of America Online, you can search the member directory and find out. You can look for a member by his or her real name or "screen" name. You also can examine members' online profiles, if they've posted one, and update your own profile at the same time. Read Chapter 6, "Meeting People Online," for more information on this subject.

Using the Send an Instant Message Option (Ctrl+I)

An *instant message* is America Online's way of enabling you to hold an interactive "conversation" with another member, in private. Simply select this option, type the online address of the person to whom you want to send the message, and then enter your message. Click on Send or press Enter, and your message is sent almost instantaneously.

Using the Get a Member's Profile Option (Ctrl+G)

If you want to learn more about an online member, using this option is the way to do it. If the member has created an online profile, you can view it by selecting this option. You find more information on these and other special features for America Online members in Chapter 6, "Meeting People Online."

Using the Locate Member Online Option (Ctrl+F)

Not sure whether your online friend is going to "meet" you at the appointed hour? Here's how to find out whether they're online. If the member is attending a chat or an online conference, you receive a message announcing where the person is. Otherwise, you are just notified that the person is online.

When you select this option, enter the screen name of the member for whom you're searching, and press Return or Enter. If that member is online, you know about it in just a few seconds.

Using the Personal Choices Option

Keywords: Personal, Personal Choices

When you choose this command, you bring up the screen shown in figure 3.25. All the features we're about to discuss in the next few sections are accessible from this single window, plus one additional option, Marketing Preferences. The last choice lets you decide whether America Online can market your name as part of a mailing list of its members. The decision is up to you. Now we'll discuss the other choices available to you.

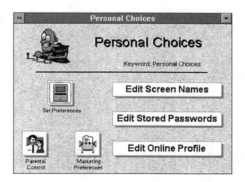

Fig. 3.25
Your America Online software preferences can be set by clicking on the appropriate icon in the Personal Choices window.

Using the Parental Control Option

This choice is only available to you when you log on with your master account (that's the first name shown in the pull-down menu of available accounts on the main screen of your AOL software). It allows you to restrict certain parts of AOL's services to one or more of the screen names on your account. We describe it in more detail in Chapter 20, "Getting Help." We'll also skip the Set Preferences option, since we discussed it in full detail earlier in this chapter.

Using the Edit Stored Passwords Option

You should use this option with care. It enables you to store one or more of the passwords you use to get online. When you select this option, a window appears in which you can enter the password for each of your screen names. The text is reflected on-screen with an asterisk, so someone looking over your shoulder can't see what you type. Your sign-on process is automatic, but if anyone else has access to your computer, storing a password enables that person to use your account without your permission. So think about it carefully before you take this step.

Using the Edit Your Online Profile Option

Your online profile is your chance to write a little bit about yourself, your hobbies, and your special interests so that other members can learn more about you. You can even make it humorous if you want, but try to be as accurate about yourself as possible. You don't have to post an online profile, of course, but it helps other members get to know you better if you do.

Using the Edit Screen Names Option

When you sign on to America Online for the first time, you give yourself a screen name—a unique mailing address that's used as the primary address on your master account. You can add up to four additional screen names to this account, perhaps for different members of your family, or to create an "alter ego" for yourself.

Please note that since all these screen names are part of the same master account, you cannot sign on to more than one of these screen names at one time.

Using the Window Menu

As you continue to travel through the America Online community, your screen will soon become cluttered with many open windows. The Window menu, shown in figure 3.26, is your tool for cleaning and clearing your screen.

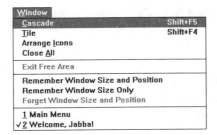

Fig. 3.26
The Window
menu is designed
for spring
cleaning, so you
can clean up a
cluttered desktop.

Setting Up

Note

Notice that at the bottom of the Window menu is a list of all open America Online
windows. After you've opened this menu, you can type the listed number to bring
that window to the front.

Using the Tile Option

As you travel online, you begin to open window after window, and finally
your desktop starts getting awfully cluttered. Tiling the windows enables you
to place them side by side, neatly.

Using the Cascade Option

Cascade is another option you can use to organize your online windows. The
Cascade option overlaps windows in neat form, from left to right, with the
title of each window clearly displayed.

Using the Arrange Icons Option

The Arrange Icons feature arranges all icons neatly within an active window.

Using the Close All Option

Everything has its limits, and your America Online software cannot just open
an unlimited number of windows without the chance that the program will
run out of memory. Periodically choosing this option to close all the windows is a good idea. It cleans up your workspace quickly.

Reopening the Welcome Window

If you've decided to do a real spring-cleaning session and close all your active
windows, the final option in the Window menu enables you to bring up your
America Online Welcome screen once again.

Using the Remember Window Size and Position Option

You might decide that the default size of an America Online message window is too small or too large for your screen. You can use this option to enable the program to recall the size and position of the type of window (E-mail, message, or whatever) that you have just chosen, so the program always opens that window in the same location and with the same window size.

This feature doesn't work for all America Online windows. If it doesn't work in a window you've opened, the option appears grayed out in the Window menu.

Using the Remember Window Size Only Option

This option is similar to Remember Window Size and Position, but as you might expect, the position of the window is not saved.

Using the Forget Window Size and Position Option

If you decide to change the window to its default size and location, choose this option.

Using The Help Window

If you hit a sticking point, and need a little more assistance in learning a particular function while using America Online's software, you'll find a lot of useful information in the Help menu, shown in figure 3.27.

Fig. 3.27
When the going gets rough, it's not a bad idea to seek out some online Help.

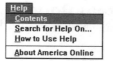

The Help menu has three parts. The first, Contents, displays a listing of the Help topics. Double clicking on the topic that interests you will provide a screen filled with the information you need. You can also use the Print Topic command to produce a paper copy of the open Help window.

The second part, Search for Help On... lets you seek information on a particular topic by typing what you want to look for in the search field.

If you're new to the Microsoft Windows environment, you may want to review the third Help selection, How to Use Help, for information on how to gain the most advantage from this feature.

Getting There By Keyboard

If you don't have a mouse hooked up to your computer, or you simply prefer using your keyboard, America Online has a host of keyboard commands that are simple to learn and use. Throughout this chapter, the keyboard shortcuts appear next to the matching menu commands, but some of the shortcuts are described in more detail in the following paragraphs.

Using the Tab Key

Suppose that you are composing a letter to another America Online member. You can use the Tab key to move from one field to another, such as from the Subject field to the field where you write your letter. The Tab key works in any area where more than one field is available to choose. Holding down the Shift and Tab keys at the same time enables you to move back to the previous field.

Pulling Down a Menu

To use the keyboard to open a menu, follow these steps:

1. Each menu bar item, such as File or Edit, has an underlined letter. If you press the Alt key plus that underlined letter, the menu drops down, and a rectangle highlights the first entry in the menu.

2. Use the down-arrow key to move the highlight down to the item you want to use.

3. Use the up-arrow key if you need to move the highlight up to the previous item.

4. Press Enter to activate the highlighted menu option.

Viewing a List of Keyboard Commands

This section contains a list of many of the keyboard shortcuts available with your America Online Windows software.

Function	Keyboard Shortcut
Access Download Manager	Ctrl+T
Cancel an action	Esc
Close a window	Ctrl+F4
Copy	Ctrl+C

(continues)

Function	Keyboard Shortcut
Cut	Ctrl+X
Find a member online	Ctrl+F
Get member info	Ctrl+G
Move to previous button	Shift+Tab
Move to next button	Tab
Move to next window	Ctrl+F6
Open a new text file	Ctrl+N
Open an existing file	Ctrl+O
Open/Browse the Departments window	Ctrl+D
Open Keyword window	Ctrl+K
Open Lobby window	Ctrl+L
Open Mail window	Ctrl+M
Paste	Ctrl+V
Read new mail	Ctrl+R
Save a file	Ctrl+S
Scroll up a page	PgUp
Scroll down a page	PgDn
Send an instant message	Ctrl+I

From Here...

In this chapter, you learned the basics of using your America Online Windows software. As you read further through *Using America Online*, you can find additional information and helpful hints to make your online sessions even more rewarding—and fun, too! You can find additional details on some of the subjects discussed so far in these chapters:

- Chapter 4, "America Online on the Road"

- Chapter 5, "Finding Your Way around America Online"

■ Chapter 6, "Meeting People Online"

■ Chapter 7, "Communicating with Others"

■ Chapter 10, "Finding Information on America Online"

■ Chapter 17, "The Internet Connection"

America Online on the Road

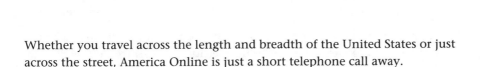

Whether you travel across the length and breadth of the United States or just across the street, America Online is just a short telephone call away.

America Online users, such as yourself, are not sedentary people. Whether you take a bus or train to work with your Macintosh PowerBook or PC laptop and a cellular modem, fly across the country on business, or simply visit friends' homes to show off your elegant example of "connectivity," you probably want to reach out to the world awaiting you on America Online, and do so from anywhere you happen to be at the time.

In this chapter, you learn how to:

■ Find your local access numbers to America Online

■ Change your access numbers in the America Online software

■ Search for other locations' access numbers

■ Find high-speed access numbers

■ Save multiple connection settings

■ Connect from hotels and offices

Finding Local Access Numbers

The cost of connecting to online services, and America Online in particular, has been dramatically cut in the last year or so. Unless you are Bill Gates, however, you still need to watch your online costs. By finding the closest number to the place from which you are calling, you do keep your telephone bills from going through the ceiling.

Although not every location in the United States has a local access number, most do, and those are the ones you want to use, wherever you might be. After you know the number, you also need to tell the America Online software that you know it. And therein lies the tale of this chapter.

First the Easy Way

In the latest releases of America Online software, for both Macintosh and Windows users, you can find a local access number not only while you're online or when you're first configuring your America Online software (see Chapters 2 and 3), but also anytime you find yourself wanting to call America Online from a location where you are not certain of your local access number.

If you have not already done so, open the America Online program, click on the Setup button to view your connection settings, and set the connection for 2400 bps access. (Note that if you change this setting, you have to reset the Connect Speed before you log on from home again.) Save that change, and then select Get Local # from the Locality pop-up menu (see fig. 4.1). If you need to dial 9 or some other access code to reach an outside line, first enter that code in your usual connection setup document. The same goes for any codes you may need to enter to disable Call Waiting. Refer to Chapters 2 and 3 for information on setting options in the Connection Settings dialog box.

Fig. 4.1
Get Local # is America Online's automated process for finding your local access number.

With your calling options now set, click on the Sign On button, or press Enter or Return, to begin the connection to America Online's toll-free number. In just a few seconds, you are looking at America Online's Access Number Location screen (see fig. 4.2). America Online asks you to enter your area code so that the program knows what area of the country to search for your access numbers. Enter the area code from which you're calling, or an area code from somewhere you plan to travel, and click on the Continue button.

The next step is to choose your first choice of connection numbers in the same way you did in Chapters 2 and 3 (see fig. 4.3).

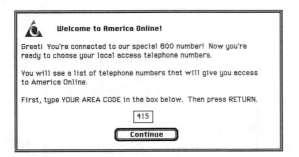

Fig. 4.2
You type your area code in America Online's Access Number Location window.

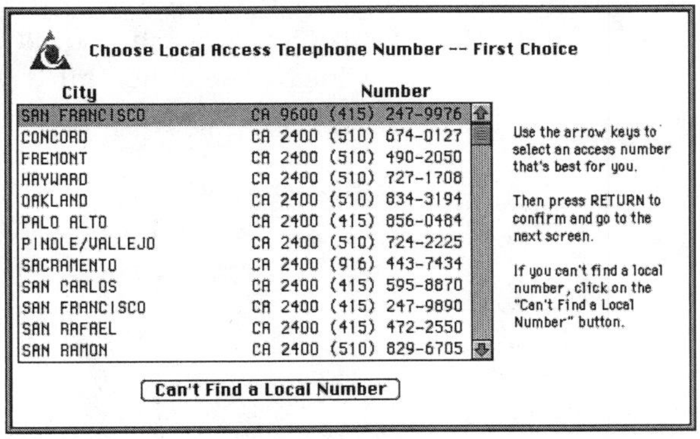

Fig. 4.3
You can choose from a list of numbers for your first choice of connection.

Double-click on the number closest to the location from which you are calling (or will be calling) to select that number as your first choice. Now the America Online host repeats the process by asking you to select a second choice number in case you're unable to connect using the first number. Double-click on your second choice number, or optionally click on the Same as First Choice button if no other number is acceptable.

Now the Magic Begins

After you confirm your choices, America Online disconnects from the toll-free 800 number and automatically presents you with a new, untitled Connection Settings window with the selected numbers already entered in their proper places (see fig. 4.4).

Fig. 4.4
The two access numbers you selected are automatically entered in their respective boxes.

First Try	**Second Try**
Connection File: SprintNet	Connection File: SprintNet
Connection Speed: 2400 bps	Connection Speed: 2400 bps
Phone Number: 591-8578	Phone Number: 637-1063

(Connection Settings — Untitled)

But I'm Already Signed On!

Great! You like to plan ahead, which is always preferable to the last-minute scramble to take care of those forgotten details. If you're already online and want to find local access numbers, enter the keyword **Access**. You then are quickly taken to a free area online that contains a database of all the access phone numbers you could ever need while traveling the United States and Canada (see fig. 4.5).

Fig. 4.5
Use America Online's local telephone access number menu.

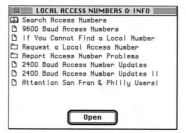

LOCAL ACCESS NUMBERS & INFO
- Search Access Numbers
- 9600 Baud Access Numbers
- If You Cannot Find a Local Number
- Request a Local Access Number
- Report Access Number Problems
- 2400 Baud Access Number Updates
- 2400 Baud Access Number Updates II
- Attention San Fran & Philly Users!

Open

These numbers are considered local telephone calls from most cities and towns and do not incur toll charges from most residential telephones. (If the nearest access number is not a local call, your local telephone service adds the per-minute charges to your phone bill. These charges are separate from the America Online connect-time charges but are usually of an inconsequential amount.)

After you arrive at the Local Access Numbers & Info screen in the free area, click on the Search Access Numbers item, and press Return or Enter on your keyboard to open the Search Access Numbers screen (see fig. 4.6).

The smaller of the two panes in the window is for you to enter the location or area code from which you are calling.

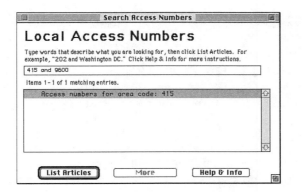

Fig. 4.6
The Search Access Numbers screen is the most versatile method of locating the access number closest to you.

America Online has arranged the telephone number database into a collection of searchable documents arranged by area code. Entering the area code from which you're calling is the fastest way to locate a nearby access number. In figure 4.6, 415 has been entered as the area code from which to connect to America Online; the entry "and 9600" indicates that the search should be for numbers offering 9600 bps access for this area code. If no 9600 bps access numbers are available in the entered area code, the search results in no matches. If 9600 bps numbers are found in the area code, then all access numbers are displayed, including lower-speed access numbers.

If you want to find a list of numbers from the area code from which you are attempting to connect to America Online, just type the area code by itself with no other search numbers or words. Then click on the List Articles button or press Enter or Return to display the matching online document containing the results of the search (see fig. 4.7).

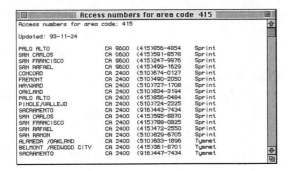

Fig. 4.7
This document title, *Access numbers for area code 415*, results from the search for numbers in area code 415 with 9600 bps access speed.

If you want to view the numbers contained in the document, double-click on the title to open a window containing the actual list of telephone numbers and the cities in which they are located.

Keep Those Numbers Handy

Tip

You also can search for an access number by typing in a city or town name, the communications carrier (SprintNet or BT/Tymnet), or even the first three digits of the telephone number.

I heartily recommend that you save the list for your area code in its entirety, and not just the number closest to your current location. If you unexpectedly find yourself a city or two away from your usual calling place, looking up the nearest number is as simple as double-clicking on the saved list. Select Save from the America Online File menu to save the list to your hard disk or floppy. Or just select the Print command to make a hard copy of your list of phone numbers.

Searching by area code is simple, offers you all the numbers serving the area in which you live, and keeps you prepared when you need to call from anywhere in your area code's coverage (and in many cases even nearby area codes).

Adding New Setups

Tip

Before you hit the trail, be sure to make a note of the local access numbers for your destination. You can find these numbers easily while you're online, as described earlier in this section.

In Chapters 2 and 3, you learned how to edit your connection (or network) setup to enter your modem's speed, the access telephone numbers, and other settings needed to connect successfully to America Online. In the preceding section of this chapter, you learned how to have the America Online software add numbers for you by searching the database of access numbers. For the *coup de grace*, you can learn one more trick: creating new connection documents by editing existing connection settings offline.

By creating new connection documents in this fashion, you are able to save various options and access numbers for simple point-and-shoot selection from the Welcome to America Online screen, as shown previously in figure 4.1. One common reason to accomplish this feat is to connect to the same access numbers from two locations, one that requires you to dial 9 to reach an outside line (such as an office, perhaps), and the other that doesn't (such as your home).

To edit a connection document, follow these steps:

1. Open the America Online File menu.

2. Select the New... option.

3. Select the Locality option from the New submenu, as shown in figure 4.8.

   Users of America Online's Windows software need to click on the Setup button on the Welcome to America Online window (described in Chapter 3, "Using Your America Online Windows Software") and then click on the New Location button. The resulting windows are similar to their Macintosh counterparts illustrated in this chapter.

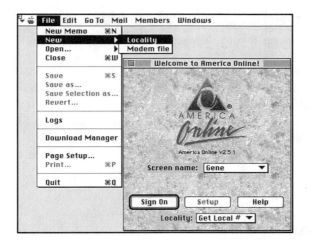

Fig. 4.8
You can create a new location profile by using America Online's new location management feature.

Setting Up

4. Enter the appropriate information, and check the options you need, as outlined here and in Chapters 2 ("Using Your America Online Windows Software") and 3 ("Using Your America Online Macintosh Software"). Don't forget to select a modem type and port, if necessary.

5. Click on the Save button to give your new setup a name and write it to your hard drive.

After saving the new setup to your hard drive, you can select it from the Locality pop-up menu that appears when you open America Online.

By this point, you have all the knowledge necessary to enter the correct information in your America Online Connection Setup documents, obtain that information from America Online, and add and change new connection documents when your travel plans dictate.

Note

Using America Online's E-mail feature is a good way to "back up" any documents that you work on while on the road. Simply attach any file that you work on to a piece of America Online E-mail (see Chapter 7, "Communicating with Others"), and send it to yourself (you may want to set up an alternate screen name so that you aren't disturbed with a Mail Waiting notice every time you log on while on vacation). The file will be waiting safely in your America Online mailbox when you arrive home. It will wait up to one month for your arrival.

Some General Advice When You're on the Road

When you book your hotel reservation, it is a good idea to ask the reservation's desk if the phones in their rooms have a "data port," a euphemism for a modem line. Many hotel phones do not have such a connection, although an increasing number do. If the room doesn't have a modem connection, but does have a standard modular (RJ-11) phone plug, you can disconnect that plug from the telephone and attach it directly to your modem (we've done it often).

But here's the important part: Double-check to see whether the hotel is using a PBX (digital) telephone system. Such a system provides state-of-the-art service, but it's also a serious problem for an analog telephone device, such as your computer's modem. Hooking up your modem to a PBX line may damage the modem. If the hotel uses a PBX installation, contact the manufacturer of your modem as to whether they have a special interface card or module for use with such services. (Macintosh users can purchase such an interface module from Global Village Corporation; the device is designed for use with their modems, but may work with other models, too.)

A final bit of advice: Some hotels will exact a large surcharge for telephone calls you make from your room (even local calls, in many cases). You may find, after your arrival, that another access number for America Online will run up a lower surcharge. At the very least, you may want to be a bit more careful about the amount of time you spend online if the hotel adds a per-minute charge for your call.

From Here...

While you satisfy your wanderlust, chances are that you want to find other America Online members who might be nearby. You can search for other America Online members not only by name, but also by hobby, special interest, occupation, and more. Wherever you travel across the United States, you can stay in touch with America Online for the latest news and information to make your trip even more rewarding.

For more information on the topics discussed in this chapter, refer to these chapters:

- Chapter 6, "Meeting People Online"
- Chapter 7, "Communicating with Others"
- Chapter 16, "The Travel Chapter"

Part II

AMERICA

Getting Your Feet Wet

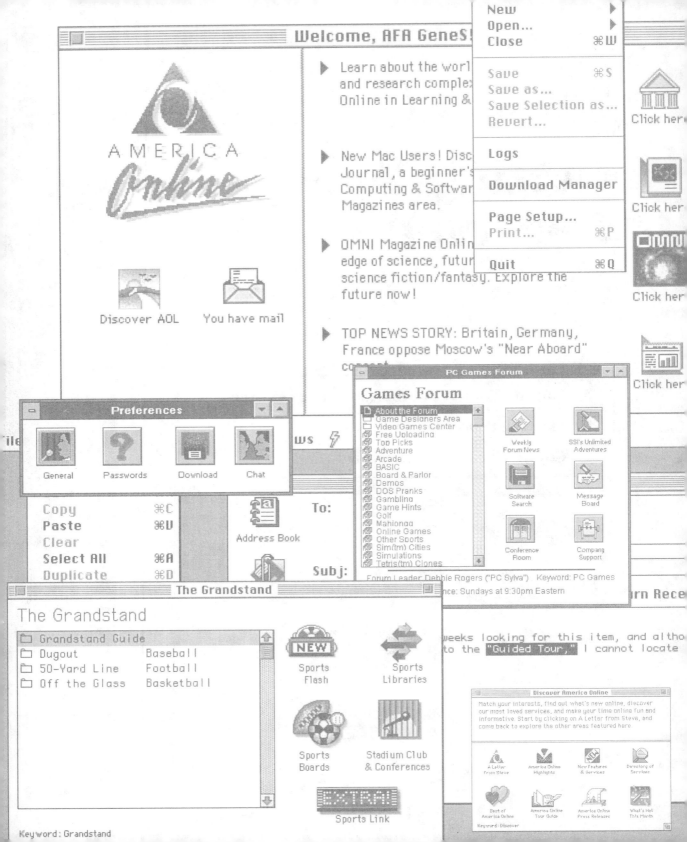

Welcome, AFA GeneS!

▶ Learn about the worl[d]
and research complex[...]
Online in Learning &[...]

▶ New Mac Users! Disc[...]
Journal, a beginner's[...]
Computing & Softwar[e...]
Magazines area.

▶ OMNI Magazine Onlin[e...]
edge of science, futur[e...]
science fiction/fantasy. Explore the
future now!

▶ TOP NEWS STORY: Britain, Germany,
France oppose Moscow's "Near Aboard"
co[...]

AMERICA Online

Discover AOL   You have mail

File menu:
- New ▶
- Open... ▶
- Close   ⌘W
- Save   ⌘S
- Save as...
- Save Selection as...
- Revert...
- Logs
- Download Manager
- Page Setup...
- Print...   ⌘P
- Quit   ⌘Q

Click here
Click here
Click here
Click here

Preferences

General   Passwords   Download   Chat

Edit menu:
- Copy   ⌘C
- Paste   ⌘V
- Clear
- Select All   ⌘A
- Duplicate   ⌘D

ws ⚡

To:
Address Book
Subj:

PC Games Forum

Games Forum

- About the Forum
- Game Designers Area
- Video Games Center
- Free Uploading
- Top Picks
- Adventure
- Arcade
- BASIC
- Board & Parlor
- Demos
- DOS Pranks
- Gambling
- Game Hints
- Golf
- Mahjongg
- Online Games
- Other Sports
- Sim(tm) Cities
- Simulations
- Tetris(tm) Clones

Weekly Forum News   SSI's Unlimited Adventures

Software Search   Message Board

Conference Room   Company Support

Forum Leader Debbie Rogers ("PC Sylva")   Keyword: PC Games
[...]nce: Sundays at 9:30pm Eastern

Click here

rn Rece[...]

The Grandstand

The Grandstand

- Grandstand Guide
- Dugout   Baseball
- 50-Yard Line   Football
- Off the Glass   Basketball

NEW   Sports Flash   Sports Libraries

Sports Boards   Stadium Club & Conferences

EXTRA!   Sports Link

Keyword: Grandstand

weeks looking for this item, and altho[...]
to the "Guided Tour," I cannot locate

Discover America Online

Match your interests, find out what's new online, discover our most loved services, and make your time online fun and informative. Start by clicking on A Letter from Steve, and come back to explore the other areas featured here

A Letter From Steve   America Online Highlights   New Features & Services   Directory of Services

Best of America Online   America Online Tour Guide   America Online Press Releases   What's Hot This Month

Keyword: Discover

Chapter 5

Finding Your Way around America Online

Once you've established your America Online account and had an online session or two, you will discover that there's a vast world of entertainment and information just waiting to be discovered.

In this chapter, we will introduce you to:

- The major departments on America Online

- Sending E-mail and instant messages

- Forum chats and conferences

- Sending paper mail and a fax to someone who doesn't have an online account

America Online Departments

Now that you've signed on to America Online, perhaps a few times, and learned how to use the software, it's time to do more than simply wet your feet.

Every time you log on to America Online, you'll see the Welcome screen (see fig. 5.1), also known as In The SpotLight, showing the major highlights, and perhaps even informing you that you have E-mail waiting.

In this chapter we'll go a bit deeper, beneath the In The Spotlight window, actually, to the Main Menu and beyond, where we'll explore the various virtual neighborhoods, known as *departments,* of America Online (see fig. 5.2).

Fig. 5.1
See the highlights
and check your
new mail when
you first log onto
America Online.

Fig. 5.2
The Main Menu is
your gateway to all
the major features
of America
Online's virtual
city.

The Main Menu is located just beneath the In The Spotlight window when
you first log onto America Online. The fastest way to bring it up front is just
to click on the shaded GO TO MAIN MENU rectangle at the bottom of your
Welcome screen.

Each of the 14 online departments shown is identified by a major topic of
interest. A department contains a number of forums, folders, services, and
other areas related (sometimes loosely) to that topic. We'll tell you more
about those areas later in this book. For now, we'll just scratch the surface.

Note

If you've closed the Main Menu during your online session, you can bring it up again
by simply selecting the Go To menu and then choosing Main Menu.

Today's News

Keyword: News

Here's your online daily newspaper. In addition to providing the top news of
the day, the Today's News department has special sections for stories related

to the U.S. and World, Business, Entertainment, Sports, and Weather. In addition, you can use the search window, located at the top right of the department window, to find stories about a particular item of interest. We'll describe this area in more detail in Chapter 14, "News, Magazines, and Business Information."

Personal Finance

Keyword: Finance

Let's consider this department an extension of Today's News (see fig. 5.3). The Personal Finance department lets you delve more deeply into all aspects of handling your personal finances, from reviewing the days business news (and how it may affect your income and investment strategies) to seeking out the profile of a company you may want to add to your stock portfolio. A surface glance at the main Personal Finance department window shows you lots of information resources, many of which we'll cover in Chapter 14, "News, Magazines, and Business Information."

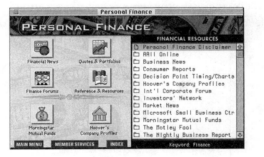

Computing

Keyword: Computing

Since we all use our personal computers to connect to America Online, the Computing department, shown in figure 5.4, is clearly one of the most popular places to visit on America Online. Whether you use an Apple Macintosh or a PC running Windows, DOS or OS/2, you'll find information, help, and huge libraries of software for you to download in this area. In addition, many of the major computer manufacturers have full-staffed support areas on America Online, where you can get quick solutions to problems with a specific product, or even advice on how to use that product more effectively. We'll tell you more about it in Chapter 11, our "Computing & Software" chapter.

Tip

Almost every area of America Online can be reached by pressing ⌘-K and typing a simple keyword. We've included a list of most of these keywords at the back of this book, in Appendix A.

Fig. 5.3

America Online's Personal Finance department has a vast storehouse of business news and advice.

II

Getting Your Feet Wet

Fig. 5.4
America Online's Computing area, one of the service's most frequently visited online departments.

Travel

Keyword: Travel

As the name implies, travelers gain gratification in the areas that comprise this department (see fig. 5.5). One of the principal services of Travel & Shopping is *EAAsy Sabre,* American Airlines' computerized travel center. You can book flights on any major airline, reserve rental cars and hotel rooms, or just check schedules and prices during your EAAsy Sabre visit. You are able to easily plan an entire itinerary simply and quickly with Eaasy Sabre.

Fig. 5.5
Book a flight or learn about your favorite tourist spot in America Online's Travel department.

Traveler's Corner brings you information from other wayfaring souls who have already braved the far corners of our country and the farthest reaches of the globe. *The Weissmann Travel Reports* bring you accurate and enticing reviews of all sorts of places, including such categories as Exotic Destinations, United States Destinations, and International Destinations. *The Weissmann Travel Reports* that you can order through America Online are the same reports used by thousands of leading travel professionals when they counsel clients. We'll cover all this and more in Chapter 16, "The Travel Chapter."

Marketplace

Keyword: Marketplace

The market place is your AOL center for shopping? Galore! Whether you are looking for America Online goodies such as T-shirts and coffee mugs, wanting to buy or sell a car, or looking for computer training aids, AOL's Marketplace department (shown in fig. 5.6) offers you these things and more. Here's a list of just some of the services offered, many of which are explained in more detail in Chapter 15, "The Shopping Chapter."

Fig. 5.6
Time to go shopping and save some cash right on America Online.

Vendor	Product
AOL Product Center	America Online products
AOL Software Upgrades	Order (or download) upgrades to AOL software
AutoVantage	Automotive buying and more
Classifieds	Buy, sell, and trade; employment
Checkfree	Pay your bills via modem
Computer Express	Computer equipment
Comp-u-Store Gateway	Computer equipment
Consumer Reports	Consumer publication
Flower Shop	Order flowers from AOL
Online Bookstore	Just what the name implies
PennyWise Office Products	Office supplies and more
PC Catalog	A fully equipped PC and software at a discount
Shopper's Advantage	250,000 brand name products discounted

II

Getting Your Feet Wet

The Newsstand

Keyword: Newsstand

It's hard to imagine what the world was like only 100 or so years ago, when almost any news of the world, or even the country, took days or weeks to reach our eyes and ears. Even 15 years ago we still waited for the morning newspapers to get more than just "headline service" about current events. In this age of the so-called information superhighway, we need not wait even that long (see fig. 5.7).

Fig. 5.7
The corner newsstand was never quite like this.

America Online's Newsstand department offers a vast amount of information about the world today, and is as current as it gets. In some cases, such as with *Time Magazine, The New York Times, The San Jose Mercury News,* and many other daily, weekly, and monthly publications, the information is on America Online before the papers themselves hit the streets.

There is so much more in AOL's Newsstand than we can possibly do complete justice to in just this section; we'll cover it in more detail in Chapter 14, "News, Magazines, and Business Information." We encourage you to explore this immense area of America Online, not only to absorb the day's news, but to expand your own knowledge about the world and current events.

Entertainment

Keyword: Entertainment

Movies, television, books, political and humorous cartoons, *Disney Adventures Magazine,* RockLink, the Trivia Forum, and LaPub—these are just a few of the Entertainment department features that draw huge numbers of the membership on a regular basis. Almost no other department online has the continuous drawing power of the Entertainment department. Both children and adults frequent Entertainment for its culturally diverse content. Be sure to stop by during your travels across America Online (see fig. 5.8).

Fig. 5.8
Just a small
portion of AOL's
Entertainment
department.

As you explore the Entertainment area, be sure to stop by LaPub for a virtual thirst quencher served by one of LaPub's congenial barkeeps. You may even find time to bounce on their trampoline or jump in the hot tub! (We'll explain what *that* means in Chapter 6.)

Education

Keyword: Education

Do you need help with that homework assignment, or do you want to take some special courses on a particular topic of interest? Well, you can do that and more in America Online's active Education department, shown in figure 5.9. Here, you can pay a virtual visit to the Library of Congress or the Smithsonian, sign up for a correspondence course, or get information about the next round of college board examinations. For now, we'll refer you to Chapter 13, "Learning & Reference," for more information.

Fig. 5.9
Sign up for a
special course, or
visit a museum
during your visit
to America
Online's Education
department.

Sports

Keyword: Sports

When America's national pastime, baseball, disappeared in the summer of 1994 due to a player's strike, the importance of sports in our lives didn't diminish one iota. We simply talked about the football season instead. America Online's Sports department, shown in figure 5.10, covers the world of sports. It's a repository of the latest sports news, plus discussion groups and regular

II

Getting Your Feet Wet

conferences on your favorite sports. And sometimes you'll be able to converse, through cyberspace, with some of your favorite sports figures too.

Fig. 5.10
If you open your newspaper to the Sports section first, you'll want to make a regular stop to this online area.

Kids Only

Keyword: Kids

We really haven't discussed special places for kids yet on America Online, but we'll remedy that right now. As shown in figure 5.11, our young people have lots of special and very friendly places to visit on America Online. *Disney Adventures Magazine* is on hand with a special forum. There's a kid's version of *Time Magazine* to explore, and also special Kids Only versions of America Online's most popular clubs, such as the Astronomy Club and the *Star Trek* club. We'll cover this all in more detail in Chapter 8, "The Entertainment Chapter."

Fig. 5.11
Kids have a special area to call their own on America Online.

...and More

By now you realize that America Online's departments contain vast areas to explore, and this chapter has highlighted only a few of them.

One of the remaining departments, People Connection, is among the most popular areas on America Online. We cover it in depth in Chapter 6. All 14 America Online departments are described in depth in the remaining chapters, but for now look around and become comfortable with their general layout. When the time comes to explore your chosen areas of particular interest, the later chapters will guide you through.

What Is E-mail?

During the first part of this book, we occasionally mentioned the information superhighway. The establishment of this national network is one of President Clinton's favorite priorities, and he has pledged to see it mature during his reign in the Oval Office.

What some of you may not yet realize is that a major chunk of this roadway has already been paved by such services as America Online and is already being traveled by you and me. One of the ways we travel this road is by using *E-mail*.

America Online's E-mail system is by far one of the most solid features the service offers and one of the most widely used (see fig. 5.12). AOL's E-mail system is simple and efficient; it can easily be scheduled to pick up mail waiting for you and deliver your outgoing mail without any intervention from you. You don't even have to lick a stamp or address an envelope.

Fig. 5. 12
The America Online E-mail form.

II

Getting Your Feet Wet

You can send E-mail at any time, day or night, and also include *attachments*—files from your computer's hard disk linked to outgoing E-mail to be delivered to someone else's incoming E-mail. To send E-mail, simply enter the recipient's screen name in the To box, type a heading in the Subject line, and type or paste in your message in the large message box. Your message can be more than 25,000 characters long.

The people to whom you are sending your E-mail may read your message, and retrieve any files you might have attached, at their leisure. You and your recipient need not be online at the same time, which saves you the aggravation and effort it would take to prearrange a time when both of you would connect your modems to complete a communication session. Using America Online's E-mail is explained fully in Chapter 7, "Communicating with Others."

What Is an Instant Message?

Regular E-mail, as we described in the preceding section, is a sort of formal and structured way of communicating messages of short to moderate length to other members, whether they are currently online or not. It's the electronic equivalent of a letter you'd send through the U.S. Postal Service.

Instant messages, or IMs for short, differ from E-mail in several ways and have distinct advantages and disadvantages. On the plus side, when using regular E-mail, you need to know only the screen names of your correspondents in order to send a message to them, and they need only to click a reply button to respond to you. The messages you exchange in this fashion do not require any knowledge on your part of the other person's activities or presence online. You can pick up mail sent to you at any time, up to a month after it was issued. Exchanging instant mail, however, requires that both you and the other party be online at the same time (see fig. 5.13).

Fig. 5.13
Instant Message Window showing a two-way mini-chat.

One large advantage of using instant messages is that both sides of the conversation take place in *real time* (while you and the recipient are online), and the topic is more easily followed without the time delays of E-mail.

Another major difference between the two types of messages is that when using E-mail, you can include as many screen names in the addressing boxes as you desire, hundreds even! On the other hand, using an instant message is just between two people, and no more. IMs are as private as AOL's E-mail. IMs are a good way to carry on an online conversation while getting to know someone better.

Yes, you may say, what about using the telephone for interactive conversation? Well, think about carrying on many phone conversations at once! That's what having a number of IM windows open at the same time means. Also, the flavor of an IM in getting to know someone better is totally different from a phone call. It's a great ice breaker too. Try it and see!

For more information on E-mail and instant messages, see Chapter 6, "Meeting People Online," and Chapter 7, "Communicating with Others."

Downloading and Uploading Files

Let's clear the air about these terms before going on. *Downloading* is the transfer of programs and files from the host computer to your computer's hard drive or floppy disk. *Uploading* is just the opposite: you send files from your own hard drive to the AOL.

There is no doubt about it; you are going to find yourself downloading files sooner or later (probably sooner). Most of us joined America Online in the first place to be able to download files. While exploring the AOL departments, you probably ran across some file libraries, and perhaps have already dabbled in downloading.

You can download files from two sources on America Online: the first is from department forums, and the other is from E-mail attachments. The way you set up a download session is slightly different between the two, but once begun, both use the same File Transfer method.

Starting the process of uploading is distinctly different, though. Using E-mail is the most straightforward of the two; simply click on the Attach button on your new E-mail window and select the file or files you wish to send to someone else.

In the Computing & Software forums, and other America Online libraries in other departments, you need to first complete a small form that requests information about the file you plan to send. We'll tell you more about it in Chapter 12, "How to Find Software."

A Brief Look at the Mail Gateway

The E-mail you send on America Online isn't restricted solely to this service. There is a vast world out there of millions upon millions of computer users, ranging from those with laptop models to folks working on huge mainframe devices. America Online offers you a method to send E-mail to others, even if they aren't members of AOL. It's done through the Internet Connection. We'll tell you more about it in Chapter 17, "The Internet Connection," but we'll give you a few highlights here.

The Internet is a vast assemblage of computers located all across the world that are linked together in a sprawling, loosely-organized series of networks. You can send E-mail to other Internet users as easily as you send E-mail to another member of America Online. The biggest limitation, at least for now, is that you cannot attach files to your Internet E-mail, but that is going to change (perhaps by the time you read this letter). Also, there is a way to convert a small file to text and send it as part of your Internet E-mail. We'll explain that in more in Chapter 17, "The Internet Connection."

America Online Paper and Fax Mail

Alright, alright, we know...the information superhighway still needs a few more on- and off-ramps for the rest of the world. When the time comes to send mail to someone who does not yet have access to AOL or other E-mail services, what can you do? Why, send regular U.S. Postal mail or a fax, of course!

Using your America Online software to send information is just as easy as sending E-mail. In fact, the real difference between E-mail and Fax/Paper Mail is how the mail is addressed. The form is exactly the same as the one you use to send E-mail to online members.

You can send paper or fax mail by following these steps:

1. From the Mail menu, select Send Fax/Paper Mail. Alternatively, from the regular mail menu, select Compose Mail.

2. In the To field, type:

   Addressee Name@usmail

   For example, to send paper mail to John Smith, type:

   John Smith@usmail

3. Type in the addressee name exactly as it would appear on an envelope, up to 33 characters. You will be prompted later for the complete mail address and your own return address.

   You are able to easily send the same message to multiple postal addresses by separating each addressee name with a comma. For example:

   **John Smith@usmail, Jane Jones@usmail,
   Mike Johnson@usmail**

> **Note**
>
> You cannot send a message to both paper mail and regular E-mail or fax mail addresses at the same time.

4. When you are ready to send your mail, select the Send Now icon.

5. You are presented with a window to enter the Return address first. Enter the address, select Continue, and type the address to which your Paper Mail should be sent.

Certain formatting rules apply to Paper Mail. You may learn more about these rules, and other information unique to Paper Mail, online by selecting Fax/Paper Mail from the Mail menu while connected to the America Online service.

Fax mail is even easier. In the Compose Mail window, type the fax address in the To or CC field in this format: **addressee@phone number**, such as **John Smith@415-555-1234**. Voila! Your fax is on its way to anywhere.

The phone number portion of the addresses must contain the area code of the receiving number and should *not* contain any other prefixes, such as a 1, before the area code. You can send Fax Mail to other fax addresses by separating the addresses with a comma, as in Paper Mail, and you can send Fax Mail to normal AOL screen name addresses by way of additional recipients listed in the To or CC boxes. As with Paper Mail, special formatting rules apply. You can learn about these rules using the same path as Paper Mail.

> **Note**
>
> When you send E-mail or an instant message, you only pay for your online time. Fax or Paper Mail is an extra cost service. You'll want to review America Online's current prices before you use this feature.

If you have general questions about the Fax or Paper Mail service or specific questions about fax or paper mail you've sent, send your questions to America Online through the free customer support area online; the keyword is *Help*.

What Is a Forum?

A *forum,* according to Webster, is a place for discussion of public matters or current issues, or an opportunity for open discussion.

This could be no truer anywhere than on America Online. Forums on America Online cover numerous topics, computer-related and otherwise. The Computing & Software department contains forums dealing with various aspects of working and playing with your computers in the information age. Some of the topics include Law and Computing, Graphic Communication, Desktop Publishing, and so much more.

Forums within America Online are usually constructed of several main areas. These are message boards, software libraries, real-time conference areas, and informational documents (see fig. 5.14).

Fig. 5.14
A typical forum in AOL's Computing & Software department.

Message boards provide a place where you post your thoughts about a particular subject for other America Online members to read and respond to. You can create and post a message in much the same way you compose E-mail. Each of the forums online contains at least one message board related to the main subject or charter of the forum's existence; many have multiple message boards containing thousands of messages.

Before posting your first message, take some time to read existing messages and see the topics being discussed. You can either respond to an existing message or create a new topic for yourself (but try to make sure it relates to the field that forum is devoted to). We'll tell you more about creating and answering messages in Chapter 7, "Communicating with Others."

Software libraries are repositories for files and programs related to each forum's purpose. For example, the Macintosh Graphics Forum libraries have a vast collection of images in the form of files that you can transfer to your own computer by way of the AOL downloading features. The Electronic Frontier Foundation, found in the Macintosh Communications Forum, offers a plethora of writings regarding the unique legal ramifications of computing in the '90s.

Conference Rooms, often called *chat rooms,* are an important area of any forum in that they provide a place for AOL members to congregate for live, real-time discussions. Depending on which forum's chat room you find yourself in, you'll be meeting other members—from just a few to hundreds. Real-time chatting is accomplished by typing your thoughts and sending them to the chat window for all to read. Similarly, other members send their thoughts for you to read (see fig. 5.15).

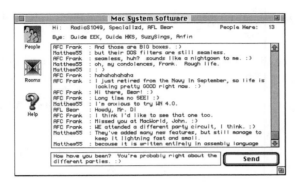

Fig. 5.15
The America Online chat window.

Conferences

Conferences are hosted not only by forums, but also by other departments of America Online. Different areas' conferences have different "flavors"—some use a formal protocol to determine who speaks at what time, some hold contests where everyone speaks (alright, they really *type*) at almost the same time. Each area's conference room usually has posted rules of conduct for members to read before entering, and you should do just that so that you will act according to local customs. To use a cliché, when in Rome, do as the Romans do.

More conference room information is located in Chapter 7, "Communicating with Others."

From Here...

In this chapter, we painted a picture of the way America Online is organized and the sorts of services offered. These services will undergo changes with time—the information superhighway is never stagnant. New areas will be added and older ones will be changed or removed.

In the remainder of this book, we'll detail each of the services we've briefly introduced here. We'll also take a task-oriented approach. We'll set a goal for you; perhaps learning more about your computer, planning a trip, or buying some merchandise. Then we'll tell you how to find the area that caters to that interest and how to use that area's resources most efficiently.

■ In Chapter 7, "Communicating with Others," we give you more information about communicating with others online.

■ In Chapter 8, "The Entertainment Chapter," we tell you more about the entertainment-related features offered by America Online.

■ In Chapter 12, "How to Find Software," we tell you how to find software for your computer.

■ In Chapter 13, "Learning & Reference," we describe many of the sources for learning and reference that you'll find in your online travels.

■ In Chapter 16, "The Travel Chapter," we help you out with your travel plans.

■ In Chapter 17, "The Internet Connection," we tell you how to participate in the world's largest computer network.

Chapter 6

Meeting People Online

One of the most enjoyable aspects of becoming an America Online member is the ability to meet others with similar interests, whether computer-related or not. A number of resources are available to aid you in your quest for meeting other online members. You find out about these features in the following paragraphs. But first, you learn how to introduce yourself to others.

This chapter tells you how to:

- Make yourself "known" to the rest of the online community

- View other members' online profiles

- Be discovered when your friends are online

- Follow proper online etiquette while meeting other members

- Find other members with similar interests

- Find online areas where you can meet people

Creating Your Online Profile

Every single member of America Online has at least one screen name. You can create up to five screen names to use when the mood strikes you or for use by other members of your family. Every member also can create an online profile for each of those online names, for other members to view (see fig. 6.1). Your first step toward meeting people is complete when you fill out your own online profile.

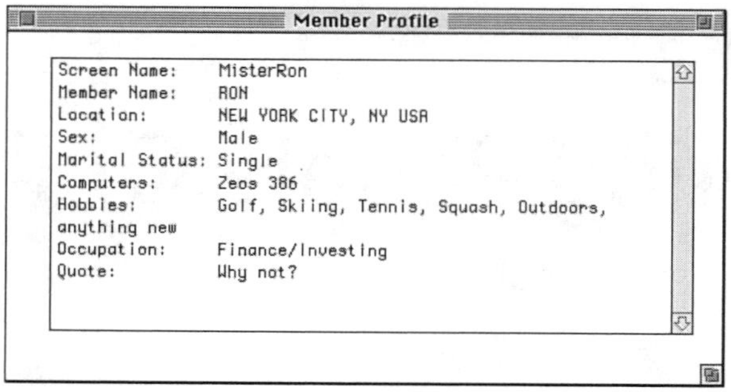

Fig. 6.1
This sample online profile shows the kind of information you can provide in your profile.

```
┌──────────────────── Member Profile ────────────────────┐
│  ┌──────────────────────────────────────────────────┐  │
│  │ Screen Name:    MisterRon                          │  │
│  │ Member Name:    RON                                │  │
│  │ Location:       NEW YORK CITY, NY USA              │  │
│  │ Sex:            Male                               │  │
│  │ Marital Status: Single                             │  │
│  │ Computers:      Zeos 386                           │  │
│  │ Hobbies:        Golf, Skiing, Tennis, Squash, Outdoors, │  │
│  │ anything new                                       │  │
│  │ Occupation:     Finance/Investing                  │  │
│  │ Quote:          Why not?                           │  │
│  │                                                    │  │
│  └──────────────────────────────────────────────────┘  │
└────────────────────────────────────────────────────────┘
```

Besides the expected information such as your real name, screen name, and location, you can enter personal information about yourself to indicate your interests to others. Hobbies, favorite quotes, your occupation, and computers you use are some of the entries you might want to provide for your profile. To create or change your profile, choose Edit Your Online Profile from the Members menu of your America Online software. A complete list of the data you can enter is shown in figure 6.2.

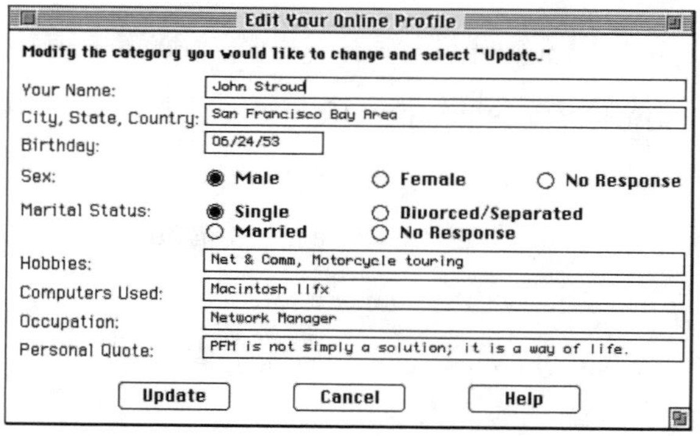

Fig. 6.2
The data-entry screen for your personal online profile.

```
┌──────────────────── Edit Your Online Profile ────────────────────┐
│ Modify the category you would like to change and select "Update." │
│                                                                   │
│ Your Name:           [John Stroud]                                │
│ City, State, Country:[San Francisco Bay Area]                     │
│ Birthday:            [06/24/53]                                    │
│ Sex:           ● Male      ○ Female        ○ No Response          │
│ Marital Status: ● Single    ○ Divorced/Separated                  │
│                 ○ Married    ○ No Response                         │
│ Hobbies:             [Net & Comm, Motorcycle touring]             │
│ Computers Used:      [Macintosh IIfx]                             │
│ Occupation:          [Network Manager]                            │
│ Personal Quote:      [PFM is not simply a solution; it is a way of life.] │
│            [ Update ]      [ Cancel ]      [ Help ]               │
└───────────────────────────────────────────────────────────────────┘
```

Caution

The first time you create a profile, it defaults to include your full name. You are free to change it to anything you want to have appear there.

As you look at the Edit Your Online Profile screen, make a note to yourself about which of the entries you want other people to be able to see when they look up your profile. You might or might not want to reveal certain information, such as your gender, real name, marital status, and so on. Fill in only the information you would not mind telling a stranger. In figure 6.2, for example, you see a user who stated his City, State, Country as a region rather than specific information about his residence.

If you do not want to reveal your gender, be sure to click on the No Response button on that line. (If your name happens to be Pat, you could sure keep 'em guessing!) Also click on No Response for your marital status if you want that information to remain undisclosed.

The remaining four fields are your basic "essay" answers. Here is where you tell other people about yourself as a person instead of simply stating factual information.

After completing your online profile, review it for spelling accuracy. This step might seem as if it would be fairly obvious, but after you look at a few random profiles, you'll know why I mention it.

After you've reviewed your completed profile and are satisfied with it, click on the Update button to finish off the job, and you can move on to more exciting online activities.

If you are not sure about your entries or have second thoughts about revealing yourself at this moment in time, you might prefer not to complete your online profile. In this case, click on the Cancel button. Your profile is not saved, and your entries vanish. If you want more information about the Edit Your Online Profile screen, click on the Help button.

Finding and Meeting Other America Online Members

Meeting people on America Online has had some interesting outcomes over the years since the online community was launched. The syndicated television program, *The Jerry Springer Show*, even spotlighted a number of AOLers who had met and married. America Online users often inhabit the various People Connection rooms, such as the Flirt's Nook and Romance Connection, in search of friendship, camaraderie, and, yes, even love.

After you've looked around at the dozens of areas where other people congregate, you'll have a hard time tearing yourself away from America Online and the friends you will soon meet!

Are you ready to dive in? Saying hello to people you meet on America Online is certainly a lot easier than opening a conversation with a stranger, because on America Online, remaining alone is difficult.

Tip
After you learn how to look up other people's profiles, take some time to look through a few other members' entries for ideas.

Tip
When you create an online profile for yourself, feel free to be humorous, but try to be accurate and truthful as well.

II

Getting Your Feet Wet

Locating Other America Online Members

You probably realize that you're not alone on America Online, right? But you might ask yourself in your first few sessions, "Where are all the rest of the people?" It's a good question. Being online is not exactly like walking into a restaurant and looking around to see whether you know anyone there. It's more akin to entering an office building; you need to know where the people are and go there before you can meet anyone.

On busy evenings in recent weeks, America Online has had literally thousands of members in "interactive areas" at one time! But as you stare at the Welcome to AOL screen, you aren't able to see any of these people. They are all behind "virtual" closed doors, and those doors are soundproof. Your first step to finding other people is to open these doors and look around. By far, the easiest place to find other members is in the People Connection area of America Online. The People Connection department houses most of the noncomputing-related chat rooms where members like to congregate and socialize. Are you ready to take a peek into one of these rooms?

First, select Lobby from the Go To menu (or simply type⌘-L). You are immediately transported to the "foyer" of America Online's People Connection, as shown in figure 6.3. This window represents a "room" in which up to 23 people can gather and get to know one another by exchanging chat. (If the Lobby is full when you enter, the room expands to additional rooms, and the room name has a number after it, such as Lobby 3.) The mechanics of chatting involve typing what you want others to see in the small box in the lower portion of the chat window and sending it by clicking on the Send button or pressing Return on your keyboard.

Fig. 6.3
America Online's Lobby in the People Connection area is one place you can chat with other members.

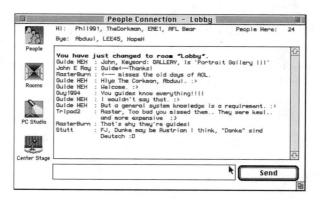

If you're like a lot of folks who are new to the online world, don't worry about starting a conversation right away; just hang around the Lobby and watch what other members type to each other. While you're lurking, chances are that someone will say hello to you. Don't worry about sending a reply if you aren't comfortable; no one will mind.

Take a moment at this time to look at your chat window, the Lobby screen shown in figure 6.3. This window contains some items of interest apart from the text you type and the text other people have typed. For one thing, now that you've located some people online, you can find out a little more about them.

Viewing Other Members' Profiles

If you want to view another member's profile, you need to know the member's screen name or be in the same chat room with that member. The Lobby is as good a place as any to start.

Members' screen names are shown at the start of each line as it is displayed in the chat window of the Lobby. At the top of the chat window are two lines of text titled Hi and Bye. These lines show you the people who have most recently entered the room and those who have recently left. You might have noticed your own screen name on the Hi line as you entered the room. As more people enter, their names appear at the start of the Hi line, and the earlier names disappear.

You also have a way to view a list of everyone in the chat room you occupy. You can view this list and practice finding out about other people by clicking on the People icon in the upper left portion of the chat window. The resulting window contains a list of all the America Online members currently in that room, as shown in figure 6.4. The list is updated as people enter and leave, so even though you might no longer see the Hi and Bye status lines, you can watch the People in this Room list to observe their comings and goings.

II

Getting Your Feet Wet

Fig. 6.4
The People list tells you which members are currently in the chat room with you.

Tip
Use the keyword *Help*, or select Members' Online Support from the Go To menu, to view and search the member directory from anywhere online at any time.

Now you can find out about someone! Select any of the names shown in the list, and click on the Get Info button on the right side of the window. If the person you selected filled out an online profile, you see it in just a few seconds. If that member has not filled out a profile, you receive a message indicating There is no profile available for that name. In that case, try using some of the other names in the list until you find someone who has provided profile information. Depending upon how much information the selected person provided, you see one or more lines of information in the Profile window.

Finding a Member Online

As you become more comfortable using the conference rooms and People Connection rooms of America Online, you will most likely begin to recognize some of the regulars. Perhaps you also know someone who uses America Online and want to find out if that person is signed on at the same time as you.

America Online provides a fast, easy method of locating people using the service. Select Locate a Member Online from the Members menu, or press ⌘-F (Ctrl+F for Windows users), and type the screen name of the person you want to locate (see figs. 6.5 and 6.6).

Fig. 6.5
Select the Locate a Member Online option to find a member.

Fig. 6.6
Enter the member's name in this Locate a Member Online window.

If a person you seek is online when you attempt to find him or her, the America Online host computer tells you one of two things: either that the person you want to find is Online, but not in a chat area, or the name of the chat or conference room where the person is currently. If the person is not online, the software tells you exactly that.

Exploring the People Connection

Of all the areas online where people congregate, the People Connection's Lobby is far and away the place you find most of the people who want to talk. On a busy evening, you can easily find hundreds of people in the various lobbies in People Connection.

Entering the Lobby

You might be saying to yourself, "Hey, wait a minute—didn't you say earlier that only 23 people can gather in a room at one time?" Well, yes, that's correct as far as it goes. What happens after the 23rd person enters the Lobby is that a new room is automatically created to hold the 24th and all the other people soon to follow. That room is called *Lobby 1*, and after it reaches 23 people, other rooms follow it with names like *Lobby 2, Lobby 3,* and so on.

The People Connection lobbies are usually bustling, crowded areas. Think Grand Central Station here; people are constantly coming and going. Often they are leaving for other People Connection rooms with specific themes or to go to Computing & Software conference rooms to discuss the latest industry news (see fig. 6.7). And private rooms are also available; you learn more about that possibility later.

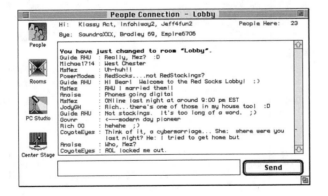

Fig. 6.7
The People Connection's Lobby area is a busy place.

As with most public areas in real life, the People Connection rooms have their own etiquette and rules of conduct. First and foremost is TOS, or Terms of Service. TOS is America Online's equivalent of real-life laws. You should take some time during your first sessions to acquaint yourself with TOS. Use the keyword *TOS* to go to AOL's free help area, and look over the Terms of Service, which are displayed in separate text files according to category. Spend at least a few minutes reviewing the contents of this area. (After all, it's free!) By making this effort now, you can feel more comfortable your first times visiting the public area rooms, and you'll have a greater understanding of how things work in general on America Online. The contents of each Terms of Service topic can be saved or printed (see Chapters 2 and 3 for an explanation as to how to save and print files in the Mac and Windows versions of AOL software).

Briefly, the most important parts of TOS simply state that you are expected to be a good citizen when you visit America Online. You are expected to refrain from using vulgar language and to respect others in the same way you expect them to respect you.

Entering the LaPub Entertainment Connection Room

As mentioned, the lobbies are the places in which you automatically arrive when you select Lobby from the Go To menu. For this reason, they are busy places. America Online's staff saw the need for regular visitors to have a place online where they could sit back, relax, and enjoy ongoing, pleasant conversation—and have some fun while there. With this idea, LaPub was born (see fig. 6.8). To get to LaPub, type the keyword **LaPub**, or enter through the Online Games Forum or Entertainment Forum.

Fig. 6.8

The LaPub is a pleasant gathering place.

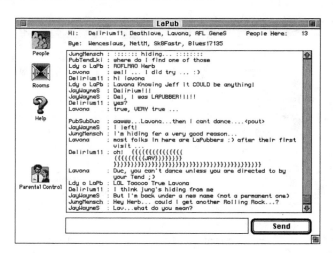

The bar was constructed, the refreshments were ordered and stocked, and the cheerful, highly capable "Pub Tenders" were rigorously trained. All this preparation for the sake of creating one of the liveliest of the People Connection areas ever seen online anywhere. The best part is that you don't have to drive anywhere; just sit in your most comfortable chair with the one-eyed monitor of your favorite computer in front of your face. Most likely, you will have at least one free "online" beverage of your choice offered on your first visit. Accept it, and enjoy!

LaPub offers more than just a place to chat with members and partake of the occasional festivities. In addition to the LaPub chat room, you find a special area, the LaPub Cellar, offering files uploaded by other LaPub patrons, including pictures of some of the regulars, sound files, and lastly, transcripts of notable LaPub events (see fig. 6.9).

Fig. 6.9
The LaPub Cellar is a collection of marvelous and entertaining files.

The LaPub Pictures library contains all the pictures of your favorite LaPub patrons, PubTends, and PubSubs—that is, if they are not shy. Ever wonder what somebody looked like offline? Then check out this library and see whether your favorite friend's picture is available. And don't forget to upload your own picture! You also might want to check out America Online's portrait library, the Gallery, which is discussed later in this chapter.

Check out the LaPub Sounds library for the latest in LaPub chat sounds. Install it with your Online Sounds, and watch the fun as some rowdy PubTend tosses a lemon meringue pie at your LaPub neighbor! (You learn how to install and use sounds while in any chat room in Chapter 7, "Communicating with Others.")

Remember that fun party last Friday night? Relive the experience by downloading the transcript of LaPub that night from the files in LaPub Transcripts. LaPub Notes also has a folder available for the discussion of LaPub Cellar. You can use this folder to announce a neat, new file you have just uploaded or to talk about the latest new file in LaPub Cellar. Archived LaPub Notes are also available within this library.

If you have any questions or comments about the contents of LaPub Cellar, feel free to E-mail your comments to the LaPub Management Team (Lavona, LaPub Hero, TallTassle, JR32, Exter). They welcome any comments you might have.

While visiting the LaPub area, be sure to check for upcoming events and contests in LaPub's schedule. You don't want to miss out on its unique happenings!

Visiting Private Chat Rooms

If you are like many of the People Connection's regular visitors, you'll eventually meet someone online with whom you want to communicate further. You want more privacy than the public People Connection rooms are able to offer, but in a fashion more convenient than instant messages and E-mail. (Instant messages and E-mail are discussed in more detail in Chapter 7, "Communicating with Others.")

Private rooms look and feel exactly like any chat room, such as the Lobby or forum conference rooms (see fig. 6.10).

Fig. 6.10

This screen shows an example of a member's private room, named "Here I Am."

The only difference between a public chat room and a private one is that the name of the room does not appear in any of the People Connection room lists. To join another member already in a private room, you must first know the exact name of that room.

The first step to creating this private area is for you or any other member to go to the Lobby in the People Connection. Then click on the Rooms icon on the left side of the Lobby chat window. Alongside the list of rooms that appears is a button titled Private Room. Click on that button. What appears then is a request for you to enter a room name (see fig. 6.11). Remember this room name so that you can send it in an instant message or E-mail to those members you care to have join you.

Fig. 6.11
You create or enter a private room by using this screen.

Entering the Center Stage Auditorium

The People Connection staff have also invited some extremely popular celebrities to pay a visit. Night Court's Harry Anderson once visited the People Connection and drew many, many people. (In the People Connection's Lobby, "many, many" means more than 23 people!)

Because the regular People Connection rooms hold only 23 folks before another room is automatically opened, a solution was needed for events that would be more popular. Another problem was that with so many people in one room, so many comments and questions would be typed by members wanting to talk to the guests that tracking the conversation with the guests could be next to impossible. To solve this dilemma, America Online and People Connection came up with a unique interactive concept: the AOL Auditorium. Figure 6.12 shows the Center Stage screen.

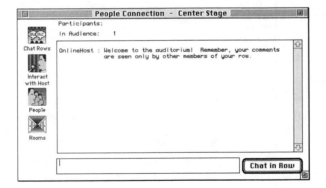

Fig. 6.12
The People Connection Auditorium is where hundreds can gather.

II

Getting Your Feet Wet

Note

America Online's Computing and Software department has a similar auditorium for large gatherings, known as The Rotunda (keyword: *Rotunda*). The instructions that follow apply equally to your visits to the Rotunda.

Center Stage is America Online's largest gathering place, capable of accommodating hundreds of guests for fun-filled game shows and special events.

When you first enter Center Stage, the service reminds you that only those in the same "row" as yours can see the text you type to the screen. If you find that the typing of members in the same rows is distracting or inconvenient to your concentration on the event, you can turn off that feature. Just click on the Chat Rows icon; then click on the Turn Off Chat button in the window that appears (see fig. 6.13). When the Chat feature is turned off, you can enjoy the event while seeing only text that appears from the "stage"—text from your hosts, guests, and contestants.

Fig. 6.13
More chat controls for the Center Stage Auditorium are found in the Chat Rows window.

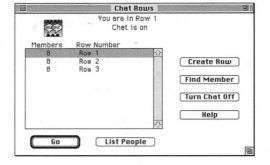

From this window, you also can look for other members who might be online (so you can tell them what a great time you're having on Center Stage), list people in your chat row or any other row, and create a new chat row.

You also can highlight selected speakers or contestants. Highlighting causes the conversations of the selected people to appear in the chat window in bold type so that you can follow the progress of the event more easily. First, click on the People icon on the left side of your Center Stage window. Then click on the Who's Onstage button. Lastly, select on the stage the individual you want to highlight, and choose the Hilite button (see fig. 6.14).

Fig. 6.14
Selecting Hilite to
highlight on-stage
guests in Center
Stage.

Entering the Gallery

The Gallery might turn out to be one of your favorite places online because
there you get to place faces with the screen names of people you meet online.
To find this interesting area, use the keyword *Gallery*.

The Gallery is a collection of photos put in computer-readable form and uploaded for all to see. Hundreds of America Online members have already
uploaded their portraits or sent their photos to the Gallery's staff to digitize
for free. As you get to know some of the regulars online, chances are good
that you'll be tempted to find out what they look like, and the Gallery is the
place.

A separate library is also included in the Gallery for family-album types
of pictures. Perhaps you should gather your own clan's photos and send
them to the gallery. You can upload the files in GIF format directory to The
Gallery's software libraries, or submit your photo to be scanned and uploaded
for you by the Gallery's staff. The address to which you should send your
photos for scanning is listed in the library.

To make viewing these photos easy for all America Online users, regardless of
the type of computer, the Gallery photos are all provided in GIF format. GIF,
short for Graphic Interchange Format, is a cross-platform image format that
offers a high-quality image with a small file size. The small size keeps your
download time short and makes it more convenient if you want to see photos
of a number of your fellow members.

The very latest versions of America Online's Macintosh and Windows software allow you to actually see a photo gradually appear on your screen while
it's being downloaded to your computer, just as we've shown in figure 6.15.
To view the photo files after you downloaded them, simply choose Open
from the File menu and then select the file you wish to see. Once the file is

Tip

Many areas besides
People Connection
hold regular chats
and conferences.
Look in Comput-
ing & Software
forums for other
chat schedules
(see Chapter 11).

II

Getting Your Feet Wet

opened (or has appeared on your computer's screen right after the download process is over), you'll be able to print it like any other document.

> **Note**
>
> If a photo has been uploaded with the newest version of AOL's software, you'll be able to see a thumbnail of the photo when you view the file description in the Gallery's libraries. Thumbnails are not available for photos sent using older versions of AOL's Mac and Windows software.

Fig. 6.15
As you download a file from The Gallery, the photo begins to display on your computer's screen. The complete photo is shown when the download is finished.

For more information about including your own photos in the Gallery, read the Get Framed document in the Gallery window.

Using Abbreviations and Shorthand Symbols

This section provides a partial listing of some of the more popular abbreviations and shorthand symbols you might see while online in the People Connection, in chat rooms, or on message boards. They have grown out of the need to show what cannot be shown when online—facial expressions and body language.

Online Abbreviations

Often when chatting, America Online members will shorten long phrases into a few letters so that they can be typed quickly. Here are some of the more common online abbreviations:

Abbreviation	Stands For...
LOL	Laughing Out Loud
ROFL or ROTFL	Rolling on the Floor Laughing
AFK	Away from Keyboard
BAK	Back at Keyboard
BRB	Be Right Back
OIC	Oh, I See
IMO	In My Opinion
IMHO	In My Humble Opinion or In My Honest Opinion
TTFN	Ta-Ta for Now
TTYL	Talk to You Later
NIFOC	Nude in Front of Computer
GMTA	Great Minds Think Alike
IHTBHWYG	It's Hard to be Humble When You're Great
<g>	Grin
GA	Go Ahead

II

Getting Your Feet Wet

Online Shorthand

When you're communicating with others online via instant messages, chat rooms, or E-mail, it's often difficult to convey body language and tone of voice. As a result, some brilliant individual invented online *shorthand*—keyboard symbols that convey human expression. Tilting your head toward the left will help you to see most of the symbols; for example, the characters :) form a sideways smiley face. Here are some common examples:

Shorthand	Symbolizes
[ ]	A hug, repeated as needed for degrees of enthusiasm, such as [[[[[[[[ ]]]]]]]]
:)	Basic smile
:(	Frown

(continues)

Shorthand	Symbolizes
:/	Ho-hum smile
;)	Winking smile
:D	Smile with a big grin
:*	Kiss
8)	Wide-eyed smile
B-)	Wearing sunglasses
[:l]	Robot
:>)	Big nose
:<l	From an Ivy League school
:%)%	Acne
=:-)	Hosehead
:-)8	Well-dressed
8:-)	Little girl
:-)-}8	Big girl
%-)	Cross-eyed
#-)	Partied all night
:-*	Just ate a sour pickle
:-'l	Has a cold
:-R	Has the flu
:-)'	Tends to drool
':-)	Accidentally shaved off an eyebrow
0-)	Wearing a scuba mask
P-)	Getting fresh
l-)	Falling asleep
.-)	Has one eye
:=)	Has two noses

Shorthand	Symbolizes
:-D	Talks too much
O:-)	Smiley face with halo; very innocent
:-()	Has mustache
:-)}	Has goatee/beard
:-p~	Smokes heavily
Q:-)	New graduate
(-:	Australian
M:-)	Saluting (symbol of respect)
8:]	Gorilla
8)	Frog
B)	Frog wearing sunglasses
8P	Bullfrog during mating season
8b	Same as 8P
I)	Salamander
:8)	Pig
3:-o	Cow
:3-<	Dog
pp#	Cow
pq'#'	Bull
}.'\	Elephant
+O:-)	The Pope
C=:-)	Galloping Gourmet
=):-)	Uncle Sam
=l:-)	Abe Lincoln
4:-)	George Washington
5:-)	Elvis Presley
7:-)	Fred Flintstone

(continues)

Shorthand	Symbolizes
:/7)	Cyrano de Bergerac
>:*)	Bozo the Clown
#:o+=	Betty Boop
>>-O->	General Custer
8(:-)	Walt Disney
>:^(	A headhunter
-=#:-)	Has wizard status
(: (=l	Going to be a ghost for Halloween
=:-H	Plays for NFL
(V)=l	A Pac-Man champion
M-):X):-M	See no evil, hear no evil, speak no evil
C):-O C):-O C):-O C):-O	A barbershop quartet
>:-(	Sick and tired of reading this nonsense
;^?	Punched out for submitting a sexist article
l-O	Bored
*-)	Shot for the last posting
~~\8-O	Needs to fix frayed cord on terminal
8-O	Took too many No Doz to work on thesis
L:-)	Just graduated
$-)	Just won the lottery
:-@	Extremely angry
:-o	Shocked
B-)-[<	Wearing sunglasses and swimming trunks
:-#	Punched in the mouth
R-)	Broken glasses
:-7	Talks out of the side of the mouth

Shorthand	Symbolizes
%')	Finished off a fifth for lunch
:-(O)	Yelling
..	Lying down
I:-)	Heavy eyebrows
{:-)	New hair style
{:-{)}	New hair style, mustache, and beard
(:-)	No hair
:~)	Ugly nose (needs a nose job)
:-E	Major dental problems
C:-)	Large brain capacity
I:-I	Excessively rigid
:-)))	Very overweight
._)	Suffers from Lorentz contractions
:-G-	Smokes cigarettes
\:-)	Wears a French hat
]:-)	Devil
8=:-)	Chef
$-)	Yuppie
{{-}}}	Refugee from the '60s
0-)	Cyclops

II

Getting Your Feet Wet

From Here...

You learn more about forum conferences, such as how to log and print conference proceedings, in the next chapter. You also find out about the formal chat protocol that many forums use and how to look up the conference schedule to find ones that might interest you.

If you have young children in your household who use America Online, read Chapter 20, "Getting Help," for information about parental controls that enable you to restrict certain features of America Online, including the types of chat rooms, if any, your children are permitted to use and whether they can use instant messages. You can find other related information in these chapters:

- Chapter 2, "Using Your America Online Macintosh Software"

- Chapter 3, "Using Your America Online Windows Software"

- Chapter 7, "Communicating with Others"

Chapter 7

Communicating with Others

Getting to know your America Online neighbors is one of the most popular activities of the AOL community. On any given evening it is not uncommon to find thousands of members in the various chat rooms of People Connection, Computing & Software conference rooms, and other online gathering places. Although you can't see E-mail, it flies across cyberspace at all hours of the day and night.

In this chapter, we explore the various areas of America Online designed to let you communicate with members who share similar interests or, in the case of the Debate Forum, even opposing views. You'll learn about:

■ Using E-mail and instant messages

■ Conferences and chats on America Online

■ The lasting power of message boards

■ Saving information for offline use

Testing the Waters: How to Write E-Mail

Of course, not everyone can be online at the same time as their friends for chats, so America Online E-mail is a busy online feature. The system is one of the best, if not *the* best, in the industry. It has proven to be extremely reliable, simple to use, and can be automated for the shortest possible connect times, saving you substantial online connection charges.

E-mail begins with a single, simple step: selecting Compose Mail from the Mail menu bar item. Keyboard enthusiasts may simply hit ⌘-M (Ctrl+M for Windows users) to begin a new mail message. The resulting form, shown in figure 7.1, is the jumping off point for all your original E-mail. Later we show you how to reply to E-mail without using a new mail form.

Fig. 7.1
America Online's E-mail form.

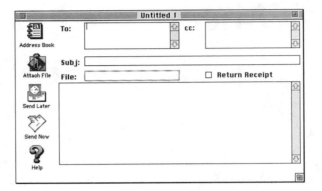

When you first conjure up a new E-mail window, the cursor is automatically positioned within the To: field of the form. Although it seems presumptuous, most folks actually do begin composing electronic mail by first addressing it. If this does not suit your tastes, simply press your Tab key to move the cursor to any of the other fields contained in the E-mail window, or click in the desired field with your mouse.

America Online is unflaggingly insistent about a few things regarding its E-mail system. You must include at least one To: address, a subject, and a message. Seems rather Orwellian, but it does make sense. After all, receiving a blank message is like picking up the telephone and finding no one on the other end.

The address fields of the E-mail window can contain literally hundreds of electronic mailing addressees. If you send a message to more than one person, each person's screen name must be separated by a comma or a Return (entered by pressing Return, not Enter; hitting Enter will send the message). When you use the Return key to separate multiple names, the window list is easier to read than when separated by commas. In the example shown in figure 7.2, the To: field shows names delimited (separated) by commas, whereas the CC: field uses the Return.

If you've entered any addresses in your AOL Address Book, you may also click on the Address Book icon to select names for this E-mail. The use of your AOL Address Book is described later in this chapter.

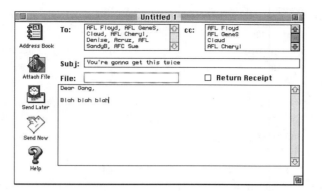

Fig. 7.2
Addressing E-mail to more than one person.

Now that you've decided to whom you will be sending your message, move to the Subject field and let the recipient know what your message is about without making them read it to find out. This step is both convenient and considered normal E-mail etiquette. After the subject, move the cursor to the message body, if you have not already done so, and compose your message.

E-Mail Styles for Macintosh Users

As we explained in Chapter 2, a unique feature of America Online E-mail—if you are using the Mac version of the software, of course—is that you may style your message by using type of different Size, Font, Style, and Color. The AOL Edit menu shows the four attributes you may change within the E-mail message (see fig. 7.3).

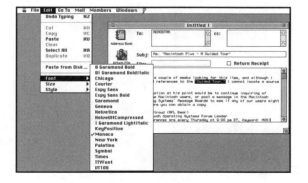

Fig. 7.3
Changing E-mail text styles using the Edit menu.

You give your E-mail more impact when using these features described, but don't overdo it; there's a limit to the number of fonts and styles which can be contained in one document, and overly complex styles look gaudy, anyway. Besides, the recipient of your E-mail won't enjoy some of your fancy special

II

Getting Your Feet Wet

effects if they're not using the same typeface you are. If you opt to vary the color of different parts of your E-mail, the recipient must have a color computer and a color monitor to see the results properly (otherwise, it'll just appear as varying shades of gray).

How to Send E-Mail

Once your E-mail is composed, you can send it along its merry way by using one of a number of methods. The easiest, if you are connected to America Online, is to click on the Send Now icon on the left side of the E-mail window. The mail is sent immediately, along with any attachments you may have enclosed. We talk more about file attachments later in this chapter.

If you composed your outgoing E-mail offline, or signed off while composing it, you may choose to use the Send Later feature that saves the outgoing mail on your hard drive. You can send your saved mail manually on your next online visit, or automatically during your next automated mail session. Note, however, that if you enclosed an attached file, you cannot move or delete that file until after you send your mail.

How to Receive E-Mail

This is the easy part! All you have to do is log on to AOL and, if you have mail, the happy guy that lives inside the AOL program tells you, "You have mail!" (that is, assuming that you have your Mail Sounds turned on in the Member Preference settings). A special mail icon is also displayed on the Welcome screen (see fig. 7.4).

Fig. 7.4
The Welcome screen indicating you have mail waiting to be read.

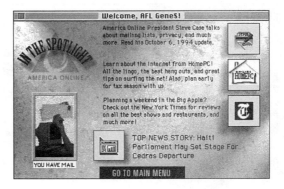

You can click on the icon directly above the YOU HAVE MAIL message on the Welcome screen, or you can press ⌘-R (Ctrl+R for Windows users) to view a list of new mail (see fig. 7.5). You can then double-click to open each piece of mail as you wish. You may also click on the Next arrow icon on the mail form to advance to the next message awaiting you (see fig. 7.6). The Previous arrow lets you move backwards through the mail. The left and right arrow keys on the keyboard are equivalent to clicking on the Next and Previous arrows.

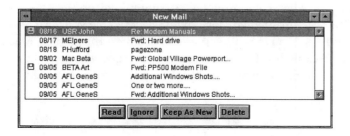

Fig. 7.5
A list of E-mail waiting to be read.

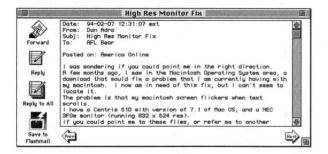

Fig. 7.6
The Read E-mail form. Note the navigating arrows in the lower corners.

As you read each piece of mail, a check mark is placed in front of the item as it appears in the New Mail window. If you do not read all your mail in one session, the pieces that have the check mark do not show up when you next open the New Mail window. Only those items you have not previously read appear there.

The Ignore button is functionally the same as reading mail, except no Read Mail window opens. Of course, the person who sent you the E-mail, if they check the status of the message, will know if you ignored the message.

The Delete button removes the message from your list of incoming mail, unread. Of course, the person who sends you E-mail will know, in checking the message status, that you have deleted the message.

The Keep As New button allows you to keep the message among your list of waiting mail even after you've read the message. It's useful if you want to use that message as a reminder of an upcoming event or as a specific bit of information you want to review the next time you visit America Online.

Tip
If you want to send a letter you just received to another online address with your added comments, use the Forward icon.

Getting Your Feet Wet

Attaching Files to E-Mail

America Online's E-mail system allows you to attach files from your computer to a piece of E-mail. When you send your E-mail, you also send the files you attached to it.

To attach a file when composing E-mail, simply click on the Attach File icon, and use the accompanying dialog box to select the file you wish to attach (see figs. 7.7 and 7.8). You may also choose to compress the file you attach by checking the Compress Files option before you click the Attach button. If you elect to attach more than one file, the AOL software automatically compresses them.

Fig. 7.7
In the AOL E-mail form, the Attach File icon is located in the upper-left margin.

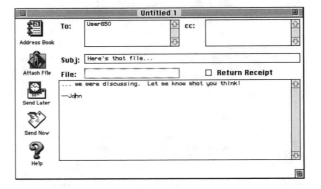

Fig. 7.8
Selecting files to attach is easy in this split window.

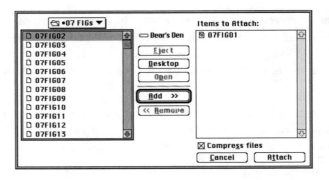

The file you attach must be on a disk drive connected to your computer or a mounted network drive, and you must attach the file before you send the E-mail. The recipient sees two extra buttons at the bottom of the received E-mail window, Download Now and Download Later. Selecting the Download Now button transfers the file from America Online's host to the recipient's computer. Selecting Download Later marks the file for your

Download Manager to transfer at a later time (see fig. 7.9). For additional information on the Download Manager, see Chapters 2, 3, and 12.

Fig. 7.9
An E-mail window containing an attachment.

When you send attached files through E-mail, you are charged only for the time needed to send your message and the attachments to the AOL mail processing area. Similarly, the recipient of the attached file is charged for the time needed to transfer the file from AOL's host to his or her computer. Because this costs money on both ends, it is a good idea not to send unnecessarily large files through E-mail.

Use file compression whenever possible, and if you believe other AOL members could make use of the file, consider posting the file to a forum library instead of sending it in E-mail. By posting the file to a forum, you are not charged for the connect time spent sending (uploading) the file to AOL's host. Read Chapter 12, "How to Find Software," for more information about uploading files to an AOL software library.

Note

If you are transferring a GIF image file to another AOL member, compression is probably not going to provide much benefit. A GIF file is already compressed all by itself.

Note

The Attach File icon changes to Detach File after you attach a file to your E-mail. In the event you decide not to send the attached file, but you still want to send the original E-mail message, you can click on Detach File to break the link between the unsent E-mail and the file (see fig. 7.10). At this point you can still attach a different file to your letter before it's sent.

II

Getting Your Feet Wet

Fig. 7.10
Detaching files is a
simple matter of
clicking the
Detach File icon,
located where the
Attach File icon
used to be.

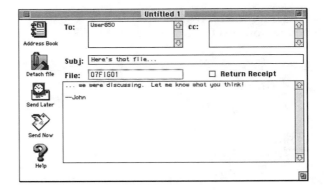

Saving and Printing for Posterity

After reading each piece of your E-mail, you have a few options. The first is to simply click the close box of the window, which sends the mail into oblivion. (Well, not quite—you can always find and read mail you've previously viewed from the Check Mail I've Read menu item, found on the Mail menu.)

Another option is to save mail to your Flashbox, a file stored on your hard drive that can hold tons of saved E-mail. To save to your Flashbox, click on the icon just above the appropriately worded Save to Flashmail legend. You can retrieve this E-mail item at any time, whether you are offline or online, by selecting Read Incoming Mail from the Mail menu.

You can also save your E-mail as an individual file. America Online has two special file types for E-mail—one for outgoing mail and one for incoming mail (see fig. 7.11). By selecting Save As from the File menu you may choose to save your E-mail as one of these types of files, or as plain text. Saving your mail as plain text allows you to view or change the contents of the E-mail in any text processor, such as your favorite word processing program.

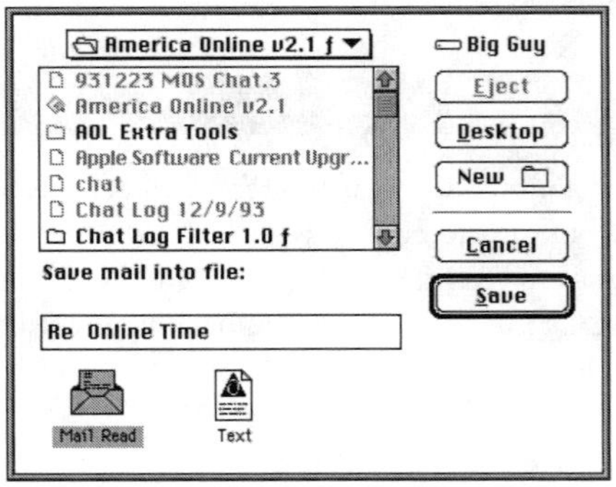

Fig. 7.11
File Save options
for E-mail.

One useful feature found in AOL is the ability to save selected text to a file. If you ever want to save some text from any of AOL's text windows, not just E-mail, simply select the text with your mouse and then select Save Selected Text As from AOL's File menu (see fig. 7.12). This feature is especially handy for saving addresses or lists contained in E-mail that you may wish to open or import into other applications.

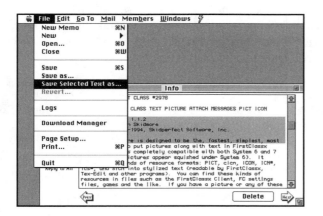

Fig. 7.12
Saving selected text from an incoming E-mail message.

Note

If you are a user of AOL's Windows software, you have to save the entire text window by using the Save As feature in your File menu, or copy and paste the text directly into another document.

Printing E-Mail

To print a hard copy of your E-mail, choose Print from the File menu. This works the same way as in almost every other application that supports printing, so we won't say any more on that. Remember, however, that if you changed printers since the last time you printed anything from AOL, you first need to select Page Setup to verify your printing options.

Note

If you are using a Macintosh and do not have a printer selected in the Chooser after you start your AOL program, you will likely not be able to print a text window; you'll just see a little flicker from the File menu when you choose the Print or Page Setup functions. Should this happen to you, log off America Online, selecting the Quit rather than Sign Off option. Then select your printer, launch America Online's software, then log on again. You should now be able to print normally.

II

Getting Your Feet Wet

Your AOL Address Book

Your America Online Address Book is the best way to store mail addresses that you use regularly so that they are available at the click of a mouse. Use this feature to build a file card system to keep track of your online friends.

Suppose for a minute that you have an online friend named Jesse Dunn. Her screen name on America Online might be Ogyr, and you exchange E-mail with her often. You'll probably find it more convenient to store her name in your Address Book rather than manually typing it each time you compose mail to her. To do this:

1. Select Edit Address Book from the Mail menu.

2. Click on the Create button. A new address entry form appears on-screen (see fig. 7.13).

Fig. 7.13
The AOL Address Book screen name entry form.

Tip
As you meet new friends and associates online, be sure to add their names to your Address Book. That way, you won't lose track of your online contacts.

3. Type the name of your friend in the Name field; for example, type **Jesse Dunn**.

4. Type the screen name of your friend in the Account field; for example, type **Ogyr**.

Now, the next time you want to send a piece of mail to Jesse, or any other person, simply open a new mail window, click on the Address Book icon on the left side of the window, and click on the name of the person to whom you will be sending this E-mail.

We mentioned earlier in this chapter that you can enter groups of people in the mail window to send a single E-mail to a number of recipients. Well, you can include group addresses in your AOL Address Book. As an example, suppose you have a group of online associates with whom you correspond regularly, perhaps your staff at work or your favorite Forum Leaders on America Online. Here's how you can create a group of addresses in your Address Book:

1. Select Edit Address Book from the Mail menu as you did earlier.

2. Click on the Create button. A new address form will appear on your
    screen.

3. Type a name for your group in the Name field; for example, type **My
    Staff**.

4. Type the screen names of all the people you would like in that address
    group into the Accounts field; for example, type **SteveC**, **TimB**,
    JohnS.

Congratulations! You set up a group address and, when you select My Staff
from your Address Book, all the names you entered for that group appear on
the E-mail address field you designate on your Mail form.

E-Mail FlashSessions for Macintosh Users

You can set a schedule for your America Online Macintosh software to log in
automatically at those times when you're too busy or nowhere near your
computer. You can even schedule these sessions for any or all your screen
names on your account (see fig. 7.14). You can elect to do one-way E-mail
transfer, read-only, or read and download E-mail and their attachments, or
any combination of the above.

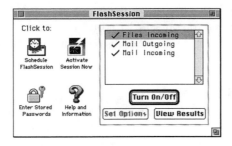

Fig. 7.14
The FlashSession
manager window.

Turning off the Files Incoming prevents the downloading of files that may be
listed in your Download Manager. Selecting Mail Outgoing and turning it off
causes your AOL software to not send any of the E-mail you may have sitting
in your outgoing FlashMail box waiting to be delivered to AOL. Turning on
the Mail Incoming item causes the AOL software to receive any E-mail you
may have waiting the next time a FlashSession takes place.

> **Note**
>
> If you click on the Options button while the Mail Incoming item is selected, you can instruct the AOL software not to download files which might be attached to incoming E-mail (see fig. 7.15). This could be a real money saver should you ever receive a large file attachment while you are in a hotel room paying exorbitant phone charges for even a local call. Would you want to have your FlashSession download the latest version of the Mac Operating System at that time? No, that would not be a good thing, would it?

Fig. 7.15
Turning the Automatically Download Attached Files feature on or off gives you control over E-mail attachments.

Turning off Automatically Download Attached Files gives you complete control over when and if you download attached files. You have the ability, for seven days after you read the E-mail, to download its attached files manually. Even easier, you can push the Forward icon on the E-mail form with the attachment and send it to yourself. Turn on the Automatically Download Attached Files option before the next connection, and the file will be downloaded at that time.

Scheduling FlashSessions

FlashSessions allow you to go online—immediately or at times you designate—to send mail you have prepared offline, retrieve any mail waiting for you, and/or download software files that you have saved to your Download Manager.

All these functions are managed from the FlashSession window. Access this feature, whether you are on- or offline, by selecting FlashSessions from the Mail menu on your menu bar.

If you wish to have your mail automated using America Online's Flash-Sessions, you are almost there. You've selected the FlashMail options in the previous section, and all that remains is to set up the FlashSession schedule and enter the passwords for the screen names used during these sessions.

If the FlashSession window is not already open, select FlashSessions from the Mail menu. Click on the Schedule FlashSession icon and look at the new window (see fig. 7.16).

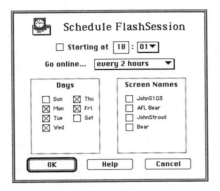

Fig. 7.16
The FlashSession scheduling window.

Now you need to follow these steps:

1. Tell the software at what hour you want to have it begin connecting automatically, using a 24-hour clock. For example, 18 means 6PM local time.

2. Select the 30-minute period of that hour in which you want the connections to begin. You can select one of two different settings that are automatically 30 minutes apart. The actual minutes, 01 in this example, vary from user to user so that not everyone's AOL software is trying to make automatic connections at the same time every hour.

3. Select the interval period between your online connections now. You set the period from a pop-up menu just below the Starting At time, and you may select every half hour, every hour, two hours, four hours, eight hours, or once per day.

4. Check the boxes to indicate what day or days of the week you want the FlashSessions to occur. Figure 7.16 shows Monday through Friday.

5. Select the screen name you want to use for FlashSessions. Check those names, and then review the form carefully.

6. Once satisfied with your settings, select the Starting At check box. This step actually enables the FlashSessions to begin automatically, according to the schedule you set. If this check box is not selected, no automated sessions take place, regardless of other settings in this window.

7. Now click the OK button to close this window and to store the settings you made.

Storing Your Passwords

This feature allows you and your family members to enter passwords for your screen names. This is necessary so that you do not have to be present for scheduled FlashSessions. Otherwise, you have to enter your password manually each time you log on to AOL. Remember that if you store your passwords, be sure that no unauthorized persons have access to your machine.

> **Caution**
>
> When you save a stored password with your America Online software, anyone who has access to your computer can log onto the service with your account, and use online time that will be charged to your monthly bill. Before using this option, be certain your computer is not easily accessible to others without your permission. You may want to consider, for example, using a security program to prevent unauthorized access to your computer.

To store your passwords:

1. Click on the Enter Stored Passwords icon and check the boxes in the FlashSessions column next to the screen names you set to connect during FlashSessions.

2. Enter your passwords in the fields next to the checked screen names. Notice as you enter your password that asterisks appear instead of the characters you type. This feature prevents others from looking over your shoulder and seeing your passwords on-screen.

3. Click the OK button to save your settings.

America Online's internal log-in calendar is now working and connects to the service at the times you scheduled. To turn off automatic connections, select the FlashSessions menu item, click on the Schedule FlashSessions icon, deselect the Starting At check box, and click OK.

E-Mail FlashSessions for Windows Users

You can schedule your America Online Windows software to log in automatically at those times when you're too busy or nowhere near your computer. To set your FlashSession preferences, select FlashSessions from the Go To menu. The first time you choose this option, America Online will guide you through the process of scheduling your automated session, using a special feature called Walk-Through, as shown in figure 7.17.

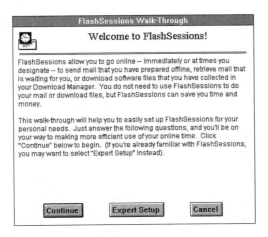

Fig. 7.17
America Online's FlashSessions Walk-Through guides you step-by-step through the process of activating automatic E-mail sessions.

Scheduling FlashSessions Using Walk-Through

The center button at the bottom of your first Walk-Through button gives the option of an Expert Setup. If you are familiar with setting up FlashSessions in the Macintosh version of America Online's software, or you've done it before in the Windows version, you may prefer to use this option instead. You'll then have the same sort of choices we describe above in configuring the Mac AOL software for a FlashSession.

Otherwise, click on the Continue button to continue your Walk-Through, which will bring up the screen shown in figure 7.18, which gives you the option of retrieving unread mail during your FlashSessions.

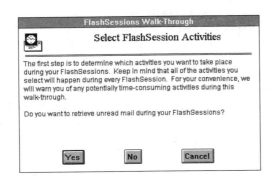

Fig. 7.18
Your first decision in preparing a FlashSession is whether you want to receive your unread mail during these automatic log-ons.

The next screen, shown in figure 7.19, only appears if you decide to retrieve incoming mail. You are then presented with another choice, whether or not to download files attached to your E-mail. If you don't accept this option, you are instructing the AOL software not to download files that might be attached to incoming E-mail. This could be a real money saver should you ever receive a large file attachment while you are in a hotel room paying exorbitant phone charges for even a local call. Would you want to have your FlashSession download the latest version of the Mac Operating System at that time? No, that would not be a good thing, would it?

Fig. 7.19

You will want to decide whether to automatically download files attached to your E-mail during a FlashSession.

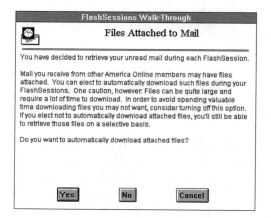

If you select the No option, you have the ability, for seven days after you read the E-mail, to download its attached files manually. Even easier, you can push the Forward icon on the E-mail you receive with the attachment and send it to yourself. Turn on the Automatically Download Attached Files option before the next connection, and the file will be downloaded at that time.

The final E-mail option, shown in figure 7.20, is whether to automatically send your outgoing mail by a FlashSession. This is a very useful choice. It allows you to compose all your E-mail while offline, so you don't incur online charges to your account. When you complete your E-mail, simply click on the Send Later icon, and it'll be added to your queue of Outgoing Mail. The only disadvantage is if you cannot select which mail to send during a particular FlashSession. It's all or nothing. But you will probably want to click on the Yes button for this option.

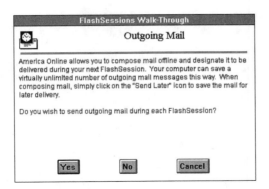

Fig. 7.20
You will want to decide whether to automatically send your outgoing E-Mail during your FlashSession.

Download Manager Preferences

The Download Manager stores a list of files you've selected using the Download Later option when you're online. This feature allows you to transfer all the files you want in a single session. The option shown in figure 7.21 allows you to retrieve all your selected files in the Download Manager automatically during a FlashSession. Since you cannot selectively download a single file this way, you may want to think a bit about this option before giving it the okay.

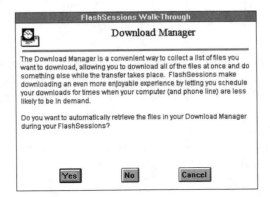

Fig. 7.21
If you say "Yes" to this choice, you'll be able to retrieve all the files selected via AOL's Download Manager during your scheduled FlashSession.

Storing Your Passwords

The next screen, shown in figure 7.22, allows you and your family members to enter passwords for your screen names. This is necessary so that you do not have to be present for scheduled FlashSessions. Otherwise, you have to enter your password manually each time you log on to AOL. Remember that if you store your passwords, be sure that no unauthorized persons have access to your machine. As you enter your password, what you type will be entered as an asterisk, so someone looking over your shoulder won't see what the password really is.

II

Getting Your Feet Wet

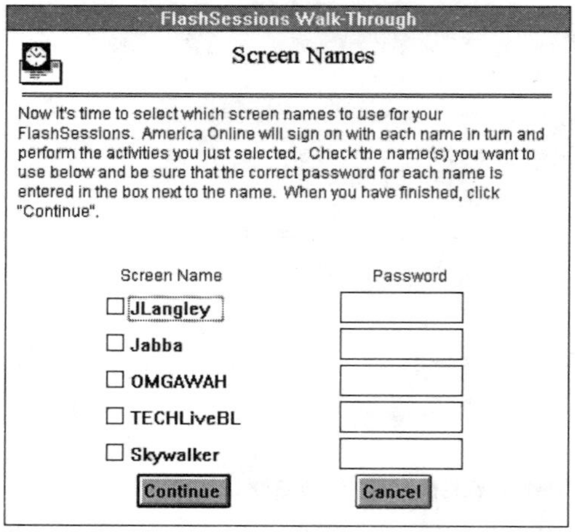

Fig. 7.22
In order to log on automatically during a FlashSession, you need to enter your password for each account for which you want to schedule your session in this Window.

Scheduling FlashSessions

Up till now, you've decided what you want to do when you run a FlashSession on America Online. There are two ways to have a FlashSession. One is simply to choose Activate FlashSession Now from the Mail menu, click on the checkboxes corresponding to the screen names for which you want to run your session, and then click on the Go Ahead button. The FlashSession will begin on the spot, using the preferences you've selected.

The second choice is to run an unattended FlashSession at regularly scheduled intervals. The next four screens of your FlashSession Walk-Through allow you to plan your FlashSessions in advance. You can change your settings at any time as your needs change. The first screen, shown in figure 7.23, gives you the option of scheduling your FlashSessions. If you opt to run the sessions manually, you just click on the No button; otherwise Click on the Yes button to continue. You then have three sets of selections to make.

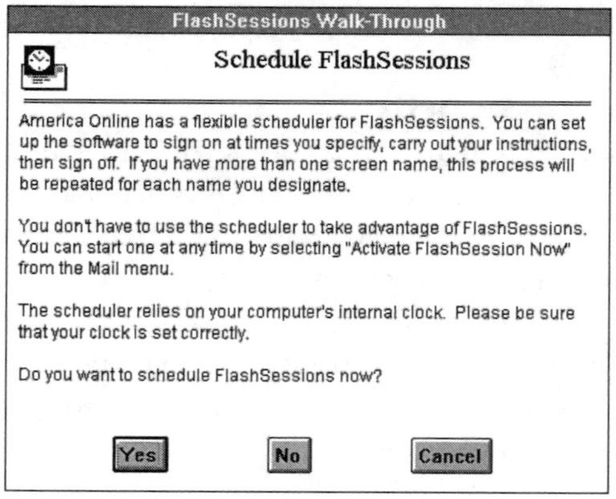

Fig. 7.23
If you want to automate your FlashSessions, click on the Yes button.

1. The first option, shown in figure 7.24, lets you choose the days of the week when you want your FlashSessions to take place. If you use your computer at work, you'll probably check only the weekdays, unless, like your cheerful authors and stressed-out editors, your work knows no such boundaries.

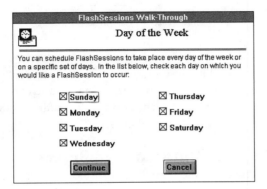

Fig. 7.24
Click on the boxes corresponding to the days of the week you want to schedule FlashSessions on AOL.

2. Your next choice, shown in figure 7.25, is how often you want to schedule a FlashSession, ranging from every half hour up to just once per day.

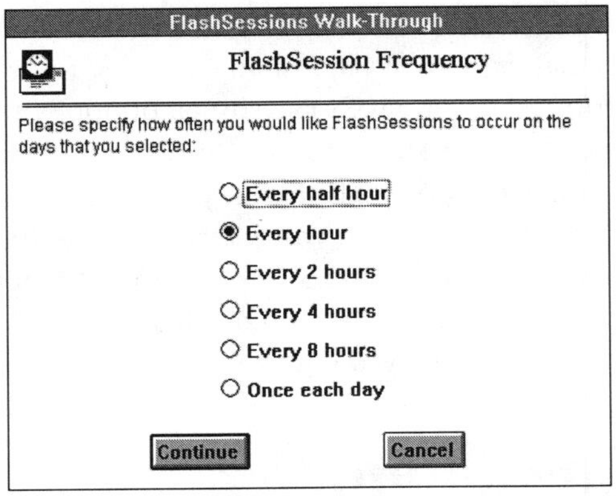

Fig. 7.25
Click on the boxes corresponding to the frequency of your FlashSessions.

3. Finally, you want to decide when your FlashSession should begin, as we've done in figure 7.26. If your computer is not on during a scheduled FlashSession, you'll receive no warning message that the session was not run. It'll simply not take place.

Fig. 7.26
Indicate the starting time for your first FlashSession for each day you've selected.

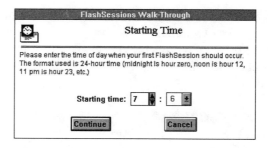

America Online's internal log-in calendar is now working and connects to the service at the times you scheduled. To turn off automatic connections, select FlashSessions from the Mail menu, click on the Schedule FlashSessions icon, deselect the Starting At check box, and click OK.

The Incoming and Outgoing Mailboxes

Each piece of E-mail you create for a FlashSession is a separate file. The mail you want to send is placed in the Read Outgoing Mail folder (or directory) which you can choose from the Mail menu. You can open individual letters to review or edit the contents. You can even delete a message should you not want to send it. Once all of your outgoing letters have been sent, the Read Outgoing Mail item is grayed out (a clear indication that it's empty).

The Read Incoming Mail folder (or directory), also available from the Mail menu, is your personal mailbox. Each E-mail letter you received from a FlashSession (or from using the Save to Flashmail option when you open a new E-mail message online) is stored in this mailbox as a separate file. To read a letter, just double-click on its listing in your incoming mailbox. You can save and print these letters when you want, or delete them when the amount of E-mail begins to get a little overwhelming. When the entire contents of your incoming mailbox have been deleted, the Read Incoming Mail selection in the Mail menu is grayed out.

Instant Messaging

Instant messages are used for two-way, immediate, private, person-to-person communication. To send an instant message while online, select Send Instant Message from the Members Menu or press ⌘-I (Ctrl+I for Windows users). You see a new window in which to address and compose your message (see fig. 7.27).

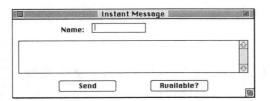

Fig. 7.27
The originator's
Instant Message
window.

If you receive an instant message, respond to it by clicking on the Respond button, entering your reply in the lower portion of the Instant Message window, and clicking on the Send button (see fig. 7.28).

Fig. 7.28
The recipient's
Instant Message
window.

Note

If you are using a Macintosh, you can press the Enter key on the numeric keypad rather than clicking the Send button to send your instant message. You cannot use the Return key to send your message because this key starts a new line in your message text. If your keyboard does not have an Enter key, use ⌘-Return. If you are using America Online for Windows, you can press Ctrl+Enter rather than clicking on the Send button.

You can have a two-way conversation with any AOL member by leaving the Instant Message window open after you send a response. When a new message arrives from your friend, it appears in that window. (If your online sounds are turned on, the arrival of the message follows a pleasant musical tone.) The actual conversation appears in the upper text field, while the responses you type appear in the lower portion of the window. You can hold numerous instant message conversations simultaneously.

America Online also provides an application Preference that keeps an instant message from appearing as the top window. Set this option to your liking by doing the following:

1. From the Members menu, select Preferences.

II

Getting Your Feet Wet

2. Select Members Preferences from the Preference Categories list.

3. Click on the Incoming IMs to Front check box to deselect that option.

> **Note**
>
> Using instant messages is a simple and unobtrusive process. If you are typing in a different window at the moment an instant message arrives, for example, you can automatically send the incoming instant message behind the top window with your next keystroke, provided you turn off the option to bring instant messages to the front (in your AOL application preferences, as we described in Chapters 2 and 3).

The option Incoming IMs to Front determines whether or not an incoming instant message appears as the frontmost window. Most people prefer that instant messages come to the front. You should select at least one of the three options under Members Preferences; otherwise, you may never realize that you have received an instant message (see fig. 7.29).

Fig. 7.29
The preferences available for instant messages.

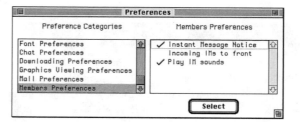

As with other types of text windows in AOL, you can print or save the Instant Message window's contents by selecting Print or Save from the File menu in your menu bar.

Forums

America Online's meeting places are called *forums*. They are places where staff and members focus on a specific interest. There are more than a dozen forums, for example, in the Macintosh side of the Computing & Software department (see Chapter 11, "Computing & Software") and a similar complement of PC and Windows forums. For a list of these forums, there is a Mac AOL Text Map in the Mac Beginners' Software library for you to open, save, and read. Find that area by entering the keyword **ABF** or **Beginners** (see fig. 7.30).

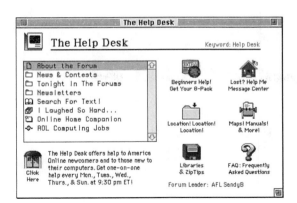

Fig. 7.30
The America
Online Help Desk.

> **Note**
>
> Macintosh forums are available to users of the Windows version of AOL software and PC and Windows forums are available to Macintosh users. But the special artwork you find in a forum isn't generally shown if you enter that forum from a computing platform other than the one it covers.

All the forums have their own chat rooms, software libraries, and message areas configured to focus on the special interests of that forum.

Forum Message Boards

The message areas are where members and AOL staff leave messages about the forum's field of interest. One advantage of message boards is that you are not constrained to communicating only with members who are online at the same time as you. When you leave a message, you can wait several minutes, hours, or even days before checking back to look for responses.

Before posting anything in the computing forums' message boards, you should learn about the forums and what their topic or subject covers. To do this, you need to explore. Most forums have a Forum Update file you can read online to find out what is new and what is happening in them. For an example, check out the Weekly Forum Update file in the Macintosh Communications Forum; the keyword is *MCM* (see fig. 7.31).

> **Note**
>
> Before you respond to a message, read the other responses first. It's possible that the message has already been answered or your question has already been dealt with by another member.

Fig. 7.31
The Macintosh
Communications
Forum.

Finding Forum Messages

To find messages in a forum that may interest you, click on the Message
Boards icon, which brings up the window shown in figure 7.32, or one very
similar to it. You see the general subject matter of the forum described briefly.

Fig. 7.32
A typical introduc-
tory message for a
computing forum.

You have four icons at the bottom of the window, one of which takes you
further along the road to finding messages you want to read. The Help & Info
icon is your route to the Macintosh Beginner's Forum (again see fig. 7.30). For
now, we'll click on the List Categories icon, which opens a list of discussion
topics (see fig. 7.33). We explain what Find New and Find Since is all about in
a moment.

Each forum divides its message boards into a group of overall topics that
relate to the forum's field of interest. If you're looking for a particular type of
message, check here for the general category. To get to the next step in your
message-reading process, click on the List Topics icon (see fig. 7.34).

In most message boards, you have a Create Topic option that allows you
to make your own folder, name it, and describe the subject matter. In the

directory shown in 7.34, you have a list of topics created by the forum staff and fellow AOL members. This list is your direct-entry point to a message on the topic you are interested in.

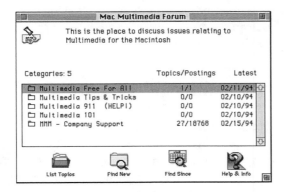

Fig. 7.33
Forum messages subdivided.

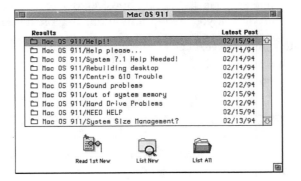

Fig. 7.34
A list of discussion topics in a message board.

Now let's get to those other icons we mentioned earlier:

■ *Find New.* This icon brings up a display of posted messages and the topics created since the last time you entered that forum (AOL's host computer keeps a record of your previous visit).

If you are visiting a forum for the first time, choosing this icon can produce literally dozens of topic folders and hundreds of messages. You may be better off using the next option.

■ *Find Since.* This icon lets you set a time for the duration of time spent searching for new messages. Its default is 1 day, but when you enter a forum for the first time, you might want to read all messages added in the previous 30 to 60 days, so you can get a taste of the flavor of the forum and the kind of messages the board contains.

- *Read 1st New.* When you open a directory of recent messages (see fig. 7.34), you can highlight a folder's name and click on this icon to see the first new message in the folder.

Tip
After you open your first message, use the arrow keys on your keyboard to move to the next or previous message.

- *List New.* This choice brings up a directory showing the subject of each message. You can review this directory and decide which messages to read. Double-clicking on the message itself opens that message window.

- *List All.* This option displays all the messages posted in a specific topic or folder, regardless of how old they are.

Posting a Message in a Forum

Posting a message is not unlike writing E-mail. You click on the Add Message icon (or Respond in some forums), enter the subject in the first field, and insert your comment in the second field. By default, the subject of the message you were reading before you choose the Add Message button appears, preceded by the reference (Re:). You can, however, delete this subject and choose one of your own, if you are not responding to a previous message.

After you write your message, click on the Post icon, and the message is added to the topic folder you were viewing. When your message is actually posted, your screen name and the time it was sent appear at the top of the message.

> **Caution**
>
> Posting a message more than once in a single forum is considered bad online etiquette. Some AOL members may even get upset at having to read the same message over and over again on billable time. When you have something to say, take a moment to choose the topic folder or directory that closely matches what you want to write about. In many forums, you can create your own topic to begin a discussion.

Tip
As with regular E-mail, it's considered good online etiquette to sign the messages you post in a message board.

A Brief Description of Message Threading

If you are a frequent visitor to user group bulletin board systems or some of the other online services, you may be familiar with a feature called "message threading." This is a technique to let you read all messages devoted to one subject in a single group, rather than having them mixed in with other messages on other subjects. When you post a message, you get the option to respond or reply to an individual message rather than just post a new one. There's an important difference between responding and posting. In the first case, your message is added to the "thread," so readers will be able to read the original message and all the responses it brings in one group. If you post a message, it is simply added to the message folder or directory in chronological order without regard to which message you're responding to. Even where message threading is available, you'll want to post a message if you prefer to begin a new topic.

You'll find message threading available in America Online's Newsgroups area (keyword: *Newsgroups*). Since we discuss Newsgroups in much more detail in Chapter 18, "The Low-Down on Internet Newsgroups," for now we'll just tell you that message threading is spreading to different message boards throughout America Online. In most ways, it's not terribly different from a regular message board. But the ability to keep all the messages on a single subject together makes browsing through messages much easier.

Conferences

This section describes the last of the four ways you can communicate on America Online—online conferences, or *chats*, as they are more commonly called.

Chats are live, interactive discussions. You and other members speak to each other by typing and sending text to a centralized display, the *chat room*. Each computing forum on AOL, and many areas in other departments, has its own chat room. People Connection (Lobby from your Go To menu), as we described in the previous chapter, also has a lot of rooms for people to chat about anything they wish. You can even start a new room for any topic of your choosing, and have other members join you for discussion.

Within the chat window, you type text in the bottom part of the window and click on the Send button to send it into the upper, main portion of the chat window. (Don't choose Send until you are sure you want to send your text.) Figure 7.35 is a typical chat window.

Some forums' chats are formalized, following chat protocol. This decreases the confusion that arises when you get 30 people trying to talk at once. When using chat protocol, if you have a question, you raise your hand by sending a question mark to the screen. The conference emcee recognizes you in order, and calls on you when it is your turn to speak. You can then send your question. Let the conference host know that you want to make a comment by sending an exclamation mark (!) for recognition rather than a question mark.

Tip
When you enter a chat room for the first time, take a few moments to see whether protocol is in effect before you send your comments.

Getting Your Feet Wet

II

Fig. 7.35
A forum chat
window.

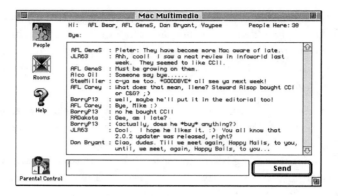

To keep a text record of the chat, select Logs from the File menu. Here you can open a chat log to record to a text file everything you see in the chat window (see fig. 7.36). We describe the logging process in more detail in Chapters 2 and 3.

Fig. 7.36
The America
Online Log
Manager window.

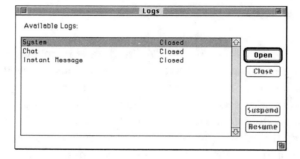

The System log records all messages received by your computer while online except instant messages and chat text. The other two logs handle those two categories.

From Here...

If the '80s was the decade of the Information Age, the '90s is the Communication Age. Instant access to people all over the world is a reality, regardless of their location or time zone.

■ For more information about E-mail and instant messages, see Chapter 2, "Using Your America Online Macintosh Software," Chapter 3, "Using Your America Online Windows Software," and Chapter 5, "Finding Your Way around America Online."

■ The America Online Computing & Software forums and forum conferences are described in depth in Chapter 11, "Computing & Software."

■ For more information about using America Online chat rooms and
auditoriums, see Chapter 5, "Finding Your Way around America
Online," and Chapter 6, "Meeting People Online."

■ For more information on message threading and using America
Online's Internet Center, see Chapter 18, "The Low-Down on Internet
Newsgroups."

II

Getting Your Feet Wet

Part III

AMERICA
Having Fun

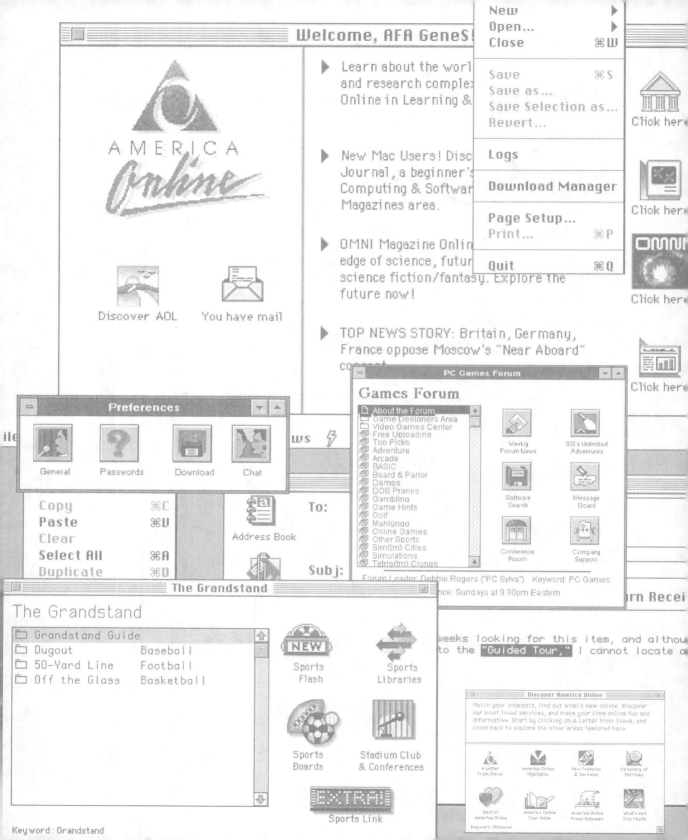

Welcome, AFA GeneS!

- Learn about the worl[d] and research complex[ity] Online in Learning &

- New Mac Users! Disc[over] Journal, a beginner's Computing & Softwar[e] Magazines area.

- OMNI Magazine Onlin[e] edge of science, futur[e] science fiction/fantasy. Explore the future now!

- TOP NEWS STORY: Britain, Germany, France oppose Moscow's "Near Aboard" cor[...]

Discover AOL   You have mail

Menu (File)

New	▶
Open...	▶
Close	⌘W
Save	⌘S
Save as...	
Save Selection as...	
Revert...	
Logs	
Download Manager	
Page Setup...	
Print...	⌘P
Quit	⌘Q

Click here
Click here
OMNI
Click here
Click here

Preferences

General   Passwords   Download   Chat

(Edit menu)

Copy	⌘C
Paste	⌘V
Clear	
Select All	⌘A
Duplicate	⌘D

ws ⚡

To:
Address Book
Subj:

PC Games Forum

Games Forum

- About the Forum
- Game Designers Area
- Video Games Center
- Free Uploading
- Top Picks
- Adventure
- Arcade
- BASIC
- Board & Parlor
- Demos
- DOS Pranks
- Gambling
- Game Hints
- Golf
- Mahjongg
- Online Games
- Other Sports
- Sim(tm) Cities
- Simulations
- Tetris(tm) Clones

Weekly Forum News   SSI's Unlimited Adventures

Software Search   Message Board

Conference Room   Company Support

Forum Leader: Debbie Rogers ("PC Sylva")   Keyword: PC Games
[Confere]nce: Sundays at 9:30pm Eastern

rn Recei[pt]

The Grandstand

The Grandstand

- Grandstand Guide
- Dugout   Baseball
- 50-Yard Line   Football
- Off the Glass   Basketball

NEW
Sports Flash   Sports Libraries

Sports Boards   Stadium Club & Conferences

EXTRA!
Sports Link

Keyword: Grandstand

weeks looking for this item, and althou[gh] to the "Guided Tour," I cannot locate a[...]

Discover America Online

Match your interests, find out what's new online, discover our most loved services, and make your time online fun and informative. Start by clicking on A Letter from Steve, and come back to explore the other areas featured here.

A Letter From Steve   America Online Highlights   New Features & Services   Directory of Services

Best of America Online   America Online Tour Guide   America Online Press Releases   What's Hot This Month

Keyword: Discover

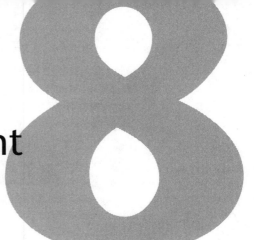

Chapter 8

The Entertainment Chapter

The world of entertainment in America Online's terms covers everything from a television show to your daily horoscope. In this chapter, you explore such diverse topics as movies, television, music, games, sports, books, kids' activities, and horoscopes. You find out what America Online has to offer in those areas and how you can find it. Wherever your interests lie, America Online surely has a place where you can find the entertainment you seek.

We'll tell you at the outset that this chapter is meant to introduce you to online areas where you can simply relax and have fun. In this chapter, we'll show you how to:

- Find the latest news from the world of entertainment

- Become a critic right here on America Online

- Find information about online games

- Access the special areas of America Online designed strictly for kids

Accessing the Entertainment Forum

Regardless of what facet of the world of entertainment interests you—catching a movie, watching a soap opera, sitting down in front of a warm fireplace with a good book in your hands, or playing a video game—America Online can be your first and best resource for information.

Start your search for entertainment-related information in America Online's Entertainment Forum. To access this area, type the keyword **Entertainment**. The directory window shows just a few of the areas you visit in this chapter (see fig. 8.1). During your online visits, you discover many more locations that provide you not only with information but also with your own opportunity to participate in discussions on a host of related subjects, and even to post your own book and movie reviews.

Fig. 8.1
The Entertainment department is America Online's gateway to the world of entertainment.

You learn about most of the places listed under Entertainment Features throughout this chapter. New features are added regularly to America Online's resource roster, so you can expect this directory to change often.

Tip
As explained in Chapters 2 and 3, you can save and print any text document you see on America Online.

> **Note**
>
> Your quick shortcut to your favorite area is a keyword. Just press ⌘-K (or Ctrl+K for Windows), enter the name of the area you want to visit (the keyword), and click OK. Then you're on your way. I've noted the keywords you need to find the features described in this chapter.

You can survey the features of the Entertainment department in two ways. There's an alphabetical listing of the areas available on the directory at the right of the screen. On the left, there are six icons that will quickly transport you to one of your favorite areas. We'll cover some of these first.

Finding Out about Movies and Television

The word *entertainment*, for many people, produces such images as huge dinosaurs roaming the earth, spaceships racing between the stars battling evildoers of all shapes and sizes, or bold adventurers seeking fame and fortune in untamed, undiscovered lands in exotic portions of the world. And these scenes describe many of the famous action movies that Hollywood has produced through the years.

Using the What's Hot Icon

This icon changes periodically, to reflect the latest additions to the Entertainment department, and areas that are running special promotions or introducing new features. As this book was written, featured areas, shown in figure 8.2, included NBC Online, MTV Online, C-Span, and Court TV.

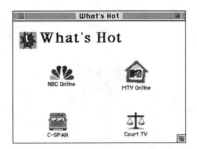

Fig. 8.2
Just some of the forums featured in AOL's Entertainment department.

Using the Movies Icon

At the left half of the Entertainment Forum window is the Movies icon. It's your gateway to news, views, and reviews about your favorite movies past, present, and future. And you can learn something about your favorite stars as well.

You also find the gateway to America Online's Critics' Choice Forum, which is discussed in more detail later in this chapter. Figure 8.3 shows the Television Highlights area you can reach directly from Critics' Choice.

Fig. 8.3
Previews and reviews of upcoming television shows are featured in Television Highlights.

III

Having Fun

Using the Television & Radio Icon

The Television icon on the bottom of the Entertainment department screen provides the same sort of information about your favorite television shows. Before you decide what you want to watch or tape, America Online gives you a chance to get a preview of what's coming up on the tube.

When you click on this icon, you see a directory that offers you several forums devoted specifically to radio and television. Let's look into the one labled *Networks* first. You can choose online forums for such diverse services as ABC Online (see fig. 8.4), Cartoon Network, Court TV, C-SPAN, Lifetime, MTV Online, NBC Online (see fig. 8.5), and The Sci-Fi Channel. And no doubt, by the time you read this book, other TV Networks, broadcast and cable, will be represented as well.

Fig. 8.4
ABC Online offers a separate double-clickable icon as a gateway to each programming feature

Fig. 8.5
NBC Online provides all sorts of information about the network's program lineup.

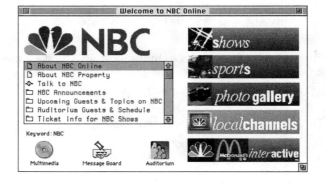

Returning to the top of the TV icon, you'll find support areas for popular programs as well. Your choices include Energy Express, The Geraldo Show, The Nightly Business Report, The Ricky Lake Show, Washington Week in Review Online, and The McLaughlin Group. Fans of daytime TV will find the Soap Opera Summaries area a useful source, giving you the latest happenings on your favorite soap operas. These summaries are especially helpful if you happened to miss a couple of shows.

Among the other forums available to you are the Critics' Choice and TV Gossip areas. The gossip section is one that needs no introduction; it's simply a place where you can exchange messages with fellow AOL members about your favorite programs, and even participate in an online chat from time to time. We'll get to Critics' Choice a bit later in this chapter.

Accessing Hollywood Online

Keyword: Hollywood

At any one time, literally dozens of current motion pictures might be playing at your local theaters. New flicks are released weekly, and during the summer and Christmas seasons, scores of pictures vie for your attention and your ticket dollars. What to do?

America Online's Hollywood Online Forum (see fig. 8.6) is the resource you can use to learn about these films before they are released.

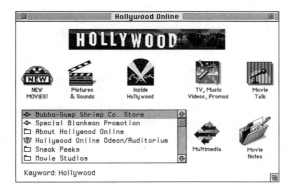

Fig. 8.6
Hollywood Online is Tinseltown's own forum on America Online.

The following paragraphs describe the features you access from the seven icons included on the Hollywood Online screen:

■ New Movies enables you to preview all the new films before they reach your local screens. When you click on this icon, you see the screen shown in figure 8.7.

Fig. 8.7
You can find the latest information about the newest releases from Hollywood's motion picture factory.

III

Having Fun

■ Pictures & Sounds is your resource library. Here you can download pictures of your favorite stars, and maybe even get a sound bite from your favorite picture. If you've never downloaded files before, you want to read Chapter 5, "Finding Your Way around America Online," first.

- Inside Hollywood is an information resource where you can learn what's really happening behind the scenes in Tinseltown. There's even an Ask The Stars feature, which allows you to post questions to your favorite stars and often get their personal answers. From time to time, motion picture executives and the stars themselves will have online press conferences and you're invited to attend.

- TV, Music, Videos, Promos gives you a chance to order exclusive promotional gifts from the movie studios. These gifts include such things as movie posters, complementary movie passes, and other items. This place is one you will want to visit often.

- Movie Talk gives you your chance to express yourself about what you like and don't like about a movie and about the performers in that movie. You also can read and respond to messages on these subjects from other America Online members.

- Multimedia accesses Hollywood Online's software library. Here you find the tools you need to view photos of your favorite stars and to see brief movie clips. You need to read Chapter 11, "Computing & Software," as well, for advice on how to download and use the software you receive from America Online.

- Movie Notes gets you a complete set of background information about current movie releases. You'll find basic production information describing the plot of the movie, plus fascinating material about the movie stars themselves. Quite recently, we read some information on how director Robert Zemeckis created some of the extraordinary screen effects in his extremely popular movie, *Forrest Gump*.

- The directory window at the lower left of Hollywood Online lists information sources for production information about existing films, news about upcoming releases, and a library of software you can use to view the GIF graphic files you download.

Accessing Your Music Resources

Keyword: Music

If you dig rock 'n roll music, or prefer country, classical, or jazz, you will appreciate that America Online's music-related forums are your resources for information and online discussion about your favorite performers. The keyword *Music* (or just clicking on the Music icon in the Entertainment department window) is just a gateway. It's a stopping-off point where you can visit the special online areas that cater to music lovers of all persuasions.

Accessing the RockLink Forum

Keyword: RockLink

When I was a kid, it was just plain old rock 'n roll. But this musical form represents many tastes and styles. So now you see references to Classic Rock, which emphasizes the music that was popular in the late 1960s and early 1970s, such as the Beatles and Rolling Stones, and Alternative Rock, representing performers at the cutting edge of musical development.

No matter what sort of rock 'n roll music you prefer, you can read about it in the RockLink Forum on America Online (see fig. 8.8). You can share your feelings about your favorite bands here, or just read reviews and gossip about them.

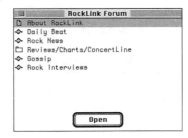

Fig. 8.8
RockLink is your source for the latest news and views on rock 'n roll.

Accessing the Grateful Dead Forum

Keyword: Grateful Dead

The Grateful Dead have the distinction of being one of the longest surviving rock 'n roll bands out there now. Their concerts are still sellouts, and so they've set up their own special area on America Online for the Deadheads among you to visit, read about the band's latest music, and even share messages with other fans (see fig. 8.9). The Winterland: Dead Chat room is just what it says: a place where you can have online chats with other members of the online community.

III

Having Fun

Fig. 8.9
Even the Grateful
Dead have their
own special place
on America
Online.

Exploring Warner/Reprise Records Online
Keyword: Warner

Warner/Reprise Records spans generations of music lovers. This forum covers
the entire Warner/Reprise artist roster (see fig. 8.10).

Fig. 8.10
This screen appears
when you visit the
Warner/Reprise
Records Forum on
America Online.

The following paragraphs describe the icons you find on the Warner/Reprise
Records Online screen and what you discover when you choose them:

■ New Releases describes the latest recordings from Warner/Reprise's vast
roster of entertainers.

■ News and Information offers text files in which you can read about
Warner/Reprise artists.

■ No doubt you've read about the Cyber-Talk area in your daily newspaper. Your favorite musical stars will, from time to time, appear online
for special interactive conferences that you can attend.

- Contents & Special Events are held from time to time when a recording artist releases a new recording or is beginning a major concert tour.

- Artists on Tour lists the touring plans of your favorite Warner/Reprise Records artists. Is your favorite entertainer coming to your hometown? Here's where you find out about it.

- As with many other America Online forums, Message Board is your place to read the views of fellow America Online members, and for you to join in on the discussions yourself.

Finding Out What the Critics Have to Say

Keyword: Critics

Like most of you, before I buy a book, see a movie, or even rent a videotape, I want to know what the reviewers have to say about it. America Online's Critics' Choice (see fig. 8.11) is a compendium of thousands of reviews and discussions about the entire spectrum of the world of entertainment.

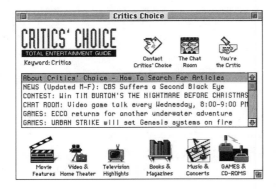

Fig. 8.11
The Critics' Choice area is where you can read what the critics say, and become one yourself if it suits you.

Here you find reviews of your favorite movies, concerts, television shows, books, and even video games. The following paragraphs describe the icons included on the Critics' Choice screen:

- Contact Critics' Choice enables you to express your own views to the forum staff.

III

Having Fun

■ The Chat Room is another one of AOL's exciting interactive chat rooms, where you'll be able to discuss your favorite books or TV shows, and sometimes even meet your favorite author or movie critic for a fun-filled conference.

■ The title *You're the Critic* means what it says. It's your chance to post a message giving your viewpoints about something you've read or seen. In figure 8.12, an America Online member gives viewpoints about a motion picture being made of a best-selling book by author Tom Clancy (who himself is an active America Online member).

Fig. 8.12
Here's your chance to become a critic.

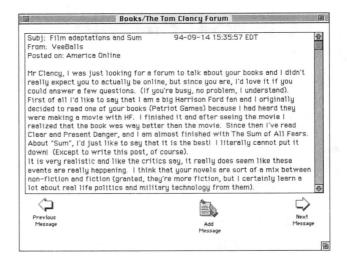

The icons at the bottom of the Critics' Choice window take you to other entertainment forums on America Online, ranging from movies, video, and TV, to books, music, and games. Nearly every forum you visit on America Online provides gateways to other areas that might interest you. It's a journey you will truly enjoy.

Playing Games

Still another icon on the Entertainment department window is Games, and it represents, among other things, one of the most popular categories of software sales. They appeal to the young and the young at heart. A computer game enables you to turn your Mac or PC into an outer-space battleground, a deep, dark dungeon, or even a maze. You can pit yourself against evil creatures and machines or even other human players in a quest to right wrongs, locate a secret castle, or save the world from destruction.

Accessing the Macintosh and PC Games Forums

Keywords: MGM, PC Games

The Macintosh and PC computing forums are discussed in Chapter 11, "Computing & Software," but the games forums deserve a special place here, because they are a special resource that any fan of computer games will want to visit often. Figures 8.13 and 8.14 show the Games Forum screens.

Fig. 8.13
The Macintosh Games Forum is for Mac games enthusiasts.

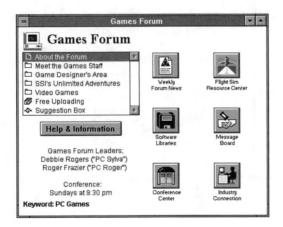

Fig. 8.14
The PC Games Forum is for DOS and Windows users.

As with other computing forums on America Online, these special areas enable you to get advice from other America Online members about their experiences with and recommendations on different game software.

The software libraries in these games forums contain demonstration versions of many popular commercial games that you might want to try. In addition, you can find a large number of freeware and shareware games (some award-winning) that can entertain you and your children for hours on end.

III

Having Fun

In Chapter 11, "Computing & Software," you find out more about all the computing and software forums. For now, feel free to explore the software libraries in the Mac and PC games forums. Check the file descriptions and download the software you want to try.

Accessing the Online Gaming Forums

Keyword: Gaming

Whether you are interested in a casual game of checkers or are involved in a heavy-duty game of strategy, The Online Gaming Forums area is a place you surely want to learn about and visit often.

As you can see from the forum's main directory window in figure 8.15, this forum serves as a gateway to many areas that deal with gaming. The following paragraphs discuss just a few of them.

Fig. 8.15
The Online Gaming Forums screen is your first stop for information on all sorts of games.

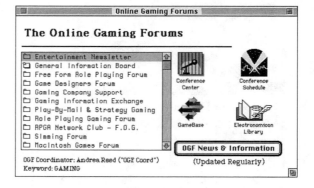

Entering the Conference Center

The Online Gaming Forums hold regular conferences. Along with online members and forum staff, you can attend these conferences and participate in chats and attend debates and panel discussions featuring experts on the subject. To enter the conference center, click on the Conference Center icon in the Online Gaming Forums main window. The screen shown in figure 8.16 appears.

You also can participate in the General Information Board (shown in the directory listing at the left of the Gaming Forum screen) area to exchange views with other America Online members. The conference schedule is updated often, so please stop by regularly. If you missed a conference, simply look up and download the log from the Conference Archives library. As with all conference logs, you can view and print them with your America Online software. Chapters 2 and 3 explain how.

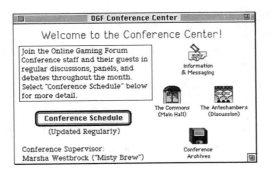

Fig. 8.16
Regular confer-
ences are held
for gaming
enthusiasts.

Exploring the GameBase Database

GameBase is a resource for information about the manufacturers of games,
new product information, and reviews from both experts and members alike.
You can search GameBase for information about your favorite products or a
new product you want to know more about. Click on the GameBase icon in
the Online Gaming Forums main window to access GameBase and display
the screen shown in figure 8.17.

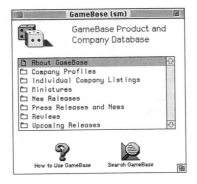

Fig. 8.17
The GameBase
resource in
America Online's
Gaming Forum
can provide you
with all kinds of
gaming informa-
tion.

Getting More Gaming Information

Returning to the main Online Gaming Forums window, you can click on the
Electronomicon Library icon to download an electronic magazine on games.

If you have a problem or question about a specific product, you can click on
the Gaming Company Support option on the left side of the main Online
Gaming Forums window for assistance.

Exploring the Electronomicon Archives

Electronomicon is an all-electronic newsletter prepared by the staff of the
Online Games Forum. Each issue is posted in the Electronomicon Library as

soon as it's "published." It is an interesting compendium of general gaming news, advice, and forum happenings. The newsletter consists of a text file that you can view and print in almost any text processing program.

Accessing the Trivia Forum

Keyword: Trivia

Okay, I admit it. I am far removed from being a chess master (or even playing a decent game of checkers). My abilities at computer games are laughable for the most part. But I do know my trivia. If trivia is one of your favorite pastimes, too, the Trivia Forum might turn out to be one of your favorite online places.

Regardless of the subject you are an expert in, whether it's *Star Trek,* radio shows of the 1940s, or famous historical figures, the Trivia Forum is where you can interact with other trivia enthusiasts. (In Chapter 7, "Communicating with Others," you learn how to participate in a message area.) The Trivia Forum has a regular schedule of nightly games in America Online's People Connection (also see Chapter 6, "Meeting People Online").

In addition to the interactive trivia games, you can participate in the forum's message area, post your own trivia questions, or answer those from other users. The Trivia Game Board provides a roster of regular games you might want to join as well. Figure 8.18 shows a typical message board sample.

Fig. 8.18
You can test your trivia knowledge on the Trivia Game Board.

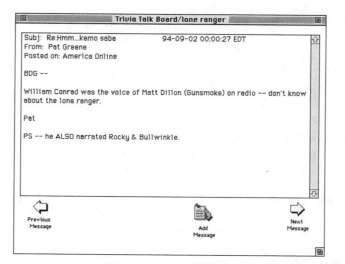

From the World of Sports

Keyword: Sports

If you played Little League sports when you were a child, have children interested in sporting activities, watch sports events regularly on television, and on a rare occasion have been known to attend a game or two, you might want to visit America Online's virtual sports page frequently. To do so, choose Sports from the AOL's Main Menu window to display the Sports department screen shown in figure 8.19.

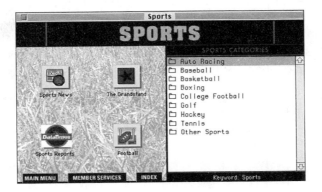

Fig. 8.19
Whatever your favorite sports activity, you'll find information about it on America Online.

The major sports are listed in the directory window at the right of the screen. To the left, you can check the latest news from the world of sports, by clicking on the Sports icon. DataTimes Sports Reports, at the bottom left, is another major sports news resource. To the right of this icon is one that relates to the most popular sport of the current season; it was football when we wrote this chapter. And then there's The Grandstand, shown in figure 8.20.

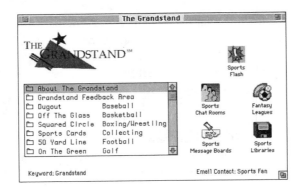

Fig. 8.20
Take your seat in The Grandstand to enjoy your favorite sport.

III

Having Fun

Sitting in The Grandstand

Keyword: Grandstand

The Grandstand is where all you sports lovers can find the latest news about your favorite games, learn how your favorite teams fared the night before, and participate in online conferences with other fans. It is the entrance to America Online's sports stadium.

The following paragraphs describe some of its most popular features:

- Sports Flash offers announcements about the long list of regular online conferences on every sport under the sun. As you can see from the screen shown in figure 8.21, (which you'll see when you click on any topic shown in the Sports Flash directory), America Online even conducts an online wrestling match!

Fig. 8.21
Sports Flash announces upcoming meetings for sports lovers.

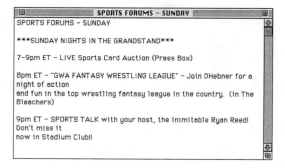

- The Sports Chat Rooms icon is your admission ticket to The Grandstand's nightly online conferences. After viewing the schedule, you can pop into the active conference room of your choice.

- Fantasy Leagues are what the title implies. Participate in your own sports league in cyberspace in the forum shown in figure 8.22. There's a league for your favorite sport. You can have a wrestling match without ever breaking into a sweat, and participate in an auto race without ever having to drive a car around a track.

- Back to the main Grandstand screen: The Sports Libraries icon accesses a huge collection of software, ranging from shareware sports games and utilities to files about your favorite teams. Please read Chapter 5, "Finding Your Way around America Online," for information about finding and downloading files from America Online. Files are available for both Mac and PC users. You'll want to visit the New Files and Free Uploads library first, for all the newest sports-related software.

Fig. 8.22
From baseball to auto racing, let your imagination be your guide.

■ Sports Boards are much like the message areas in other America Online forums. You can share your feelings with other online members, forum staff, and occasional experts on the latest information from the world of sports.

At the left side of the main Grandstand screen shown in figure 8.23 is a list of special sports-related forums that you might want to explore. Each forum has its own schedule of conferences, active message boards, and software libraries. Just double-click on the forum that interests you.

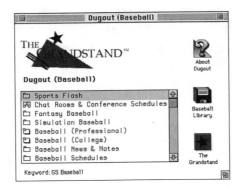

Fig. 8.23
All the popular sports get their own forums on America Online.

III

Having Fun

Delving into Books

Keyword: Books

To many of you, the best entertainment is probably sitting down with a good book in hand. But the selections at your favorite bookstores have become daunting. Literally thousands of new works are on the shelves, ready for you to make your choice. Where do you begin?

Whether you prefer fiction or nonfiction, you want to check the Book Bestsellers first to see how your favorite author's works are faring in the marketplace. Choose Book Bestsellers from the main Entertainment Forum window to display the Book Bestsellers screen shown in figure 8.24. From there you can find out more about this area of America Online, check out the bestseller lists, and see what's soon to be released. Your Book Reviews is the place to post your own book reviews and read about the choices of other members of the online community.

Fig. 8.24
Book Bestsellers provides the latest information about best-selling books and upcoming works.

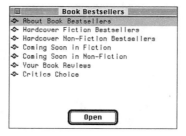

Note

Notice that the last option on the Book Bestsellers screen is Critics Choice. That topic is discussed in more detail previously in this chapter (see "Finding Out What the Critics Have to Say").

You can order your favorite books online as well, from America Online's Online Bookstore. Chapter 15, "The Shopping Chapter," tells you how. That chapter even takes you step by step through the ordering process.

Finding Fun for Kids of All Ages

Keyword: Kids, KOOL

America Online is not just a place for adults. The service offers a wide variety of healthy online activities for your kids as well, and the gateway to that area is AOL's Kids Only department, shown in figure 8.25. Not only can they have fun, but they also can learn a few things and become more adept at working with a computer.

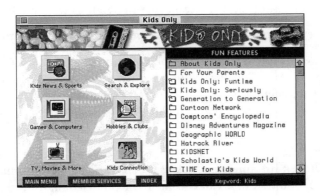

Fig. 8.25
Kids Only is a special place for your children to participate in healthy activities right on America Online.

Many of the areas we've discussed so far in this chapter have special kids-only departments as well, with areas developed strictly for our young people. The Kids Only department window in figure 8.25 shows just a few of the areas available, all specially designed for kids ages 5 through 14. We'll discuss some of these places in the following pages.

As with all America Online sessions, I suggest that you teach your children how to conduct themselves online. You should go over with them the basics of using America Online software, such as navigating through the network, reading and posting messages, and participating in online conferences. Your child should know how to act responsibly online and to refrain from the use of vulgar language. In addition, you should establish limits as to the amount of time your children spend online, because you are responsible for any charges they run up during their time.

III

Having Fun

> **Note**
>
> America Online also gives you the right to exert Parental Control on your account. As described further in Chapter 20, "Getting Help," you have the right to block access to instant messages, People Connection rooms, member rooms, and many Conference Rooms. By giving your child a special screen name under your online account, you can set special restrictions for that screen name.

Let's highlight a few of the areas available through Kids Only on AOL:

- Kids News & Sports covers the news and the day, with a youthful slant.

- Search & Explore is a learning tool. You can open the pages of the huge Compton's Encyclopedia online to search for information on a homework assignment, or just to learn more about our incredible universe. Additional learning resources include the *National Geographic* magazine and the Scholastic Network.

- Games & Computers provides another resource for gaming information on AOL, but this time just for kids. There's also a lot of information on how our young people can become more proficient at using a personal computer (and it's not long before they match and beat their parents in computer-related skills).

- The Hobbies & Clubs icon takes you to special groups that are just for kids.

- The TV, Movies & More area covers children's programming, family movies and other areas of interest. There's even a forum devoted to DC Comics (such as Superman, Batman, and others).

- And then there's the Kids Connection, a variation of America Online's People Connection area that we discussed in Chapter 6, "Meeting People Online."

We'll devote a few more pages to cover some more forums on America Online that are just for kids.

Exploring the Disney Adventures Magazine Forum
Keyword: Disney

Every month, *Disney Adventures* contains exciting adventures and stories for your children (see fig. 8.26). America Online is the place for your child to read about those many adventures and learn more about our world. The magazine even offers online conferences, D.A. Live, which take place in the forum's Odeon Auditorium, where your child can meet other kids with similar interests and enjoy an online chat.

Fig. 8.26
Disney Adventures magazine is a special resource for your child on America Online.

The Disney Adventures Magazine Forum is structured much like any other online forum, so the same skills you learned about in Chapters 2, 3, and 5 will be valuable for both you and your child as you journey through this area. You see, for example, the following:

■ D.A. Live, as mentioned previously, is your gateway to *Disney Adventures'* online conferences.

■ Search D.A. Articles enables you to use America Online's Search function to look for articles in previous issues.

■ The Message Board enables your child to post messages, just as you do, and to read messages from other young online members.

■ The D.A. Library contains software of interest to your child.

■ And if you want to see a copy of the magazine in your own home, click on the Subscribe To D.A. icon to find out how you can subscribe.

Accessing the Cartoons Network
Keyword: Cartoons

I can't conclude this brief discussion of America Online's offerings for kids without mentioning the Cartoons Forum (see fig. 8.27). Cartoon entertainment appeals to the young at heart of all ages, from children to adults.

III

Having Fun

America Online has a special library of cartoon art in GIF (Graphic Interchange Format) format. See Chapters 7 and 12 for more information on how to create and view GIF files.

Fig. 8.27
America Online didn't even forget cartoons.

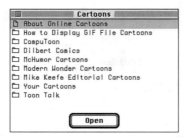

A number of special libraries in this forum contain professional cartoon artwork that you can download to your computer, view, and print (at least for your personal use).

The Cartoons Forum is also a resource for all you online cartoonists to create and post your own artwork so that others can see it. The Toon Talk section is a message area where you can discuss your favorite cartoon characters.

Viewing Your Horoscope

Keyword: Horoscopes

Well, some of you probably don't believe that a horoscope is a way to foretell your future. And some of you do depend on the readings of the stars to guide many aspects of your daily life. Whether for fun or information, you will want to view your daily horoscope on America Online. Although your cheerful authors are on the fence about this issue, it is no coincidence that Virgo is highlighted in figure 8.28; sometimes we read our horoscopes, too.

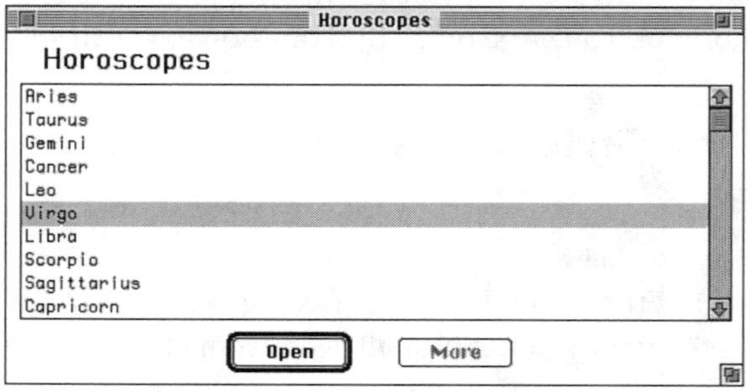

Fig. 8.28
You can use America Online's Horoscopes feature to find out what the stars predict for you.

From Here...

As with other areas on America Online, you don't have to restrict yourself to searching one area for the information you want. For more useful stuff on entertainment-related subjects, refer to these chapters:

- Chapter 9, "Lifestyles & Interests"
- Chapter 11, "Computing & Software"
- Chapter 12, "How to Find Software"
- Chapter 13, "Learning & Reference"
- Chapter 14, "News, Magazines, and Business Information"

III

Having Fun

Chapter 9

Lifestyles & Interests

You can explore the stars, upgrade the sound of your stereo, research your family history, and debate with other America Online members on subjects ranging from the top news of the day to whether your Macintosh or PC is a better computer. It can all happen in the various Lifestyles forums on America Online.

In this chapter, you learn how to:

- Locate the latest information on health-care issues

- Find information about things to do in various areas of the country

- Interact with other members on hobbies ranging from cooking to science fiction

- Discuss the important issues of the day with other members

Figure 9.1 shows the Clubs & Interests main window, which you can find by typing the keyword **Clubs**. As you can see, the features you can reach from this point are numerous, diverse, and intriguing.

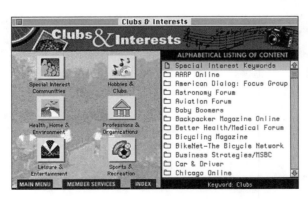

Fig. 9.1
The Clubs & Interests department on America Online leads you to a diverse group of features.

When I sat down to write this chapter, I spent many, many hours exploring all the areas on America Online that cater to lifestyles, hobbies, and special interests. Some of these places have already been discussed in Chapter 8, "The Entertainment Chapter." You learn more in this chapter, and finish the little tour in Chapter 14, "News, Magazines, and Business Information."

My little survey proved to be never-ending. For this reason, this chapter just touches on the highlights of America Online's Lifestyle areas, and the rest is left for you to explore at your leisure.

To make it easier to find an area that caters to a specific interest, all the forums in this area of AOL are grouped by category, as shown in the icons at the left of the Clubs & Interests screen. Let's explore the highlights.

Special Interest Communities

There are a number of areas on America Online that cater to special interests, covering a wide range of subjects. Here's just a few of them:

Exploring the Baby Boomers Forum

Keyword: Baby Boomers

What is a baby boomer? It's a term that refers to the huge numbers of people who were born after World War II, right up through the 1960s. People who were born during this time share a unique range of experiences ranging from the advent of television to the Korean War, Vietnam, the Kennedy assassination, and more pleasant things such as Elvis Presley and the Beatles.

The focus on this forum is strictly interaction. You can share your experiences on a host of subjects with others who were born in the same frenetic generation. Figure 9.2 shows the Baby Boomers directory.

Fig. 9.2
The baby boomers generation has its own hangout on America Online.

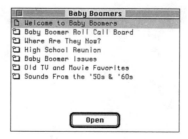

Entering the National Multiple Sclerosis Society Forum

Keyword: NMSS

Many of you might not have paid much attention to multiple sclerosis until you read, as I did, that actress Annette Funicello—the young woman who starred in those beach movies of the 1960s—now suffers from this crippling disease.

The National Multiple Sclerosis Society has set up this forum on America Online to provide information about the disease, including updates on medical research into finding a cure. As you can see in figure 9.3, a host of information is available for you to read. You also can find a message center and health & medical chat rooms where you can interact with other members, including health-care professionals.

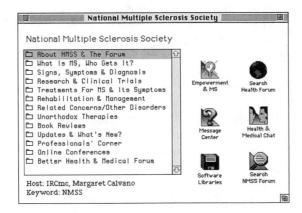

Fig. 9.3
NMSS is another area on America Online that provides health information.

There are other areas on America Online that are devoted to health interests too, such as the United Cerebral Palsy Association's own forum, which is devoted to informing everyone about progress in finding a cure for that debilitating disease.

Joining the Religion & Ethics Forum

Keyword: Religion

The Religion & Ethics Club, shown in figure 9.4, doesn't favor a particular religion or belief system. It has message boards devoted to many faiths, including New Age philosophies. In the Religion and Ethics Message Center, you can debate with other online members.

III

Having Fun

Fig. 9.4
The Religion &
Ethics Club is a
special place to
reflect on your
religious beliefs.

The Religion Library Center includes a collection of software with a religious orientation. Included are educational games, Bible search programs, and more. You also can search the contents of the Bible for specific references and passages in a searchable database.

The Front Porch Room is a special locale for impromptu chats or for regularly scheduled meetings on a host of fascinating subjects.

Exploring SeniorNet Online

Keyword: SeniorNet

SeniorNet Online should demonstrate to everyone that reaching one's senior years is often when life truly begins. In a special Computer Learning Center, you can learn how to master your computer. SeniorNet Online also includes active message areas, a Community Center where you can interact with other online members and forum staff, and a wealth of information you can read and download (see fig. 9.5).

Fig. 9.5
SeniorNet Online
provides a special
meeting place for
senior citizens on
America Online.

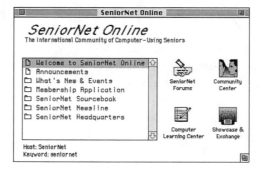

SeniorNet is also a membership organization that offers special benefits and merchandise discounts to its members. You aren't required to join in order to participate in the forum, but a membership application is there in case you want to learn more about the organization.

Hobbies & Clubs

Whether your interest is recreational or professional, America Online has a hobby or club forum for you.

Joining the Astronomy Club (a.k.a the Astronomy Forum)

Keyword: Astronomy

When I was a child, I was absolutely fascinated by the mysteries of the stars and planets and the incredible goings-on in our universe. So I joined a local astronomy club and even bought myself a little telescope so that I could view the planets in our solar system up close and personal.

America Online's Astronomy Club (see fig. 9.6) is hosted by a real astronomer, Mr. Astro, better known as Stuart Goldman. Mr. Goldman works for *Star & Telescope* magazine as an associate editor.

Fig. 9.6
You can explore the stars with a little help from America Online.

If you want to learn more about the stars and planets, explore the Ask Mr. Astro message board. There you can interact with other America Online members who share an interest in astronomy, or even ask experts such as Mr. Astro about what is on your mind.

You can meet fellow astronomers, amateur and professional alike, for their weekly conference in the Planetarium.

Joining the Cooking Club

Keyword: Cooking

Whether your efforts at cooking are limited to boiling water and warming a TV dinner, or you are a culinary expert, you can find a wealth of useful information in America Online's Cooking Club (see fig. 9.7).

III

Having Fun

Fig. 9.7
The Cooking Club is your resource for cooking tips and tricks on America Online.

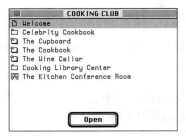

The message boards are places where you can share your favorite recipes or pick up a tip or two from other online gourmets. You can even enter a conference room, the Kitchen, where regular meetings are held on food preparation or new recipes.

Exploring the Exchange

Keyword: The Exchange

The Exchange is a place where you can express yourself on a wide variety of special interests. To make it easier to find discussion groups that interest you, click on the icons shown in the main Exchange forum window, in figure 9.8. There are discussion areas related to men's and women's issues, gardening and other outdoor activities, politics, philosophy, crafts, careers, coin collecting, and many other topics of discussion.

Fig. 9.8
The Exchange is America Online's meeting place for online discussions of all sorts.

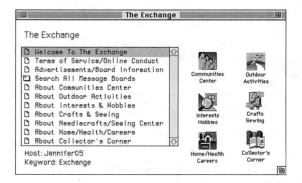

As with other areas on America Online, make sure to approach the debate with care. Don't use vulgar language, don't insult other America Online members (even though the discussions have been known to get hot and heavy), and, most importantly, just have a good time.

The Capital Connection

Keywords: capital, politics

You can find information and debates on all sorts of issues in many places on America Online, from company support forums in the Computing & Software section to the special places that are devoted solely to news and debate about the issues that affect us the most. The Capital Connection is one of those special places (see fig. 9.9).

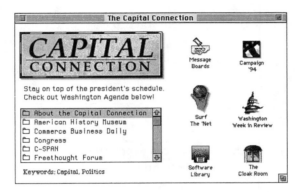

Fig. 9.9
America Online's Capital Connection area gives you a chance to speak your mind about the important issues of the day.

Better than a talk show? Yes, because here's where you can jump right in and express yourself, without waiting for a moderator to pick up a phone or call your name.

To give you an idea of what you can find in Capital Connection area, let's visit the Message Boards, where you can debate the issues with fellow AOL members.

Dozens of folders are devoted to specific subjects. If you don't find anything that interests you, feel free to start your own topic. As a sample, figure 9.10 shows a typical message from a user of the Apple Macintosh who is putting down users of IBM PCs and compatibles. Rest assured, PC users had a sharp and ready response in the next message.

Joining the Genealogy Club

Keyword: Roots

This special corner of the America Online community, the Genealogy Club, provides advice and useful information to help you search your family tree (see fig. 9.11). In active message areas, you can share information and experiences with other online members as you try to find just who your ancestors were.

III

Having Fun

Fig. 9.10
Mac versus PC might not be as important as the state of the economy but is an issue just as hotly contested.

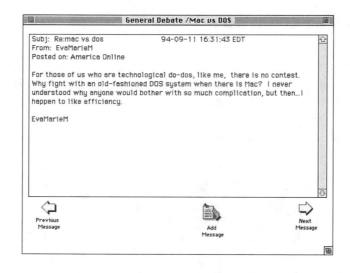

Fig. 9.11
Get some tips on searching your family tree.

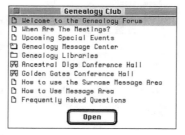

The software library includes programs that help you catalog information about your family history. You can review the findings of many genealogy experts who assist you in your quest. Or you can attend the regular chats in the Ancestral Digs Conference Hall to interact with other online members.

Joining the Ham Radio Club

Keywords: ham radio, radio

Ham (or amateur) radio enthusiasts are a breed apart from those of you who sit in front of a CB radio and exchange 10-4s with a friend. A ham radio operator uses a shortwave radio setup to communicate with another radio enthusiast on the other side of the world. In times of natural disasters, Hams worldwide have used their equipment to get information about the situation to the outside world.

The Ham Radio Club (see fig. 9.12) includes a special area devoted to those who like to listen to shortwave radio. With a shortwave radio, which you can buy at many consumer electronics outfits, you can hear actual broadcasts from other parts of the world. Many countries in the farthest corners of the globe have special English-language radio shows and music programs designed to present news about their cultures and politics. These programs are different from the capsule summaries you get on network television programs.

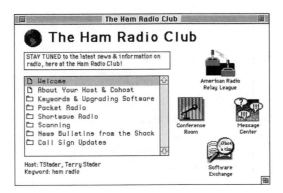

Fig. 9.12
America Online's special forum for the world of radio communications is the Ham Radio Club.

The American Radio Relay League, which has an area of the Ham Radio Club, is an organization devoted strictly to the interests of amateur radio enthusiasts. The group's work also includes setting up networks to offer communications in the event of a local emergency.

Entering the Kodak Photography Forum

Keyword: Photography

Photography is not just for professionals. All you need is a camera—any camera, a little advice, and your own imagination, and you can produce some good photos.

The Kodak Photography Forum, shown in figure 9.13, is conducted by Ron Baird, a photography specialist from Kodak who writes many of their technical manuals. Ron, along with fellow online members, provides you with hints and tips that can make your picture-taking experience more rewarding. If you're looking to sell that old camera and get something better, you can even check out a buy/sell section.

The Photography Chat Room is your place to receive online help and advice when you have a question. You also might want to check the schedule for upcoming conferences. Of course, because the forum is sponsored by Kodak, a special folder is devoted strictly to Kodak's product line.

III

Having Fun

Fig. 9.13
America Online's
Kodak Photogra-
phy Forum is
the place for
shutterbugs of all
kinds.

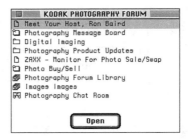

Exploring the Science Fiction & Fantasy Area

Keyword: Science Fiction

Science fiction is the art of taking present-day science, imagining how it will develop in the future, and building an exciting story around that sort of speculation. America Online's Science Fiction & Fantasy section is an active pit stop for fans of books, comics, movies, and TV programs. You can share your views and learn about upcoming events. Figure 9.14 shows the main Science Fiction & Fantasy directory window.

Fig. 9.14
From comic books
to movie theaters,
you can explore
the world of
science fiction and
fantasy on
America Online.

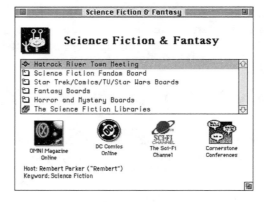

For information about OMNI Magazine Online, which features science fiction tales, see Chapter 14, "News, Magazines, and Business Information."

Joining the Star Trek Club

Keyword: Star Trek

When the original *Star Trek* TV show (a wagon train of the stars) was canceled by NBC in the mid-1960s, few envisioned that it would become a cultural phenomenon that would spread to all aspects of our society. Star Trek now encompasses TV shows, movies, books, magazines, and conventions, too.

Star Trek has made almost all of you aware of the possibilities of space exploration. It presents a truly optimistic view of our future, professing that our present conflicts and strife will eventually disappear and that humans will all learn to work together in harmony. That hopeful view probably explains some of its vast appeal.

America Online's Star Trek Club is a meeting ground for Trekkers, where you learn about upcoming TV shows and conferences and can participate in discussions and chats with other fans (see fig. 9.15). One chat I recently attended featured one of the special effects experts on the *Star Trek: The Next Generation* program, who let us in on just how those incredible visual illusions on the show are created.

Fig. 9.15
Beam to the bridge of the starship Enterprise on America Online.

Health, Home, & Environment

Here are the parts of America Online that are devoted to the subjects that are uppermost in the minds of most of us.

Visiting the Better Health & Medical Forum

Keyword: Health

Whether you are a health-care professional or are just seeking the route to better health and a longer, more productive life, the Better Health & Medical Forum is a place you might want to visit often.

As you can see in figure 9.16, the Better Health & Medical Forum contains a large store of text files on all sorts of health-related issues. It's not intended to replace a regular visit to your family physician but is designed to give you a better range of knowledge about the issues that are of the most importance to you.

A useful database you might want to check is the Home Medical Guide, which provides brief text files on common illnesses, their causes, and the common remedies (see fig. 9.17). The information you receive when you search the Home Medical Guide listings is not intended to encourage self-medication but to help you give more information to your doctor in times of illness, or just for general information.

Fig. 9.16
This special area on America Online is for consumers and health professionals.

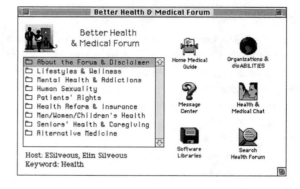

Fig. 9.17
The Home Medical Guide is not a virtual doctor but a source for information on common illnesses.

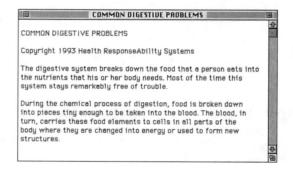

The forum also has regular conferences (check the forum for the schedule) and an active message center where you can interact with other America Online members on a whole range of health-related subjects.

Visiting the Environmental Forum
Keyword: eforum

The news media refers to the 1990s as the Decade for the Environment. The Environmental Forum is America Online's response to the attention on the environment (see fig. 9.18). This forum has an active message board divided into four main categories. And because the best way to deal with environmental concerns can become hotly contested at times, one board is called The Water Cooler. There you can approach all these subjects with calm and reason.

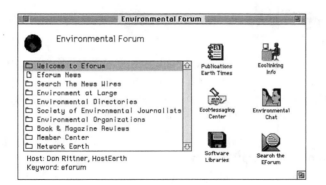

Fig. 9.18
The Environ-
mental Forum is
America Online's
center for the
Decade for the
Environment.

The Environmental Chat room holds regularly scheduled meetings that feature noted scientists and other experts on the environment. Check there often for chat schedules and the guest list.

Studying Issues in Mental Health

Keyword: IMH

Relationships are probably the most difficult problems you are asked to face. Whether it's your spouse, your children, or just coping with each day's events, the task often can be challenging.

Issues in Mental Health (see fig. 9.19) is a place where you can learn about how to deal with everyday problems. Active message boards enable you to interact with other online members and professionals on the problems of daily living.

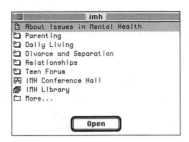

Fig. 9.19
The complex issues
of relationships are
discussed on
America Online.

III

Having Fun

You also might want to explore the forum's vast library of mental health reference materials and attend regular conferences where you can discuss problems and solutions.

Exploring Network Earth Online

Keyword: Network Earth

Network Earth is a weekly television program broadcast on the Atlanta-based TBS super station, which is offered through cable TV systems around the country. This program features reports about the progress made in dealing with the problems of the environment.

You can read about the program in America Online's Network Earth Online area, download transcripts of previous shows, and check the schedule for upcoming broadcasts (see fig. 9.20). Click on the News & Resources icon to learn more about the fight to clean up the environment and also to locate other environmentally aware organizations you want to learn more about. As with other online forums, you can attend regular chats featuring Network Earth staff people by entering the Conference Hall.

Fig. 9.20
Turner Broadcasting's Network Earth Online gives you important information about the environment.

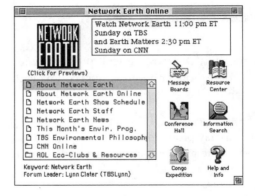

Visiting the Pet Care Forum

Keyword: Pet

Most of you probably think of a pet as a dog or a cat or even a fish, but many other animals qualify for pet status. The Pet Care Forum on America Online is devoted to helping you find better ways to care for all your animal friends (see fig. 9.21).

The forum is hosted by veterinarians and is frequented by professional breeders and fellow pet owners. You can participate in active discussions about the common problems you might face in bringing a pet into your home. You can use the Animal Talk Chat Room for a spontaneous chat with a fellow animal lover or to attend one of the forum's regular conferences.

Fig. 9.21
Learn more about
caring for your pet
in America
Online's Pet Care
Forum.

Professions & Organizations

Many professional societies have formed special areas on America Online that
cater to members as well as casual visitors who want to learn more about a
specific topic. We'll discuss a few of them in the pages that follow.

Joining the Aviation Club

Keyword: Aviation

Whether your interest in aviation is limited to reading about it in your living
room, building a model plane, or piloting a craft yourself, the place where
you can find others who share your interest is America Online's Aviation
Club (see fig. 9.22).

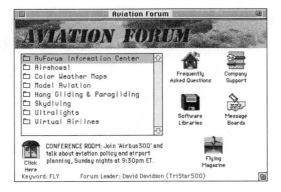

Fig. 9.22
The Aviation Club
is for armchair and
active aviators.

One of the club's most popular spots is its active message boards. There you
can find ongoing discussions about commercial aviation, military aviation,
and even model planes.

III

Having Fun

The Aviation Libraries feature both GIF and text files that you can download and view on your computer. As mentioned in Chapter 6, "Meeting People Online," a GIF file is a multiplatform format that enables you to view and print photos on your computer.

> **Note**
>
> If you can't find the specific forum that interests you on America Online, try locating it with a keyword. Most keywords either contain the name of an area or its subject, so if you don't know which keyword is correct, don't hesitate to try a few out for size. Suppose, for example, that you want to learn more about Dolby Surround sound. Type the keyword **Dolby** and guess what? It takes you directly to the Dolby Audio/ Video Forum on America Online.

Visiting the Emergency Response Forum

Keyword: Emergency

This special area of America Online isn't just devoted to health professionals, fire fighters, or law enforcement personnel. It's for everyone seeking information on how to deal with common household emergencies that can become disasters if you don't act quickly. The main Emergency Response Club window is shown in figure 9.23.

Fig. 9.23
The Emergency Response Club is a special forum for online members who work in the emergency services field.

As with other forums on America Online, the forum features an active message area and a library containing text files you can transfer to your own computer for later viewing and printing.

Joining the Military & Vets Club

Keyword: Military

America Online's Military & Vets Club (see fig. 9.24) is dedicated to those of you who have served the country in the armed forces, whether in times of war or peace. You can find message areas for both veterans and for those still serving in the military.

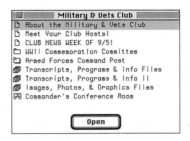

Fig. 9.24
Armed forces,
actives, and
veterans have their
interests addressed
in the Military &
Vets Club.

One of the most interesting places to visit is the Images, Photos, & Graphics Files libraries, which include image files not only of places where military encounters took place but also of aircraft and ships. I even saw a picture there of an enemy star cruiser from the TV series *Star Trek*.

Joining the National Space Society

Keyword: Space

The National Space Society is devoted to promoting research and exploration of space (see fig. 9.25). Its Board of Governors features such luminaries as Hugh Downs, Arthur C. Clarke, Jacques Cousteau, John Glenn, Nichelle Nichols, and Alan Shepard.

Fig. 9.25
America Online's
center for space-
related research is
the National Space
Society.

III

Having Fun

If space exploration interests you, you're invited to join the organization. But even as a nonmember you can participate in roundtable discussions or regular chats and can even download GIF photos showing the stars, the planets, and our own space probes. (As mentioned elsewhere in this book, a GIF file is a cross-platform graphic format that enables you to view and print photos with your own computer.)

Leisure & Entertainment

Of course, not every part of America Online is quite as serious as the places we've just discussed. Here are some examples that provide a more entertaining outlook on life.

Visiting Car and Driver Online

Keyword: Car and Driver

Before you buy a new car, you'll want to keep up to date about the new models and how they perform on the road. *Car and Driver* is one of the oldest magazines that caters to automobile enthusiasts. Their online forum, shown in figure 9.26, includes feature articles from the magazine itself, complete test reports of the hot new models, and an active message area where you can learn about the experiences other AOL members have had with these models. Oh, and by the way, we don't want to ignore it, but *Car and Driver's* sister magazine, *Road and Track* has its own AOL forum, too. The keyword is *Cars*.

Fig. 9.26
Learn how the new cars really perform before you take that test drive.

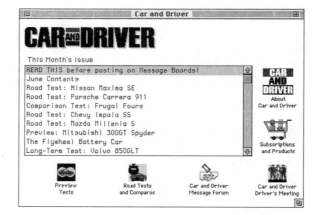

Visiting Chicago Online

Keyword: Chicago

Much like the city for which it's named, this forum is a huge, sprawling place with many areas to visit. This section just covers the highlights and leaves you to explore the rest at your leisure.

When first visiting Chicago Online, click on the Chicagoland Calendar listing in the main forum directory (see fig. 9.27) for the latest news and event information. If you're traveling to Chicago for business or pleasure, you'll probably want to read the Chicago Tribune News & Features area (which we'll get to shortly) for latest forecasts and for important information you need to know when you get there.

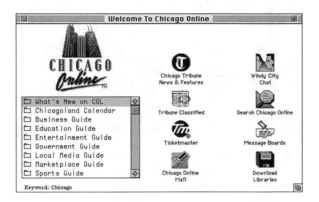

Fig. 9.27
Chicago Online is the gateway to information about happenings in the Windy City.

The Ticketmaster icon takes you to the Ticketmaster gateway, a special area where you can learn about concerts and other special events not only in Chicago, but in the state of Florida, too (and it's expanding to other parts of the country as time goes on). Once you've found the event you want to attend, you can order your tickets right from the keyboard and mouse of your personal computer.

Chicago's Education Guide is a special area in Chicago Online, with information about the city's vast array of educational opportunities. You find previews of special events at different educational institutions, along with detailed enrollment information.

Reading the Chicago Tribune

Keyword: Chicago Tribune

One of the biggest challenges for the large daily newspapers has been to decide just how to deal with the Information Superhighway. The Chicago Tribune Forum (see fig. 9.28) is the way one publisher is meeting the challenge.

The Chicago Tribune Forum (run by the sponsors of Chicago Online) delivers the same news, sports, and features that you find in the printed editions. One section is even devoted to classified ads. You can view, save, or print text files that you select. And you can search the contents of each daily edition for specific news items.

By far the most unique aspect of your virtual daily newspaper, though, is its message board. It's far more than a Letters to the Editor column because you

III

Having Fun

can interact directly with other readers and with the newspaper's editorial staff. You can find discussions on the news of the day and many other subjects. The board recently featured a discussion about the newspaper's design, including input from readers and some of the reporters, too.

Fig. 9.28

You can read an entire daily newspaper online.

Visiting the Dolby Audio/Video Forum

Keyword: Dolby

The name Dolby was originally synonymous with techniques to provide better-quality sound with reduced background noise (or hiss) on audio compact cassettes and professional studio recordings. It also describes the technology Dolby Surround that provides uncanny realism in your favorite motion pictures. If you've ever watched a movie in a theater equipped with Dolby Surround, you heard sounds emanating not only from your screen but also from your left, your right, and behind you.

The Dolby Audio/Video Forum on America Online (see fig. 9.29) features experts from the audio and video industries and active fans who interact on a whole range of issues, ranging from where to hear the best movie sound to how to set up a Surround sound installation in your home.

Fig. 9.29

The world of Dolby Surround sound is brought to your home in the Dolby Audio/Video Forum on America Online.

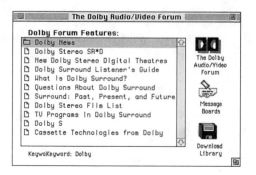

The forum also includes a big library of text files you can read and download. These files explain what the various Dolby sound-enhancement techniques are all about and provide helpful hints on how you can get the best sound and video in your own home.

Entering the Gadget Guru Electronics Area

Keyword: Gadget Guru

Figure 9.30 shows the Gadget Guru Electronics Area's directory window. The Gadget Guru, also known as Andy Pargh, is a fellow who travels across the country in search of new and fascinating devices that eventually end up on the shelves of your favorite stores.

Fig. 9.30
Consumer electronics gets its own forum on America Online.

The Gadget Guru Message Board is a forum for America Online members to discuss their likes and dislikes on various gadgetry. I have spent quite some time there reading messages from folks who still remember the good old days when electronics used tubes, not solid-state devices.

You also can find reviews of upcoming products so that you can learn all about them before they hit the marketplace.

Using the Mercury Center

Keyword: Mercury

Like Chicago Online, Mercury Center is a resource run by a large daily newspaper, in this case the *San Jose Mercury News*. As you can see in figure 9.31, Mercury Center is designed to provide a full range of information about the San Francisco Bay area (which includes the Silicon Valley).

When you first visit Mercury Center, you might just want to look at the top news, shown in the What's New Today listing at the right of the Mercury Center screen, which you can view online or save and print, the same as any other text document on America Online.

Fig. 9.31
Mercury Center is the center for news, views, and more for visitors to the San Francisco Bay area.

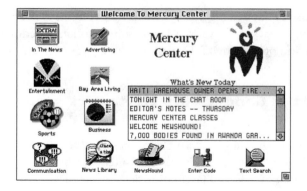

Each icon on the main Mercury Center screen takes you to another special part of Mercury Center. You can check the latest Bay Area entertainment news and then review the Bay Area Living section for a list of things to do when you visit the area, including a list of popular restaurants.

Other sections are devoted to sports and business information and another of America Online's unique message boards, where both fellow members and Mercury Center staff discuss the important issues of the day, or whatever else is on their minds.

One really fascinating feature is Newshound (shown in the Mercury Center window in fig. 9.31), a search tool that will seek out information from the *San Jose Mercury News* and other sources behind the scenes. When the information is found, it'll be sent directly to you via E-mail. Give it a try and see.

Reading the San Jose Mercury News

When you click on the In the News icon on the main Mercury Center screen (see fig. 9.31), and then click on the Extra icon that appears in the next window, you bring up a copy of the current edition of the *San Jose Mercury News* (see fig. 9.32). You can read the entire news, sports, and features sections and interact with the paper's editors.

Reading The New York Times Online

Keyword: Times

Start spreading the news and be a part of it. *The New York Times* is on America Online (see fig. 9.33) with an emphasis on the top features and lifestyle news from each daily edition of the paper. All the top stories from the newspaper itself are available for you to read online, or save and print for later review.

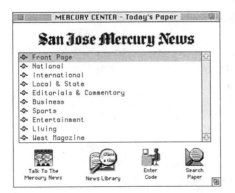

Fig. 9.32
Your virtual daily
newspaper comes
right to your
America Online
doorstep.

Fig. 9.33
The *New York
Times* offers the
best of its daily
editions on
America Online.

Caution

When you want to find *The New York Times* on America online, don't forget the
keyword is *Times.* If you forget the *s*, and type **Time** instead, you'll be taken to the
Time magazine forum instead.

If you live in New York, or are planning a visit, click on the Leisure icon.
You'll find news and views about the top dining and entertainment spots in
New York. And don't forget to check out In The Region, a special area de-
voted to the rest of the tri-state New York metropolitan area.

Exploring Wine & Dine Online

Keyword: Wine

This forum caters to all of you who are interested in fine food and drink,
whether it involves home cooking or a visit to your favorite restaurant.

From the right side of the main forum window (see fig. 9.34), you can access a collection of columns from Jerry D. Mead, a syndicated writer in wines, and a Reading Room & Reference area featuring articles that cover everything from wine and food basics to such topics as How To Buy Wine Futures.

Fig. 9.34
From wine tasting to fine dining, Wine & Dine Online is your information source.

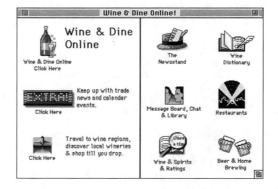

You can find a diverse array of resources that extend from reviews of fine restaurants to a message center where you can exchange news and views with fellow online gourmets. Wine & Dine Online also offers a service to help you locate and purchase wines of rare vintage.

The Extra icon alerts you to upcoming events, such as wine tastings and other gatherings of interest.

Sports & Recreation

We've covered some of America Online's sports-related forums in Chapter 8, "The Entertainment Chapter." Here are some more areas you'll want to visit:

Exploring BikeNet: The Bicycle Network

Keyword: BikeNet

The Bicycle Network on America Online is sponsored by a number of bicycle organizations in North America. It's a database for publications and text files on bicycle-related information (see fig. 9.35). A Rides & Events Calendar keeps you up-to-date on happenings in this field, and the network also includes a regular schedule of conferences and an active message board. Even if your bike riding is limited to Sunday afternoons in a local park, you'll be interested in visiting this forum often.

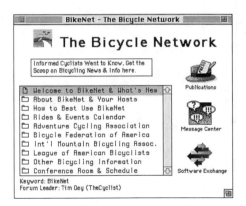

Fig. 9.35
BikeNet is the
online source for
information for
bicycle riders.

Going Scuba Driving

Keyword: Scuba

Like me, I'm very sure most of you have become familiar with scuba diving
through many of the exciting movies where characters perform many of their
incredible stunts underwater. If you've entertained the idea of trying this
sport, pay a visit to AOL Scuba Forum (see fig. 9.36). You'll find a full directory of places where you can learn scuba diving yourself. If you are already a
participant in this exciting activity, you'll also find helpful tips here to help
you really hone your skills.

Fig. 9.36
Underwater
sports can be
truly exciting,
whether you
watch or partici-
pate yourself.

From Here...

New Clubs & Interests forums are being added regularly to America Online,
so if you don't find an area that caters to your special interest, check back
often. Many of the special forums mentioned briefly in this chapter and
other information pertinent to your Lifestyles & Interests needs are also discussed in more detail in the following chapters:

III

Having Fun

- Chapter 8, "The Entertainment Chapter"
- Chapter 10, "Finding Information on America Online"
- Chapter 13, "Learning & Reference"
- Chapter 14, "News, Magazines, and Business Information"
- Chapter 20, "Getting Help"

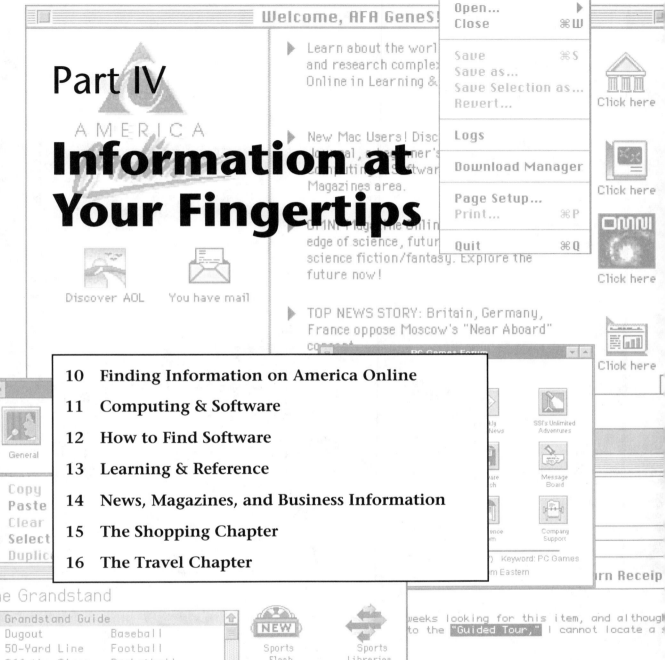

Part IV
A M E R I C A
Information at Your Fingertips

Discover AOL You have mail

Welcome, AFA GeneS!

- Learn about the worl... and research comple... Online in Learning &...

- New Mac Users! Disc... ...al, ...mer's ...ting ...twar... Magazines area.

- OMNI Mag: The Onlin... edge of science, futur... science fiction/fantasy. Explore the future now!

- TOP NEWS STORY: Britain, Germany, France oppose Moscow's "Near Aboard" con...

New ▶
Open... ▶
Close ⌘W

Save ⌘S
Save as...
Save Selection as...
Revert...

Logs

Download Manager

Page Setup...
Print... ⌘P

Quit ⌘Q

Click here
Click here
Click here
Click here

PC Games Forum

...kly ...News SSI's Unlimited Adventures

...re ...ch Message Board

...rence ...m Compang Support

Keyword: PC Games
...m Eastern

General

Copy
Paste
Clear
Select
Duplic...

The Grandstand

📁 Grandstand Guide
📁 Dugout   Baseball
📁 50-Yard Line   Football
📁 Off the Glass   Basketball

NEW
Sports Flash

Sports Libraries

Sports Boards

Stadium Club & Conferences

EXTRA!
Sports Link

weeks looking for this item, and althoug... to the "Guided Tour," I cannot locate a s...

Discover America Online

Match your interests, find out what's new online, discover our most loved services, and make your time online fun and informative. Start by clicking on A Letter from Steve, and come back to explore the other areas featured here.

A Letter From Steve   America Online Highlights   New Featured & Services   Directory of Services

Best of America Online   America Online Tour Guide   America Online Press Releases   What's Hot This Month

Keyword: Discover

Return Receip...

Keyword: Grandstand

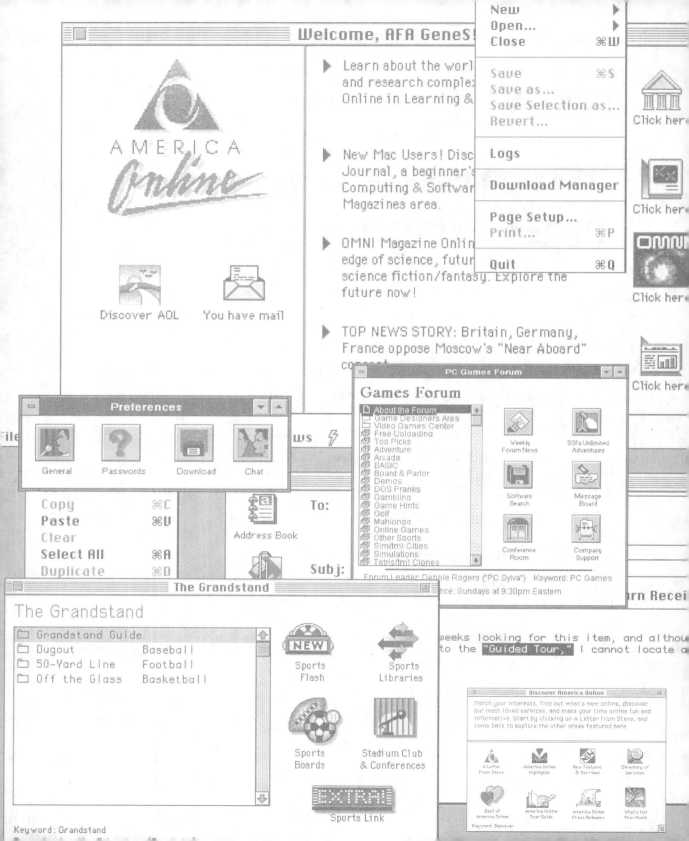

Welcome, AFA GeneS!

AMERICA
Online

Discover AOL   You have mail

▶ Learn about the worl
and research comple:
Online in Learning &

▶ New Mac Users! Disc
Journal, a beginner's
Computing & Softwar
Magazines area.

▶ OMNI Magazine Onlin
edge of science, futur
science fiction/fantasy. Explore the
future now!

▶ TOP NEWS STORY: Britain, Germany,
France oppose Moscow's "Near Aboard"
c

File menu:

New	▶
Open...	▶
Close	⌘W
Save	⌘S
Save as...	
Save Selection as...	
Revert...	
Logs	
Download Manager	
Page Setup...	
Print...	⌘P
Quit	⌘Q

Click her
Click her

OMN
Click her

Click her

Preferences

General   Passwords   Download   Chat

Copy	⌘C
Paste	⌘V
Clear	
Select All	⌘A
Duplicate	⌘D

ws

To:
Address Book

Subj:

PC Games Forum

Games Forum

- About the Forum
- Game Designers Area
- Video Games Center
- Free Uploading
- Top Picks
- Adventure
- Arcade
- BASIC
- Board & Parlor
- Demos
- DOS Pranks
- Gambling
- Game Hints
- Golf
- Mahjongg
- Online Games
- Other Sports
- Sim(tm) Cities
- Simulations
- Tetris(tm) Clones

Weekly
Forum News

SSI's Unlimited
Adventures

Software
Search

Message
Board

Conference
Room

Company
Support

Forum Leader Debbie Rogers ("PC Sylva")   Keyword: PC Games
nce: Sundays at 9:30pm Eastern

rn Recei

The Grandstand

The Grandstand

- Grandstand Guide
- Dugout   Baseball
- 50-Yard Line   Football
- Off the Glass   Basketball

NEW

Sports
Flash

Sports
Libraries

Sports
Boards

Stadium Club
& Conferences

EXTRA!
Sports Link

Keyword: Grandstand

weeks looking for this item, and althou
to the "Guided Tour," I cannot locate a

Discover America Online

Match your interests, find out what's new online, discover
our most loved services, and make your time online fun and
informative. Start by clicking on A Letter from Steve, and
come back to explore the other areas featured here.

A Letter
From Steve

America Online
Highlights

New Features
& Services

Directory of
Services

Best of
America Online

America Online
Tour Guide

America Online
Press Releases

What's Hot
This Month

Keyword: Discover

Chapter 10

Finding Information on America Online

Your computer is crashing over and over again, you need to check your stock portfolio, research a high school report for a history class, or schedule that long-delayed vacation to Europe. You can do it all on America Online but first you have to know where to find the information you need.

In this chapter, we give you a brief overview of how to:

- ■ Search the resources available on America Online
- ■ Quickly find the newest services on America Online
- ■ Find the most popular America Online services
- ■ Get a status report on the services that will be introduced in the future

Navigating Across the America Online Superhighway

Until now, we've discussed in-depth how to use America Online software, how to send E-mail, how to attend and participate in chats, and how to use some of the sources for entertainment and lifestyle information that might appeal to you.

Since America Online's information superhighway has an ever-changing landscape, we devote this chapter to telling you how to find the services that do exist and how to keep abreast of the new areas that are being opened on almost a daily basis.

So let's consider the following section a pit stop. If you follow our step-by-step instructions here, in a short time you'll be a seasoned traveler across the superhighway.

America Online Departments

Whenever you log on to America Online, the In The Spotlight window highlights some of the newest services, in addition to displaying the top news headlines. This display changes several times a day and is updated with the latest window every time you log on (but it doesn't update during your online visit).

Right beneath the In The Spotlight screen is the Main Menu, your principal gateway to the different areas in America Online. Click on the Departments icon to view AOL's departments (see fig. 10.1). Simply click on the icon you want and explore at will.

Fig. 10.1
America Online is divided into 14 main information areas.

Discover America Online

Keyword: Discover

Another valuable resource of information is the Discover America Online window (see fig. 10.2). It takes you to out-of-the-way spots along the information superhighway, spots that you might otherwise neglect.

We first introduced you to this area in Chapter 1, "Getting Started on America Online," where we gave you the road map for a quick guided tour of the service. Now we want to cover in more detail just what some of those nice-looking icons contain. Begin by clicking on the New Features & Services icon.

Fig. 10.2
Let's Discover
America Online.

New Features & Services

The New Features and Services icon is your shortcut to checking out the latest additions to your online information roster. Double-clicking on the item that interests you transports you directly to that area (see fig. 10.3).

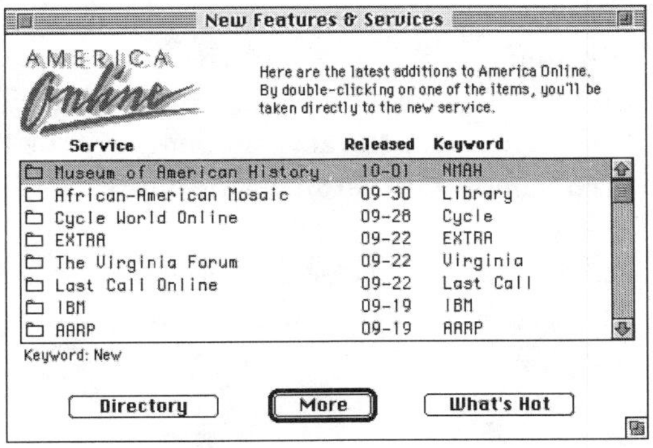

Fig. 10.3
Here's how to find out what's new on America Online.

Tip
As with all America Online text windows, you can save the text to your computer's disk or print the text file. Read Chapters 2 and 3 for more information on how to do this.

Figure 10.4 shows the sort of information services that America Online is adding regularly. If your children are engaged in a homework or special studies project (or you are working toward advancing your own education), here's one place where you can find help. You'll also want to read Chapter 13, "Learning & Reference," for more details on the learning tools provided by America Online. To get there, use the keyword *TLC*.

Fig. 10.4

One of the areas you can visit with two clicks of your mouse.

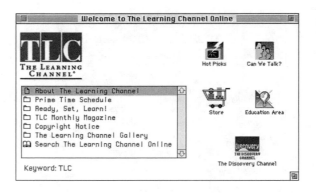

Best of America Online

At the lower-left side of your Discover America Online window is an icon consisting of two hearts (they're red and violet on a color screen). Click on that icon to discover the fast route to the most popular America Online services.

The Best of America Online list changes often (see fig. 10.5). All you have to do is double-click any item in this list that interests you and you'll be taken directly to that area. The one we've highlighted is America Online's rapidly growing Internet Connection (use the keyword *Internet*). The Internet is a gateway between online networks that spans the entire world.

Fig. 10.5

A quick way to locate America Online's most popular services.

Although the Internet can seem like a very confusing place in which to seek out information and services, America Online has made it easy. Chapter 17, "The Internet Connection," and Chapter 18, "The Low-Down on Internet Newsgroups," focus on the Internet, so if we've piqued your curiosity, we suggest you go right to those chapters for more information about this exciting, sprawling, and rapidly growing service.

Directory of Services

Keywords: Dir of Services, Directory

We can only hope to capture a small part of the vast array of services and information sources that America Online offers in this book. As we've explained, the service is undergoing regular revisions. More and more new services are added, sometimes on a daily basis, and older ones are modified quite often. Here's a fast route to seeing whether the service you are seeking is available.

- The main window of America Online's Directory of Services area helps guide you to locating the information you want (see fig. 10.6). If you need additional assistance, read the How to Search the Directory text file, which you can save and print for later review, if you prefer.

Fig. 10.6
How to find whether America Online has the information you want.

- A Calendar of Events is available that reports on interesting things coming up in the near future, such as a special chat or the introduction of a new service.

- We've talked quite a bit in this book about keywords, shortcuts that take you to the areas you want to visit so that you don't have to meander through a number of different menus. Here's one of many places on America Online where you can get a list of keywords. You'll want to update that list regularly. In Appendix A of this book, we've included the keywords that were active at the time this book was published.

If you want to see whether or not a particular service or information source is available on America Online, simply enter the topic you want to know about in the field on the first line of the Directory of Services window.

If your family enjoys visiting new restaurants in your hometown or while traveling, you can select *food* as the topic of your search of America Online's vast information database (see fig. 10.7). After you enter the topic you want to know more about, click on the List Articles button.

Fig. 10.7
Well, how about food?

If the service is available, you see a listing in just a few seconds. You can activate the text window that interests you by double-clicking on that item. In this case, we chose Wine & Dine Online (see fig. 10.8). If you're curious about this service, just read the preceding chapter on lifestyles and interests for more details.

Tip
If your first search doesn't bring the result you want, try a different word or phrase.

Fig. 10.8
A description of the Wine & Dine Online service.

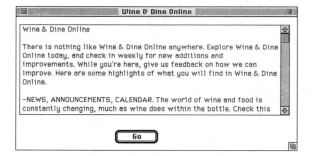

What's Hot This Month

When you select the What's Hot This Month icon, you see a list of the most popular online features. Figure 10.9 illustrates just a sample of the things you might find when you select this icon. It was current when we wrote this book, but you can expect to see it change regularly as new services are added and older services are improved.

Just double-click the name of the topic you want to explore further, or highlight that item and click on the Open button. You see a small text file explaining what the topic is about. We were very curious to learn just what was meant by the topic "Get Your 'Out of the Sun' Demo." As it turns out, it describes a demonstration version of a hot new Macintosh game (see fig. 10.10).

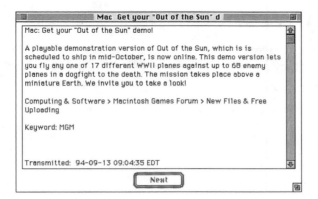

Fig. 10.9
What's hot?

Fig. 10.10
Find out about
downloading the
demo of a hot new
computer game.

If you enjoy games (and who doesn't?), the Mac and PC Games forums have
software libraries filled not only with demonstration software, but freeware
and shareware games for you to download. And there are message boards
filled with tips and tricks about your favorite computer games. We used some
of those tips to learn how to get to the Mechanical Age in Broderbund's
popular CD-ROM game, Myst.

America Online Press Releases

Because America Online is a publicly traded company, there are frequent
press releases about the status of the network and about major new features
being added (see fig. 10.11).

America Online president, Steve Case, regularly writes a letter to members,
with a status report on the service and about plans for the future. You'll see a
new message every month or so in the Discover America Online window, and
you're always welcome to send E-mail to Steve with your suggestions.

Tip
For up-to-date
information about
happenings in the
computer industry
at large, type the
keyword
Newsbytes.

Fig. 10.11
Regular status reports from America Online's press relations folks.

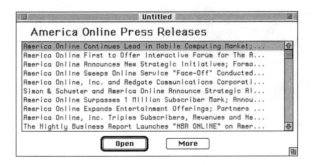

From Here...

In this chapter, you learned how to seek out the many America Online services that you may not be aware of, simply by clicking one of the many fancy icons that grace your computer's screen when you first sign on.

In the chapters that follow, we discuss some of the most popular information services in more detail, plus give you helpful hints on how to get maximum benefit from your America Online experience.

- For information on computers and software, see Chapter 11, "Computing & Software."

- For advice on how to locate and download software, see Chapter 12, "How to Find Software."

- For information on educational and reference materials available on America Online, see Chapter 13, "Learning & Reference."

- For the latest in news and magazines, and for information for your business, see Chapter 14, "News, Magazines, and Business Information."

- For a quick shopping tour, see Chapter 15, "The Shopping Chapter."

- For advice on how to plan your travel itinerary online, see Chapter 16, "The Travel Chapter."

- To learn how you can participate in the largest computer network in the world, read Chapter 17, "The Internet Connection" and Chapter 18, "The Low-Down on Internet Newsgroups."

- For information on how to get further help to make your online sessions more enjoyable, see Chapter 20, "Getting Help."

Chapter 11

Computing & Software

Because you interact with America Online by computer, the online service is a natural place to learn more about your computer, too. Whether you want to download a fancy new shareware program, or you're looking for advice on how to upgrade your computer for better performance or to solve a specific problem, America Online can help you find the answers.

Suppose, for example, that you try to run a new program and your computer crashes every time. It's Friday evening, and the manufacturer's technical support people have gone home for the weekend. You need that new software to finish a special project. What to do?

Log on to America Online, where you can find both members and manufacturer's support people ready and willing to help you out of your jam.

Or suppose that you're looking for a program that can help remind you of special events. Relief is just a download away in America Online's vast software libraries. You have a software selection numbering in the tens of thousands, and more is being added daily.

In this chapter, you learn how to:

- Find computing advice and software

- Find free support

- Ask for help with a computer-related problem

Previewing Computer Books & Magazines

When you want to learn more about how your computer works, find out how to use a specific piece of software, or just sneak a preview of upcoming products, you are likely to venture into your local bookstore and purchase a book such as this one.

America Online gives you a chance to preview some of those publications before you buy them. You can even search through back issues of many of your favorite computing magazines for a specific article of interest, all during your online session.

Looking at Home Office Computing

Keyword: Home Office

If you, like many people, work from an office located in your own home, you might want to read *Home Office Computing*. This magazine caters to small-business folk, offers advice on buying new hardware and software, and provides helpful tips on making your office run more productively (see fig. 11.1).

Fig. 11.1
Home Office Computing's forum on AOL is a valuable resource for small businesses.

You also are invited to participate in the magazine's active message board, where readers and editors alike discuss how to get the most mileage out of your computer purchase.

Reading HomePC Magazine

Keyword: HomePC

The personal computer has taken over almost every area of our lives. Our children work with computers at school, and low-priced computers are now available not only at specialty stores, but from discount stores and consumer electronics chains. *HomePC* magazine (see fig. 11.2) is for users of both the Apple Macintosh and IBM PCs and compatibles, with an emphasis on the home rather than business user.

The Ask Dr. PC section provides answers for common problems one faces in learning more about a computer. The HomePC Forum also provides a special section covering the latest and greatest children's software products, and helpful advice you'll want to read about before you make your next (or first) home computer purchase.

Fig. 11.2
HomePC magazine takes a personal approach to the world of personal computing.

Reading MacHome Journal

Keyword: MacHome Journal

If you are new to the world of desktop computers and find such jargon as CPUs, RAM, hard drive access speeds, and other phrases to be a foreign language, you need to read *MacHome Journal*. This publication is designed for those of you who want to learn how to use your computer more effectively without wading through confusing paragraphs of technical material (see fig. 11.3).

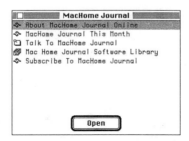

Fig. 11.3
You don't have to be a technological wizard to find valuable information in *MacHome Journal*.

As with other online magazines, you can preview the latest issue of the magazine, exchange messages with fellow America Online members and editors, and download useful software. If you like the magazine well enough to want a copy in your home, you even find a convenient way to order a subscription.

Exploring MacTech Magazine

Keyword: MacTech

If you want to write software for the Macintosh, you'll want to check out *MacTech* magazine. This publication caters strictly to the interests of developers and programmers. Each issue is filled with helpful information to help you learn programming, and advice on how to debug your software and even suggestions on finding a solution to a sticky coding problem.

MacTech also distributes regular CDs filled with advice for programmers and sample source code that you could use when developing your own software.

Exploring Macworld

Keyword: Macworld

When you buy a new Apple Macintosh, you get a free trial subscription to *Macworld*. But even if you haven't made a new computer purchase lately, you might want to keep up-to-date on all the new hardware and software products. *Macworld* contains special sections, Macworld News and New Products, where you can learn just what Apple has up its corporate sleeve for the newest generation of Macintosh computers. The Macworld screen is shown in figure 11.4.

Fig. 11.4
Macworld
magazine is
highlighted on
America Online.

In Touch with Macworld is a message board with breezy and sometimes heated discussions on all sorts of computer-related subjects involving America Online members and *Macworld*'s writers and editors.

Macworld's Software Library is a repository of unique shareware reviewed by the magazine and other special files that might interest you. One file, in fact, puts grammar-checking software through a genuine torture test—something you want to think about if you want to buy a program to help you improve your writing skills.

Exploring Mobile Office Online

Keyword: Mobile, Portable

The proliferation of Macintosh and PC laptop computers has made it possible for you to do your work most anywhere in the world, even in the middle of a desert, so long as you have a spare set of batteries or an available source for AC power. Mobile Office Online, as shown in figure 11.5, is the AOL counterpart of the popular newsstand magazine that caters to this new generation of traveling workers.

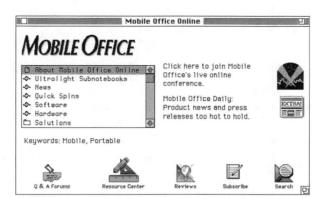

Fig. 11.5
Mobile Office magazine keeps tabs on the growing world of laptop computing.

In addition to reading the top features from the magazine itself, there's a special area, Mobile Office Daily, that contains hot news that just can't wait for the next issue. The Q&A forums give you a chance to offer advice, ask questions, and share information with fellow AOL members and the magazine's friendly editorial staff.

Visiting PC World Online

Keyword: PC World

PC World magazine is *Macworld*'s sister publication. It provides its own unique slant to information on new PC hardware and software products. A typical visit to the forum might offer you news about a special contest, a new family of chips from Intel, or the latest operating system upgrade from Microsoft. The PC World Online screen is shown in figure 11.6.

Virtually the entire text of the current issue of *PC World* is at your fingertips for review. A large software library of useful PC utilities is available. You are also invited to attend special conferences featuring fellow America Online members, editors and writers, and visiting experts.

Fig. 11.6
PC World Online is an information resource for users of IBM PCs and compatibles.

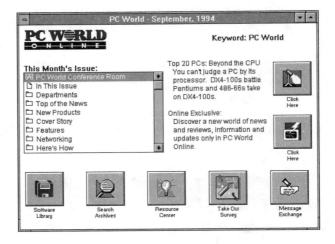

The Online Exclusive area contains the latest computer news and information—before it appears in the magazine itself. Because a magazine must be prepared a month or two in advance, America Online members get a jump on newsstand buyers by learning about new developments in computing first.

Visiting Redgate Online

Keyword: Redgate/INN Online

If you're looking for a particular Macintosh hardware or software product, and you don't know if it exists, or how to contact the manufacturer, *The Macintosh Product Registry* will probably have the information you want. Redgate/INN Online, shown in figure 11.7, has a huge database showing virtually every existing Macintosh product. In addition, there's a directory for PC Multimedia products.

Fig. 11.7
The Redgate Registry is a database of information about thousands of computing products.

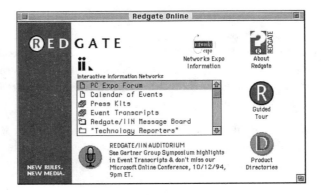

The Redgate/INN Online Forum also schedules regular conferences with major leaders in the computing industry, so you can learn about special product introductions, and gain insights into future developments. There's also a special library that contains complete press lists describing new computing products that you will surely want to check out.

Looking at IYM Software Review

Keyword: IYM

IYM Software Review is an online publication that reviews new PC software products and gives you useful information before you lay down your hard-earned dollars for a purchase. The review also includes a library of useful software that can enhance the productivity of your computer.

You can interact with IYM's writers and fellow America Online members on a variety of computer-related subjects.

Visiting WordPerfect Magazine Online

Keyword: WPMag

If you are a user of WordPerfect, the popular cross-platform word processing program published by Novell, the monthly *WordPerfect* Magazine, shown in figure 11.8 is your source for advice and information about this popular word processing program. It comes in two flavors. The regular version, and a special Windows edition.

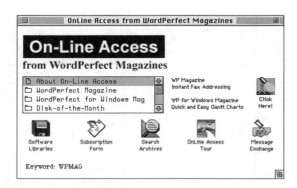

Fig. 11.8
OnLine Access features *WordPerfect* Magazine.

Text-based copies of the latest issue, and recent issues, are available for you to view and read at your leisure. The Software Library features special files, such as handy macros, that will help make your experience with WordPerfect software more productive. The Message Exchange is a gathering place for readers and editors to offer advice and provide time-saving tips and tricks.

Exploring the Computing & Software Forums

Keyword: Computing

If you want to learn to use your computer more effectively, or just talk computers with fellow online members, visit America Online's Computing & Software forums often.

The following paragraphs briefly highlight many of the forums. Because a picture is truly worth a thousand words, look closely at the figures throughout this chapter for a list of many of the services that the forums offer.

As you can see in figures 11.9 and 11.10, both the Mac and PC versions of the Computing department screen provide a gateway to America Online's computing and software forums and other valuable information resources. You can find special areas devoted to specific aspects of computing, updated computing news, company support forums, and schedules for upcoming chats that you don't want to miss.

Fig. 11.9
The Macintosh Computing & Software screen is your gateway to the Mac software forums on America Online.

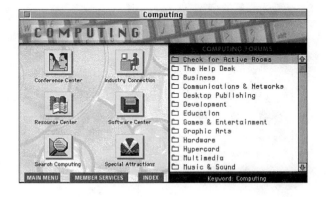

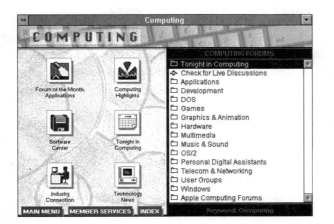

Fig. 11.10
The PC Comput-
ing & Software
screen is your
gateway to the PC
software forums
on America
Online.

Visiting the Macintosh Help Desk

Keyword: Help Desk

Every Mac computing forum on America Online has a little icon with a
shaded question mark. It's labeled Help & Information, and it's your entry to
the Help Desk (see fig. 11.11).

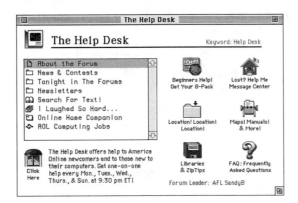

Fig. 11.11
When you need a
helping hand, the
Mac Help Desk on
America Online is
there for you.

Tip
Before you post a
question, read
older messages in
the same message
folder or in other
message areas
dealing with a
similar topic.
You might find
a response and
a solution to a
question much
like yours.

If you've just bought your first computer, you might want to visit this forum
often for advice on how to get over the rough spots and become more comfortable with your new purchase. In the Frequently Asked Questions area
(often called *FAQ*), you can find ready answers to your most common questions. We especially recommend Beginner's Help! Get Your 8-Pack! a special
set of helpful documents that will really get you over the rough spots.

If you need further assistance, visit the Message Center and post your question. America Online members and the forum's knowledgeable staff are on hand to help. Five conferences, called *Help hours,* are held every week. There you can find helping hands with a ready solution to guide you through a nagging problem.

Visiting the PC Help Desk

Keyword: Help Desk

Every one of us was a beginner once. I remember my first visit to America Online, back in the fall of 1989. I was a new owner of a computer, and had just installed the software and logged on for the first time. It was like visiting a strange, vast and unknown world for the very first time. I needed a little guidance to find out how to navigate through the uncharted waters, and some suggestions about the best places to visit.

As with the Macintosh Help Desk, the PC Help Desk, shown in figure 11.12, is a rich information resource. You'll find helpful text material answering common questions you may have about using your PC to explore the highways and byways of America Online. Armed with that resource, plus a copy of this book at hand, you'll have a safe and pleasant trip across the information superhighway.

Fig. 11.12
The PC Help Desk (also known as the Beginners' Forum) is there to help you get going when the going gets rough.

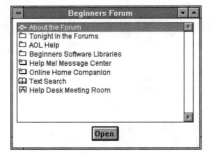

Exploring the PC Applications Forum

Keyword: PC Applications

The market offers a bewildering array of PC applications. Knowing which word processor to choose, which financial planning software works best, and which spreadsheet crunches numbers most efficiently is difficult to determine. The Applications Forum tries to bring a little order and helpful advice in its active message board.

This forum is also a repository of thousands of public domain and share software files for PC users, separated by category (see fig. 11.13). Feel free to browse through the libraries, which are separated by topic. Each file has a full description that you need to examine before choosing the files you want to download.

Fig. 11.13
The Applications forum is your own virtual software store.

If you have a problem with a specific program or just need some interactive advice before deciding which one is right for you, attend the Applications Forum's weekly chat.

Visiting the Macintosh Business Forum
Keyword: MBS

You might be seeking a better spreadsheet program to display those all-important numbers. Or perhaps you're looking for software that can help you build a mailing list or prepare invoices for your clients.

The Mac Business Forum is your center for information and advice on how best to select and use the software on which your business depends (see fig. 11.14). On an active message board, fellow users and experts discuss tips and tricks to get the best performance. You learn how to create presentations that sell your product or service, or even whether a new tax preparation software product can make things a little less unpleasant at tax time.

You can share your thoughts with other members, forum staff, and visiting experts at the weekly conferences. And you might want to join Special Interest Groups that cater to specific categories of business computing.

Fig. 11.14

From spreadsheets to financial planners, your source for business-related programs is the Mac Business Forum.

Visiting the Computing Resource Center
Keyword: CRC

This forum has three different faces, depending on which of the three buttons shown in figure 11.15 you select. The first, which we are picturing here, shows Resources. There are also selections for searchable databases and publications. Depending on which button you select, you can just click on the appropriate directory listing to visit the area that's shown.

Fig. 11.15

Find a vast resource of information in one place in AOL's Computing Resource Center.

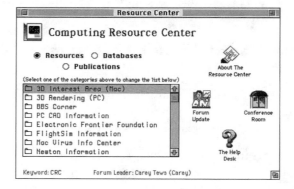

In addition to these information resources, you will also be able to visit Special Interest Groups (SIGs) that are devoted to a specific topic of personal computing. Regular conferences are scheduled where you can share information with forum staff and fellow AOL members.

As this book went to press, the Computing Resource Center was in its embryonic stages of development, and additional features, including full message boards, were being phased in.

Exploring the Telecommunications Forums

Keywords: MCM (Macintosh), PC Telecom (Windows)

If you're thinking of buying one of those newer, high-speed modems, or finding a better way to network your computer with a printer or another computer, pay a visit to the Telecommunications forums on America Online. Figure 11.16 shows the Communications Forum screen for Macintosh users; figure 11.17 shows its PC counterpart, the Telecommunications and Networking Forum screen.

Fig. 11.16
The Communications Forum is your America Online headquarters for Macintosh modem and networking issues.

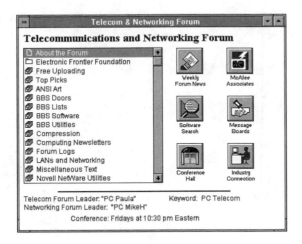

Fig. 11.17
This forum is the telecommunications and networking headquarters for DOS and Windows users.

Using a modem isn't always a cut-and-dried process. A modem might take just a few seconds to plug in, but then you have to deal with such issues as communications software (if you're not logging on to America Online) and such arcane subjects as configuration and initialization strings. Your America

Online Telecommunications forums are your sources for helpful advice and useful information of all sorts to get you on your way to confident telecommunications.

When you hook up your computer to even a single printer or to another computer for exchanging files, you've established a network. Also, offices these days commonly have Macs and PCs working side by side, and the networking issues often can get complex. You need a place where you can get some helpful advice to get you over the rough spots. As with other forums, the Telecommunications forums schedule regular conferences—and frequent special events—that you probably want to attend.

Visiting the Macintosh Desktop Publishing Forum
Keyword: MDP

Desktop publishing owes its lineage to traditional typesetting. But instead of producing text with machines that melt down hot sticks of lead, or on expensive minicomputers that generate characters on photosensitive paper with flashing lights and lenses, you now can create professional publications—like this book, for example—on a desktop computer.

The Macintosh Desktop Publishing Forum, whose main screen is shown in figure 11.18, caters to beginners and professionals alike. You can find helpful advice on how to select publishing or word processing programs, what sort of fonts you need, and even the best printer to buy.

Fig. 11.18
Desktop publishing is the descendant of traditional typesetting, and a whole forum covers it on America Online.

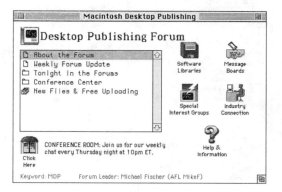

Every week, the forum holds a conference where you can ask questions of the forum's expert staff or special guests. The message boards are one of the most popular in the Computing & Software areas of America Online, and you'll want to participate as well.

Visiting the Developers Forum

Keywords: MDV (Macintosh), PC Development (Windows)

If you want to write your own software, or you're a professional looking for advice on dealing with a specific problem in writing code, America Online's developers' forums are resources you can use again and again. Figure 11.19 shows the Developers Forum screen for Macintosh users; figure 11.20 shows the PC version, the Development Forum screen.

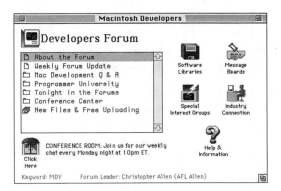

Fig. 11.19
When you want to write your own Mac software, the Developers Forum is a place you want to visit.

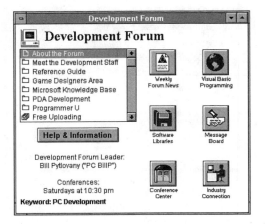

Fig. 11.20
Whether your software is earmarked for DOS or Windows, you can seek out advice from the experts.

A huge store of information helps budding programmers deal with the rough spots. The software libraries contain resource tools that help you create better, more efficient software. You can exchange views and share knowledge with fellow America Online members, forum staff, and many of the software engineers (programmers) who write your favorite software.

You also can bring your questions and problems to the forums for assistance during their weekly interactive conferences. And because Mac developers often want to develop a Windows version of their software (and vice versa), you might want to make a regular visit to both developers' forums.

Visiting the DOS Forum

Keyword: DOS

When Microsoft introduced MS-DOS 6.0, America Online established a special Resource Center in the DOS Forum to offer advice and suggestions on updating your PC computers to take the best advantage of this new operating system. You can even download the latest DOS update and take advantage of the new features and bug fixes that are offered.

The DOS Forum on America Online (see fig. 11.21) is not just an information center to help you make your computer run more efficiently. You can check out the forum's huge libraries of public domain and shareware to find that special utility you've been seeking, to manage memory more effectively, or to help you back up your daily work.

Fig. 11.21
Advice and updates are available on America Online's DOS Forum.

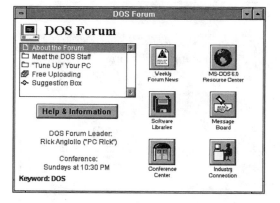

If you've got a particularly annoying problem and you need a helpful response, visit the forum's message board or drop into the weekly conferences for interactive discussions with fellow America Online members and visiting experts.

Exploring the Macintosh Education Forum

Keyword: MED

More and more young people are using computers in the classrooms. Even those in kindergarten and first grade more and more often find a small desktop computer on a teacher's desk. And as your children grow older, they might find a computer lab available in their school as well.

The Macintosh Education Forum is a resource for students, educators, and parents alike to help our youth learn more about how to use their computers and to learn from them (see fig. 11.22). The forum also includes a library of software with an educational slant.

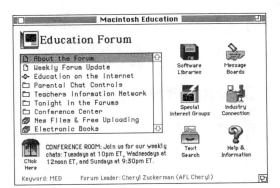

Fig. 11.22
When you use your computer for education, visit the Macintosh Education Forum.

The forum features a special information section devoted to Parental Chat Controls. This resource is provided on America Online to restrict your children's access to some areas of the online community. Chapter 20, "Getting Help," contains more information about this important tool.

Exploring the Games Forums

Keywords: MGM (Macintosh), PC Games (Windows)

In Chapter 8, "The Entertainment Chapter," you were introduced to many of the ways you can have pure, simple fun on America Online. The Games forums contain shareware games, add-ons, and demos of many popular commercial games, and, just as important, helpful advice on how to make your playtime (for adults and children) more rewarding. Figures 11.23 and 11.24 show the Macintosh and PC Games Forum screens. (For more information, refer to Chapter 8.)

Fig. 11.23

You have time for a little fun with a game downloaded from the Macintosh Games Forum.

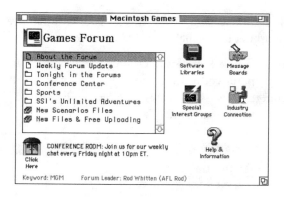

Fig. 11.24

You can make your PC more fun to use with a game from America Online's PC Games Forum.

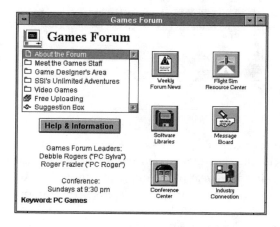

Using the Graphics Forums

Keywords: MGR (Macintosh), PC Graphics (Windows)

If you are a computer artist or want to become one, you need to drop in to visit the Graphics forums on America Online. These forums contain huge resources of information to help you learn your craft and produce better work (see figs. 11.25 and 11.26).

Even if your drawing or image-editing skills are limited to a few simple shapes or scanning artwork with your desktop scanner, you can find useful advice and information in the Graphics forums.

You might want to attend the regular weekly conferences and become involved in some of the Special Interest Groups (SIGs). These groups are devoted to specialized areas of graphics expertise or users of a particular program.

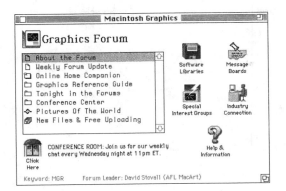

Fig. 11.25
The Macintosh
Graphics Forum
is AOL's resource
for Macintosh
graphics profes-
sionals.

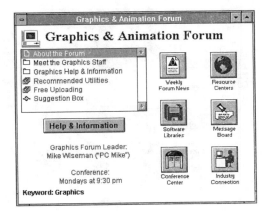

Fig. 11.26
PC computer
artists should
check out the
Graphics and
Animation Forum.

Visiting the Hardware Forums

Keywords: MHW (Macintosh), PC Hardware (Windows)

New computers are coming out so often that keeping a scorecard is difficult.
Before you buy a new model only to learn that it will be outdated the next
day, check out America Online's Hardware forums, shown in figures 11.27
and 11.28.

These forums feature an active message boards area, with special areas devoted to the newest CPUs, upcoming products, hardware expansion, modems, printers, and other issues. You can communicate with other America
Online members, the forum's own staff (which includes representatives of
some of the hardware manufacturers), and visiting experts.

Whenever a major new product is announced, you can hear about it first in
the Hardware forums. If you have a problem getting a computer, hard drive,
or printer to work correctly, for example, these forums give you a resource to
go to for further help.

Fig. 11.27
If you're buying a new Macintosh computer, you need to visit the Mac Hardware Forum first.

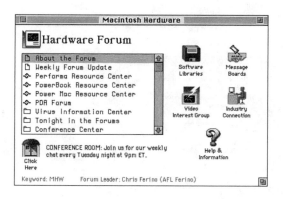

Fig. 11.28
Find out which PC can run Windows faster in the PC Hardware Forum.

Visiting the Macintosh HyperCard Forum
Keyword: MHC

HyperCard is your own personal, easy-to-use programming language that you can use to build your own programs based on the metaphor of a stack. A stack is like a Rolodex card, containing useful information that you can read or print or that enables you to perform a particular function. Unlike the often arcane, difficult-to-master programming language used in commercial software, HyperCard programming often requires only a little practice.

The HyperCard Forum on America Online is the place where you can learn how to develop your own HyperCard stacks or just download ones from other enterprising programmers (see fig. 11.29). You have a whole range of stacks from which to choose, from simple information resources to mailing list software. You can find a wealth of information, sage advice, and useful software for your computer.

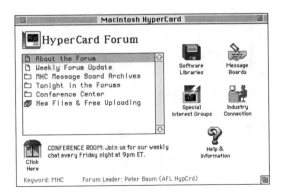

Fig. 11.29
The HyperCard
Forum gives
you help with
HyperCard, your
personal program-
ming language.

Using the Multimedia Forums

Keywords: MMM (Macintosh), PC Multimedia (Windows)

The word *multimedia* has been bandied about the computer world for quite a
number of years. Multimedia refers to the marriage of audio and video (still
or moving) on your desktop computer. As computers have become more and
more powerful, the tools to manipulate the sometimes huge audio and video
files have become cheaper and easier to use.

Major movie production houses have been using desktop computers for their
work. The newest models from Apple Computer such as the Power Macintosh
line, with the AV option, offer special tools for multimedia use, such as the
ability to capture video images without having to buy extra hardware (other
than a video source, of course). America Online's Multimedia forums (see figs.
11.30 and 11.31) are meeting grounds for both amateurs and professionals to
share experiences and learn more about this growing art.

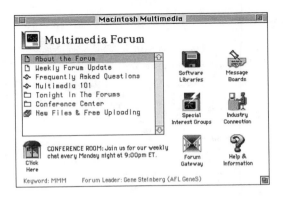

Fig. 11.30
Video and sound
combine to
produce multi-
media, and this
forum is where
you can keep
up-to-date with
the emerging
technologies.

Fig. 11.31
America Online's resource for PC multimedia users is the PC Multimedia Forum.

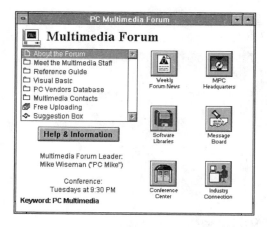

You can attend regular chats and special workshops to hone your skills, whether you just like to play with a QuickTime movie clip, manipulate some sounds, or are a seasoned professional.

Exploring the Music and Sound Forums
Keywords: MMS (Macintosh), PC Music (Windows)

In the 1980s, music came into its own on a desktop computer. More and more recording artists (some whose names are household words) have begun to use personal computers to create and store sounds. With a few inexpensive add-ons, you can even make your computer into a miniature, multitrack recording studio and produce digital-quality audio.

The Music and Sound forums on America Online provide helpful advice and tips on how you can use these tools to create professional-sounding music presentations (see figs. 11.32 and 11.33).

Fig. 11.32
The Macintosh Music & Sound Forum is for professional musicians and amateurs alike.

Fig. 11.33
The PC Music and
Sound Forum on
America Online
gives PC music
buffs a chance to
explore musical
tools.

If you simply want to add a few convenient sounds to make your computer more fun to work with, the Music and Sound forums can help you, too. You can explore their libraries of entertaining and sometimes funny sound clips.

Visiting the Macintosh Operating Systems Forum

Keyword: MOS

The operating system is usually the most invisible part of your computer's software. But every function, from turning on your computer to moving and copying files, is managed by the operating system. The software you use to do your work uses tools provided by the operating system for many of its functions.

The Macintosh Operating Systems Forum is your information center for System 6, all flavors of System 7, and Apple's UNIX front end, A/UX (see fig. 11.34). The forum's expert staff advises you on how to solve your computer's problems, such as frequent crashes or other strange behavior, and helps you make your computer work better and faster.

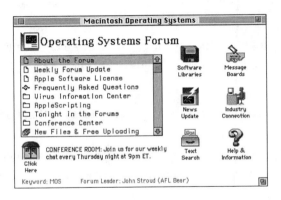

Fig. 11.34
Your computer
can't even start
without its
operating system,
the subject of this
forum on America
Online.

The forum's Apple software libraries contain the latest updates from Apple, including the newest printer drivers, system updates, and special programs to enhance performance.

Visiting the OS/2 Forum
Keyword: OS 2

IBM's OS/2 is an efficient multitasking operating system that is gaining more and more popularity in the PC world. Even if you aren't ready to switch just yet, you might want to visit America Online's OS/2 Forum to learn just what all those computer magazines are writing about and find out whether OS/2 is something you want to use. Figure 11.35 shows the main OS/2 Forum window, from which you can access all the forum's resources.

Fig. 11.35
The ins and outs of OS/2 are explained in this America Online forum.

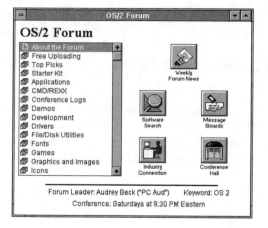

If you already run OS/2, this forum can serve you as a helpful information center where you can interact with fellow America Online members, forum staff, and industry experts on how to make your computer run faster or more efficiently.

As with other computing and software forums on America Online, a huge library of files, ranging from basic utilities and configuration files to games, is available.

Exploring the Personal Digital Assistants Forum
Keyword: PDA

PDA is an abbreviation for Personal Digital Assistants, and it refers to a computer that you can hold in the palm of your hand, such as a Sharp Wizard or an Apple Newton. Whether you have just bought one of these neat examples of electronic wizardry in action or you are wondering whether it's something other than a high-priced toy, you can visit this forum to learn more (see fig. 11.36).

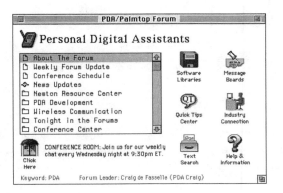

Fig. 11.36
Learn about hand-held computers in this America Online forum.

The PDA Forum is multiplatform and has active message boards for both Macintosh and PC users who want to learn more about these handy little devices. The News Update section offers the latest news about new product releases, including software that makes your PDA do more things. You also can find a busy, rapidly growing software library with system updates, information managers, games, and other useful utilities.

Some industry analysts are stating now that the PDA represents the future of personal computing, that in years to come, even your desktop computer will fit in the palm of your hand. Sound intriguing? Then visit the PDA Forum to learn more.

Using the Macintosh Utilities Forum

Keyword: MUT

A utility can be a program that enhances your computer's operating system—such as a screen saver, an address book, or a reminder program—or software that diagnoses the condition of your computer's hard drive and fixes minor problems.

The Macintosh Utilities Forum, shown in figure 11.37, is your gathering place for information and advice about those little programs that you might often take for granted but that can make a huge change in the way your computer works.

Fig. 11.37
One of America
Online's most
popular Mac
computing forums
is the Utilities
Forum.

A software library contains thousands of useful programs you might want to check (they're updated daily). And you can interact with fellow America Online members and visiting experts twice a week at the forum's regular conferences.

Visiting the User Groups Forum

Keyword: UGF

When you first buy a personal computer, you're no doubt anxious to meet other computer owners to receive advice and share tips and tricks to make your computer run more effectively. A *user group* is a club, pure and simple. It's an organization consisting of computer owners, usually devoted to one specific platform, such as Macintosh or PC.

America Online's User Groups Forum is a special resource for user group members (see fig. 11.38). You can have your organization listed so that others in your area can learn about it. The forum also features a database of news articles that contain helpful material you might want to include in your newsletters, and the library of useful software offers files that you can download and incorporate into your organization's own monthly software disks.

Fig. 11.38
Meet with fellow
computer owners,
right here on
America Online.

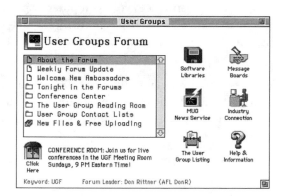

You can attend the weekly chats to talk with fellow members of groups from around the country, and if you aren't a user group member yet, you can consult the forum's User Group Listing for a place to join in your hometown.

Visiting the Windows Forum

Keyword: Windows

Microsoft Windows has caught the PC world by storm, providing an easy-to-use point-and-click metaphor to the way you interact with your computer. Many of your favorite programs are now available in both Macintosh and Windows versions, sporting similar interfaces and similar learning curves. If you review Chapters 2 and 3, for example, you can see that the Macintosh and Windows versions of America Online software are quite similar in the way they're used. They differ mostly in features that support one computing platform or the other.

America Online's Windows forum provides an extensive library of public domain and shareware, an active message board, and regular conferences where you can interact with fellow members and experts alike (see fig. 11.39). As Microsoft's Windows 95 moves into full gear, this is the place where you'll find out what it means for your computing experience.

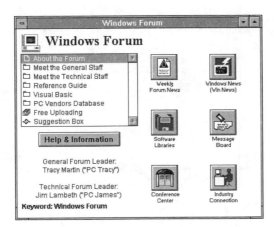

Fig. 11.39
You can make Windows work better by consulting the Windows Forum.

Accessing the Software Center

Keyword: Software

You have several ways to locate software on America Online. One is by doing a file search, which is described in more detail in the next chapter, "How to Find Software." Another method is to visit a forum that caters to that software category. Still a third is the Software Center, which is a repository for popular software from across the entire America Online community. Figures 11.40 and 11.41 show the Software Center screens for Macintosh and PC software.

Fig. 11.40
You can find your favorite Macintosh software all in one place.

Fig. 11.41
You can find your favorite PC software all in one place.

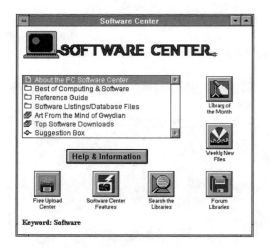

The Software Center is your gateway not only to software in individual forum libraries but also to a number of Specialty Libraries as well, featuring software that's available nowhere else. You also can find a folder of helpful hints that help you deal with problems you might face in finding and transferring software to your computer.

Seeking Company Support

Keyword: Industry Connection

If you've ever waited long minutes listening to voice mail when you try to reach a hardware or software manufacturer for some help, you'll appreciate America Online's solution. More than 100 firms, ranging from small utility software publishers to the major manufacturers of computer hardware, are represented in America Online's Industry Connection areas, as shown in figure 11.42.

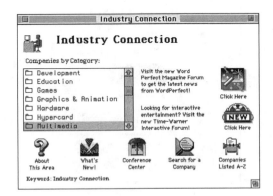

Fig. 11.42
Get help right from the source, using America Online's Industry Connection.

These support forums are places where you can get advice on how to use a company's product more effectively and how to solve problems when they arise. The company's own support personnel usually staff the forums, and they are often ably assisted by knowledgeable America Online members.

Software publishers often give you free maintenance updates to their products in their support areas, so you don't have to wait for that product update to be mailed to you. You also want to check the software libraries often in case they contain an update that you need.

Finding a Company

Not every firm is represented on America Online yet, but more are being added regularly. You can find computing industry support areas in the computing and software forums that cater to the kind of product the companies support. Suppose, for example, that you want to access a modem manufacturer in the Hardware and Communications forums. Click on the Industry Connection icon to see whether the firm is represented.

If you can't find the company you're looking for in a computing forum's directory, you can type the keyword **Industry**, which takes you to America Online's Industry Connection section (shown in fig. 11.42). Then click on the Search for a Company option. If the firm is represented on America Online, it'll be listed in the search window.

But the fastest route might simply be to use a keyword to go directly to the firm you want. If you want to find Claris, Apple Computer's cross-platform software subsidiary, for example, type the keyword **Claris**. In just a few seconds, you are transported directly to the front door of the company's America Online support forum (see fig. 11.43).

Fig. 11.43

Apple's Claris software division publishes software for both the Mac and Windows platforms.

Using Industry Connection Help

A technical support person can't help you solve your problem if you don't give enough information about your setup and the difficulties you're having with the product. This typical letter is often found in the message boards:

```
Help! My computer is crashing all the time. I can't get any work
done when I use your software. I need help.
Signed: Harried Harry
```

This sort of letter is only going to postpone the process of helping you, because the letter lacks any information to enable a technical support person to diagnose and, if necessary, try to reproduce your problem. Remember that the only information a manufacturer has to go on is what you provide in your letter, because they aren't present at your worksite to see what exactly is going wrong.

> **Note**
>
> Don't cross-post. In other words, don't post your message in more than one message folder in a single forum. America Online members don't always take kindly to reading the same message over and over again. Before you issue your plea for help, take a few moments to find the right place to post it. Look for a computing forum or a company support area that's appropriate (the Hardware forum, for example, for a malfunctioning printer), and leave your message there.

The following list gives you some helpful hints on how to ask a company support person for help:

1. Describe the kind of computer you have, including the model number.

2. Briefly describe your setup, including the operating system version and the amount of installed RAM, and list the accessories attached to it, such as a video card or an additional hard drive.

3. Identify the manufacturer's product by model or version number. Quite often a problem might affect only a single version of a program or piece of hardware.

4. Describe the kind of problem you're having. If your computer is crashing, report whether an error message appears on your computer's screen. That kind of message might be crucial to finding out what went wrong.

5. If the problem can be reproduced, describe the steps you've taken to reproduce it. That way, if the problem is unique to your setup, the steps can give a clue for the support person to attempt to reproduce the problem.

6. If the problem started after you made a change in your setup, such as a new hardware addition or a software installation, mention that, too. That new installation might have caused your troubles.

7. And, finally, don't expect miracles. These products are manufactured by human beings, too, and they have the same shortcomings as the rest of us. No hardware or software product is ever perfect, but you want to get it to work as efficiently as possible in your home or office.

Sometimes a problem is just too complex to deal with by E-mail or a message board. In that case, the company invites you to contact its technical support people directly for further assistance.

From Here...

If you want to learn more about your computer and how to use it more effectively, America Online is your best resource for interacting not only with hardware and software manufacturers but also with many savvy computer users. For more information on setting up America Online on your computer, finding the software files you want, and getting help, refer to these chapters:

- Chapter 2, "Using Your America Online Macintosh Software"

- Chapter 3, "Using Your America Online Windows Software"

- Chapter 12, "How to Find Software"

- Chapter 20, "Getting Help"

Chapter 12

How to Find Software

America Online has a library of tens of thousands of Macintosh and Windows software for you to download. The libraries are expanding daily. Whether it's an arcade game, a program that lets you create a to-do list, or an update to commercial software you own, America Online is the place to find it.

In this chapter, you'll learn:

- How to quickly and easily find software in America Online's libraries

- How to transfer that software directly to your computer

- What kinds of software you can find on America Online

- How to upload your own files to America Online's huge software libraries

America Online's Software Libraries

When I first joined America Online in 1989, I was the owner of a brand new computer, and I wanted to stock up on software. As an inveterate software junkie, I was a frequent visitor to the service's vast software libraries. It took me a while to discover the rich array of information services available elsewhere online.

Before we go on, let's define a couple of computer terms you'll see often in this chapter.

- *Downloading* a file is simply the act of transferring a file from America Online's host computer, through the telephone lines, and to your computer by way of your modem.

- *Uploading* a file is the process of sending a file from your computer directly to America Online.

Virus Protection

Because there is always the danger that a file can be contaminated by a computer virus, America Online's forum staff checks all uploaded files with an up-to-date virus detection program before posting them online. You should, however, always install and use the latest virus detection software so that all your files are safe and sound.

Using File Search

The fastest way to locate software you want is to let America Online's host computer do the searching for you. So let's bring up America Online's File Search window:

1. Press ⌘-K (Ctrl+K for Windows) and type the keywords **File Search** (see fig. 12.1).

Fig. 12.1
Your gateway to America Online's convenient software database.

2. In seconds you see a large window on your computer that gives you a number of search options (see fig. 12.2).

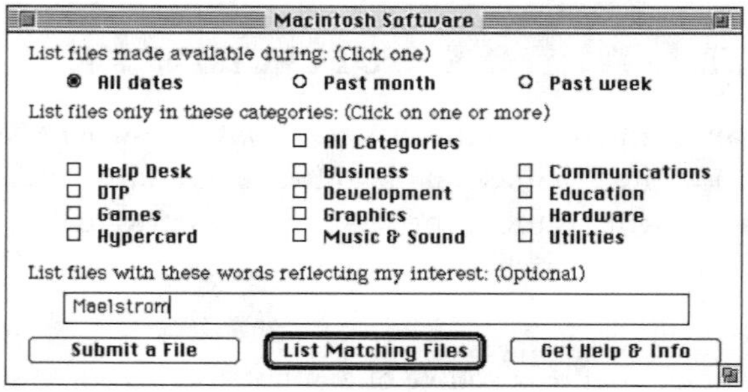

Fig. 12.2
Finding the software you want.

IV

3. You can search for software in many ways. You can limit your search to a specific category, such as Games or Graphics. You can even restrict the search to a specific time frame; for instance, perhaps you only want to find a file that was posted in the past month.

4. If you want to locate a file by name or subject, enter the information in the List files field. If you want to find a screen saver, for example, you'll enter *screen saver* as the subject of your search.

   In this example, we'll try to locate a copy of the popular Macintosh shareware arcade game *Maelstrom*, written by programmer Andrew Welch.

5. If files matching your description cannot be found, you'll see a window that notifies you.

6. If files meeting your description are located, you'll see a File List window on-screen (see fig. 12.3). A file may be listed more than once, because it is in more than one library on America Online. Because only 20 files are loaded to the File List at one time, you might need to click on the List More Files button to see additional entries.

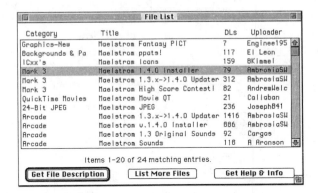

Fig. 12.3
Success! The files you are looking for are listed here.

7. To learn more about the file that interests you, either highlight the file name and double-click on it, or select the Get File Description button, either by clicking on it or by pressing Return or Enter. You'll see a window very much like the one shown in figure 12.4.

Fig. 12.4
Review the file
description first.

How to Download a File

Tip
Before download-
ing a file, check
the File Descrip-
tion. This descrip-
tion not only tells
you more about
the file, but con-
tains information
about what kind
of computer it
works on.

Now that you've found a file you'd like to download to your computer, the next step is to start the download process. Your first option is to create a file *queue*, which is a list of files to download. That list or directory will be stored in AOL's Download Manager (which we'll describe in more detail later in this chapter). Your second option is to download the file immediately.

1. The default selection in the software list, at the bottom of the window, is Download Now, which brings up a window that allows you to indicate where you want to store the file that's being transferred to your computer (see fig. 12.5). You can select the download location in either the Macintosh or Windows version of America Online's software.

Fig. 12.5
Select the place
where you want
the file sent.

2. You have the option to rename the file.

3. Click on the Save button or hit the Return or Enter key to begin the download process (see fig. 12.6).

Fig. 12.6
The download in
progress.

4. When your file download begins, you see a progress bar showing approximately how much of the file has been sent, and an estimate of how long it will take to transfer that file to your computer.

5. Macintosh users of System 7 or MultiFinder under System 6, can click on the desktop and resume other work while the download is in progress. (Windows users may press Alt+Tab to switch from one application to another.) Avoid CPU-intensive tasks, such as calculating a spreadsheet, while downloading. Doing so could slow down or even interrupt the download process.

6. When the file has been transferred, America Online's friendly narrator will (if the sounds are enabled) announce File Done.

Tip
To speed up file
transfer times, you
may want to log
on to America
Online at a
nonpeak hour,
perhaps early in
the morning,
when network
traffic is less busy.

Note

If you decide you don't want to download the file after all, hit the Finish Later button. In a minute or two, the download will stop. If you intend to resume the download at a later time, *don't* delete the partial file that has been transferred to your computer; if you do, the Download Manager cannot resume downloading at the point where it left off.

The Download Manager

You can build a download queue or list by using the Download Manager, and you can start the download any time during your online session or when the session ends. When you add a file to the list, you see the acknowledgment shown in figure 12.7.

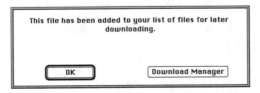

Fig. 12.7
Another file added
to the download
queue.

To use the Download Manager, choose the second option available to you when downloading a file—Download Later.

Check the Download Manager any time after adding files to the queue to see if you want to make changes in the lineup before downloading begins.

Caution

If you log onto America Online as a guest using another member's software, the Download Later function will not work nor will you be able to use AOL's FlashSession feature.

America Online's Download Manager lets you manage the entire download process from a single window. You can open the Download Manager window when notified that a file has been added to the download queue by selecting the Download Manager button, or you can use America Online's File menu. The Download Manager displays all files you've selected for downloading (see fig. 12.8).

Fig. 12.8
The Download Manager.

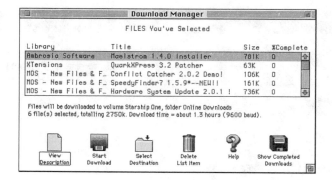

- *View Description*, your first option (bottom left of the window), gives you the chance to check whether you really want to download the file. If the file transfer process will take a long time, you probably should review the file descriptions before beginning a download.

- *Start Download* allows you to begin the entire download process immediately.

- *Select Destination* allows you to select a new default location (folder or directory) on your computer's drive in which to store the downloaded files. All files selected for download by the Download Manager will always be sent to this location.

■ *Delete List Item* allows you to remove a selected item from the Download Manager's queue if you decide you don't want to download the file after all.

■ *Help,* as with many other areas on America Online, produces America Online's comprehensive Help menu, with instructions and quick tips to help you get the most efficient use of your online visit (see fig. 12.9).

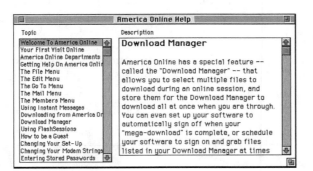

Fig. 12.9
Getting Online
Help.

■ *Show Completed Downloads* allows you to view a list of files you've downloaded. You can check the file description again or remove the file from the list.

The Download Manager window lists the total size of the files you've selected for transfer to your computer and gives an estimated transfer time at your modem connection speed. Downloads can take a little longer than the estimate during the evening prime-time period or when there is noise on your phone line. At other times, you may find your downloads moving more swiftly than estimated.

Tip
Any text window on AOL, even a File Description, can be printed or saved to your computer's disk. See Chapters 2 and 3.

How Do I Use the Files I've Downloaded?

Most larger files in America Online's software libraries are compressed to save disk space and to reduce transfer time, thereby reducing online charges.

Note

If you get a message on your Macintosh that the application that created your downloaded file can't be found, log on and check the file description, or view it offline in the Download Manager's list of Completed Downloads. You may need other software to use the downloaded file, either to decompress it or to run it after it's decompressed.

Both Macintosh and Windows America Online software can be set to automatically expand files that you've downloaded, as soon as you log off. Because some files may be compressed in a format that isn't supported by the software, those files will have to be expanded before you use them.

Before you pick a file to download, read the file description carefully to make sure that your computer, operating system, and software setup are compatible with those of the file. If you make a mistake and download a file you can't use, type the keyword **Credit** to request a rebate to your account for the time you wasted online.

If you get a message that the file has been damaged after download, you need to remove the file from your computer and download the file again. Although files are not damaged often, sometimes a file may not arrive in perfect condition due to noise on the telephone lines or to a network-related problem.

Caution

If your download is interrupted for any reason (perhaps your connection was terminated because of poor phone-line conditions), a fragment or partial file is left on your computer's drive. If you want to resume the download when you log on again, *don't* delete or move the partial file. Otherwise, you won't be able to resume your download where it left off.

What Kind of Software Is Available?

Before you begin to fill your software library, let's discuss the kinds of software that are available and the types of software you are apt to find on America Online.

Commercial Software

Commercial software is a retail product. You can find it at your local computer dealer, software reseller, or at one of the mail order firms that cater to this type of merchandise. You can even order commercial software on America Online through a publisher's company support area or through forums devoted to shopping (see Chapters 11 and 15).

You will not find commercial software in America Online's software libraries, but you can, from time to time, locate a free update program. The author or publisher of a software product can make an update program available so that you can revise your copy of the software to a newer version, usually to fix some bugs.

Like most software, commercial software is covered by a license agreement. Though licenses vary from product to product, in most cases, the license states that you are not buying the software itself, but the right to use it. The agreement spells out what those rights are. For most of you, those rights include being allowed to use the software on a single computer at a time and to make backup copies in case the master disks are damaged.

Because many of us use laptop computers for travel, some software licenses allow you to install the software on both your home or office computer and a portable, assuming that not more than one person will use the software at the same time. If you're going to install the software on multiple computers, you need to buy a site license from the author or publisher.

Demoware

Demonstration software is designed to let you try out all or most of the features of a software product before you buy it. Demoware, as it's known, may be either a commercial or a shareware program. In most cases, you can use the software for a limited period of time, ranging from a few days to a week or two; it then expires and you cannot use it again until you buy a copy. Some demoware may simply lock out some program features (such as the capability to save and print a document), which become available in the version you buy, or by typing in a password on the demo application.

Shareware

Shareware exemplifies the original try-before-you-buy concept. The author or publisher of a software product gives you a fully functional version (though a feature or two may be restricted). You can try it out on your computer for a period of up to a month. When that period expires, you are asked to pay the author or publisher a small fee for a license to continue to run the program.

Shareware is one of the last vestiges in our society of an honor system. The publisher has no way of knowing whether you are continuing to use the software. If you decide to continue to run it, consider the time and energy the author put into writing and testing that software. Also consider how you would feel if you were not paid for your work.

Shareware is often less expensive than commercial software because it lacks fancy packaging, manuals, and a fully-staffed technical support department. Some shareware, however, has become commercial, such as the compression software America Online uses for its Macintosh version StuffIt. StuffIt was first written by a 15-year-old high school student. It's now published in shareware form, as StuffIt Lite, and as a more fully-featured commercial product, StuffIt Deluxe (published by Aladdin Systems).

Freeware

This category covers a wide range of products. Freeware is available to you without cost, but the author retains all rights to the program, including how it is to be distributed. Freeware may include a fully functioning program or an update to an existing product. Don't attribute cost to value. You can often find a wealth of very useful programs in this category.

Public Domain Software

Public domain software can be used and distributed freely. The author has given up all rights to this program.

Uploading Files to America Online

America Online's computing and software forums have a special department labeled *New Files and Free Uploading.* This department allows you to upload software to America Online's software libraries without being charged.

Caution

Demoware and shareware can contain restrictions on whether they can be uploaded by anyone other than the author, so read the instructions that come with the software before you decide to upload it to America Online. In general, commercial updates, such as system-related software from Apple Computer, may be uploaded to America Online only by the publisher.

Where to Upload

You must do a little research to find out the appropriate place to upload the file and to verify that you have the right to send it. Each computing and software forum has a description file that tells you its purpose and the kind of software wanted. Rather than waste your time and the forum's by uploading to an inappropriate location, read the description files to be sure that you are uploading your software to the most suitable forum. A screen saver, for example, will likely go in a Utilities forum.

Before uploading the file— especially if you are not the author—use America Online's File Search feature (described in the section "Using File Search," earlier in this chapter) to make sure that the file you want to send isn't already posted somewhere on America Online.

How to Upload

When you visit a computing and software library (see Chapter 11), you'll see a button at the bottom of the software directory labeled *Upload File*. When you want to send your file, click on the button, which opens the window shown in figure 12.10.

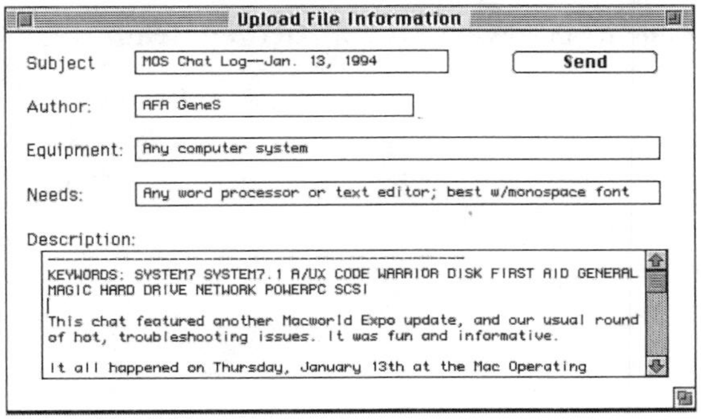

Fig. 12.10
Entering information about the file you're sending.

The Upload File Information window has several fields that you need to fill out. Enter the title of the file, the author of the file, and the kind of equipment needed to use it. Next, give a brief description of the file you're sending. You can enter a list of suggested keywords so that others can locate the file easily.

When you upload the file, you'll see a File Transfer window that's very much like the one displayed when you download a file (refer to fig. 12.6). After the file is received, it is reviewed by forum staff who decide whether it's suitable for their forum. The file description you give may be edited.

Because many of the staff members who review these files are volunteers, expect several days to pass before you hear of the forum's decision. If posted, your file will turn up in their New Files and Free Uploading library.

Tip
Before filling out the Upload File Information window, review the descriptions of other software to become familiar with the way the descriptions are written and the kind of information required.

IV

Info at Your Fingertips

From Here...

Okay, now you have the basics on how to get software and other files from America Online, and how to post your own files as well. For more information, see the chapters listed below.

■ For further assistance in using your America Online software, see Chapter 2, "Using Your America Online Macintosh Software," and Chapter 3, "Using Your America Online Windows Software."

■ Chapter 11, "Computing & Software," highlights America Online's Computing and Software forums.

■ Have a problem? Read Chapter 20, "Getting Help."

Chapter 13

Learning & Reference

Combine the vast resources of a major encyclopedia, home study schools, libraries, museums, and dozens of other information centers, and you can learn something about almost anything on America Online. In the previous century, your resources for learning were confined to written material, such as books, newspapers, and magazines, or verbal descriptions. The twentieth century brought into play the audio and visual mediums as well. But interactive learning capabilities have come into their own with the advent of an online service such as America Online.

In this chapter, you learn how to:

- Seek help with your child's homework

- Tap the resources of huge libraries

- Take diploma- and degree-granting courses without ever visiting a classroom

- Interact with other parents on America Online

- Learn more about dealing with the common problems of raising children

Because of the extent and scope of the educational resources available on America Online, a separate chapter would be needed for each of the Learning & Reference forums just to contain the full scope of their services. So just consider this chapter a get-acquainted visit. The Learning area (known as Education on America Online) and the Reference department are separate on America Online, although their interests often converge, so we'll describe them separately, too.

Exploring the Reference Desk

Keyword: Reference

The Reference Desk is your gateway to many of the areas that provide information for you on America Online. Many of the services listed in figure 13.1 are no doubt familiar to you. Some of the magazines, such as *Consumer Reports* and *Disney Adventures*, are discussed in more detail in other chapters. Other services offer huge databases of information that you'll want to explore in careful detail. The Internet Gopher & WAIS databases are described in Chapter 17, "The Internet Connection," so we'll leave this subject for that chapter. For now, stay with us if you want to begin a little sojourn for knowledge.

Fig. 13.1
The Reference Desk on America Online offers you a wide variety of information resources.

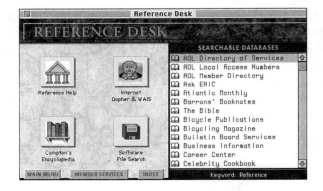

AskERIC

Keyword: AskERIC

ERIC is not a person, it is an Internet-based information center, an electronic library containing thousands of information for educators (as shown in fig. 13.2). There's also a resource to have your education-oriented questions researched and answered by the ERIC staff.

Fig. 13.2
AskERIC is a question-answering service and information library for parents and educators.

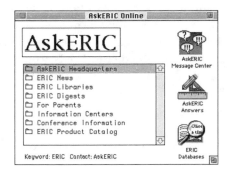

One particular item of special interest is the For Parents folder, an information repository containing common questions and answers on how parents can better involve themselves with their children's education. Recently we read an article in that folder describing how parents can help prevent drug abuse in our schools.

Reading Barron's Booknotes

Keyword: Barrons

As you might already know, Barron's guides are useful abstracts about the great literary works. And you can search the vast library of Barron's Booknotes on America Online (see fig. 13.3).

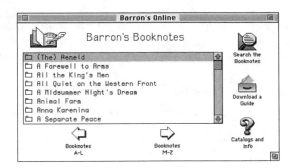

Fig. 13.3
Barron's Booknotes is your source for abstracts on great literature.

The abstracts are grouped by title, and each title contains useful text files describing the highlights of great works ranging from Shakespearean plays to classic best-sellers. As you read these books, you can use these text files as a guide to a better understanding of what made such great literature so memorable that it has survived decades and sometimes centuries.

Accessing Compton's Encyclopedia

Keyword: Comptons

Not so long ago, looking up something in an encyclopedia meant a trip to the public library or purchasing a huge set of books for your home. Although you might not want to replace those voluminous, color-filled works on your bookshelves, consider America Online your second reference resource.

Compton's Encyclopedia has placed its huge database of information on America Online (see fig. 13.4). All you have to do to tap that database is click on the Search Encyclopedia Articles button, and choose Open (or press Return or Enter).

Fig. 13.4
The resources of a huge encyclopedia are at your fingertips.

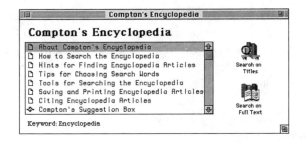

Follow these steps to continue your search for information:

1. Enter the topic or a description of the information you want in the text entry field near the top of the screen.

2. Within seconds, if articles are available on the subject, you see a list of matching entries (see fig. 13.5). If the entry has a folder icon, it means that the entry contains a number of text reports on the subject.

Fig. 13.5
Searching your virtual encyclopedia is an easy task.

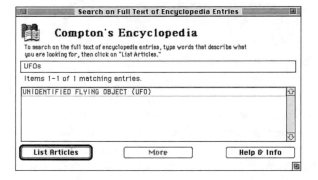

3. In the directory listing, double-click the entry you want to explore (or highlight it and choose the List Articles button), and you see the names of all the articles related to the subject. You can view each article online (see fig. 13.6), or you can save or print the article for reading at your leisure.

Visiting the Career Center

Keyword: career

One of the hardest tasks many young adults have to face is deciding what line of work to enter. Although some of you might have chosen your career during your early childhood, others work hard and long to find the line of work for which they are suited.

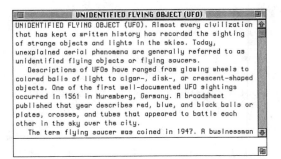

Fig. 13.6
Viewing an article online.

America Online's Career Center is an electronic career and employment guidance forum (see fig. 13.7). The forum features an extensive lineup of services that can help you find the right career or even tap a huge database of available jobs.

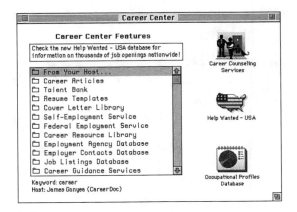

Fig. 13.7
America Online offers a center for career counseling and employment opportunities.

The Career Center also offers you personal career counseling services, where you can exchange E-mail with an experienced counselor or schedule an interactive one-on-one session right on America Online. To access these services, click on the Career Counseling Services icon.

A database of Occupational Profiles enables you to view on your own computer the requirements and opportunities offered by a particular line of work. If you are job hunting, a library of Resume Templates is available for you to tailor to your personal needs.

Accessing Court TV

Keyword: Court TV

For most of us, knowledge about the workings of the court system is limited to such TV programs as Matlock or Perry Mason. In real life (as opposed to reel life) trials are not resolved in 55 or so minutes plus commercials. The legal process is complex and convoluted and often difficult for the layman to understand.

The intense national attention over the O.J. Simpson murder case has placed such Cable TV sources as Court TV (shown in fig. 13.8) into the spotlight. Court TV is a 24-hour network devoted solely to the legal process and how it works. While the Simpson matter was at its highest prominence, a special area was established (shown by the icon in the Court TV main screen) for the latest information about the case.

Fig. 13.8
Court TV is the popular cable TV network devoted to the legal system.

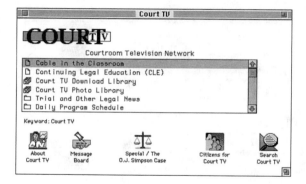

Click on the icon labeled Citizens for Court TV, by the way, and you'll see an invitation to receive the network's free newsletter, which provides insights into how the network works and how it will be developing over time.

Accessing C-SPAN

Keyword: CSPAN

Whenever an important hearing is being held in Congress, or a major address by the President or another important government figure is being given, C-SPAN (short for Cable-Satellite Public Affairs Network) is often there with gavel-to-gavel coverage.

C-SPAN is available through most cable TV networks (you might want to check to see whether it's offered in your area). Not only do you see hearings and press conferences, but you also can find a huge schedule of public affairs programming. The C-SPAN online area gives you the daily schedule, some background information on the service, and guides to help make your viewing (at home or in the classroom) more informative. Figure 13.9 shows the C-SPAN Online welcome screen.

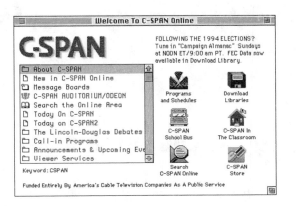

Fig. 13.9
You can learn all about C-SPAN from your computer.

In the active message area, you also can contact other America Online members about the issues being presented on C-SPAN and can even interact with C-SPAN's own staff.

Accessing Smithsonian Online

Keyword: Smithsonian

Most of you probably never hear much about the Smithsonian Institution except when reading news about a particular exhibit that's on display. When visiting the Smithsonian Museums in person isn't possible, a visit to the Smithsonian Online Forum on America Online provides a useful substitute (see fig. 13.10).

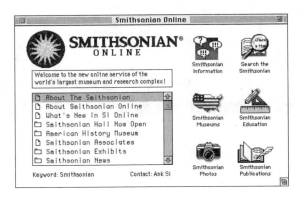

Fig. 13.10
You can visit the world's largest museum on America Online.

Here you can read about many of the Smithsonian's exhibits, order one of the Institute's publications, or even see photos of these exhibits. The photos are all available as graphics interchange format (GIF) files, a cross-platform format that enables you to view and print the photo from your computer.

> **Note**
>
> GIF files are discussed in more detail in Chapter 6, "Meeting People Online." To recap briefly, the current versions of America Online's Macintosh and Windows software can open and view GIF files.

Exploring the Education Center

Keyword: Education

America Online's Education Department, shown in figure 13.11, complements the Reference Desk and provides a wide range of information and tools to advance your education. In the following pages, we'll describe just a few of the resources available. Some are shown with colorful icons at the right of the Education department's main screen. Other facilities are available in the directory listing at the right (which, when you scroll down the directory window, offers a huge array of education services).

You'll notice that some of the facilities offered are shared with the Reference Desk, since they cover both areas. We'll cover some of the highlights here.

Fig. 13.11
You can consider the Education department an online educational institution.

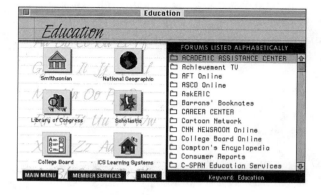

Visiting the Academic Assistance Center

Keyword: homework

Whether you are pursuing higher education, preparing for the College Board exams, or just trying to figure out how to do a teacher's homework assignment, consider the Academic Assistance Center as one of your resources for some help (see fig. 13.12).

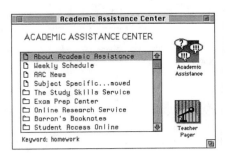

Fig. 13.12
America Online can give help to the harried student.

One of the special features of the center is the Exam Prep Center, which you access by clicking on the corresponding directory listing of the right of the center's main screen. Here is a place where you can post messages to receive help with a particular problem, maybe when you're researching that term paper or writing a book report. You also can access a library of text files on common subjects that you can download.

But suppose that the paper or assignment is due tomorrow. You have worked for hours trying to put it into shape, and you still have questions you need solved. Just click on the Teacher Pager icon on the Academic Assistance Center screen, and you receive directions on how to get interactive help from teachers who are online to assist you.

First type the keyword **Teacher Pager**, which brings up the special message window shown in figure 13.13.

Suppose, for example, that your child, a grade school student, asks the question posed in figure 13.13: "How do you add and subtract numbers with more than a single column?" You ask your question, and then click on the button that reflects the grade level. Also indicate the time you want to meet with your online teacher. When you or your child asks the question, stay online for at least five minutes, because more often than not, your answer will be there in a jiffy in your mailbox. If not, you have the chance to meet with the instructor at the appointed time. In some cases, the student is invited into the Homework Help conference room for a one-on-one tutorial session.

Fig. 13.13
View the Teacher
Pager in action.

Exploring the ASCD

Keywords: ascd, curriculum, ed tech

The ASCD, Association for Supervision and Curriculum Development, is an
area meant for professional educators. ASCD is a nonprofit organization designed to improve all aspects of education, from curriculum development to
such nuts-and-bolts issues as the structure of our schools. The ASCD America
Online area contains a library of resources that educators will find useful and
also offers direct, online enrollment in the organization (see fig. 13.14).

Fig. 13.14
ASCD is a special
development
center for
educators.

Visiting the CNN Newsroom

Keyword: CNN

CNN Newsroom is a daily 15-minute news program that is offered to schools
by Ted Turner's Cable News Network. The online CNN Newsroom focuses on
that program and related issues (see fig. 13.15). The forum has message areas
where you can communicate with other America Online members or with
CNN staff. You also can participate in the regularly scheduled conferences
that feature CNN representatives.

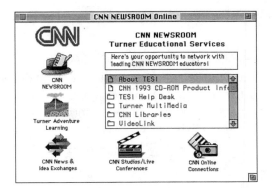

Fig. 13.15
Visit the CNN
Newsroom online.

Using College Board Online

Keyword: College Board

The College Board is a national organization devoted to the interests of secondary and higher education. You can use the online forum to order books and other materials to help prepare you or your child for college entrance exams and to deal better with some of the tougher academic subjects. Figure 13.16 shows the College Board Online screen.

Fig. 13.16
College Board
Online is a source
of advice and
assistance to
students.

The College Handbook is a database providing informative profiles of many colleges and universities. The Ask the College Board area is a regular America Online message board where you can post questions and receive responses from College Board staff. You also might want to check the Conference Hall for information on the regular schedule of online conferences.

Exploring the Electronic University Network

Keyword: eun

Although attending college is often viewed as an exciting time for most students, sometimes traveling to classes just isn't possible. Work and family commitments might be preventing you from attending class for an advanced degree, new career studies, or a much-needed remedial course. If so, the Electronic University Network might be able to help you. It's a group of educational institutions that offer interactive learning programs on a variety of subjects (see fig. 13.17).

Fig. 13.17
You can go to college and stay home at the same time.

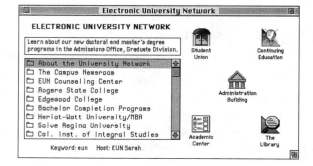

You can consult the Electronic University Network's huge library of educational materials, check on available courses, and even enroll online, from the convenience of your home.

Attending International Correspondence Schools

Keyword: ICS

You might recall seeing ads for International Correspondence Schools in many magazines. For quite some time, they have offered a whole range of home-study courses, which award diplomas in a host of fields, from computer servicing to TV repair. You don't have to attend a classroom. You can handle all your studies in your own home at your own pace.

In the past, correspondence with your assigned instructor was restricted to the U.S. mail. Because no teacher was at hand to explain the concepts to you, your text responses had to be self-contained and written in a clear, direct language that would be accessible to almost anyone.

Well, times have changed, and ICS is one of a growing number of educational institutions that use America Online to interact with the student body. In the

International Correspondence Schools Forum, you can learn about ICS's courses, inquire about further information, or even submit your registration (see fig. 13.18).

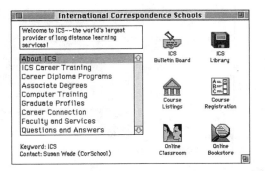

Fig. 13.18
The online meeting place for ICS students is the International Correspondence Schools Forum.

If you are a student, you can interact with your teachers, review supplementary course information, or even purchase additional text materials in the ICS Online Bookstore.

Attending the Komputer Clinic

Keyword: Komando

Kim Komando is a newspaper columnist and radio talk show host who has developed a line of tutorial videos designed to make the sometimes obscure world of personal computing understandable by using simple words instead of complex "technospeak." You may have even seen the TV commercials about these tapes, entitled "Komputer Tutor." The Komando Forum is a resource of tips and secrets to help you use your computer more effectively (see fig. 13.19).

If you need help with a computer-related problem, you can leave a message for Kim and her assistants, who respond in the forum or by E-mail (click on the Leave Questions Get Answers icon). You also can order from her line of tutorial videotapes, books, and other merchandise through the Komando Mall (click on the Online Shopping icon).

Exploring the Library of Congress Online

Keyword: Library

One of the largest information centers in the world is owned by the U.S. government. It's the Library of Congress, and if you are ever in Washington,

D.C., you can visit its teeming information archives in person. You also can explore this huge resource on America Online, from right in front of your computer (see fig. 13.20).

Fig. 13.19

The Komputer Clinic is a place to get help with your computer-related troubles.

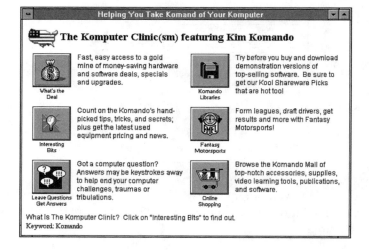

Fig. 13.20

You can tap the huge information resources of the Library of Congress online.

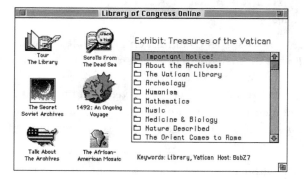

The Tour the Library icon in the forum's main window gives you a brief overview of the Library of Congress's resources.

After you get familiar with the resources available, you might want to click on the icons that identify the exhibits that are being highlighted. In addition to being able to view, save, and print text reports on the subjects that interest you, you'll find a Voices message board, where you can read the text of debates on various subjects by noted scholars.

Since the Dead Sea Scrolls were discovered in the Judean Desert in 1947, scholars have spent countless hours researching their scope and meaning.

This area of the Library of Congress Forum, which you access by clicking the Scrolls from the Dead Sea icon on the main forum window, enables you to review the scholars' findings as well, plus learn the exciting background of this extraordinary archaeological find (see fig. 13.21).

Fig. 13.21
The secrets of the Dead Sea Scrolls are available for you to explore on America Online.

Exploring NCTENet

Keyword: NCTE

NCTE is the National Council of Teachers of English, an association dedicated to teaching English and language arts. The organization offers continuing education, discussions, and books to help educators improve their skills. You can access NCTE resources online through NCTENet (see fig. 13.22).

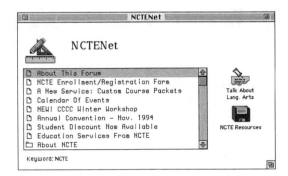

Fig. 13.22
Another America Online resource for professional educators is NCTENet.

Visiting the NEA Public Forum

Keyword: NEA Public

The NEA, National Education Association, is another online resource for professional educators who want to hone their teaching skills and interact with their peers.

The NEA's online organization offers a message area where teachers can discuss the major issues affecting curriculums and other important topics. And you can use the Professional Library, which contains useful material that you can download for later reference. Access the wealth of information from the NEA Public Forum screen shown in figure 13.23.

Fig. 13.23
The NEA Public Forum is a resource for 2.2 million teachers on America Online.

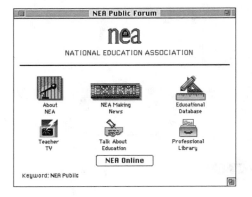

Joining the National Geographic Society

Keywords: geographic, ngs

No doubt you have seen the elaborate, colorful *National Geographic* magazine at your local public library. The magazine represents just a portion of the National Geographic Society's work, which is represented in its online forum, National Geographic Online (see fig. 13.24).

Fig. 13.24
Unique online resources are provided by the National Geographic Society.

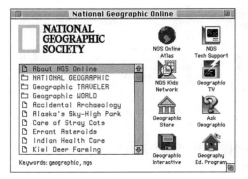

The society has a huge database of files for you to download and read. One of the most striking features is its NGS Online Atlas library. It's distilled from the society's CD-ROM Picture Atlas of the World, which contains hundreds of interactive maps and photos. A number of maps, representing a cross-section of those available on the CD, are available for you to download directly to your computer. They're saved in GIF format, the cross-platform format that enables you to view and print an image file easily without needing an expensive image-processing program.

Other features of the National Geographic Online Forum include the NGS Kids Network, an active message board on which you can exchange views with other America Online members and society staff, and other useful information resources.

The Geographic Store is an online shop where you can place your order for the society's magazine and other publications.

Accessing National Public Radio Outreach

Keywords: NPR, radio

When you tire of silly disk jockey chatter, the same repetitive music over and over again, or endless confrontational and sometimes exploitive talk shows, and you want something a little more stimulating, National Public Radio is the way to go. It's not available in every town—but it should be.

The National Public Radio Outreach forum on America Online is your way to interact with this public broadcasting network (see fig. 13.25). If you cannot receive their broadcasts in your area or you've missed a show, you can even place an order for transcripts of the shows. You also can find up-to-date station listings, so you can see whether the programs are indeed available on a radio station that you can hear. This broadcast network is a different sort of network and isn't always meant for casual background listening, but it is worth checking out. In the meantime, the NPR Outreach forum on America Online is your way to stay in touch with the network's activities.

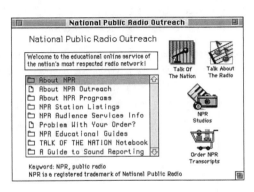

Fig. 13.25
National Public Radio even has an online support area on America Online.

Exploring the Parents' Information Network

Keyword: Parents

In Chapter 8, "The Entertainment Chapter," you learned about the special areas on America Online devoted to children. The Parents' Information Network is a place where you can learn more about special programs designed strictly for your children (see fig. 13.26).

Fig. 13.26
Information for parents on America Online is found in the Parents' Information Network.

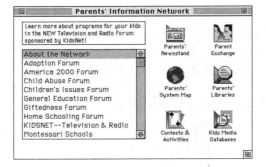

The Parent Exchange icon brings you to message areas that enable parents to interact with each other about dealing with the often complex issues of bringing up a child in our often-confused society. And libraries of useful information are available for you to download and read at your leisure.

The network also has special forums that deal with such important issues as adoption, child abuse, home schooling, and working with gifted children.

Exploring Princeton Review/Student Access Online

Keyword: Student Access

If you're attending college or seeking career-related information, Student Access is a special center that's meant for you. It's sponsored by *Princeton Review* magazine and offers special resources for all visitors to the forum.

The forum also features a number of members-only departments (see fig. 13.27), which you can access only if you join the organization. But even if you don't sign up, you can exchange messages with other students, download useful material from the forum's software libraries, and even leave classified ads that are of interest to other students.

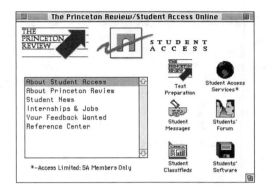

Fig. 13.27
Student Access is a special online area for those seeking higher education.

Visiting the Scholastic Forum

Keyword: Scholastic

The Scholastic Network Sampler is an online resource for teachers and students (see fig. 13.28). Professional educators can interact with their peers, and if you are a teacher, you can even join the network online.

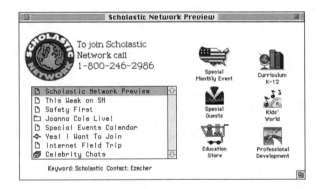

Fig. 13.28
From your child's classroom to America Online, the Scholastic Forum is the place for educators.

The forum is a center to discuss curriculum planning, purchase professional literature, and participate in live conferences on a host of subjects related to educating our youth.

One of the most popular areas in the Scholastic Online Forum is Kids' World, a part of the Scholastic Network. It's a place where children can have fun and learn at the same time.

Visiting the Afterwards Cafe

Keyword: Afterwards

Having spent these many hours deeply immersed in your studies on one subject or another, the time might come when you want to relax and perhaps meet with other students for a chat.

America Online's Afterwards Coffeehouse and Cafe is a pleasant, relaxing environment for serious discussions about all sorts of topics, from current events to literature and the arts. After you're there for a few moments, you will actually be able to imagine its decorative surroundings and comfortable seating. It's a place to get a virtual cup of coffee or a soft drink after completing a day's hard work. Figure 13.29 shows the Afterwards Coffeehouse directory screen.

Fig. 13.29
When your studies are done, you can relax at the Afterwards Cafe.

From Here...

America Online's resources for education and reference aren't confined just to the forums mentioned so far in this chapter. The repositories are so huge that the surface has barely been scratched. You need to dig in and explore further on your own to find out what gems of knowledge you can find.

Both newspapers and magazines are valuable learning tools, too, and online resources for both are described in the next chapter. In addition, you'll want to check out these chapters for related information:

■ Chapter 8, "The Entertainment Chapter"

■ Chapter 10, "Finding Information on America Online"

■ Chapter 20, "Getting Help"

Chapter 14

News, Magazines, and Business Information

A visit to America Online is like having many magazines and newspapers at your beck and call. You can find a summary of the top news of the day, commentaries from your favorite columnists, or updates on how your stock portfolio is doing.

In previous chapters, we introduced America Online as a friendly community where you can meet and talk with your friends. We showed you where to find information from the world of entertainment, and about your hobbies and special interests. We showed you how to use your computer more effectively and how to use America Online as an educational institution.

In this chapter, we open up the pages of many magazines and newspapers. We also examine resources for investment information and tax preparation information. We'll show you where to find:

- Information resources

- News and opinion journals

- Advice and information about business, stocks, and bonds

- Country-wide real estate listings

- Helpful hints at tax time

Today's News

Keyword: News

When you first sign on to America Online, you're greeted with the friendly, familiar In The Spotlight Welcome window and voice message—if you've got your computer's sound turned on, of course. The Top News Story of the day is always featured (and it may change from hour to hour, depending on new developments). You can see the major headlines by clicking on the Top News icon (see fig. 14.1). What you have here is organized very much like the sections of your daily newspaper. We'll read through each section and give you an idea of what information you can find.

Fig. 14.1

America Online's Today's News department is organized in much the same way as a typical daily newspaper.

When you bring up the Today's News screen, you'll see the major stories of the day in a directory window, which you can scroll through for additional information. By double-clicking on a story listing, you'll be able to read the text of that news item. As with other America Online text windows, you can save the story or print it for later reference.

U.S. & World News

Keyword: US News

Now that you've read the front page, let's examine the table of contents of your daily newspaper and check out some of the other features (see fig. 14.2). During your online travels, you can set aside pages for reading later. The news of the world, for example, is organized by category. There are separate folders for National News, Washington News, Europe, and other categories. If you are seeking information about a particular topic, you'll want to click on the News Search icon.

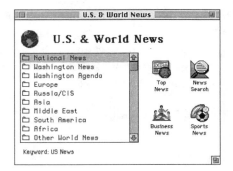

Fig. 14.2
Your online
newspaper's index.

As with other searchable databases on America Online, looking for a news item is a simple process. Just bring up the search window, enter the topic of your search, and you'll see a display of the available articles on that subject as long as there are articles available, of course.

You'll note that many of the news-related forums on America Online are interrelated. So if you open one screen, there will be icons that will allow you to switch to another area that has related information. An example is the Top News icon at the right side of the U.S. & World News screen.

Business News

Keyword: Business News

Let's turn now to the business section (see fig. 14.3). All the information is divided into convenient categories, so you can easily locate material on a particular topic. The News Search icon at the upper right allows you to quickly access all the articles on a single topic. The Market News icon is useful for checking the goings-on in the world's various stock markets. The Top Business icon provides up-to-date news from the financial world.

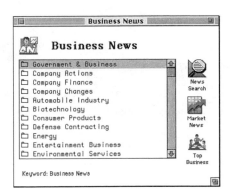

Fig. 14.3
Here's your online
financial section.

As an example of the sort of information one finds in the Business News area, we selected the High Technology pages, where headlines separate current developments (see fig. 14.4). You can select an article, double-click on the title, or click on the Read Article button. The entire article can be saved as a text file for printing later or for offline reading.

Fig. 14.4
News with a technological bent.

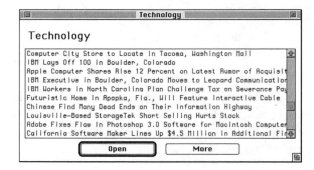

Weather News

Keyword: Weather

Since we already read the sports and entertainment pages in Chapter 9 (yes, we read them first, too!), we'll skip the Entertainment and Sports icons in the Today's News screen and move on to the final category.

Although we can't do much to change the weather, we can at least be fully informed about it. By turning to the weather section in our virtual newspaper, we can review both articles and special forecasts countrywide (see fig. 14.5).

Fig. 14.5
When severe weather has a major impact, AOL has the latest information.

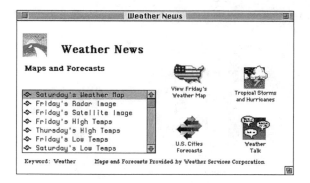

You can also see maps of weather trends right on your own computer, simply by selecting and downloading them. The forum updates the weather maps daily. You can see them in full color if you have a color screen. Choose from a satellite view, radar displays, and view charts of maximum and minimum temperatures not only for today, but for tomorrow and the next day as well (see fig. 14.6).

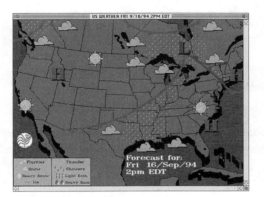

Fig. 14.6
See the weather displayed on your computer.

The forum offers these maps in the cross-platform GIF format (short for Graphic Interchange Format). Once you download the file to your computer, you can use the latest versions of AOL's Macintosh and Windows software to open and view the file.

During the summer and fall season, there is a special area devoted to Tropical Storms and Hurricanes. You will want to check this section to see if any severe weather is expected in your area, and what the trends are for the very near future (within the limits of the science of weather forecasting, of course).

U.S. Cities Forecasts

Whether you are a regular traveler or a vicarious sojourner, you're no doubt curious as to the weather in other parts of the country. No problem, America Online's weather page has information about that too, grouped by country or continent and updated regularly. If you're planning a trip abroad, consult this area before you pack your bags (see fig. 14.7).

Fig. 14.7
If you are travel-
ing, review these
areas.

```
┌─────────────────────────────  Arizona ─────────────────────────────┐
│                                                                      │
│ DOMESTIC CITY WEATHER FORECASTS  --  PROVIDED BY WEATHER SERVICES     │
│ CORPORATION                                                          │
│                                                                      │
│ LEGEND:              TEMPERATURES ARE IN DEGREES FAHRENHEIT           │
│ PC  -PARTLY CLOUDY      S  -SUNNY       C  -CLOUDY      R  -RAIN       │
│ SH  -RAIN SHOWERS       SN -SNOW        SF -SNOW SHOWERS I  -ICE       │
│ T   -THUNDERSTORMS      W  -WINDY                                     │
│                                                                      │
│ FORECAST FOR:   HI/ LO/WX  HI/ LO/WX  HI/ LO/WX  HI/ LO/WX  HI/ LO/WX │
│                 SATURDAY   SUNDAY     MONDAY     TUESDAY    WEDNESDAY  │
│                 17-SEP-94  18-SEP-94  19-SEP-94  20-SEP-94  21-SEP-94  │
│   *** ARIZONA ***                                                    │
│ FLAGSTAFF       75/ 44/PC  76/ 58/T   76/ 43/T   75/ 41/T   74/ 42/S  │
│ GRAND CANYON    75/ 44/PC  76/ 58/T   76/ 43/T   75/ 41/T   82/ 47/S  │
│ MESA           100/ 75/S  101/ 77/T  102/ 73/T  101/ 72/T   99/ 72/S  │
│ PHOENIX        100/ 75/S  101/ 77/T  102/ 73/T  101/ 72/T   99/ 72/S  │
│ TUCSON          99/ 69/PC 100/ 71/T   96/ 68/T   95/ 67/T   94/ 67/S  │
│ WINSLOW         80/ 49/PC  81/ 63/T   81/ 48/T   80/ 46/T   84/ 54/S  │
│ YUMA           100/ 75/S  101/ 77/T  102/ 73/T  101/ 72/T  101/ 74/S  │
│                                                                      │
│ FORECASTS ARE COPYRIGHTED BY WEATHER SERVICES CORPORATION, BEDFORD    │
└──────────────────────────────────────────────────────────────────────┘
```

The Newsstand

Keyword: Newsstand

Having read the latest news of the day, let's now pay a visit to America
Online's huge newsstand. We described three of the major daily newspapers, the *Chicago Tribune,* the *San Jose Mercury,* and *The New York Times* in
Chapter 9, "Lifestyles & Interests." There, we focused on the features you find
in daily newspapers. A click on the handy icon at the right of the Newsstand
screen, shown in figure 14.8, will return you to those newspapers. Now we'll
cover some other parts of our virtual news dealer. Some of these publications,
by the way, exist solely in cyberspace. You won't find them at your corner
newsstand.

Fig. 14.8
The list of
available maga-
zines on AOL's
newsstand is
increasing rapidly.

The Atlantic Monthly Magazine

Keyword: Atlantic

Several important magazines regularly appear online at the same time they
appear in your favorite bookstore. One of these is *The Atlantic Monthly* (see
fig. 14.9).

Fig. 14.9
Read *The Atlantic Monthly* on AOL.

Founded in 1857, *The Atlantic Monthly* is a journal of literature, entertainment, and opinion. Highlights of the latest issue appear online, including features, letters to the editor, and many of the articles that appear in the printed edition.

The Message Board is your chance to communicate with editors, writers, and other online members. As with any magazine of opinion, the discussions can become very active indeed. The Atlantic Auditorium hosts special gatherings involving both editors and writers.

Bicycling Magazine Online

Keyword: Bicycling

We discuss AOL's special forum for cyclists in Chapter 9, "Lifestyles & Interests." But check out *Bicycling*, too (see fig. 14.10).

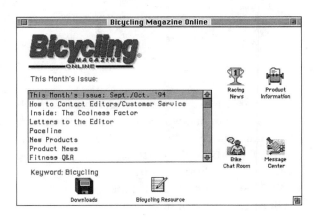

Fig. 14.10
Advice and information for anyone who rides a bike.

Whether you're in the market for a new bike, or you want some advice about how you can use your bike as part of a physical fitness program, you can find the bicycling information you need in this forum. There's news about new products, racing information, and an active message center for you to interact with fellow cyclists.

We wondered just what sort of stuff you'd find in a Downloads library for a bicycling publication, so we checked it out. We found GIF files of some really nice new racing bikes, and a copy of the text of the magazine's annual *Ride Guide*, which is a comprehensive survey of riding tours in which you might want to participate.

Columnists & Features Online

Keyword: Columnists

We exposed you to the latest news and business reports in the Today's News department earlier in this chapter. Now let's pause for a few moments to review some commentary and opinion on the feature pages. Rather than poring through a pile of newspapers to find your favorite columnists, look in Columnists & Features Online (see fig. 14.11).

Fig. 14.11
Your online features page on AOL.

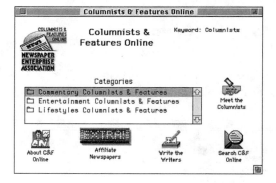

Newspaper Enterprise Association (NEA) sponsors this forum where you can read the regular features from many of your favorite writers. Read commentaries from such luminaries as Hodding Carter, William Rusher, and Nat Hentoff. You can read reports on the latest happenings from the world of show business and your daily horoscope (it's called *Astrograph*, from writer Bernice Bede Osol). If you have a question about personal finance, radio personality Bruce Williams will answer it for you.

You also have the opportunity to interact with many of your favorite writers, review back columns, and consult from the list of affiliate newspapers to find out which paper carries your favorite writers.

Compute

Keyword: Compute

Compute magazine actually no longer exists in printed form (see fig. 14.12). This magazine officially ceased publication in September, 1994. Yet it still exists as an online information resource for PC users. Just like the magazine you used to buy on the newsstand, *Compute* online contains news, features, and product reviews designed to make your computing experience more enjoyable and surely more productive.

Fig. 14.12
Now published just in cyberspace, *Compute* magazine.

There are special sections devoted to tips and tricks from the magazine's editorial staff and fellow computer users. Message boards are filled with valuable exchanges of information and views upon a host of computer-related issues. You'll also find hot news about the newest operating system developments from IBM and Microsoft, and about the latest new product releases.

Consumer Reports

Keyword: Consumer Reports

Before you make a single purchasing decision, read *Consumer Reports*. This magazine offers comprehensive reviews on major new products of all types, from dishwasher detergents to new cars (see fig. 14.13).

One of the most popular issues, much of which appears online, is the annual automobile issue, printed in April of each year. It's a valuable resource you can refer to before you plunk down hard-earned dollars for a new or used vehicle.

Fig. 14.13
A major resource
for product
information.

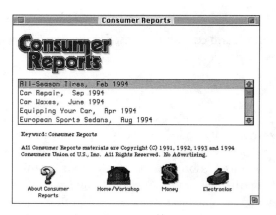

Many of the regular columns in the magazine are available on AOL. You can
save or print the text windows for reading at your leisure, as you can with
other text files on America Online.

Cowles/SIMBA Media Information Network
Keyword: CowlesSIMBA

The word *media* connotes a variety of industries, from advertising agencies to
broadcasting and publishing businesses. The Cowles/SIMBA Media Information Network is a major resource for information about this challenging and
ever-changing business field (see fig. 14.14).

Fig. 14.14
Your source
for the latest
media-related
information.

Whether you want to know about the latest deal to acquire a big entertainment conglomerate, or about how your favorite magazine is faring, consult
Cowles/SIMBA for current information in an easy-to-read form.

In addition to reviewing the news online, you can order Cowles/SIMBA's business publications, review their vast libraries of information, or interact with other members and industry observers on active message boards.

The New Republic

Keyword: New Republic

The New Republic is a magazine of opinion that takes an unabashedly liberal viewpoint of the nation and the world. It covers politics, literature, and the arts with its own unique slant. The magazine is interesting, controversial, and always entertaining, whatever your political leanings (see fig. 14.15).

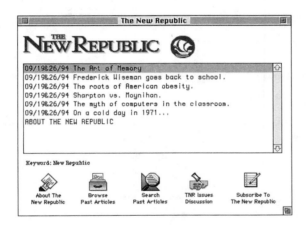

Fig. 14.15
Whether you agree or disagree with the views offered, *The New Republic* is a magazine many opinion-makers read.

The online forum for *The New Republic* contains a selection of articles from the latest issue, plus a built-in search feature, which you can use to browse and read past articles. The magazine's active TNR Issues Discussion message board hosts lively discussion and debate.

OMNI Magazine Online

Keyword: OMNI

Whether interested in space exploration or in UFOs, you can explore scientific interests by visiting the OMNI Magazine Forum on AOL (see fig. 14.16).

In addition to reading many of the features from the latest issue of *OMNI*, you can attend a number of regular chats. The forum always posts the schedules, and the chats feature not only the magazine's editorial staff, but visiting experts of all sorts. One exciting and controversial section of *OMNI* is the Antimatter department, which explores the frontiers of science and features reports about psychic phenomena and strange things seen in the skies (generally referred to as UFOs).

Fig. 14.16
Science fact and science fiction combined in *OMNI* magazine.

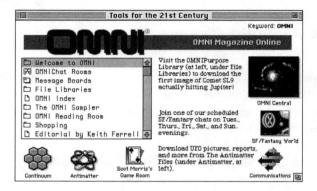

Saturday Review Online
Keyword: Saturday Review

Many of you probably remember *The Saturday Review* as a magazine of arts and culture that existed for many, many years and folded in 1986. During its over half a century of existence, this journal covered such subjects as politics, science, business, literature, and even the world of entertainment.

So what is a magazine that no longer exists doing on America Online? Well, unlike the other online magazines we've discussed so far in this chapter, Saturday Review Online doesn't exist as a printed publication. It's strictly an electronic magazine brought to you by the publishers of *OMNI* and *Compute* (see fig. 14.17).

Fig. 14.17
The Saturday Review reborn as an electronic magazine on America Online.

In the tradition of the magazine originally edited by Norman Cousins, this twenty-first century counterpart contains articles of both fact and fiction. It reviews current events in detail from the perspective of many noted writers. As with other online publications, you can participate in its active message boards to share your views with writers and editors. Reading this revived publication is a unique experience indeed.

Stereo Review Online

Keyword: Stereo Review

It started out years ago as *Hi-Fi Review,* and then it was *Hi-Fi/Stereo Review* when stereophonic audio became popular in the early 1960s. Now it's just *Stereo Review* (shown in fig. 14.18), and it remains one of the most popular consumer audio magazines in the USA. If you are looking to buy a new stereo system, exploring the frontiers of home theater (surround sound), or you just want to read reviews about the latest recordings, you'll want to visit Stereo Review Online.

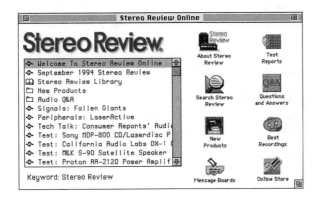

Fig. 14.18
Learn all about home audio in *Stereo Review* magazine on AOL.

You'll find all of the content of the newsstand issues online for you to read, including thoroughly researched product test reports from the magazine's staff of audio professionals. Sometimes audio fans can get sharply opinionated about their favorite hardware, and *Stereo Review's* active message board is a place where you'll find animated discussions about such diverse subjects as tube amplifiers and the best budget-priced loudspeaker systems.

TIME Magazine Online

Keyword: Time

When you want to find out how long you've spent on America Online, you might be inclined to type the keyword **Time** (rather than **Clock**, which is

IV

Info at Your Fingertips

the correct choice). Instead of seeing time spent, you'll see the very latest issue of *TIME* magazine. The full content of the current issue is posted on America Online before the printed magazine hits the newsstands (see fig. 14.19).

Fig. 14.19
An issue of *TIME* on AOL.

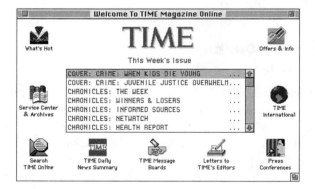

TIME magazine, because it is weekly, analyzes current events with a special perspective. But that doesn't mean stories are dated—the magazine is often reworked just before deadlines approach, when the press of news events changes things. In addition to reading the latest issue, you can browse through past issues online.

You even have some additional resources that you won't find in the news-stand version. For example, you can examine the International Editions of *TIME* that often contain stories that aren't included in the USA edition. The Time Auditorium hosts regular conferences featuring writers and notables. You can submit letters to the editor for publication in the magazine or participate in active message boards.

Windows Magazine
Keyword: Winmag

How can you get the best performance from your Windows PC? What will Microsoft's next version of Windows mean to you? Will programs be compatible or have to be updated? Which new word processor is right for you? The Windows Magazine Online Forum answers these and many more of your Windows computing questions.

This forum allows you to review the regular contents of the magazine from features to product reviews and letters and to download selected shareware and other utilities that enhance your computer's performance (see fig. 14.20).

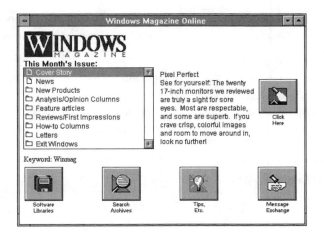

Fig. 14.20
Windows Magazine on America Online.

This forum has regular conferences, an active message exchange, and a special section devoted just to tips that help you get the most from your computer investment.

Wired Magazine

Keyword: Wired

The rise of the information superhighway means that we are all truly connected by telephone line, by satellite, or by our computers talking to one another. *Wired* magazine explores what it calls the Digital Generation, who have grown up and experienced the joining of computers, telecommunications, and the media (see fig. 14.21).

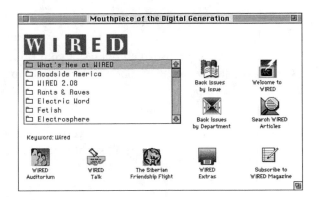

Fig. 14.21
The voice of the Digital Generation on AOL.

Wired is not necessarily for the casual reader, because its articles are strong and blunt and often controversial. Quoting the editor's demands of its writers, "Amaze us."

Rather than try to explain what this magazine is all about, we suggest you spend a few moments reading the latest issue online. Or search through articles from past issues. The magazine's very individual approach is best exemplified in its message areas or in its regular chats. This forum will not bore you in the least.

Worth Magazine

Keyword: Worth

Here's a different approach to presenting financial information. Rather than deal with business news in a cold, dry, analytical fashion, *Worth* magazine attempts to take into account what it considers one's personal needs in providing financial information (see fig. 14.22).

Fig. 14.22
A different slant on your finances.

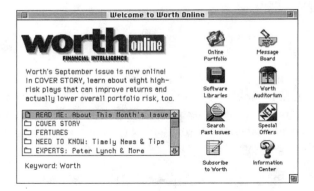

Each issue contains advice on dealing with all phases of your financial picture, from taxes and real estate to stocks and bonds. *Worth's* online forum offers feature articles and key reports from past issues that you can search by topic or content.

The Software Libraries include files with advice on investing, plus huge numbers of articles that you can download and read at your leisure.

Personal Finance

Keyword: Finance

Now that we've read the latest news and browsed through the magazine racks, let's deal further with important information about the world of business. America Online's Personal Finance department, shown in figure 14.23, isn't just for your business activities, however. You'll find resources here that will help you take charge of your personal finances too. Let's look over some of them in the final section of this chapter.

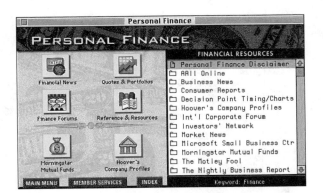

Fig. 14.23
America Online's Personal Finance department with an emphasis on money-management.

Before going on, though, let's take note of the first item shown in the directory listing, Personal Finance Disclaimer. The purpose of this forum is to give you information about various aspects of financial management, but they are not responsible for the way you use that information to conduct your personal finances. Okay, let's go on now.

Hoover's Company Profiles

Keyword: Hoover

Before you decide to invest in a company's stock, you want to know something about that company and the related industries. AOL's Company Profiles Forum is an important resource (see fig. 14.24).

The forum lists company profiles alphabetically, by industry, or by location. Choose the search technique that best suits your needs. To give you an idea of the kind of information you can find, we looked up the profile for one major company (see fig. 14.25).

Fig. 14.24
Your online
resource when you
want a company
profile.

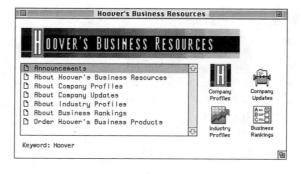

Fig. 14.25
Detailed but
concise summaries
of a major
company.

Caution

The company profiles offered are, of course, not guaranteed 100%. The firms who provide these reports post online terms and conditions that you will want to read before reviewing the profiles themselves. If you want to learn more about a specific company before investing, you may also wish to secure the company's annual report and do additional research before making a financial decision.

Company profiles are brief but sharply focused to give you the information you need to make important decisions about the future prospects of a company.

Investors Network

Keyword: Investors

Some people liken the process of making the correct financial investment to fortune-telling. Because you cannot easily predict the outcome of an invest-ment, you need as much information as possible before you make a decision (see fig. 14.26).

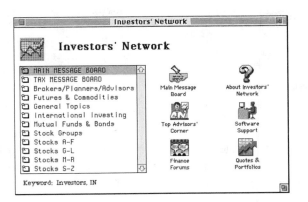

Fig. 14.26
This network provides help when you want to know where the best investments might be.

The Investor's Network is a resource that you can visit for information before you make a decision. The Main Message Board hosts brisk debates on the state of the financial markets and offers helpful advice.

During this forum's regular chats, you can consult with fellow AOL members and financial experts about the best investment prospects.

Microsoft Resource Center

Keyword: Microsoft

In addition to providing popular software for the Macintosh and Windows platforms, Microsoft has a huge library of information on all aspects of computing. Whether you have a hardware-related problem or have difficulty using your Microsoft software, you'll probably find the information you need in its online database (see fig. 14.27).

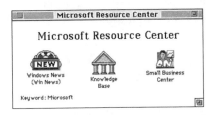

Fig. 14.27
A vast storehouse of business-related information.

The information you want is conveniently catalogued by topic, or you can search for particular articles that might interest you. As with any text file on America Online, you can read it online, or save or print the file for offline review.

The Win News area provides updated press releases and information about the newest version of Microsoft Windows and useful information about other

Microsoft software products. The Microsoft Small Business Center provides a huge library of text information and an active message area where you can receive tips on how to make your business run more efficiently and profitably.

Morningstar Mutual Funds

Keyword: Morningstar

A mutual fund is a way to reduce the risk in your investments, by investing in a portfolio of a large number of stocks, rather than two or three. Morningstar Mutual Funds (shown in fig. 14.28) is an independent company that tracks the progress of some 3,400 different mutual funds.

Fig. 14.28
For information as to how your favorite mutual fund is doing, check out the Morningstar Mutual Funds forum on AOL.

To learn how the service works, click on the Guided Tour button. It'll take a few minutes of your time, but it will provide valuable advice to consider if you want to get involved in this sort of investment or just track the progress of mutual funds in which you already invest. A handy text-based User Guide is online so you can learn how best to track the progress and history of a mutual fund.

Quotes and Portfolios

Keyword: Stocklink

How well is your stock portfolio doing? Is your stockbroker's phone busy, or do you just want to see how your favorite stocks are doing before you decide whether to invest? Check out AOL's StockLink forum (see fig. 14.29).

Because America Online's stock is quite popular, we decided to check its present value. Figure 14.29 shows its price and related statistics. Checking the value of stock is easy. You first have to enter the stock's symbol, because market entries are usually identified in abbreviated form. The Lookup Stock

Symbol feature lets you quickly find the correct symbol. The Add to Portfolio feature is simply a convenience measure, so you can easily track your favorite stocks, whether your interest in the market is from an armchair or as an active investor.

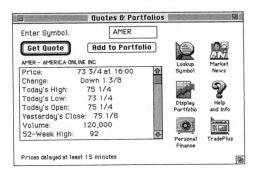

Fig. 14.29
Keeping your stock portfolio current.

If you want to learn more about a company, look at the Company Profiles section (described in an earlier section). The Market News icon takes you to AOL's business news area, an online equivalent of a newspaper's financial pages.

Real Estate Online

Keyword: real estate

Selling your home, or looking for a new residence in your hometown or in another state? Whatever your interest in real estate, pay a visit to Real Estate Online. Here you'll find an interactive Multiple Listing Service, which you can check for available homes nationwide (see fig. 14.30).

Fig. 14.30
Your forum when real estate is on your mind.

If you are looking to finance or refinance your home, consult the listing of current Mortgage Rates. The Ask OurBroker message board lets you get expert advice from a real estate professional.

Consult the forum's library for lots of useful information and its folders upon folders filled with advice and tips on all sorts of real estate-related issues.

For more assistance, attend this forum's regular conferences.

From Here...

In this chapter we describe America Online as—in part—one huge newsstand, with magazines and newspapers available online for you to browse and read at your leisure. We also show the many business resources online that help you manage your stock portfolio and perhaps make it easier to navigate through your tax returns.

- For an overview of the educational tools and research materials America Online has to offer, review Chapter 13, "Learning & Reference."

- In Chapter 15, "The Shopping Chapter," we take a breather and go on a shopping spree.

Chapter 15

The Shopping Chapter

Do you want to save a few dollars on your next purchase? Perhaps you just want to get the most up-to-date information about a particular product or service before you decide whether or not to buy. America Online is the place to do both.

Up till now we have devoted much of this book to telling you how you can locate information resources on America Online. For this chapter, we're just going to take an enjoyable shopping trip across the information superhighway. We'll make several brief stops at different shops in our online mall, and we'll even buy a few items along the way.

In this chapter, we'll show you how to:

- Search for particular products from a variety of online databases

- Buy the items you want while logged on to America Online

- Join a service that will help you save money on your next car

- Place your own classified advertising, free of charge

- Tap a huge database of employment opportunities

Your Virtual Marketplace

Keywords: Marketplace, Shopping

America Online's Marketplace department, shown in figure 15.1, is a gateway to AOL's huge shopping mall. The next chapter is devoted to using America Online for your travel plans; we'll confine this little excursion to the items that strictly concern shopping.

Fig. 15.1

The Marketplace department is your gateway to AOL's online mall.

AOL Product Center

Keyword: AOL Products, America Online Store

America Online has its own custom line of merchandise, which you can wear, send as a gift, or just keep as a souvenir (see fig. 15.2). Since I collect fancy T-shirts myself, let's order one. First we'll click on the America Online Six Color T-Shirts listing.

Fig. 15.2

Here's where you can order custom America Online products.

Okay, I prefer X-Large myself. But I'm curious to know more about this T-shirt, to see if it's something I'd really want to buy. So I click in the directory listing for X-Large (see fig. 15.3).

Fig. 15.3

Pick your size.

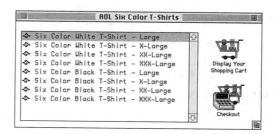

The descriptive window gives you the very same sort of information you'd find in a mail-order catalog (see fig. 15.4). The description is just enticing enough to give you a pretty fair picture of what the shirt really looks like. I think I'm going to order one, so let's select the Add Product To Cart button.

Fig. 15.4
Ready to order?

After you've selected the merchandise you want to order, you will probably want to examine your shopping cart to make sure that you've selected the correct item. Click once on the Add Product to Cart button to confirm your selection, as shown in figure 15.5.

Fig. 15.5
Your selection confirmed.

Click once on the Display Your Shopping Cart icon to bring up a window that allows you to review your order before it's placed (see fig. 15.6). You can double-click on the directory listing to review the product description.

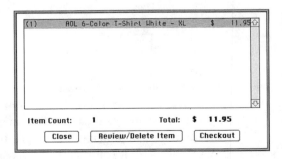

Fig. 15.6
This shopping cart has one T-shirt in it.

Now that you have chosen your merchandise, this is the time to make sure that your mailing address is correct. Click once on the Checkout button. By default, the address listed for your online account will be listed for AOL merchandise (see fig. 15.7). If you want to ship the products to a different location, here's your chance to change the listing. Click the Continue button to bring up a window that will request your billing information. You can bill your purchase either to your online account or to a credit card.

Fig. 15.7
Completing the
order.

```
┌──────────────── Shipping Information ────────────────┐
│  First Name            Last Name                      │
│  GENE                  STEINBERG                      │
│                                                       │
│  Street                                               │
│  THE BRIDGE                                           │
│                                                       │
│  City                         State    Zip Code       │
│  STARSHIP ENTERPRISE          AZ       1176b          │
│                                                       │
│  Daytime Phone                                        │
│  555-1212                                             │
│                                                       │
│            ┌──────┐   ┌──────────┐                    │
│            │ Stop │   │ Continue │                    │
│            └──────┘   └──────────┘                    │
└───────────────────────────────────────────────────────┘
```

Tip
Before visiting your
online shopping
center, have your
credit card handy
so that you can
enter your billing
information with-
out delay.

Now that we've ordered a new T-shirt, let's start looking for a brand new car.

AutoVantage

Keyword: AutoVantage

AutoVantage is both an online database of new and used car information and a center where you can arrange to service your car, buy accessories, and even order your new vehicle at a discount price (see fig. 15.8).

Fig. 15.8
AutoVantage is
your online
resource for
automobile
information.

Tip
As with all online
information, feel
free to save and
print the text
window when-
ever you want.
(See Chapters 2
and 3 for further
information.)

AutoVantage provides a face that's very different from other areas on America Online, so we'll go into it in detail. If you are using the Windows version of America Online software, you are no doubt familiar with the command-line (text) interface in DOS. This interface will probably seem a bit strange to Macintosh users, but AutoVantage makes it really simple to navigate through. You are prompted every step of the way, and your answers will govern the information that's presented.

To take advantage of AutoVantage's services, you have to join, but there's almost always a low-cost introductory membership available, so let's dig in.

1. Double-click on the Access AutoVantage (Non-Members) line (again see fig. 15.8).

2. The first window you'll see is a request to specify how long your row of text should be. A good size is 40, 60, or 80 characters. The narrower the screen, the longer it takes to scroll through the section. If you don't make the right selection, just close the window, open it again, and start over.

3. The Main Directory lists the services available to non-members (see fig. 15.9). Since this is a text-based interface, you cannot just double-click on the item you want to select. You have to let the descriptions in the text window guide you on what to do next. In this case, you have 13 items from which to choose. You simply enter the number of the item you want to learn more about, and either click on the Send button or press the Enter or Return key.

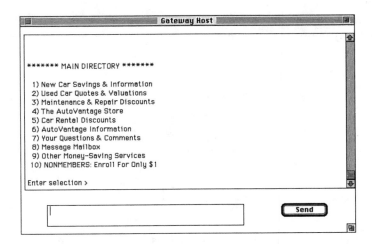

Fig. 15.9
Typical
AutoVantage
directory window.

4. For each selection, you'll be asked to enter a number or further information. If you want to join, you'll be presented with a brief questionnaire that asks for your name, mailing address, and billing information. Pressing Enter or Return when you've finished entering the requested data will send it to AutoVantage's gateway, and you'll then be prompted for further information.

5. Once you have completed your visit to AutoVantage, you can close the window to leave the text-based service behind and return to your familiar America Online icons and windows.

Checkfree

Keyword: Checkfree

The routine sounds familiar. Once or twice a month, you gather your monthly bills in a big pile, and write checks for each and every one, place the checks in the envelopes along with the billing stub, and mail them. If you're using a personal finance program, you can do the check-writing routine on your computer, but the checks that come out of your printer still have to be placed in envelopes and sent via snail mail.

With Checkfree (shown in fig. 15.10) you don't have to worry about bill stubs, and stamps and envelopes. It's a service that allows you to do all your checkbook transactions electronically, via modem. Using Checkfree Corporation's Macintosh or Windows software, you enter the payment information, which is then transferred to a central processing center. The software adjusts your checkbook balance automatically. You can even schedule fixed monthly payments to be automatically deducted from your checkbook balance.

Fig. 15.10
Checkfree
eliminates checks,
stamps, and
paperwork when
you pay your bills.

A demonstration version of the Checkfree Macintosh and Windows software is available for download. You can also order the regular version at a discount price.

Computer Express

Keyword: Computer Express

Maybe you want to buy that neat new computer game, you need some hard drive utility software, or it's time to replace that old modem with one of those spanking new high-speed models (and take advantage of America

Online's 9600 bps service). Computer Express is your resource for discount prices on all sorts of computer-related merchandise.

Computer Express lets you search for a specific product or check the newest software titles and special Hot Deals (see fig. 15.11).

Fig. 15.11
A source for computer software and accessories.

If you've decided to look for a new modem, simply bring up the Search Products window by double-clicking on it; then enter modems in the information field. Click on the List Articles button, and you'll soon see a list of related products (see fig. 15.12). In this case, we found 228 of them, but you have to hit the More button a few times to be able to scroll through the entire list of available products.

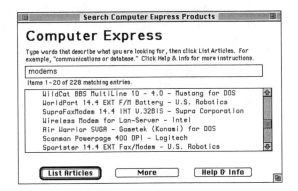

Fig. 15.12
Computer Express merchandise database.

Double-click on the item that interests you to get detailed descriptions, product specifications, and the latest prices.

As with all stores in America Online's shopping mall, entering your order is simply a matter of naming the items you want to buy. Computer Express lists them by Part Number—a five-digit number in the product description. Type the Part Number in your order form, below the name of the product (see fig. 15.13). Click on the Continue button to select additional merchandise or to tally up your order.

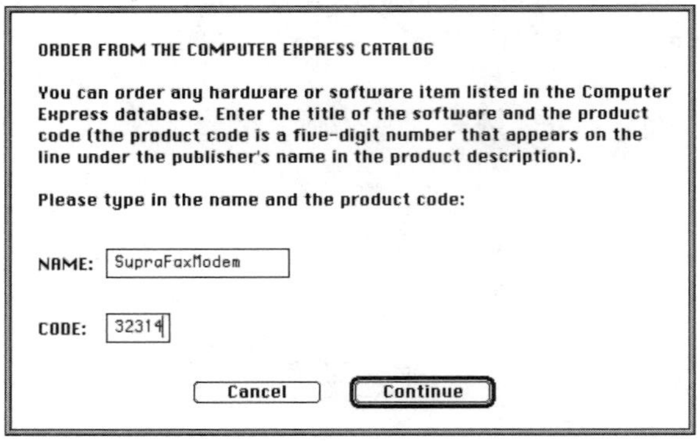
ORDER FROM THE COMPUTER EXPRESS CATALOG
You can order any hardware or software item listed in the Computer Express database. Enter the title of the software and the product code (the product code is a five-digit number that appears on the line under the publisher's name in the product description).
Please type in the name and the product code:
NAME:
SupraFaxModem
CODE:
32314
Cancel
Continue

Fig. 15.13
Getting ready for the checkout counter.

Flower Shop

Keyword: Flower Shop

Our next stop along the information superhighway shopping mall is that cute little flower shop shown in figure 15.14. Maybe a friend or relative is having a special occasion, or you want to give a bouquet of roses to your significant other. You can place your order at the Flower Shop. That order will then be transmitted to a local florist near the home of the person who will be receiving the flowers. That florist will deliver your order in person.

Flower Shop
Long Stem Roses
Single Rose
Delivery/Price Information
About the Flower Shop
Open

Fig. 15.14
Say it with flowers.

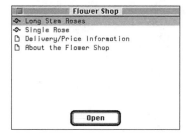

Online Bookstore

Keyword: Bookstore

America Online's Bookstore is stocked with shelves and shelves of the latest titles, both fiction and nonfiction, in all the major categories (see fig. 15.15). There's a special database that allows you to search for a specific title; select the Search for Books icon in the top right corner of the Online Bookstore forum window. The Special Requests and Questions icon takes you to a message area where you can post your request for a book that may not be in stock, or simply to ask for additional information about available volumes.

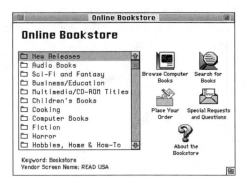

Fig. 15.15
Looking for that best-seller.

The main directory window displays the latest releases, plus listings in all the major publishing categories. Once you bring up a directory of available books, double-clicking on the title gives you a brief description of what the work is about and its price.

The ordering window for the Online Bookstore is a bit different from those available in other America Online stores (see fig. 15.16). The window allows you to select up to three titles at a time and to enter your shipping and billing information. If you want to order additional titles, simply bring up the order window again. And, yes, last time we checked, the latest edition of a certain book on how to use America Online was available there.

Fig. 15.16
Time to tally up your order.

ORDERING INFO:

Full Name:	Gene Steinberg	Ph: 555-1212
Street Address:	Starship Enterprise	
City/State/Zip:	Space 1999	

	Item	Product Number	QTY	Price
Prod #1:	Using AOL	156529727-X	1	$17.50
Prod #2:				
Prod #3:				

Method of Payment? VISA (MC, VISA, AMEX)
Credit Card Number: 0000-0000-0000-0000   Exp. Date: 9/99

Send   Cancel

PC Catalog

Keyword: PC Catalog

PC Catalog is devoted strictly to products for IBM PCs and compatibles (see fig. 15.17). You will receive discount pricing on hardware, software titles, and accessories. But it is not really a store or mail-order catalog in the same sense as the other places we've visited so far in this chapter.

Fig. 15.17
A different sort of buying service on America Online.

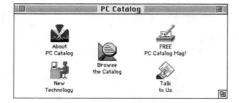

Unlike the other stores, PC Catalog is a buying service. When you browse through its listings, you'll see a list of products, prices, and the name of the vendor offering that product. The list is updated weekly.

You don't actually place your product order directly with PC Catalog. Instead, you contact the vendor mentioned in the product description, who will fill your order for the selected item at the advertised price. The product information is provided as a service, and the seller of the product is responsible for taking the order and shipping your merchandise.

Penny Wise Office Products

Keyword: Penny Wise

For our final visit on this shopping trip, we'll stop over at Penny Wise Office Products to pick up a new toner cartridge for my laser printer and maybe get a box of envelopes and some copy paper (see fig. 15.18).

Fig. 15.18
America Online's source for discount office products.

Penny Wise offers a free catalog too, but you can simply select all the office supplies you need during your America Online visit.

A quick way to find the merchandise you want is to select the Search for Office Products option. The window that appears is typical of the search windows you'll find on America Online.

First enter the name of the product in the field; the directory window will display a list of what's available (see fig. 15.19). If you double-click on the item, you'll get a brief description of the product and its price.

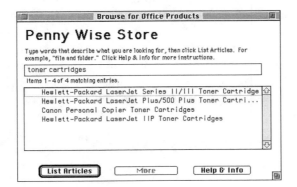

Fig. 15.19
Searching for laser printer supplies.

The ordering process is very much the same as other America Online shopping areas. Select the Place Your Order option, then enter the information required to identify the product you want to buy. Then add or confirm your shipping address. Once the information has been sent, your order will be processed and the merchandise will be delivered directly to your specified shipping address.

Using Shoppers Advantage Online

Keyword: Shoppers Advantage

Shoppers Advantage, shown in figure 15.20, is a discount buying service that lets you purchase any one of up to 250,000 different items right from the comfort of your personal computer. Like AutoVantage, which we described earlier in this chapter, the interface for Shoppers Advantage is text-based. That is, you navigate through the service by entering simple commands in the text field. By choosing numbers or typing simple words, you are able to view the vast catalog, check product descriptions and place your order for prompt shipment to your home or office.

Fig. 15.20
Shoppers Advantage Online is your interactive discount mail order catalog.

When you look over a product's description, you'll see two prices. One is for members, the other, somewhat higher, is for non-members. When you find a product you want to order, you'll find out quickly enough whether the low membership fee is covered by the purchase of a single item (and quite often it is). Members also get a two-year warranty on the products they buy. Our recent online shopping trip for a new computer brought us a huge list of choice products from Apple Computer, IBM, and other manufacturers.

Using the Classifieds Online

Keyword: Classifieds

America Online's Classifieds forum is your place to post your own ads or to check advertising from fellow members and commercial outfits. You aren't limited to just the computer-related merchandise shown in figure 15.21. You can place ads for home appliances, electronics, and other types of merchandise.

Fig. 15.21
America Online's buy/sell/trade center.

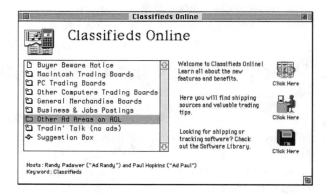

The guidelines for this area are few and very simple. When you post an ad, describe the merchandise you are selling as accurately as possible, including the warts (like that little scratch at the side of the case). Review other ads of the same sort of merchandise to set a fair price, or do as I have done in the past when I've offered merchandise for sale—let your fellow members make their best offer.

There are thousands of ads in the Classifieds message area. Most of them are placed by well-meaning firms and individuals, and in most cases you will receive the exact merchandise you order. But as with all mail-order transactions, approach the deal with some healthy skepticism. It's a good idea, for example, to use a credit card when you make your purchase. That way, if you are not satisfied with the product or service, the credit card issuer will usually investigate the transaction on your behalf and even credit your account if necessary.

IV

Info at Your Fingertips

Other Services

No doubt you are faced with a bewildering array of choices when you want to buy something new. Well, we're going to discuss one resource, here, where you might find a little help in making your buying decision. Then we'll discuss another kind of shopping, job hunting.

Consumer Reports

Keyword: Consumer Reports

We wrote about Consumer Reports and other online magazines in much more detail in Chapter 14, "News, Magazines, and Business Information," so we'll just remind you that Consumers Union is a non-profit product test and research center you can use for up-to-date information before you buy.

You'll find product reports and special columns in its America Online support area, shown in figure 15.22.

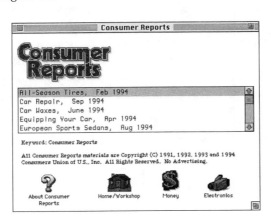

Fig. 15.22
Consumer Reports reviews new products.

Job Listings Database

Keyword: Jobs

America Online features job listings from two large help-wanted databases: E-Span and Help Wanted-USA. If you are seeking employment in your present field or are seeking a new occupation, you can examine this database for possible job openings. The listings are updated weekly, so you can expect to find jobs that are still available.

The Search Help Wanted USA window is typical of most database resources on America Online. Just enter the field in which you seek a job, and if there are any opportunities in the database, you'll find a listing within just a few seconds (see fig. 15.23). Simply double-click on the listed item or highlight the item and press Enter or Return to get more information about the employment opportunity.

Fig. 15.23
Looking for a
new job.

From Here...

Sometimes shopping is a headache, especially when you have to fight through heavy traffic and search for parking spaces at a crowded suburban shopping mall. On America Online, however, there are no crowds and no waiting lines. Simply browse through the virtual shopping isles at your leisure, take the time you need to decide what you want to buy, and place your order. You can even get information about your next car.

■ You'll find some helpful shopping advice in AOL's online newsstand. We tell you how to get there in Chapter 14, "News, Magazines, and Business Information."

- In Chapter 16, "The Travel Chapter," we prepare for a vacation or business trip, without ever leaving the computer screen, simply by logging on to America Online.

- In Chapter 20, "Getting Help," we give you a few tips on finding more money to make that purchase, with advice on how to reduce your online bill.

IV

Info at Your Fingertips

Chapter 16

The Travel Chapter

For this chapter, just imagine that you're visiting a travel agency. The difference is that your travel agency is America Online's host computer. From the comfort of your own home or office, you can pick a spot for a family vacation and find out information about the place you're going to visit. You can select a hotel, make reservations, and even rent a car.

In this chapter you learn how to:

- Find out about attractions in your destination city

- Prepare your travel itinerary right on your computer

- Use American Airlines' Eaasy Sabre gateway

- Check flight schedules and fares

- Make your airline, car, and hotel reservations

Suppose, for example, that your children, like my son, have never visited California, and have wanted to go there for a long time. This chapter uses Los Angeles and San Francisco as sites for a sample vacation plan. Of course, you can travel virtually anywhere in the world by using the same techniques discussed in this chapter.

Accessing the Travel Department

Keyword: Travel

Your first step in preparing for this vacation is to pay a visit to AOL's Travel department. To access this area, click on the Travel icon in the Main Menu or just type the keyword **Travel**. You then see the screen shown in figure 16.1. We'll spend the next few pages describing some of the online areas available in this department.

Fig. 16.1
The Travel department on AOL provides the resources you need before making that business or vacation trip.

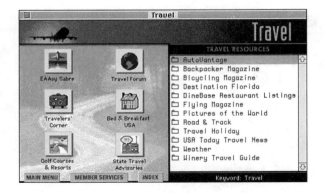

Using the Eaasy Sabre System

Keyword: Eaasy Sabre

Tip
If you have a Macintosh with a color monitor, first download a file containing color versions of the icons you see in the Eaasy Sabre area. This file, named *Online One*, is placed in the Online Files folder.

To get from the Travel & Shopping window to the Eaasy Sabre main menu, first click on the Eaasy Sabre icon. Then, in the Eaasy Sabre window that appears, select Enter Eaasy Sabre. In the following window, if this is your first time, select Visitor; in the next window, you can read the terms and conditions of Eaasy Sabre, or you can continue to the Eaasy Sabre main menu.

Visiting American Airlines' Eaasy Sabre Forum is much like visiting your local travel agency (see fig. 16.2). You can look up the current weather in the cities to which you are traveling. You can check on the availability of airline flights, hotel rooms, and rental cars. Not only can you find out flight schedules, but you also can check for the lowest available fares and even examine the fine print that lets you know whether you're eligible for a discount.

Fig. 16.2
America Online's Eaasy Sabre gateway is your entrance to a text-based reservation service.

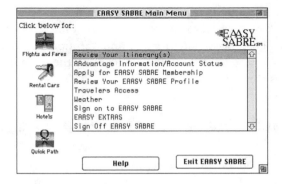

When you've located all the information you want, you can even make your reservations, confirm those reservations, and bill the charges directly to your credit card. Your plane tickets and confirmation information are mailed to your home or office.

Macintosh users on America Online can use Eaasy Sabre's unique graphic menu to navigate the service. If you've used Eaasy Sabre on other services, you can opt for the standard text menu instead.

Applying for Membership

Feel free to browse through the Eaasy Sabre Forum to see what features it offers. Because membership is free and without any obligation, however, you probably want to become a member so that you can make your reservations whenever you want. When you click on the Apply button in the Eaasy Sabre main menu, you are taken through a brief questionnaire that asks for your name, address, telephone number, and information about the credit card you want to use for billing (you don't have to include this information, of course).

For security reasons, you are given your personal membership identification number. You can select your own password, too, so that nobody else can make reservations and bill charges in your name.

In a few weeks, you get a membership kit with further information on using the service.

Tip

If you have a special preference for seating, such as a nonsmoking window seat, or if you are on a special diet, you need to list those preferences in your application. Getting correct reservations is much easier this way.

Viewing Weather Reports

The Eaasy Sabre main menu gives you a number of options to help you find the information you want. When you click on the Weather selection, you are asked to name the city for which you want to check the weather. Then you receive information not only about the current weather, but also about that day's forecast and the expected weather on the following day (see fig. 16.3).

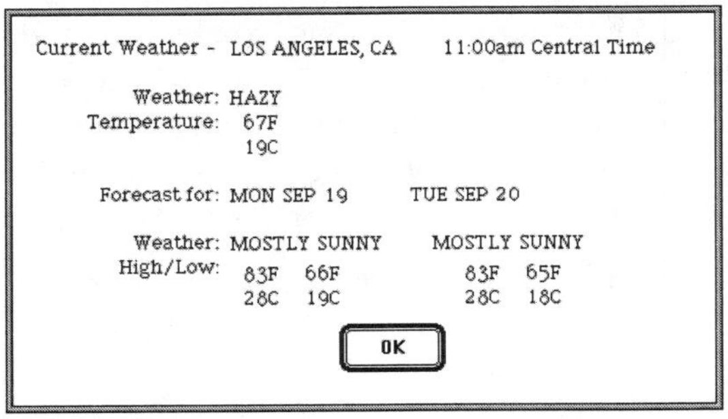

```
Current Weather - LOS ANGELES, CA      11:00am Central Time

       Weather: HAZY
   Temperature: 67F
                19C

   Forecast for: MON SEP 19       TUE SEP 20

       Weather: MOSTLY SUNNY    MOSTLY SUNNY
     High/Low:  83F   66F         83F   65F
                28C   19C         28C   18C

                        [ OK ]
```

Fig. 16.3
Eaasy Sabre provides the latest weather information on the places you want to visit.

Finding the Best Fares or Flights

The airline price wars have made just about everyone (your cheerful authors included) confused about airline fares. Each airline has its own schedule, with specific rules to obtain those highly desired discount fares.

So the first thing to do is click on the Flights and Fares icon on the Eaasy Sabre main menu screen. On the Flight Res. & Info window that appears, select the Fare icon. In the next window, enter the requested information about your flight. You are asked the name of the city from which you're leaving, the final destination of your flight, and the dates you plan to travel, along with the time you want to leave.

You can conduct your search in two ways:

■ If you're looking for the cheapest available flights, you want to check fares first. After you've entered the information about your flight, choose OK. You are then presented with a window of the fares that apply to the flight you've specified, as shown in figure 16.4, along with the name of the airline (which can be defined in a separate window). Double-click on the fare to learn about the restrictions. The buttons at the right enable you to locate additional information about the flights covered by these fares.

Fig. 16.4
You can check fare information with Eaasy Sabre.

■ If you need to depart at a specific time, you first need to see what flights are available to you at that time. The buttons at the bottom of the window, as shown in figure 16.5, enable you to figure out what those arcane travel codes mean and to check which fares and seating arrangements are offered.

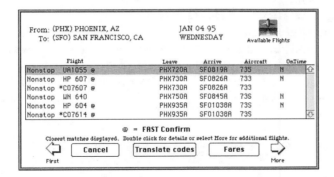

Fig. 16.5
Here's your flight
schedule.

After you've found the flight and fare information you need, you can book
your flight then and there, through Eaasy Sabre, and have the tickets sent
directly to you. Or you can use the information you've found to book flights
directly with the airline or with your favorite travel agency.

Booking Hotel Rooms

Now that you know how you're getting to Orlando, you need a place to stay.
Because hotel rates might vary during the year (they're higher during the
peak travel season) and because special promotions are offered from time to
time, you need to make your reservations as far in advance as possible. Click
on the Hotels icon on the Eaasy Sabre main menu screen to search for information about hotels and rates. You are asked basic information about your
travel itinerary. After you've described your plans, choose OK to bring up
your hotel choices, as shown in figure 16.6.

Fig. 16.6
Making hotel
reservations is easy
with Eaasy Sabre.

With the New Preferences button at the bottom of the window, you can list
how many are in your party and describe the kind of room you want. After
you've received the hotel information you want, you can go ahead and make
your reservations through Eaasy Sabre or directly with the hotel.

Making Car Reservations

Although many cities across the country offer public transportation, you can find no substitute for sightseeing in your own car. And if your visit is for business purposes, a rental vehicle is an added convenience. You can make your car rental selection with Eaasy Sabre. The information in figure 16.7 is available when you select the Rental Cars icon from the Eaasy Sabre main menu screen.

Fig. 16.7
Getting your car reservations.

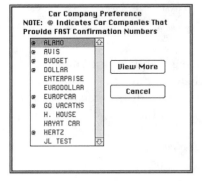

Because car rental rates are nearly as volatile as airline fares, you need to check rates and confirm your reservations as far in advance of your trip as possible.

> **Note**
>
> The national daily newspaper *USA Today* is a great source for up-to-date news for travelers. You can read, save, and print the latest news before planning your trip. Just select the USA Today Travel News folder from the main menu of the Travel & Shopping window (you probably have to scroll down to see the folder). You then see a list of travel articles.

Visiting the Travel Forum

Keyword: Travel Forum

The Travel Forum consists of a wealth of resources containing much of the information you need to know before planning your trip (see fig. 16.8). The main window of this forum contains useful articles on many related travel subjects. If you're going to travel by air, you receive up-to-date information on the lowest fares. When you travel abroad, you need to know specific things about the country you are going to visit.

Fig. 16.8
America Online's Travel Forum is your first resource for information about the places you want to visit.

Because you're in a traveling mood, take a brief tour of the Travel Forum:

- The Welcome window (at the top right) gives you a brief overview of the Travel Forum and the features it offers.

- What's New & Events is in many ways similar to your daily or weekly travel newspaper, with the latest tips and information useful to all travelers.

- The main directory (center window) consists of articles with useful information on many travel-related subjects.

- If you want to meet other online travelers, stop over for a while in the Travel Cafe (at the lower left of the forum window). The Travel Cafe is the Travel Forum's online chat room, where you visit with fellow travelers and discuss your experiences and share information. From time to time, regular conferences feature guest experts in the travel industry, so stop by and check the conference schedules.

- The Travel Board is your own set of message resources. It's divided into three sections: World Traveler, U.S. Traveler, and Caribbean Traveler. Here, you can exchange travel advice with other America Online members. And one more message area, Travel Tips, gives you helpful up-to-the-minute advice from online members and experts alike.

- The Travel Library is a special resource of files that you can download to your computer. Hundreds of files here cover every aspect of travel lore. Feel free to browse through the file descriptions before downloading the files of your choice. (See Chapter 12, "How to Find Software," for advice on how to download files from America Online.)

Tip
As with all America Online text windows, you can save the window by using the Save command, or you can print the text window.

■ Since the world situation is apt to change at any moment, you'll want to view the official State Department travel advisories (see fig. 16.9). You can tap into a huge database of information that covers the entire world, and learn if there are any special considerations for traveling to a specific country.

Fig. 16.9
The State Department's travel advisories can be searched on AOL.

The U.S. State Department Warnings folder contains the latest alerts about problems and limitations of traveling to specific parts of the world. You'll want to review these text files before you plan your travel itinerary.

■ The last department, Travel Books, contains concise news and reviews of the latest books on travel. If a visit to your local bookstore or public library has left you overwhelmed about which book you need, America Online's Travel Books section is where you can find suggestions about the one that's right for you.

> **Note**
>
> If you are traveling with America Online and plan to stay at a hotel, be sure to ask in advance for a "computer ready" room. Most hotels are happy to offer you a room with an extra phone jack for your modem. If your hotel does not have special rooms for computer users, in most cases you can simply remove the cable for the phone from the phone jack and insert your modem cable.

Visiting the Travelers' Corner

Keyword: Travelers Corner
The next stopping point in this tour is the Travelers' Corner. In addition to using the Travelers' Corner keyword, you can choose the Travelers' Corner

icon in the Travel & Shopping window to reach this area. This forum is hosted by the editors of *Weissman Travel Reports*. The Corner's main focus is comprehensive profiles about major U.S. and international destinations. You get a brief overview about the high points of a specific city and a list of its main attractions. The report not only describes these attractions, but also suggests the kinds of folks who would most like to visit them. This information is especially important if you're taking your children with you.

To visit the Travelers' Corner, choose that icon from the Travel & Shopping window. The Travelers' Corner screen that appears is shown in figure 16.10.

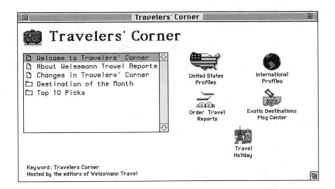

Fig. 16.10
The Travelers' Corner profiles your favorite travel spots.

The profiles contain lists of dos and don'ts so that you can learn more about the local culture and etiquette of your destination. This kind of help is especially useful if you're traveling to a foreign country.

The Travelers' Corner screen includes separate icons for the kinds of profiles you want to review, domestic or international. You can even find a message center describing exotic destinations you might want to visit. You can stop over in this area to learn about the experiences of other online travelers, both America Online members and *Weissman Travel Reports* editors.

But because the sample travel plan is taking you to Orlando, Florida, choose the United States Profiles icon to bring up the list of United States profiles (see fig. 16.11). The window gives you two ways to search: by city name (the Search icon) or by the letters of the alphabet. Profiles contain five or more pages of valuable information about your favorite destination.

The final icon in the Travelers' Corner, Order Travel Reports, gives you a special offer to purchase comprehensive professional profiles of the places you want to visit. These profiles are the same ones that are available through your local travel agency.

Fig. 16.11
You have two ways to search for a profile of your destination.

Using the Bed & Breakfast USA

Keyword: Bed & Breakfast

If all those hotels and motels have begun to look the same to you during your trips around the USA, perhaps you want to consider a very attractive alternative. Bed & Breakfast refers to a special kind of lodging that consists of private homes that rent out rooms to travelers, or inns that provide extra-special personal service. Sometimes they're referred to as Guest Houses or Tourist Homes. The Bed & Breakfast USA Forum, shown in figure 16.12, provides an up-to-date listing of this unique kind of accommodation from across the country.

Fig. 16.12
Bed & Breakfast USA offers an alternative to conventional hotel/motel lodging.

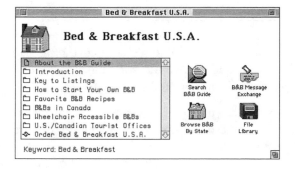

AOL's Bed & Breakfast USA Forum contains the regularly updated text of the same guidebook that you can find at your local bookstore. You can examine listings by state, review information on how to seek out the best accommodation for you, and share experiences with other AOL members about your favorite lodgings. If you intend to travel to Canada, there's a special listing showing bed and breakfast lodgings divided by province.

Visiting the Golf Courses & Resorts Forum

Keyword: golfis

If your golf bag is never far from you when you travel, you'll want to visit the Golf Courses & Resorts Forum on AOL, shown in figure 16.13. Sponsored by the Golf Information Source, the forum maintains a list of thousands of golf courses and resorts. A current list of golf tournaments is offered too, in case your aspirations spread beyond the putting green.

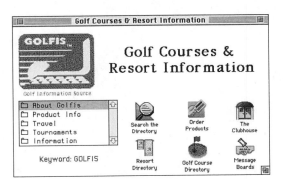

Fig. 16.13
Browse through a list of thousands of golf courses and resorts.

Quite often the best guide is the personal experience of others who've visited these golf courses. And the message board is a place where you can read the experiences of others and share yours as well. There's even a message folder dedicated to golf humor.

From Here...

Exploring America Online's resources for travelers is fun, not just for the vicarious voyagers among you, but for those of you who are planning a vacation or business trip. Because travel brings out most people's desire to shop as well, you might want to read these chapters:

- Chapter 14, "News, Magazines, and Business Information"

- Chapter 15, "The Shopping Chapter"

- Chapter 20, "Getting Help"

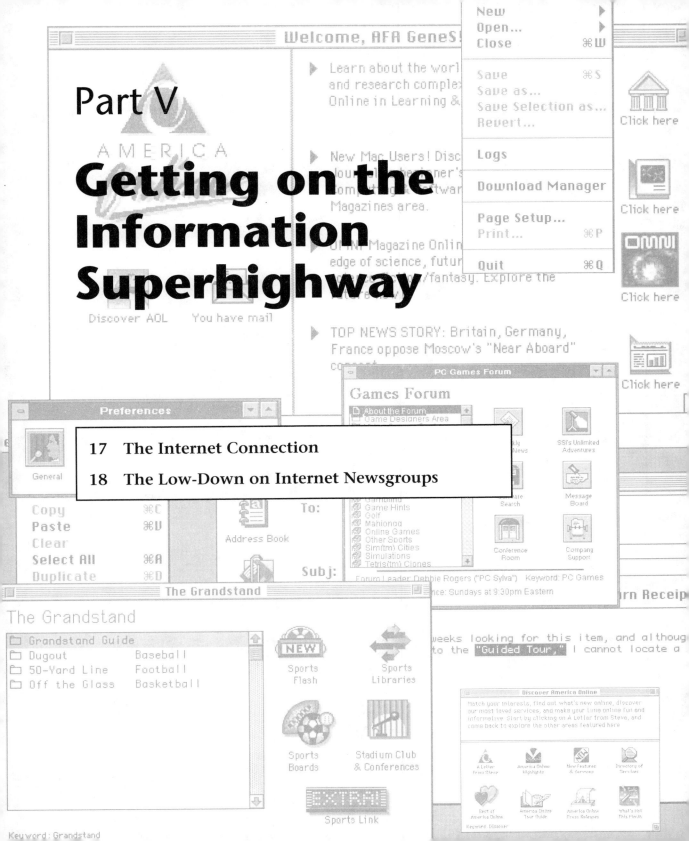

Part V

Getting on the Information Superhighway

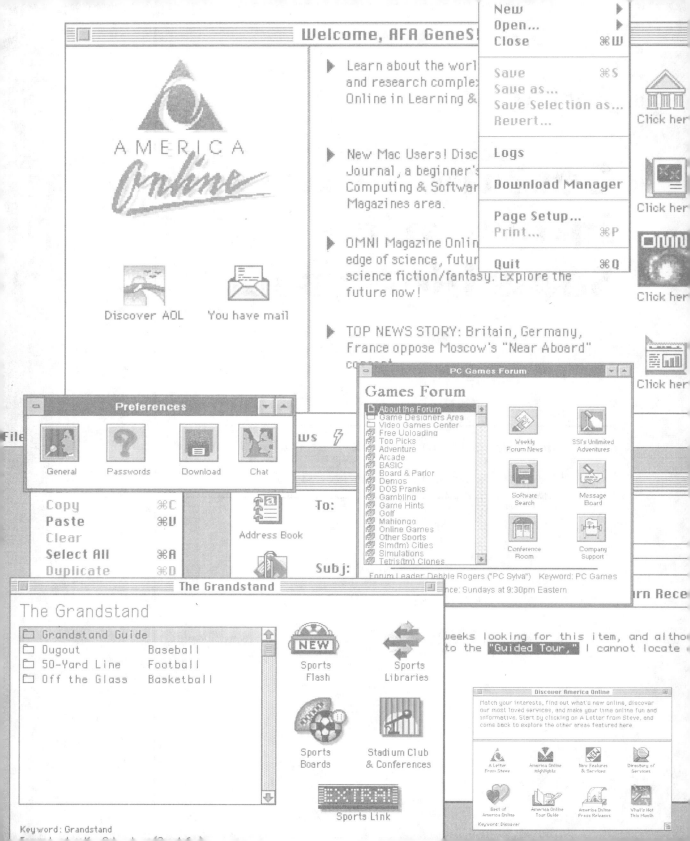

Welcome, AFA GeneS!

New
Open... ▶
Close   ⌘W

Save   ⌘S
Save as...
Save Selection as...
Revert...

Logs

Download Manager

Page Setup...
Print...   ⌘P

Quit   ⌘Q

▶ Learn about the worl
and research comple
Online in Learning &

▶ New Mac Users! Disc
Journal, a beginner's
Computing & Softwar
Magazines area.

▶ OMNI Magazine Onlin
edge of science, futur
science fiction/fantasy. Explore the
future now!

▶ TOP NEWS STORY: Britain, Germany,
France oppose Moscow's "Near Aboard"

Click her

Click her

Click her

Click her

AMERICA
Online

Discover AOL   You have mail

Preferences

General   Passwords   Download   Chat

File   ws ⚡

Copy   ⌘C
Paste   ⌘V
Clear
Select All   ⌘A
Duplicate   ⌘D

To:

Address Book

Subj:

PC Games Forum

Games Forum

- About the Forum
- Game Designers Area
- Video Games Center
- Free Uploading
- Top Picks
- Adventure
- Arcade
- BASIC
- Board & Parlor
- Demos
- DOS Pranks
- Gambling
- Game Hints
- Golf
- Mahjongg
- Online Games
- Other Sports
- Sim(tm) Cities
- Simulations
- Tetris(tm) Clones

Weekly Forum News

SSI's Unlimited Adventures

Software Search

Message Board

Conference Room

Company Support

Forum Leader: Debbie Rogers ("PC Sylva") Keyword: PC Games
nce: Sundays at 9:30pm Eastern

rn Rece

The Grandstand

The Grandstand

- 📁 Grandstand Guide
- 📁 Dugout   Baseball
- 📁 50-Yard Line   Football
- 📁 Off the Glass   Basketball

weeks looking for this item, and altho
to the "Guided Tour," I cannot locate

NEW
Sports Flash

Sports Libraries

Sports Boards

Stadium Club & Conferences

EXTRA!
Sports Link

Keyword: Grandstand

Discover America Online

Match your interests, find out what's new online, discover
our most loved services, and make your time online fun and
informative. Start by clicking on A Letter from Steve, and
come back to explore the other areas featured here.

A Letter From Steve   America Online Highlights   New Features & Services   Directory of Services

Best of America Online   America Online Tour Guide   America Online Press Releases   What's Hot This Month

Keyword: Discover

Chapter 17

The Internet Connection

America Online has brought you into an exciting new universe. You are already a member of not only America Online, but also of the exciting Internet, your gateway to communicate with millions of fellow computer users from across the globe. America Online's Internet Connection provides information and access into what have been described as the Internet's most popular features—*E-mail*, *database searching*, *mailing lists*, and *Newsgroups*.

Over time, America Online will be providing you with instant access to even more features of the Internet. The best news is that the new features won't require you to learn about a whole new environment. America Online has designed the new areas to look and feel very similar to the message boards already on the service, the very same message boards we've been describing throughout this book.

In this chapter, you will discover:

- What the Internet is

- How to send and receive Internet E-mail

- How to use Internet mailing lists

- How to learn more about the Internet

- A glimpse of future AOL Internet services

What Is the Internet?

Simply stated, the Internet is the largest, most complex computer network in the world. The Internet is also one of the oldest existing networks, has the unique distinction of having no hubs or central control point, and was designed with the assumption that the rest of the network was totally unreliable.

What began as a military project idled along for a number of years, slowly growing to encompass educational and business communities in addition to the military. The last five years have seen an enormous growth in the Internet, and now, "being on the net" is almost a necessity for the millions of users throughout the world. Business people are scrambling to add their Internet address to their business cards to join the cadre of folks already using the Internet to send and receive electronic mail (E-mail), keep current with special interests, search databases, and do their day-to-day business.

The concept of a global information superhighway is one that excites even experienced computer users. There are, however, a few thresholds to cross so that you can begin to use the Internet.

Because the Internet has no central control, and no authority to train and guide new users, it can readily appear a daunting giant to everyday business people. Those of you who have become accustomed to the graphical interface of Macintosh and Windows computers might easily be put off by the enormous architecture of the Internet. Unless you are connected to an academic or research institution, it can be hard to get connected, as well.

America Online's *Internet Connection* is the solution you need to overcome the obstacles presented by the Internet network (see fig. 17.1). Every America Online member is already a member of the Internet. Soon you will be able to travel the length and breadth of the Internet just like you use any other part of America Online.

Fig. 17.1
America Online has a special department devoted strictly to Internet access.

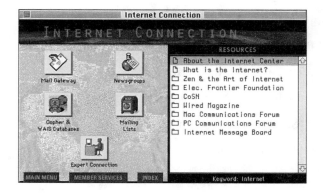

Sending and Receiving E-Mail Over the Internet

Not coincidentally, E-mail is one of the most popular uses of not only America Online, but also the Internet. Right now, you can send electronic mail to, and receive it from, *anyone* connected to the Internet. It makes no difference whether they use America Online or not. If you have friends who use one of the other online networks, such as Prodigy, CompuServe, MCI Mail, AT&T Mail, AppleLink, and others, you can send them E-mail by using America Online's normal E-mail windows (see fig. 17.2). America Online handles in excess of 100,000 pieces of Internet mail daily.

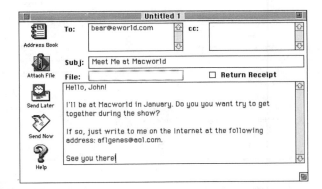

Fig. 17.2
The look of Internet E-mail isn't terribly different from regular America Online E-mail.

V

Information Superhighway

Sending E-Mail

Sending E-mail over the Internet works no differently than the normal America Online E-mail you send to other members; you just type in the Internet address of your intended recipient rather than typing the America Online screen name you normally use to send mail to other AOL members.

Addressing Internet mail is that simple. There are a couple of rules to follow, however, and once we show you those rules, you'll be sending worldwide E-mail with ease.

An Internet address never contains any spaces. If someone's mail system does allow spaces at the receiving end, the spaces are automatically replaced by underscores (_) in the Internet Address; for example, you might see john_smith@hugecorp.com, where the space between the user's first and last name is closed up with an underscore character.

Also, every Internet address must have the user name and domain (location) specified. For our purposes, the user name is everything to the left of the

Tip
The best way to learn the address of an Internet correspondent is to simply ask him or her for it.

@ symbol, and the domain is everything after the @ symbol. In the domain, a company name is followed by a suffix that describes what type of organization it is. A business, for instance, uses the suffix *com,* educational institutions use *edu,* military sites use *mil,* and government offices use *gov.*

We've created the following table to show you how you can send Internet E-mail to your friends on other online services. If you follow the format we've provided, you can easily address other services in much the same manner:

Location	Long Address	Abbreviation	Example
AppleLink	applelink.apple.com	apple	name@apple
AT&T Mail	attmail.com	att	name@att
BIX	bix.com		BIXname@bix.com
CompuServe	compuserve.com	cis	12345.678@cis
Delphi	delphi.com		name@delphi.com
eWorld	eworld.com		name@eworld
GEnie	genie.geis.com	genie	name@genie
MCI Mail	mcimail.com	mci	name@mci

Tip

To learn people's addresses without asking for them, we suggest a book called *A Directory of Electronic Mail !%@:: Addressing & Networks* by Donnalyn Frey and Rick Adams, available in most bookstores. We also suggest New Riders' *Internet Yellow Pages* by Christine Maxwell & Czeslaw Jan Grycz, which is available for business addresses.

Note

Each online service has its own requirements and limitations as to how the Internet services it offers work. AOL's Internet Connection contains a number of help texts that will help you address your E-mail to other services. As other services change their Internet offerings, these help texts will also be revised.

Receiving E-Mail

To receive mail from the Internet, you need to know your own Internet address, just as you need to know a recipient's. Your address is simply your America Online screen name, with any spaces removed, plus *@aol.com.* If your screen name is *John User,* for example, your Internet address is *johnuser@aol.com.*

As of this writing, there is one other caveat to sending and receiving E-mail: You cannot enclose (attach) files in your E-mail to others on the Internet, nor can you receive files as attachments. There is a way to include files as part of your Internet E-mail, but it can be a bit cumbersome and it works best with small files.

> **Note**
>
> Internet addresses are almost always expressed in lowercase letters. While this is not an absolute requirement, we recommend that you follow this convention for clarity and consistency with existing Internet practices.

The Internet sends your E-mail in text form. To include a file as part of your message, you need to convert that file to text as well and paste it into the body of your message. To do that, you need a program that converts binary files to hex-encoded text. The process of converting the files so they can be transferred as part of your Internet mail is called *uuencode*. The process to restore those text files to regular binary files is called *uudecode*.

America Online's software libraries, both Macintosh and Windows, have programs that will do this kind of conversion. You can use AOL's File Search utility, described in Chapter 12, "How to Find Software," to locate programs of this sort.

Although they do work, these programs have their limitations. AOL's Internet gateway will split long files into small parts, which you have to reassemble and save as text in your word processing program before you can convert them back to their original format. To send larger files, you would want to do it via *FTP*, a process we'll describe in more detail a little later in this chapter.

Mailing Lists

Keyword: Mailing Lists

Internet mailing lists are E-mail discussions exchanged by using the Internet among groups of people who share similar interests. Using regular Internet E-mail, information is exchanged in a continuing, interactive fashion with people all around the world.

Dozens and dozens of Internet Mailing Lists exist today, encompassing almost every imaginable topic: computer technology, American literature, philosophy, cooking, chess, motorcycling, sports, environmentalism, rock music, UFOs, alternative life styles—take your pick.

The Internet Mailing Lists area has a number of helpful text articles containing background and instructions on using the Mailing Lists features of the Internet Connection (see fig. 17.3).

Fig. 17.3
America Online's
Internet Mailing
Lists window.

To locate specific mailing lists that might appeal to your interests, click on the Search Mailing Lists icon. You'll discover a database of mailing lists you can search by entering descriptive words (see fig. 17.4).

Fig. 17.4
The Mailing List
database search
window.

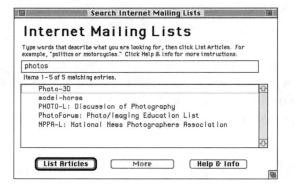

Once a list of entries that match your search description appears, simply click on the List Articles button (or press the Return or Enter key). The items that appear after a successful search from this window contain the descriptions of Internet Mailing Lists available from the matches of your search words entered in the search window (see fig. 17.5).

These descriptions contain instructions on how you can subscribe to the mailing lists that interest you by using your America Online Internet E-mail address. Follow the instructions carefully; they tend to differ slightly from list to list. Remember also to note how you can unsubscribe from any lists you join, in case you change your mind later. Most of these lists generate a large amount of mail and can quickly fill your online mailbox if you do not check in on a regular basis.

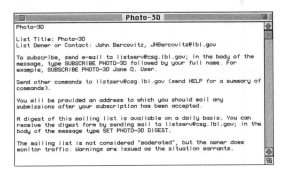

Fig. 17.5
The results of a search on the word photo.

Internet Databases

Keywords: Gopher, WAIS

The Internet contains hundreds of free databases on topics as diverse as home brewing, NASA news, recipes, Congressional contact information, and the works of Shakespeare. These databases are indexed, meaning that you can search them for information simply by using key words and phrases, just as you would search for files on America Online by using the File Search feature, described in Chapter 12. If you've been following current Internet news, you may have heard these databases called *WAIS databases* (see fig. 17.6). WAIS is an abbreviation for *wide area information server,* one of the many tools available on the Internet for searching databases.

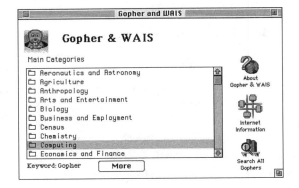

Fig. 17.6
AOL offers Gopher and WAIS database search capability.

Since most of the databases are run by unpaid enthusiasts, the nature and content quality can vary from excellent to inconsistent. Determining the

V

Information Superhighway

mechanics of searching the databases can also get complicated, but America Online's Internet Connection makes it easy to find and use Internet databases.

Using AOL's Gopher Database Searching

The best way to show you just how an Internet database search works is to conduct one for you. America Online's Gopher and WAIS center offers a list of common topics you might want to search. If the topic you want information about isn't shown in the listing, just click on the Search All Gophers icon, as we've done in figure 17.7, and enter the topic of the subject you want to learn more about.

Fig. 17.7

You can begin a Gopher search of the Internet by entering the topic in the list field.

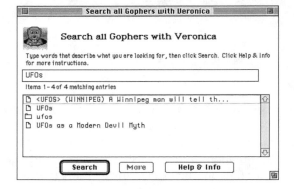

The difference between Gopher and WAIS is that the former technique doesn't actually search the contents of a file, just its title. The mechanism used to conduct this search is called Very Easy Rodent Oriented Internet-wide Computer Archive, or *Veronica* for short.

Using AOL's WAIS Database Searching

The best way to describe the difference between Gopher and WAIS is that the former is similar to a book's table of contents. The latter is somewhat like the book's index, much more detailed, capable of providing a more sharply defined range of information. The beauty of America Online's Internet search interface is that it makes the underlying process transparent to the user. You just check the topics shown in the directories, or enter the topic you want to know more about in the search screen. AOL and its Internet gateway will do the rest for you behind the scenes, without you having to use any additional software or learn arcane Unix-based text commands.

America Online's Internet Connection will, from time to time, be adding a selection of some of the best databases available on the Internet. Each will have an easy-to-use front end, just like those used on databases throughout America Online. The encyclopedia in America Online's Education & Reference Departments is a good example (see Chapter 13, "Learning & Reference"). As the number of databases available on the Internet grows, so will the number available on America Online.

AOL's TCP/IP Connection

Computers that hook up directly to the Internet speak a language called *TCP/IP*, short for Transmission Control Protocol/Internet Protocol. A number of computer networks (perhaps at your office) have direct Internet connections via this protocol (they don't come cheap, but they are capable of really fast performance).

If your computer network is hooked up to the Internet, here's an ultra-fast way to experience America Online without going through the usual local access phone numbers. Both the Macintosh and Windows versions of America Online's software offer a TCP/IP connection tool. To use it, you need to change your modem setup, just as we describe in Chapter 2, "Using Your America Online Macintosh Software" and Chapter 3, "Using Your America Online Windows Software." Instead of picking SprintNet or BT/Tymnet from the connection files offered, you choose TCPack instead, just as we've done in figure 17.8.

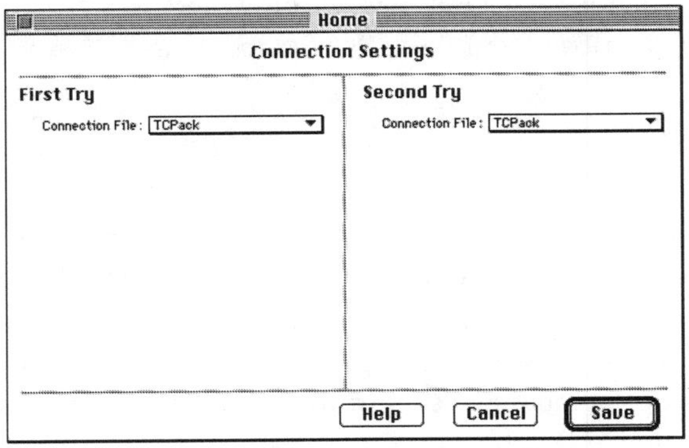

Fig. 17.8
Set up your AOL software to connect directly through TCP/IP via the Internet.

When you log onto AOL using the TCP/IP connection, performance will be limited only by the speed of your network. It can be several times faster than your present telephone connection. If you have direct TCP/IP access, give it a try and see.

> **Note**
>
> Macintosh users need Apple's MacTCP software to take advantage of AOL's TCP/IP capability. MacTCP is available as part of System 7.5 and separately through Apple's FTP sites or by calling Apple Customer Assistance at 800-SOS-APPL.

File Transfer on the Internet

Earlier in this chapter, we described how you can include files as part of your Internet E-mail, with some limitations. There is yet another, more efficient way of doing this sort of file transfer.

As you have discovered or will discover, America Online's forum software libraries contain thousands of files of all types that you can download from America Online's computers to your own hard disk. Scattered throughout computers on the Internet are many thousands of such files and programs. One of the ways Internet users can access these files is through a process known as *FTPing,* the Internet's equivalent of file transfer methods, similar to those used on America Online (FTP stands for *file transfer protocol*).

America Online's Internet Connection is bringing FTP access online. This means that you can tap a huge source of software libraries that provide files not yet available on America Online. Access to these files will not be much more complex than locating and downloading files on AOL's own software libraries. We'll describe one of these FTP services here.

Anonymous FTP

Keyword: FTP

America Online's Anonymous FTP area (see fig. 17.9), part of the Internet Connection, is an easy and convenient way to receive files from remote computers worldwide. By "anonymous," we mean that the operators of these sites will let you log on as a guest, without having to select a special password. AOL offers a list of popular FTP sites to which you can connect simply by selecting the name of the site, and then clicking on the Connect button.

If the FTP site to which you want to connect isn't shown, you can click on the Other Site button, then enter the address of the cite in the text field, as we've done in fig. 17.10. As with any Internet address, you have to enter the name accurately, or you will not be able to make a connection.

Fig. 17.9
AOL's Anonymous
FTP area maintains
a list of popular
FTP sites for your
downloading
pleasure.

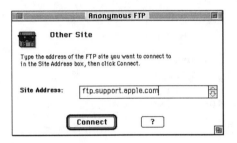

Fig. 17.10
The name of a
popular FTP site
available through
AOL's Internet
Connection.

V

Information Superhighway

Once you've connected to an FTP site, the next step is to look through the
file directory to locate files you wish to retrieve. Unlike America Online's own
software libraries, you cannot attach one of these files to your FlashMail session. They can only be received one at a time, while you are actually logged
onto the FTP site. In figure 17.11, we've selected a file to retrieve.

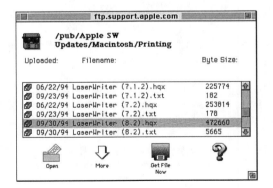

Fig. 17.11
Choose the file
you wish to
download.

As we said, the process of downloading files via FTP is somewhat different
from doing it direct from a software library on America Online. Quite often
the FTP sites consist solely of a lone personal computer that can only handle

a small number of users at the same time. Don't be surprised if you get a message that the site is busy and you need to log on again. The best times are late at night and in the early morning, when network traffic is apt to be light.

> **Note**
>
> Files at FTP sites are stored as "encoded" text files. As we explained earlier in this chapter, you will need to translate these files after they are downloaded in order to make use of them.

If you want to locate an FTP site that caters to a particular category of software or information, and you don't know its exact address, you can use AOL's Gopher search feature, which we just described.

You'll want to watch the Internet Connection on AOL for news and details on the new features as they become available.

Welcome to the information superhighway!

From Here...

As you can see, sending and receiving E-mail on the Internet is hardly more complicated than sending E-mail to another America Online member. And, from the comfort of America Online's graphic interface, participating in all the Internet's exciting features is just as easy.

- For more information on using America Online's E-mail features, read Chapters 2, 3, and 7.

- For information on locating files on America Online, see Chapter 12, "How to Find Software."

- For more information on tapping America Online's huge resources of educational and reference information, read Chapter 13, "Learning & Reference."

- For information on how to join and participate in Internet Newsgroups, see Chapter 18, "The Low-Down on Internet Newsgroups."

- If you need further assistance with using your America Online software, read Chapter 20, "Getting Help."

- And to keep up-to-date on America Online's fast-growing Internet connection, simply type the keyword **Internet** and explore the Internet Connection.

Chapter 18

The Low-Down on Internet Newsgroups

Some of the most interesting parts of the wide world of Internet are Newsgroups, also known as *USENET Newsgroups*. Newsgroups are popular and active exchanges; they are also the Internet counterparts of message boards on America Online. Just like mailing lists, there are Newsgroups covering almost any topic you can think of, and then some.

In this chapter you will discover:

- What Internet Newsgroups are

- What Netiquette really means

- How to find Internet Newsgroups

- How to participate in Internet Newsgroups

Internet Newsgroups—the Ground Rules

Before you begin to examine Internet Newsgroups for yourself, it is a good idea to acquaint yourself with the ground rules. In some respects, Newsgroups are quite different from America Online's own message boards. First, they are usually not moderated, which means there is no staff person to examine the structure of the message boards, and to remove messages that contain inflammatory, irrelevant or vulgar statements. As a result, participants in Newsgroups take quite a free-wheeling approach to participating in these areas, and sometimes they are a little slow to welcome new visitors, or newbies, as beginning Internet surfers are called. This doesn't mean, however, that you should abandon considerations of good taste when posting in such areas. We'll explain some of the things you need to know, Netiquette, later in this chapter.

Of course, a smaller number of Newsgroups do have moderators, somewhat equivalent to the forum staff on America Online, but they exercise a greater measure of control over what appears in their message boards. Each and every message that you post is reviewed by the moderators for content, and they will censor ones that they don't consider relevant to the topic at hand.

America Online's Internet Center provides access to literally thousands of Newsgroups. Using AOL's Newsgroups area, shown in figure 18.1, you will be able to select the Newsgroups that interest you and place that list of Newsgroups in a customized list. America Online keeps a database of popular Newsgroups, but as we'll explain later in this chapter, you can seek out others that interest you too.

Fig. 18.1
One of the most exciting Internet features—Newsgroups.

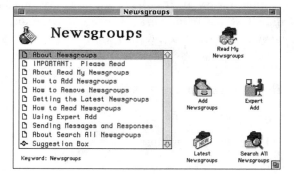

Once you've subscribed to a list of your favorite Newsgroups, you need only click on the Read My Newsgroups icon to keep current on your favorite topics. Using this message board, you will be able to discuss your special interests with people from all over the world.

Before you begin to add Newsgroups to your lists, you'll want to take a few moments to review the text files displayed in the main forum directory window (again see fig. 18.1). You can read these text files while you're online, or you can save and print them for later reference. These files contain all the simple instructions you need to become an expert user of this remarkable Internet feature.

Some Advice on Netiquette

When you first visit AOL's Newsgroups area, you'll want to jump right in and participate in a discussion board yourself. Before you do so, however, you should learn something about Newsgroups in general and how to introduce yourself to a particular discussion group. Over the years, the Internet, though largely unregulated and unsupervised, has developed some forms and conventions you should know about first.

So here are a few tips based on experience on the net.

- You will be tempted to jump in on a discussion that interests you. Our advice is *don't*. Spend a little time reading messages or following discussions. Quite often there will be a set of *FAQs* (Frequently Asked Questions), text files that will provide a list of ground rules for a specific discussion group, and responses to typical user questions. Once you've developed a feel for the flavor of a particular group, then it's time to consider posting a message of your own.

- There are literally thousands of Newsgroups. The number of messages you are likely to encounter will be in the hundreds of thousands. You can quickly become overwhelmed by the sheer volume of information if you don't pick and choose carefully. To begin with, you should restrict yourself to only a small number of discussion groups, take time to digest the messages, and only add more when you feel you can devote the time necessary to follow up on all the information you'll receive.

- When you respond to a message, consider that you are not just posting a response to a single person, but to an audience that could number in the millions. If you decide you want to restrict your audience to a single person, send that person E-mail instead.

- Before writing your message, carefully choose the appropriate forum. It wouldn't necessarily be a good idea to promote the use of a Macintosh in a discussion group oriented towards users of Microsoft Windows, for example, unless you want to risk generating a lot of ill-will.

- Show respect and be polite when you post a message. If you disagree with someone's statement, try to stick to the issues, and refrain from personal attack. Such attacks are regarded as flaming, and while they may be entertaining on some television talk shows, they are not considered good taste on the Internet.

- When responding to someone else's message, quote the relevant portions of that message at the beginning of your response, or before each

V

Information Superhighway

part of your message that refers to that message. The usual convention is to place a forward sign, to signify a quote mark, at the beginning of each line, as we've done here:

> I've access to a Mac Centris 610.

> When I try to run Norton Speed Disk,

> I get "System files not supported in System 7"

> Where can I get an update of Norton, or

> is this software now obsolete/upgraded/replaced??????

■ It is customary to use your Internet address (which we described in Chapter 17, "The Internet Connection") as your personal signature, but your name and affiliations may be placed there as well, just as we've shown in figure 18.2. Some users will also include their addresses and phone numbers, but before you do this, consider whether you feel that you'd want to really give this information out to millions of strangers. Others will add a statement or motto that reflects some aspect of their personalities. Before preparing your own signature, you might want to see how others do it first.

Fig. 18.2
Typical Usenet Newsgroup signature. The information below the signature is the long and twisted path taken by that message before it reached its destination.

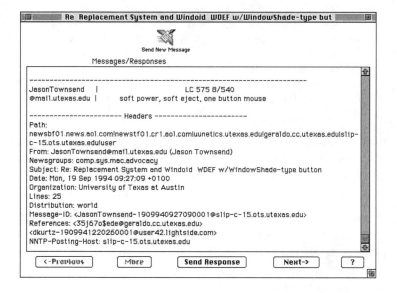

■ Keep your messages short and to the point. You are reaching an audience of millions of people, and you don't want to waste anyone's time, since many users pay high charges for Internet access. Also try not to cross-post and send your message to more than one Newsgroup at a time (unless you feel it's really necessary).

■ Choose a subject title that really describes the topic of your message. It is better to use "Type 1 Crash in System 7.1" then "System Crash" if you are seeking advice on solving a problem in a Macintosh Newsgroup.

■ Express emotions and humor with care. When you speak with someone in person, very often body language and the inflection of your voice would reveal whether you are serious or not, or whether you are angry or happy about something. Your words alone must be the mirror of your feelings. Experienced online users will express emotions with smileys :). See Chapter 6, "Meeting People Online," for a list of common smileys and emoticons.

■ Before you respond to a message, take the time to see if someone else has already answered it. Time on the busy Internet is at a premium, and reading the same sort of message over and over again wastes everyone's time, including your own.

How to Add Newsgroups

As we said at the beginning of this chapter, there are thousands upon thousands of Newsgroups, catering to interests of all sorts. Many Newsgroups overlap in terms of content too, so you will probably want to select more than a single Newsgroup that caters to topics in which you're interested.

America Online maintains a listing of the most popular Newsgroups in its own database. Just click on the Add Newsgroups icon, and you'll see a directory listing, shown in figure 18.3, that displays a number of subjects of interest.

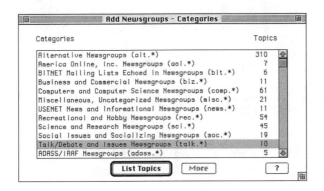

Fig. 18.3

The first step in locating a Newsgroup to join is to get a list that caters to your favorite subjects.

Once you've picked a subject, click on the List Topics button to bring up a list of Newsgroups that fit the description. To find the actual Newsgroup itself, click on the listing once more, and then you'll see the display shown in figure 18.4. Now we get to the heart of the matter.

Fig. 18.4

Here's a list of Newsgroups catering to one area of interest.

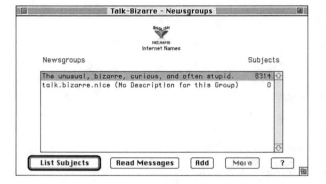

Now you don't have to join that Newsgroup yet, though if you want to plunge in, clicking on the Add button will automatically subscribe you to that Newsgroup. If you'd rather sample the flavor of a particular discussion group, just click on its name and you'll see a listing of the available messages, shown in figure 18.5. You can read those messages, but since you are just sampling the Newsgroup for now, you cannot actually post a response to a message or create a topic of your own. To do that, you must actually add that Newsgroup to your list.

Fig. 18.5

Before you actually join a Newsgroup, you may want to look over some of the messages first.

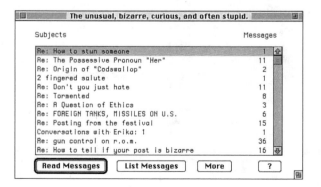

When you've actually added a Newsgroup, it'll appear under the Read My Newsgroups listing, which we'll discuss a bit later in this chapter.

How to Search All Newsgroups

If you don't find a Newsgroup that interests you, do a more thorough search of the ones that are available. Just click on the Search All Newsgroups icon, to bring up a search window (see fig. 18.6). Enter the subject for which you want to locate a Newsgroup in the list field.

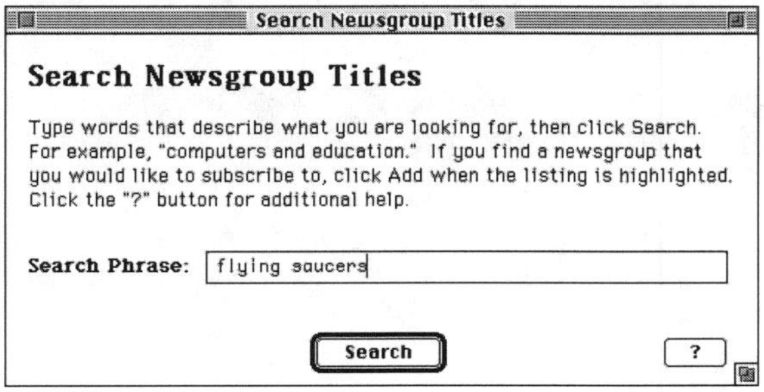

Fig. 18.6
Search from among thousands of Newsgroups for one that piques your curiosity.

If there is a Newsgroup that meets your search criteria, and sometimes you have to refine the phrases a bit or even try related ones, it'll appear in a window, from which you can read a capsule description by double-clicking on the Newsgroup's title. You'll find, however, that many Newsgroups do not actually have any description other than the title itself, which they usually consider sufficient to describe what it's all about.

Unlike the Add Newsgroups feature, the searching mechanism doesn't give you the ability to sample a Newsgroup before adding it to your list. Since you can remove a Newsgroup later if you choose, by the simple click of a button, this is not a major shortcoming.

Using Expert Add

As with E-mail addresses, the titles of Newsgroups are identified by a special syntax, with words generally separated by a period. An example is *comp.sys.mac.advocacy,* which as the title suggests, is a discussion group with active debates on the subject of the Apple Macintosh versus other computing platforms. If you know the exact title of a Newsgroup, you can bypass the search mechanism or America Online's own listing, and use the Expert Add feature, shown in figure 18.7.

V

Information Superhighway

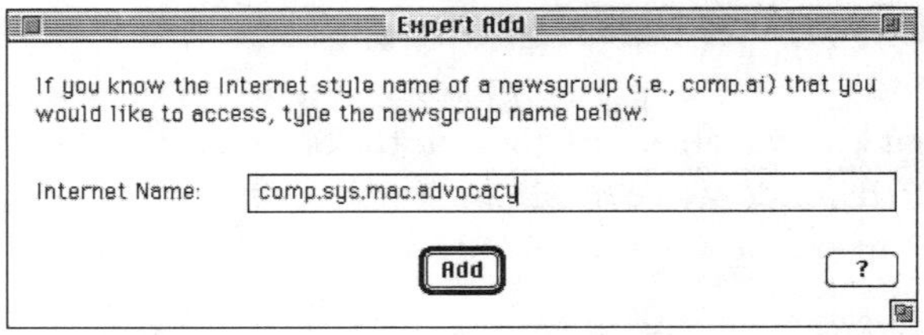

Fig. 18.7
If you know the name of the Newsgroup you want to join, enter it here.

Note

America Online's Expert Add feature is quite literal. For it to work, you need to enter a Newsgroup's name using the exact spelling and punctuation. Otherwise, the Newsgroup won't be located, or, worse, you'll add the wrong Newsgroup.

After you've subscribed to the Newsgroups that interest you, it's time to read the messages.

How to Participate in Newsgroups

Click on the Read My Newsgroups icon at the main screen of the Newsgroups area, and you'll see a listing of all the Newsgroups to which you've subscribed, as shown in figure 18.8. When you enter this area for the first time, you'll see a list of popular Newsgroups that America Online has automatically included, but you can remove them at any time, simply by highlighting the name of the Newsgroup and clicking on the Remove button. The Mark Read button allows you to flag the messages in a selected group as read without actually opening the messages themselves (so use this feature with caution if you want to read those messages at a later time).

Fig. 18.8
Here are the Newsgroups you've joined.

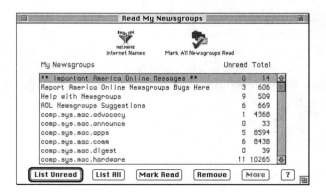

Before you begin to read the messages in your selected Newsgroups, review the section on Netiquette earlier in this chapter. Once you've done that, take some time to read the messages themselves. The first time you read the messages, you may find there are literally thousands in a single Newsgroup alone. But since they are grouped by topic (also known as *message threading*), as we've shown in figure 18.9, you'll be able to easily pick the messages that you want to actually read.

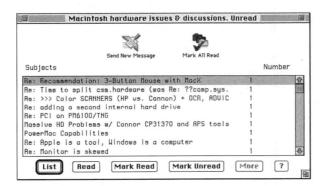

Fig. 18.9
Newsgroups messages are threaded—grouped according to topic.

How to Follow a Message Thread

All Newsgroup messages are sorted by date and then by topic. The process of organizing the messages into topics is known as *threading*, and it allows you to read messages and responses about a single topic, without having to pour through messages on other subjects.

Once you've read all the messages in a single thread, the next message you come to, by clicking on the Next button, will take you to a brand new thread. If you want to bypass that subject, just close the message window, and look over the directory of unread messages for another topic you want to follow.

> **Note**
>
> Since messages in a single thread are often posted at widely varying times, you might actually find two or more listings for messages concerning a single topic.

Using the List All Feature

When you first open your personal Newsgroup list and select a topic, double-clicking on the topic name or pressing the Return or Enter key will bring up a list of unread messages. If you want to review messages you've read previously, click on the List All button instead, which will bring up a display of all messages available in that Newsgroup, whether you've read them or not.

How to Reply to a Newsgroup Message

After you've read the messages in your favorite Newsgroup, no doubt you'll be tempted to respond to a particular message. The Reply button is used to add your message to the existing thread, so that others reading about a particular topic will also see your response. There are two ways to respond to a message. First is simply to click on the Reply button, which will bring up the screen shown in figure 18.10. If you want the author of the original message to receive a reply by E-mail, check the box at the lower-left corner of the message window.

Fig. 18.10
Responding to someone who has written a Newsgroup message.

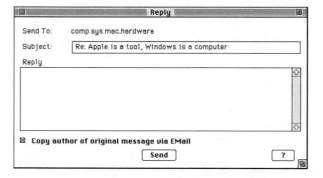

Tip
America Online's software libraries contain software that will automatically insert Internet quotation marks ahead of material you want to quote in a Newsgroup message. For Macintosh users, the shareware Signature Quote is an easy-to-use tool for quoting messages and also to automatically insert your Internet signature.

The second option is Reply to Author, which allows you to send your response as E-mail instead, but you still have the choice of having the same message posted in the Newsgroup, by clicking on the checkbox in the Reply to Author window.

Before actually writing your response, it's customary to first quote the relevant passages of the original message you are writing about. We further describe this technique earlier in this chapter, in the section about Newsgroup Netiquette. It is common for Newsgroup subscribers to quote several passages of a previous message and intersperse their own comments between them.

How to Post a Newsgroup Message

If you are not responding to a message in a particular thread and you want to create a new topic, click on the Send New Message icon, at the top of a message window. This will bring up a blank message window, into which you can insert the topic, and then the body of your message.

Once you've finished reading the messages in your selected Newsgroup and responding to the ones that interest you, click on the Mark All Read icon, at the top of the directory of available messages. That way, you won't be presented with the same list of messages next time you visit your Newsgroup.

> **Caution**
>
> When you are in the Read My Newsgroups window, before actually selecting an individual Newsgroup to browse through, the Update All As Read icon will mark all messages in all the discussion groups on your list as having been read. So be careful when you choose this option, otherwise none of the messages in those Newsgroups will be available for reading, unless you select the List All option. The latter forces you to plough through literally thousands of messages (even ones you've read before).

A Long and Circuitous Route

When you click on the Send button, your message begins its long journey through cyberspace. The Internet is a sprawling network, and your message will pass through many host computers before it's finally posted in your selected Newsgroup. It may take a few minutes for your message to appear. It make take a few hours, and sometimes it'll take a day or more, for it to travel to the remote reaches of the world and be available for reading by millions of Internet users.

From Here...

Internet Newsgroups are one of the most popular features of the information superhighway for good reason. The messages are informative, angry, funny, happy, and sad, but always interesting. You'll want to visit America Online's Newsgroups area often.

- For more information on tapping America Online's huge Internet resources, read Chapter 17, "The Internet Connection."

- If you need further assistance with using your America Online software, read Chapter 20, "Getting Help."

- And to keep up to date on America Online's fast-growing Internet connection, simply type the keyword **Internet** and explore the Internet Connection.

V

Information Superhighway

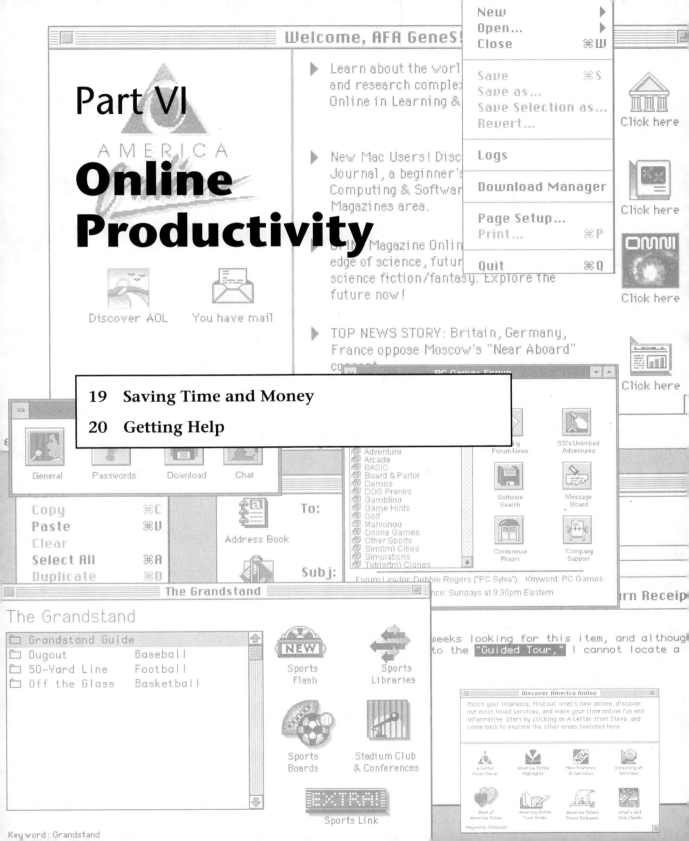

Part VI

A M E R I C A
Online
Productivity

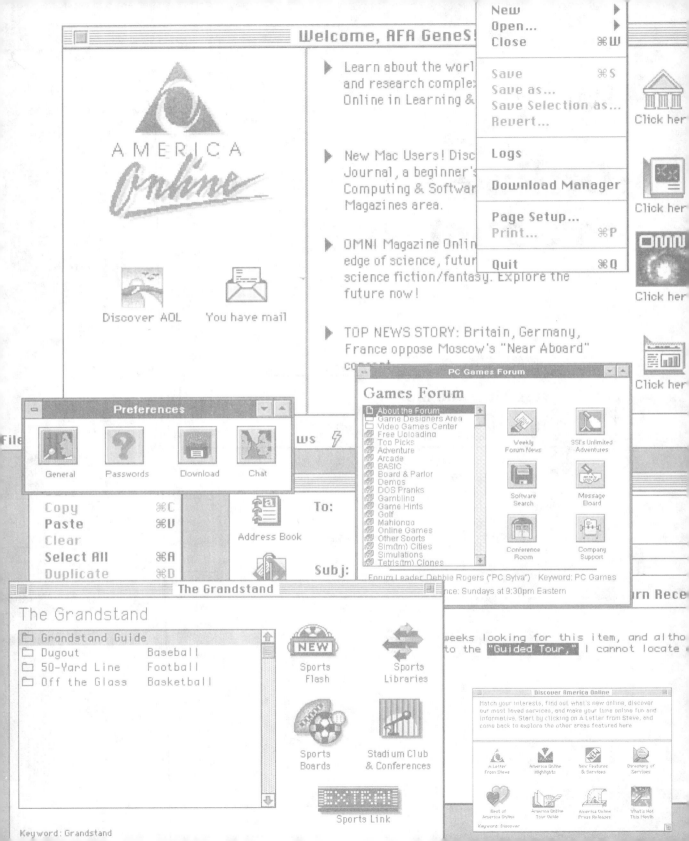

Welcome, AFA GeneS!

New ▶
Open... ▶
Close ⌘W

Save ⌘S
Save as...
Save Selection as...
Revert...

Logs

Download Manager

Page Setup...
Print... ⌘P

Quit ⌘Q

AMERICA
Online

Discover AOL   You have mail

▶ Learn about the worl
and research comple
Online in Learning &

▶ New Mac Users! Disc
Journal, a beginner's
Computing & Softwar
Magazines area.

▶ OMNI Magazine Onlin
edge of science, futur
science fiction/fantasy. Explore the
future now!

▶ TOP NEWS STORY: Britain, Germany,
France oppose Moscow's "Near Aboard"
concept.

Click her

Click her

Click her

Click her

Preferences

General   Passwords   Download   Chat

Copy   ⌘C
Paste   ⌘V
Clear
Select All ⌘A
Duplicate   ⌘D

File   ws ⚡

Address Book

To:

Subj:

PC Games Forum

Games Forum

- About the Forum
- Game Designers Area
- Video Games Center
- Free Uploading
- Top Picks
- Adventure
- Arcade
- BASIC
- Board & Parlor
- Demos
- DOS Pranks
- Gambling
- Game Hints
- Golf
- Mahjongg
- Online Games
- Other Sports
- Sim(tm) Cities
- Simulations
- Tetris(tm) Clones

Weekly
Forum News

SSI's Unlimited
Adventures

Software
Search

Message
Board

Conference
Room

Company
Support

Forum Leader Debbie Rogers ("PC Sylva")   Keyword: PC Games
nce: Sundays at 9:30pm Eastern

The Grandstand

The Grandstand

- Grandstand Guide
- Dugout   Baseball
- 50-Yard Line   Football
- Off the Glass   Basketball

NEW
Sports
Flash

Sports
Libraries

Sports
Boards

Stadium Club
& Conferences

EXTRA!
Sports Link

Keyword: Grandstand

rn Rece

weeks looking for this item, and altho
to the "Guided Tour," I cannot locate

Discover America Online

Match your interests, find out what's new online, discover
our most loved services, and make your time online fun and
informative. Start by clicking on A Letter from Steve, and
come back to explore the other areas featured here

A Letter
From Steve

America Online
Highlights

New Features
& Services

Directory of
Services

Best of
America Online

America Online
Tour Guide

America Online
Press Releases

What's Hot
This Month

Keyword: Discover

Chapter 19

Saving Time and Money

In earlier chapters, we discussed places on America Online where you can save money when going shopping or planning a trip. In this chapter, we're going to discuss one more place where you can save money—and that is with America Online itself.

In this chapter, you learn how to:

- Make your online visits more productive by doing your online work when you're offline
- Speed up the time it takes to download files
- Actually get free online time

Saving Time Online

When you end your online visit, you see a summary of the total duration of your session. This summary includes both the time spent in the free (support) areas and the regular areas for which you are billed.

Using Your Online Clock

Whenever you want to see just how long you've spent online, type the keyword **Clock**, which brings up a display showing the time that has elapsed since you originally logged on. When you are watching your budget, this is a sure way to keep track of the duration of your online session.

Compose E-Mail Offline

We described how to use AOL's E-mail capability in previous chapters, but you don't have to be online to create an E-mail message. Just open your E-mail "compose" window and type your message. You can create as many messages as will comfortably fill your computer's screen.

After you've written your E-mail, log on to America Online and send all your mail. When you use America Online's handy *FlashSessions* feature (see the following section), you can mail all your letters in a single step.

FlashSessions

Tip
AOL's computing and software libraries have a number of shareware alarm clock and reminder programs you can use to track your online session. (Also see Chapter 12, "How to Find Software.")

We described the ins and outs of FlashSessions in detail in Chapter 7, "Communicating with Others," so we simply restate its benefits here. It allows you to automate the process of sending and receiving E-mail. You can write your messages offline and then save them to FlashMail. You can activate a FlashSession at any time or simply have the sessions take place at the hours you select.

During your FlashSession, you are logged online automatically on the account name you specify. If you have more than one account, you can designate FlashSessions for them too. Your prepared E-mail, along with any attached files, will be sent, and your incoming E-mail and any attached files—if you select the Files Incoming option—will be received, all automatically (see fig. 19.1).

Fig. 19.1
Configuring your AOL FlashSessions.

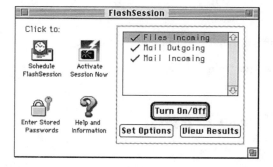

The greatest benefit here is time. You can compose your mail offline and read your new mail offline. This helps reduce online charges.

Creating Session Logs

Tip
System performance may be slower during early evening hours when online traffic is heavy. If you want to download software, choose a nonpeak hour, such as early in the morning.

You will often spend a lot of time online simply reading text messages while the online clock is ticking away. If you create a System Log, your America Online software acts like a tape recorder (see fig. 19.2). You will be able to scroll through the text, an information window, or even a message area, and a file will be created containing all the material that's being sent to your computer. (We discussed this subject in more detail in Chapter 2, "Using Your America Online Macintosh Software," and Chapter 3, "Using Your America Online Windows Software.")

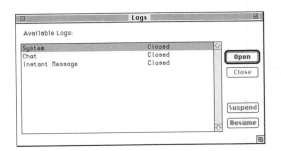

Fig. 19.2
Opening a
Session Log.

When you are offline, you can read this log at your leisure. This process doesn't work as efficiently when you want to post a message, since you will want to return to the location where the original message appeared to post a response to it, but otherwise, this is another technique to freely speed up your online session.

> **Note**
>
> As America Online software development progresses, you will be able to automate a FlashSession to include your favorite message boards, too.

Other Ways to Save Money

So far in this chapter, we've discussed techniques to reduce the amount of time you spend online, which reduces your monthly bill. Now we discuss ways in which you can actually receive free time during your online session.

Signing Up Friends

Keyword: Friend

Your cheerful authors find that using America Online is an enjoyable and rewarding experience, and we spend many hours online throughout the week. If you treasure your online experience as we do, you will want to have your friends share in the experience as well.

What's more, you can become eligible to receive free online time simply by signing up your friends as members. America Online doesn't charge you for the time you spend signing up your friends.

Your first step is to select a software kit that is compatible with your friend's computer and operating system (see fig. 19.3). There are kits available for Macintosh, DOS, and Windows. Be sure to choose the correct floppy disk size when you order the DOS or Windows versions of the software. Macintosh users may receive the software on 1.4M (high density) floppy disks or on the 800K variety (depending on what type of floppy drive your Mac-user friend has).

Fig. 19.3

Choosing an AOL membership kit.

This offer changes from time to time, so don't be surprised if it's a bit different when you decide to enroll your friend as a member (see fig. 19.4). The conditions are very simple. At the time this book was published, the following offer was in effect: *You are limited to ordering 12 membership kits per month. Also, your friend must register and maintain an online membership for at least 30 days for you to qualify for free time.*

Fig. 19.4

Here's the offer.

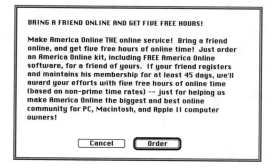

Winning Contests

Here's a method that isn't guaranteed, but if you are a regular visitor to online chats and conferences, no doubt you've seen the forum staff holding a contest or two from time to time.

These contests may result in the giveaway of free time or even some merchandise (including new books and newly released software), depending on the forum.

As an example, here's the text we logged from a recent chat that explains just how a typical contest is conducted. We've left in some of the humorous asides to preserve the flavor of this particular session. So pay attention, you may find yourself winning some free time on America Online some day. (*Online Host*, by the way, is text that's been generated by the AOL host computer with the keystrokes that are described in the following session log.)

Name	Conversation
AFA GeneS:	Since we are near the top of the hour I'll turn the mike over to AFL Bear...
AFL Bear:	Thank you, thank you!
AFL Bear:	It's that time again for someone to win three free AOL hours! So we will be rolling the old AOL dice again to determine the winner!
JLR63:	Hey, I want new dice...these are loaded!
MIKEL617:	Yeah!!!
AFL Bear:	Does anyone here NOT know how to roll the AOL dice?
AFA GeneS:	And Peter loaded them. Blame him!
OnlineHost:	AFL Bear rolled 6 12-sided dice: 12 11 7 9 9 5
TishTash:	Just repeat the command just in case, please.
AFL Bear:	I guess everyone knows the rules, then! The command is //roll only with no leading space, then hit the Return key.
TishTash:	Thanks.
JLR63:	Bear, set a good example!
OnlineHost:	MIKEL617 rolled 2 6-sided dice: 3 5
OnlineHost:	KevinY1 rolled 2 6-sided dice: 5 4
OnlineHost:	Kevin W46 rolled 2 6-sided dice: 4 3
OnlineHost:	TishTash rolled 2 6-sided dice: 2 3
AFL Bear:	OK, you must wait until I say GO! Any ties will be broken by...
AFA GeneS:	A sledgehammer.
AFL Bear:	A roll-off of the tying folks.

(continues)

VI

Online Productivity

Name	Conversation
AFL Bear:	Ready? Get set...GO!
OnlineHost:	KevinY1 rolled 2 6-sided dice: 2 4
OnlineHost:	MIKEL617 rolled 2 6-sided dice: 1 2
OnlineHost:	Imma rolled 2 6-sided dice: 5 4
OnlineHost:	TishTash rolled 2 6-sided dice: 2 2
OnlineHost:	StewMiller rolled 2 6-sided dice: 1 3
OnlineHost:	Kevin W46 rolled 2 6-sided dice: 2 5
OnlineHost:	ChuckS3257 rolled 2 6-sided dice: 5 5
OnlineHost:	JLR63 rolled 2 6-sided dice: 6 3
OnlineHost:	MIKEL617 rolled 2 6-sided dice: 3 4
OnlineHost:	IKEL617 rolled 2 6-sided dice: 1 5
OnlineHost:	JLR63 rolled 3 6-sided dice: 6 3 2
OnlineHost:	ChuckS!!!!! You win!!!!!
ChuckS3257:	Bear, thanks.
AFL Bear:	Say a few words, Chuck!
ChuckS3257:	This is my first win. Thank you.

Oh yes, one little point. There is truly a secret to rolling more than two "virtual dice" on America Online. If you catch us online some time, we'll let you in on how to do it (or you can simply take a peek at this book's glossary, where we've placed the information).

Get a New Modem

When I first bought a desktop computer, a 2400 bps modem cost several hundred dollars. Today, modems with speeds of 9600 bps data capability and more cost much, much less. America Online has been rolling in 9600 bps service around the U.S. since early 1994 and is also adding 14,400 bps in many selected cities.

If you have a 2400 bps modem, switching to 9600 means that your files transfer four times as fast and that text scrolls in a text window at a much speedier rate. Going to a 14,400 bps modem (where the service is available), provides incredibly fast throughput. Moreover, even if you log on at a higher speed, you pay exactly the same hourly rate you pay now. If you spend a lot of time online—and we hope you do—buying a high-speed modem more than pays for itself in just a few months.

With the arrival of low-cost 28,800 bps (V.34) modems, America Online has been exploring even faster ways of delivering the service to its members. In the years to come, America Online will be offering a rich array of multimedia tools (sound and picture) that will make your online visits more rewarding than ever.

From Here...

We've had some innocent fun in this chapter, but we've also given you some solid time-saving information that will allow you to get the most from your visits to America Online.

- See Chapter 5, "Finding Your Way around America Online," for advice on how to quickly navigate your way through AOL's online community.

- See Chapter 12, "How to Find Software," for quick tips on how to locate software you can download to your computer direct from America Online.

- In Chapter 20, "Getting Help," we tell you about America Online's own support area, a forum you can visit without incurring online charges. We also give you some troubleshooting hints, in case you encounter any problems during your online sessions.

VI

Online Productivity

Chapter 20

Getting Help

By now you've most likely visited a number of online areas and found America Online to be quite an interesting and entertaining place to explore. If you're like most of us, though, you have some questions or would like more information about using America Online. The following pages answer some of those questions, but more importantly, show you how to locate additional information, both online and off.

You can check your America Online bill, find out how to set up a new modem for use with America Online, or even get live help online during certain hours of the day, seven days a week.

In this chapter, we show you how to find information about:

- Using the AOL Help menu

- Troubleshooting download and other file transfer problems

- Reporting errors and other problems using AOL

- The free Members Helping Members message area

- Using AOL's Parental Controls to guide your children's online activities

- Getting live online technical assistance

The AOL Help Menu

If you find yourself needing additional information about America Online services or features, make your first stop in the extensive information area of AOL's own Help menu. Whether you need to know how to use the Download Manager or are connecting to America Online for the first time, this area most likely has the answer you need. For information about AOL's software features, see Chapter 2, "Using Your America Online Macintosh Software," and Chapter 3, "Using Your America Online Windows Software."

If you are signing on to America Online for the first time, take a moment and open the Help window from your Apple menu on your Macintosh (see fig. 20.1) or open the Help menu from your PC's menu bar with Windows (see fig. 20.2).

Fig. 20.1
Activating
Macintosh AOL's
extensive Help
features.

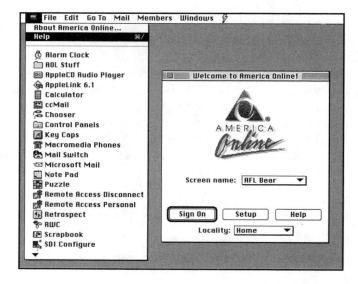

Fig. 20.2
Activating
Windows AOL's
extensive Help
features.

America Online's Macintosh Help window is a treat to work with because of its logical organization. The left panel of the Help window lists the various topics for which detailed information is available without even signing on to the service. To use the Help feature, simply click once on any one of the topics shown. The contents for that topic appear in the panel on the right side of the Help window (see fig. 20.3).

Tip
You can save and
print any text item
in the Help menu
for later reference.
Just click on the
text item first.

America Online's Windows Help window is organized pretty much like the Help menu you'd find in any Windows application. Your first Help screen, labeled *Contents* (see fig. 20.4) displays a list of the topics available. You may scroll through the window to display additional topics. Clicking on any topic will bring up a screen offering easy-to-read advice on that subject. You may also print any topic for later review.

Fig. 20.3

The America
Online Macintosh
Help window.

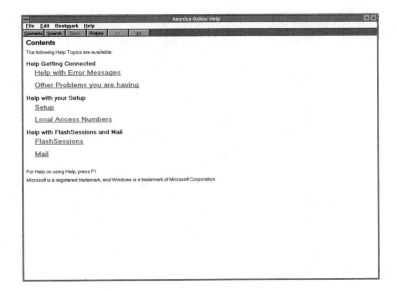

Fig. 20.4

The Help menu on
America Online's
Windows software
displays the table
of contents.

Members' Online Support

Once you establish your connection and explore America Online's areas, you
will probably find yourself less interested in the "how" of AOL's workings
and more concerned with the content of the numerous areas on AOL in
which you're interested. We covered many of those online places in previous
chapters, and more are being added almost every day.

As you wander around the virtual world of AOL and make use of its services,
questions may arise that are not covered in the offline Help features. Or you
may want to find out more about your own online status. America Online
provides a free area online dedicated to providing you with information
about its services and your account. You are not charged for the time you
spend in that support area.

VI

Online Productivity

To go to the free area, follow these steps:

1. Select Members Services from the Members menu, or use the keyword *Help* from anywhere online while you are connected to the service (you can also use the keyword *Hotline*).

2. You are asked whether you want to enter the free area. If you okay the message, all the windows that may have been open when you selected Members Services are temporarily closed. They appear again when you leave the free area.

3. You see the comprehensive online help forum, which includes live technical support (see fig. 20.5).

Fig. 20.5
America Online's
Members Services.

Your Online Bill

Keyword: Bill

Tip
The quickest route to your online billing summary is to type the keyword **Bill**.

The most widely used section of Members' Online Support is the Accounts & Billing area. (Maybe that's why they put it at the top of the icon stack?) It is here that you find out how much time you've spent online during the current billing month, how much your current bill is from the beginning of your monthly billing cycle, and information about past bills. You may also change your billing method and your personal information, including your billing address and contact information.

If you have moved or changed your telephone number, open the first item in the Accounts & Billing window to update the information stored about you in AOL's billing records (see fig. 20.6). To change your payment method, double-click the Modify Billing Information item.

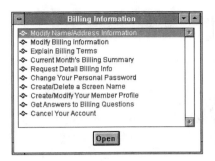

Fig. 20.6
The Accounts &
Billing area.

Obtaining information about your online account is as simple as opening the Current Month's Billing Summary. This summary will list your account usage for the current month, as well as how much time has been spent online by the other screen names you've created for your account.

As an additional service to aid you in better reconciling your online time, you may request a detailed billing accounting from America Online by double-clicking the Request Detail Billing Info item. You may then request details for either the current billing cycle or the previous one.

Also, you may change your password while visiting the Accounts & Billing area, create or delete screen names, edit your online profile, or cancel your account (and we certainly hope we don't have to explain how to accomplish that).

If you find yourself unclear on any of the billing functions or want to know more about how America Online charges you, open the Get Answers to Billing Questions item in the Accounts & Billing area. It provides answers to the most commonly asked billing questions, such as how much AOL charges, where you may check your bill, which areas of AOL incur extra charges, how you may choose to pay for AOL, how you can tell how long you've been online this session, and how to obtain credit for disconnected sessions or bad downloads (see fig. 20.7).

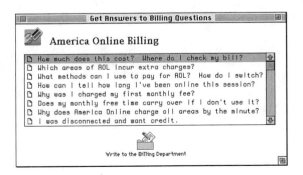

Fig. 20.7
Commonly asked
questions have
answers in AOL's
Accounts & Billing
area.

If your question remains unanswered after all of this, you may choose to write to AOL's billing staff by clicking on the Write to the Billing Department icon in this window. A staff member will retrieve the request for information and provide an E-mailed response, usually within eight business hours.

Help with Downloading

America Online's software makes downloading files to your hard drive a simple task, but at one time or another you might have questions about downloading. Perhaps your downloads are taking longer than their time estimates, or you are being disconnected during file transfers. If so, getting to the right place for assistance is a three-step task (though it takes less time to get from here to there than to describe it). First, use the keyword *Help* to reach the Member Services area, then click on the Members' Online Support icon, and, finally, click on the Downloading Help button there. The resulting window contains a comprehensive guide to downloading. There you'll find answers to some of the commonly asked questions about the files on America Online and downloading, including explanations about file compression, how to request credit for unusable downloads, and more (see fig. 20.8).

Fig. 20.8
The Downloading
Help window.

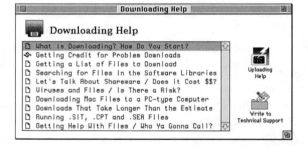

Tip

If a Macintosh file you've downloaded has a "zero" file size, it's probably corrupted. Download it again and request credit (type the keyword **Credit**) for the bad download.

You can also find help with AOL E-mail in the Members' Online Support window, plus help in working with the Internet gateway, modem and connect help, getting around on AOL, and more. (For more extensive information on the Internet gateway, see Chapter 17, "The Internet Connection." and Chapter 18, "The Low-Down on Internet Newsgroups.")

If you are having difficulties with any of these subjects, we encourage you to explore these areas for possible solutions before writing to the AOL staff for answers. A full 95% of members' questions to AOL's support staff could have been answered without a call or without waiting for an E-mailed answer by simply reading this section of AOL. (And remember, it's free of connect charges!)

Resuming a File Download

Once you've been disconnected during a file download, all is not usually lost. You can usually reconnect to AOL and resume the file download at the point where you were disconnected.

To do this, first check your Download Manager to verify that the file is still listed there. Pull down the File menu and select the Download Manager option (see fig. 20.9).

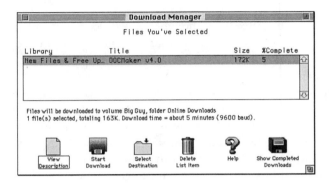

Fig. 20.9
The AOL Download Manager.

If the partially downloaded file is present, reconnect to America Online, perhaps using a different access number, and click on the Start Download button in the Download Manager window. The file should resume transferring in a few seconds.

In order to resume a download successfully, you must not throw away or move the file that represents your partially completed download. This file is usually located in the Online Downloads folder for Mac users, or the C:\WAOL\DOWNLOAD directory for Windows users. On the Mac, this partial file has the same name as the file you are downloading, and its icon shows a torn or jagged edge to indicate that it's incomplete.

If you intentionally or inadvertently discarded this file, the partially completed download is still listed in the Download Manager, and you will not be able to resume the download using the Download Manager. Simply select the item in the Download Manager list, and then click the Delete List Item icon to remove the entry from the Download Manager's list of files.

VI

Online Productivity

Tech Help Live

Keyword: CSlive

When text files don't give you the assistance you need, interact with a live AOL representative about your problem on Tech Live. The Tech Live Auditorium is open from 9AM to 2AM Eastern time, Monday through Friday, and 12 noon to 9PM Saturday and Sunday. Here, you can get live help from AOL's experienced Customer Relations staff in the free Members' Online Support area of America Online.

When you seek interactive help, though, you will see several information screens describing AOL's live technical service when you opt to enter the Tech Live area (see fig. 20.10). These information screens will offer to take you to the Members' Online Support area and other parts of AOL's member's support services, where you may review a large collection of information that may very well offer the answer to your question or problem. The support staff collected some of the most frequently asked questions and answers and compiled them into these text documents. Save yourself some time by looking for a possible solution here, because you otherwise need to wait your turn when entering the live help auditorium (and it can get a bit crowded in there sometimes).

Fig. 20.10
The Tech Help
Live area.

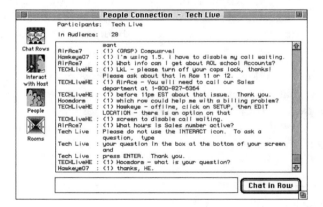

Parental Chat Controls

As any concerned parent, you may want to restrict the access of your child to certain areas of America Online. That's the purpose of Parental Chat Controls. This feature permits the original account holder (the screen name created when you first established your AOL account) to block access by users of other screen names on your AOL account to certain areas and features on America Online (see fig. 20.11).

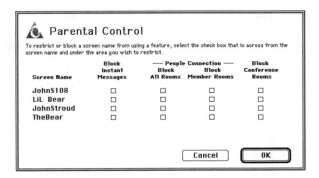

Fig. 20.11
The Parental
Control window.

Parental Control can be activated simply by selecting that command from the Members menu while you're logged on with your master account name (that's the name that's listed first among your list of available accounts on the main window of your AOL software). It's also available by clicking on the icon that appears to the left of most chat room windows. But the best route to selecting Parental Control is free—just click on the Account Security icon after entering the free Member Services area.

You can establish controls for just one or all screen names on your account. Once Parental Control is set for a particular screen name, it is in force every time that screen name logs on. Changes to Parental Control settings can be made by the master account holder at any time.

While you are logged on with your master screen name, you can activate one or more of the following Parental Control features:

- *Block Instant Messages.* Turns off Instant Messages—the immediate, one-to-one communications that can only be viewed by you and the receiver.

- *Block All Rooms.* Blocks access to the People Connection—the live, interactive chat area of America Online, but not including chat rooms in the Computing & Software areas.

- *Block Member Rooms.* Only blocks access to the member-created rooms within the People Connection. Other People Connection rooms, such as the Lobby, Romance Connection, and so on, are still accessible when this Parental Control feature is activated.

- *Block Conference Rooms.* Blocks access to the more focused rooms found around various departments on America Online, such as the classrooms in Learning & Reference, the technical forums in Computing & Software, and the NeverWinter Nights role-playing game in Games & Entertainment. It does not affect access to rooms in the People Connection.

VI

Online Productivity

Easy Troubleshooting Guide

In this section, we cover some common problems you might encounter during your online visits. Maybe you upgraded your modem and now AOL won't connect, or maybe you didn't change anything and you are unable to make the connection for no apparent reason. Perhaps you are able to get online, but not for long periods without being disconnected. We try to provide some insights to help you if you ever face these troubles, as there are often some simple things to check and adjust before you call the AOL support staff.

Setting Up a New Modem

Technology is no longer creeping up on us—it is approaching at the speed of a runaway train! Modems are becoming more complex and faster all the time. As modems become faster, connecting at the same slower speeds to which we are accustomed becomes an exercise in learning complicated modem commands.

Thank goodness someone out there had a sense of fair play, though, as most of the commands seem to have remained the same throughout the evolution of today's blazingly fast modems.

The first place to look for help in setting up a new modem is in the offline Help window, found under the Apple menu. You can also press ⌘-/ (Ctrl+/ for Windows users) to bring up the offline Help screen (see fig. 20.12).

Fig. 20.12
The AOL Help screen (the Mac version).

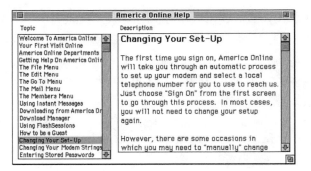

Another, and little known, help resource is AOL's own Technical Support BBS, which you can call with any of the numerous terminal program or telecommunications packages available for your computer. The America Online BBS supports modem speeds of up to 14,400 baud and is available 24 hours a day. You can find local access numbers, modem strings, and other connecting and troubleshooting information. The BBS number is toll-free: 1-800-827-5808.

The Technical Support BBS is not a part of the America Online service, so you won't need your screen name(s) or other account information when calling. The information on this BBS is provided to help you only with problems connecting to America Online and using the AOL software.

The communications program you use, such as ZTerm for the Mac or Windows Terminal, should be set to use 8 data bits, 1 stop bit, and no parity. If you're using a Macintosh terminal program that can display ANSI graphics, select Yes when asked. If you are unsure or are using a Windows Terminal, choose No when asked if you can display ANSI graphics. If you aren't certain how to use these programs, check your instruction manuals very carefully. They aren't as intuitive as AOL's graphical software.

If you can get onto the America Online service, you can also get detailed modem assistance from the Members' Online Support area by clicking on the Technical Help icon on the right side of the Support window. Much of the information found here is the same as on the AOL BBS—modem setting strings, connecting tips, and some basic troubleshooting tips (see fig. 20.13).

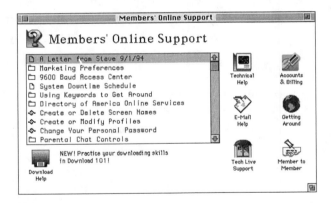

Fig. 20.13
AOL's free modem help available online in the Members' Online Support area.

If you have a modem that isn't listed in the Setup box of your America Online software, you'll may find a modem driver for that make and model available for download in this area. At the very least, you'll find advice on how to customize the existing profiles to work better with your modem.

Handling Connection Problems

The America Online network is one of the most reliable of today's large computer networks. It handles millions of connections every weekday, not only for connecting to America Online, but to other computers used throughout the country and overseas.

VI

Online Productivity

Because the amount of information being carried on computer networks is growing every day, and more people are traveling the information superhighway, you may occasionally be confronted with delays when attempting to sign on to America Online. In these cases the AOL software simply tells you that the circuits connecting to its host are busy, or that its own resources are busy and unavailable to additional users.

Of course, you usually won't get a message to the effect, "Sorry folks, we're busy. Call back later." Instead you might see such messages as:

```
All phone lines to America Online are currently busy. Please wait a
few minutes and try again.
Your local access number is not answering. Verify the access number
and try again.
We are unable to connect to America Online through your selected
access number.
```

Sometimes the message simply states that a "timeout" has occurred, meaning that your local carrier was not able to get a connection with America Online's host computer quickly enough. If this is true, take a breather and try again in a few minutes. If, however, you feel that the difficulty you are experiencing is not related to the amount of network traffic, you can try the two simple remedies that follow.

First, back in Chapter 4, "America Online on the Road," we explained how you can look for other local access numbers to connect to AOL. You see, sometimes a local connection point becomes congested, like a traffic jam at an intersection, even though the national network still has plenty of "room on the road." If this is true, trying a different access number may provide you some relief.

Are you trying to connect to America Online during the day? If so, you need to know that daytime hours are the busiest for the computer network, but not necessarily for America Online. AOL's busiest hours are from 6PM to midnight. For this reason, difficulty connecting during the day can often be overcome with a different access number.

Note

America Online will usually shut down the service once or twice a week for two to four hours early in the morning to install system upgrades or to conduct routine maintenance and repair work on the host computer system. Usually you'll get a message screen announcing that the service is temporarily shut down when logging on during this period, along with the time when service is expected to be restored. Sometimes you won't. But if you cannot get past the Connecting to America Online screen when logging on, the best thing to do is wait an hour or two and try again.

What to Do If You Become Disconnected

Suppose that you have connected to America Online, but are getting disconnected (or "bumped") right after you've seen the Welcome screen and heard the friendly welcome that greets you with every sign-on. What can you do then?

> **Note**
>
> Do you have call waiting? Be sure to disable it before you connect to AOL (use the setting in your modem Setup box). If a call comes while you're connected, you can be disconnected.

Well, first of all, think about any changes to your local setup you may have made recently. Did you add a new modem? Did you change your modem setting strings? Sometimes the factory setting of modems can actually work to prevent reliable connections, so be sure to check the modem settings database area described earlier. If you can't find the information you want there, you might want to review the manual that came with your new modem, or contact the manufacturer's technical support people for advice.

Are all your cables firmly in place? A loose modem cable can mimic a noisy telephone line, as can a loose telephone cord. Do you have regular telephones sharing the same line as your modem? Some of these devices can cause interference with your data transmissions. Try temporarily disconnecting those phones to see if it improves your connection.

Also, there are a number of variables not within your control that can cause the system to appear slow at your end, or even disconnect you. If you have answering machines or cordless telephones connected to your telephone line, you should disable or disconnect them, because they can also create line noise.

Another common cause of problems is the utilities that many of you add to your systems, such as those little programs known as CDEVs, INITs, or Extensions on a Macintosh. Each of these usually adds an icon that appears when you start up your Macintosh or start up Windows on your PC. You may want to try disabling all such utilities. If your problem goes away, try to put them back one at a time until you find the culprit. For more information about how CDEVs and INITs affect your system, visit the Macintosh Operating Systems Forum on AOL Macintosh. PC users can visit the DOS Forum or Windows Forum, as appropriate.

Some Macintosh users have attempted to download files in the background by using programs such as AOL Aid or Window To Back. While AOL does not block the use of such utilities, it does not support them either. You will see

VI

Online Productivity

more disconnected sessions and slower host response when attempting to download in the background. The host software is simply not designed for this type of multitasking.

The bottom line on disconnected sessions is that America Online wants your online experience to be enjoyable. If you feel your online time has grown much longer because of slow performance, or you've been unable to get a successful file transfer to your computer, America Online provides you with adjustments to your bill. Use the keyword *Credit* to request a billing adjustment if you are disconnected during a download and are unable to recover, or if a file you've downloaded seems to be corrupted. You'll need to supply information about the file and what time you were downloading, as well as the access number you used to connect to AOL. The support staff will check to make sure any trouble is resolved if there is something which needs adjustment or repair.

How to Handle a System Crash

The least favorite thing in your life while using your computer is likely a system crash. Although they come in a variety of flavors, most system crashes taste pretty bad.

If you experience a system error while connected to America Online, turn off your modem. This will disconnect you from America Online before much bad data can be sent to AOL, which can happen during some types of crashes. A data storm, or random data, sent in AOL's direction might confuse the host into not recognizing that you have left and prevent you from signing on again after you have restarted your computer. This does not happen often, but it can be quite annoying to see a message stating that you can't sign on because you are already using AOL. If a simple application error occurred, and if that application was not AOL, you may be able to return to AOL long enough to log off. Then reboot your computer.

Advice for Macintosh Users

If the error was with the AOL application or occurred while AOL was the frontmost application, chances are you cannot resume or save any work that may have been in progress. In this case, you should simply select the Restart button in the error message. If you are a System 7 user—and who isn't these days?—look in your Trash for a Rescued Items folder after your machine restarts. If any of your open applications were using temporary files, you may be able to recover some or all the data you lost from this folder.

If you cannot get the Restart button in the bomb window to work, try a force quit, holding down the ⌘-Option-Escape keys. If that doesn't free the frozen application, read your Macintosh manual for instructions on activating the reset switch (on some models it's down via keyboard command) to get your Mac to reboot as painlessly as possible.

Advice for Windows Users

If your America Online Windows software crashes with a General Protection Fault error, try to exit the AOL application, then exit any other active applications after saving any documents that are being worked on, and then exit Windows. If you cannot exit Windows or if attempts to resume working in Windows after restarting do not succeed, turn off your computer, and then turn it on again.

If you experience a total system lockup, sometimes you can exit a crashing application by pressing Ctrl+Alt+Delete (all at the same time). Your next step is to exit Windows and restart. If you cannot exit from a locked application, or Windows is not running in a stable manner, turn off your computer and turn it on again.

When you power up your computer, run the CHKDSK /F command in MS-DOS before restarting Windows. This function allows MS-DOS to check the integrity of your hard drive in case the drive's directory was damaged as a result of the crash.

Reinstalling America Online

What happens if you experience repeated and confusing errors, such as random data in the window where your screen names appear, or your modem lights up like the Fourth of July but never dials or gives an error message? If this is happening to you, it's possible something in your AOL's files that store your individual data has become corrupted, especially if you had a recent bout with system crashes.

If you suspect that your America Online software is corrupt, you should reinstall your AOL software. Doing this is a fairly simple task. You can do this in one of two ways—perform a clean installation, where you start your AOL connection from scratch, or perform an update installation, where you throw away only those files you suspect of being corrupted. We recommend the clean installation as the best and easiest method of isolating intermittent problems with the AOL software.

To perform a clean installation on a Macintosh, move your existing America Online software to a folder where it can rest undisturbed by the upcoming installation. Then insert your original AOL software diskette into your floppy drive and launch the installer found on the disk. Select a folder or directory

Tip

For Mac Users: Before reinstalling your AOL software, save or delete all incoming mail received during a FlashSession (in the Read Incoming Mail list in the Mail menu).

VI

Online Productivity

that will not overwrite your existing AOL software and click the Install button. For complete information on installing your AOL software, read Chapter 1, "Getting Started on America Online."

To perform a clean installation on your Windows-equipped PC, run the program setup in the normal way, just as we described in Chapter 1, "Getting Started on America Online." When the installer program detects another installed copy of America Online's software around, the America Online Setup screen will appear, telling you that `You have a previous copy of America Online`. Normally, the settings in the other copy of the software will be transferred to the new version. But if you delete the directory name shown at the bottom of the Setup screen, a fresh installation will take place, none of your previous settings will be retained, and there will be no risk of copying damaged file resources to your new software.

Once your software has been installed, launch the newly installed program and begin the sign-on process we described in Chapter 1. When you see the sign-on screen that requests you to enter a Certificate Number and Password, type in any one of the screen names you use in the Certificate Number box and your regular password for that screen name in the Password box. Your connection is then established and all your account information is transferred to the new software.

If the problems that caused you to reinstall your software in the first place do not recur, you can continue setting your preferences and options in your freshly installed software. For all the information about configuring your AOL software to your taste, see Chapter 2, "Using Your America Online Macintosh Software," or Chapter 3, "Using Your America Online Windows Software."

If, however, the original symptoms persist, the problem probably isn't caused by corrupt AOL software. You can discard the new software and restore the original software to retain your old E-mail and other settings—or to be safe, you may prefer to just continue working with the new copy of your AOL software and discard the older version.

From Here...

You'll most likely be able to easily resolve any bumps in the road by following the suggestions we've offered in this chapter. If you cannot remedy your problems, but you can get online, write to Customer Service from the free Members' Online Support area for further help. If you have a problem with a particular downloaded file, write to the author of the file (usually named in the file's instructions) or to the staff of the forum from which you obtained it.

AOL staff and members are some of the most cheerful and helpful people you will ever encounter. Don't hesitate to call on their collective expertise!

For more information about:

- Installing America Online software, see Chapter 1, "Getting Started on America Online."

- Downloading and uploading files, see Chapter 5, "Finding Your Way around America Online," and Chapter 12, "How to Find Software."

- Sending and receiving E-mail, see Chapter 7, "Communicating with Others."

- Changing your modem setup, see Chapter 1, "Getting Started on America Online," Chapter 2, "Using Your America Online Macintosh Software," Chapter 3, "Using Your America Online Windows Software," and Chapter 4, "America Online on the Road."

VI

Online Productivity

Appendixes

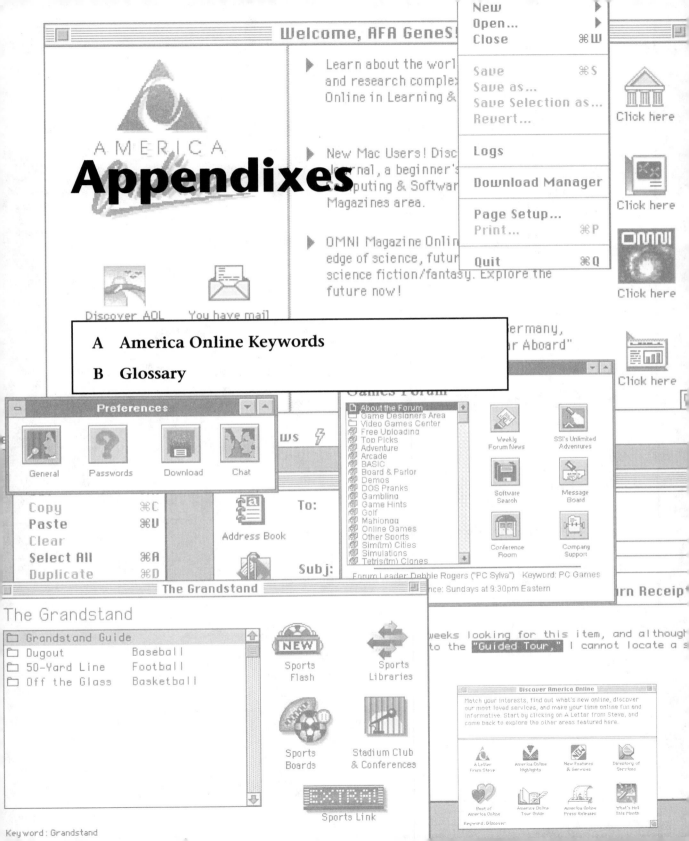

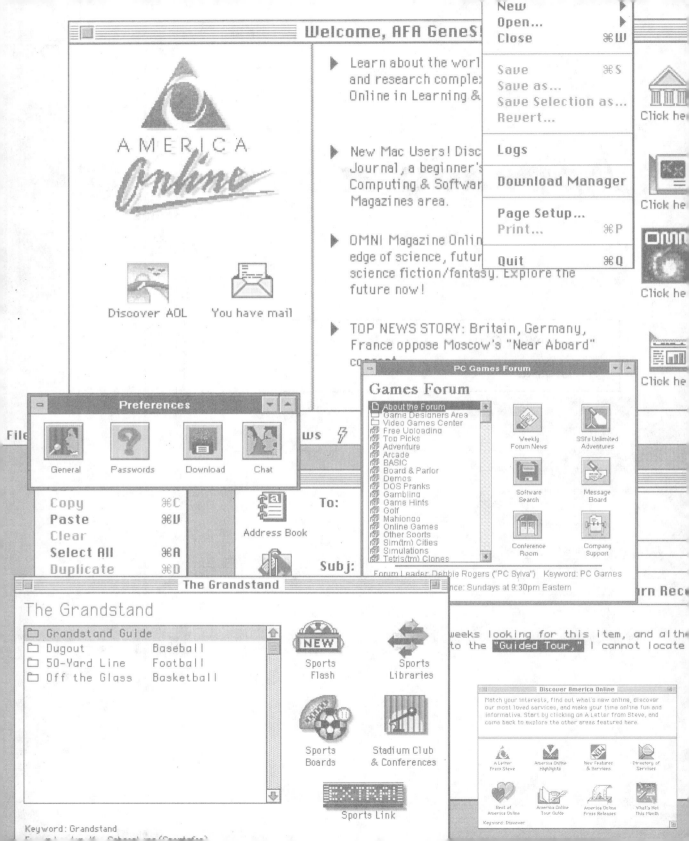

Welcome, AFA GeneS!

▶ Learn about the worl
and research complex
Online in Learning &

▶ New Mac Users! Disc
Journal, a beginner's
Computing & Softwar
Magazines area.

▶ OMNI Magazine Onlin
edge of science, futur
science fiction/fantasy. Explore the
future now!

▶ TOP NEWS STORY: Britain, Germany,
France oppose Moscow's "Near Aboard"

AMERICA
Online

Discover AOL   You have mail

Menu:
New ▶
Open... ▶
Close   ⌘W

Save   ⌘S
Save as...
Save Selection as...
Revert...

Logs

Download Manager

Page Setup...
Print...   ⌘P

Quit   ⌘Q

Click he
Click he
Click he
Click he
Click he

Preferences

General   Passwords   Download   Chat

File   ws ⚡

Copy   ⌘C
Paste   ⌘V
Clear
Select All   ⌘A
Duplicate   ⌘D

To:

Address Book

Subj:

PC Games Forum

Games Forum

About the Forum
Game Designers Area
Video Games Center
Free Uploading
Top Picks
Adventure
Arcade
BASIC
Board & Parlor
Demos
DOS Pranks
Gambling
Game Hints
Golf
Mahjongg
Online Games
Other Sports
Sim(tm) Cities
Simulations
Tetris(tm) Clones

Weekly
Forum News

SSI's Unlimited
Adventures

Software
Search

Message
Board

Conference
Room

Company
Support

Forum Leader: Debbie Rogers ("PC Sylva")   Keyword: PC Games
ence: Sundays at 9:30pm Eastern

rn Rec

The Grandstand

The Grandstand

Grandstand Guide
Dugout   Baseball
50-Yard Line   Football
Off the Glass   Basketball

NEW
Sports
Flash

Sports
Libraries

Sports
Boards

Stadium Club
& Conferences

EXTRA!
Sports Link

weeks looking for this item, and alth
to the "Guided Tour," I cannot locate

Discover America Online

Match your interests, find out what's new online, discover
our most loved services, and make your time online fun and
informative. Start by clicking on A Letter from Steve, and
come back to explore the other areas featured here.

A Letter
From Steve

America Online
Highlights

New Features
& Services

Directory of
Services

Best of
America Online

America Online
Tour Guide

America Online
Press Releases

What's Hot
This Month

Keyword: Discover

Keyword: Grandstand

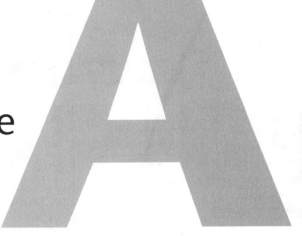

Appendix A

America Online Keywords

Keywords are shortcuts that enable you to move quickly from one area of America Online to another area or to a department. The keywords presented here are current as this book is published, but because services are frequently added and changed on America Online, keywords may change as well.

If you are using America Online for Macintosh, follow these steps to use keywords:

1. From anywhere on America Online, press ⌘-K or select Keyword from the Go To menu.

2. When the Keyword window appears, type the keyword of the department or area you want to go to, and choose GO.

If you are using America Online for Windows, follow these steps to use keywords:

1. From anywhere on America Online, press Ctrl+K or select Keyword from the Go To menu.

2. When the Keyword window appears, type the keyword of the department or area you want to go to, and choose GO.

Tip
If the keyword for the area you want isn't listed in this appendix, just improvise. Enter a keyword for the name or topic of the area you're looking for. More than likely, if that area exists, you can find it this way.

Tip

If improvising a keyword fails to bring a result, click on the Search button in the Keyword window, rather than on the Go button, to bring up a list of possible matches to the keyword you typed.

AOL General Keywords

Forum	Keyword
9600 Baud Access Center	9600
Access Numbers Database	access
AOL Software Ordering	upgrade
AOL Press Releases	press
Cancel your account	cancel
Check your bill	billing
Credit for lost time online	credit
Customer Service Live	cslive
Discover America Online	discover
Gopher/WAIS (Internet)	gopher, wais
Guide Pager	guide pager
Help Online	help
Internet Center	internet
Newsgroups (Internet)	newsgroups
New Mail System Features	newmail
Parental Control	parental control
Prodigy Refugees Forum	prodigy
Sign on a friend and get free time	friend
What's hot online this month	hot

Games and Entertainment Keywords

Area	Keyword
AD&D Neverwinter Nights	oadd, neverwinter, nwn, add
Atlantic Monthly Online	atlantic, atlantic monthly, atlantic online
Adventures By Mail	Adventures By Mail, ABM, Quest, Monster Island

Area	Keyword
Book Bestsellers	books
Broderbund's Darts	darts
Broderbund's MasterWord	mw, mword, word library
Bulls and Bears	bulls and bears
Cartoons	cartoons, yourtoons
Classifieds	classifieds
Compute Magazine Online	compute, compute magazine
Court TV	court tv, courtroom television
Critic's Choice	critics
Disney Adventures Magazine	disney, disney adventures
Free-Form Gaming Forum	rdi, ffgf
Gamebase(sm)	gamebase
Gaming Company Support	gcs
Gaming Information Exchange	gix
The Geraldo Show	geraldo
Grandstand	grandstand
Hatrack	hatrack
Hollywood Online	hollywood
Horoscopes	horoscopes
Improv "SHTICKS" Forum	improv
Lapub	lapub
Lifetime Television	lifetime, lifetime television, lifetime tv
MasterWord	mw, mword, word library (DOS and Windows users only)
Movie Reviews & News	movies
Music News & Forums	music
NBC Online	nbc

(continues)

Appendixes

Games and Entertainment Keywords   (Continued)

Area	Keyword
Neverwinter	oadd, ad&d, nwn, add
Omni Magazine Online	omni, omni magazine
Online Gaming Forums	gaming, ogf
Phantasy Guild	guild, rpg, phantasy guild
Play by Mail	pbm, play by mail
The Ricki Lake Show	ricki lake
RPGA Network—F.O.G.	rpga, fog
RockLink	rocklink
Role-Playing Games Forum	rpg
Scifi Channel	scifi channel
Showbiz Notes	entertainment
SOL III Play-by-Mail Game	sol iii
Television	television, tv
Trivia Club/Quiz	trivia

Learning & Reference Keywords

Forum	Keyword
1492: An Ongoing Voyage	library
Academic Assistance Center	homework, tutoring
Academic Research Service	research
Achievement TV	achievement tv
Adult Literacy Forum	read
Afterwards Coffeehouse	afterwards, arts
Apple Classrooms of Tomorrow	acot
AskEric Online	eric, accesseric, askeric

Forum	Keyword
Assoc. for Sup. & Curric. Dev. (ASCD)	ascd, curriculum
Barrons Booknotes	booknotes, Barrons
Bull Moose Tavern	bull moose
The Capital Connection	debate, politics
Career Center	career, careers
Cartoon Network	cartoon network
CNN Newsroom Online	cnn, cnn newsroom
College Board	college, cb, college board
CSPAN Online	cspan
Disney Adventures Magazine	disney, disney adventures
Diplomats in the Classroom	diplomats
Educational TV & Radio	kidsnet
Electronic Schoolhouse	esh, schoolhouse
Electronic University Center	university
Electronic University Network	eun
Encyclopedia	encyclopedia, comptons
Exam Prep Center	exam prep
Giftedness Forum	gifted, mensa
Interactive Education Services	ies, courses, classes
International Correspondence Schools	ics
International House	international
Job Listings Database	jobs
KIDSNET	kidsnet
Kids Only Online	kool, kids
Kim Komando: Komputer Tutor	komando
Library of Congress Online	library, loc, soviet, vatican

(continues)

Learning & Reference Keywords   (Continued)

Forum	Keyword
The Multimedia Exchange	multimedia
Nat'l Council of Teachers of English	ncte
National Education Association	nea public
National Geographic Online	geographic, ngs, national geographic
National Public Radio Outreach	npr, totn
Online Research Service (Academic Ass't Cnt)	tutoring
Parents' Information Network	parent, pin
Registration Center (IES)	register
Saturday Review Online	saturday review, sat review, sro, literature, reading, society, theater, theatre
Scholastic Network/Scholastic Forum	scholastic
School Networking Forum	cosn
Smithsonian Online	smithsonian
Student Access Online/ The Princeton Review	student
Study Skills Service	study
Substance Abuse Forum	substance abuse, prevention
Summer Semester Classes	register
Teachers' Forum	ttalk
Teachers' Information Network	tin, teacher, teachers
Teacher Pager	teacher pager
Teachers' Newsstand	tnews
TERC LabNet	labnet

Lifestyles & Interests Keywords

Forum	Keyword
American Dialogue	dialogue
Astronomy Club	astronomy
Aviation Club	aviation
Baby Boomers Club	baby boomers
Better Health & Medical Forum	health
Bicycling Magazine	bicycling, bicycling magazine, bicmag, mountain bike
Bicycle Network	bikenet, bicycle
Chicago Online	chicago
Chicago Online Ticketmaster	ticketmaster
Disabilities Forum	disabilities
Dolby Audio/Video Forum	dolby
Electronics Forum	electronics
Environmental Forum	lifestyles
Ethics and Religion Forum	religion
Emergency Response Club	emergency
The Exchange	exchange
Gadget Guru Electronics Forum	electronics
Gay and Lesbian Forum	gay, lesbian, gicf
Geneaology Club	genealogy
Grandstand	grandstand
Hatrack River Town Meeting	orson scott card, hatrack
Ham Radio Club	ham radio
Homeowner's Forum	home, homeowner, homeowners, UHA
Inside Technology	inside technology
Issues in Mental Health Forum	imh

(continues)

Appendixes

Lifestyles & Interests Keywords   (Continued)

Forum	Keyword
IYM Software Review	iym
Kodak Photography Forum	kodak
Mercury Center	mercury
Military and Vets Club	military
Microsoft Knowledge Base	microsoft
NAMI Forum (Nat'l Alliance for the Mentally Ill)	nami
LaPub	lapub
Mercury Center	mercury, mercury center, mc news, mc classified, mc entertainment, mc library, mc business, mc talk, mc living, mc sports
Military and Vets Club	military
National Space Society	nss, space
National Alliance of Mentally Ill	health, nami
Network Earth	network earth
Pet Care Club	pet care
Photography Forum	photography, kodak
Real Estate Online	real estate, mls
Rocklink	rocklink
Science Fiction and Fantasy Club	sci fi
Science Fiction Forum	science fiction, asimov, analog
Scuba Club	scuba
SeniorNet	seniornet
Sports Link	sports
Starfleet Academy	academy
Star Trek Club	star trek
Student Access Online/ Princeton Review	student

Forum	Keyword
Trivia Club	trivia
Warner/Reprise Records Online	warner, warner music, reprise
Wine & Dine Online	wine, dine, restaurant, beer
Writers Club	writers

News & Finance Keywords

Forum	Keyword
Atlantic Monthly Online	atlantic, atlantic monthly, atlantic online
Bulls and Bears	bullsandbears, bulls and bears
Business/Finance	business
Business News	business news
Chicago Online	chicago, chicago online, col
Chicago Tribune Ads	trib ads
Classifieds Online	classifieds, classified, classifieds online
Color Weather Maps	color weather maps, weather maps
Columnists & Features Online	columnists, columns, features
Company Profiles (Hoover's)	company
Cowles/SIMBA Media	cowles, simba, cowlessimba
CSPAN Online	cspan
Editorial Cartoons	keefe
Political Information, Discussion, & Debate	captital, politics, debate
Information Network	media information
Entertainment	entertainment, games, rec center, recreation
The Exchange	exchange
Fax/Paper Mail	fax, usmail, paper mail

(continues)

News & Finance Keywords (Continued)

Forum	Keyword
Federal Careers	career
The Independent Traveler	traveler
Internet Mail Gateway	internet
Mercury Center	mercury, mercury center, san jose
Advertising	mc ads
Bay Area Living	mc living
Business & Technology	mc business
News	mc news
Michigan Governors Forum	michigan
Microsoft Business Center	business center, small business, msbc, msbiz
Morningstar Mutual Funds	morningstar, mutual funds, mutual fund, funds, fund
Movies	movie reviews, movies
News/Finance	finance, news, news room, news&finance
NewsBytes	newsbytes
NewsLink	headlines, newslink, our world, topnews
News Search	newswatch
Other Sports	tennis, golf, boxing
PC Classifieds	pcclassifieds
Reuters News	topnews, headlines, ourworld, newslink
RockLink	rocklink
Sports	sports talk
Sportslink	sports, sportlink, sports club
Sports News	sports news
Strategies for Business	businessknowhow
StockLink	portfolio, stocklink, stocks, stock
Stock Marketing Timing and Charts	stock timing
Talent Bank	career

Forum	Keyword
Tax Forum	tax
Television	television, tv
TIME Online	TIME
Today's News and Weather	top news
White House Forum	white house, clinton
World Weather	weather

Newsstand Keywords

Forum	Keyword
The Atlantic Monthly	atlantic
Backpacker Magazine	backpacker, outdoor gear, vacations, trailguides, conservation, ecotourism, hiker, hiking, trails, wilderness, camping, backcountry
Bicycling Magazine	bicycling, bicyclingmagazine, bicmag, mountain bike
Car and Driver Magazine	car and driver, racing, driving
Chicago Tribune	tribune
Columnists & Features	columnists
COMPUTE Magazine	compute
Consumer Reports	consumer
Cowles/SIMBA Media Info	cowles, simba, cowlessimba
Disney Adventures Magazine	disney
Flying Magazine	flying, flying mag, flying magazine
Home Office Computing	home office
Home PC Magazine	homepc
MacHome Journal	machome
MacTech Magazine	mactech

(continues)

Appendixes

Newsstand Keywords (Continued)

Forum	Keyword
Macworld Magazine	macworld
Mobile Office Online	mobile, portable, portable computing
National Geographic	geographic, ngs
The New Republic	tnr, the new republic
Omni Magazine	omni
PC Novice and PC Today Online	pc novice
PC World Magazine	pc world
Popular Photography	cameras, photos, photography
Road and Track	cars, autos, road, road and track
San Jose Mercury News	mercury, san jose
Saturday Review Online	saturday review, sat review, sro, literature, reading, society, theater, theatre
Smithsonian Online	smithsonian
Museum of American Art	nmaa
Stereo Review Online	stereo review, stereo, audio, home theater
TIME Magazine Online	time
Windows Magazine	windows magazine, windows mag
Wired Magazine	wired
Worth Magazine	worth

People Connection Keywords

Forum	Keyword
Advice & Tips	tips
Ask the Doctor	health
Cartoons	cartoons, yourtoons
Celebrity Cookbook	celebrity cookbook, cookbook

Forum	Keyword
Center Stage	centerstage, auditorium, shows
Classifieds	classifieds
CompuToon	computoon
Court TV	lawyer
The Crystal Ball	crystal ball, tarot
The Gallery	gallery
Games Parlor	parlor
LaPub	lapub
Online Tonight	online tonight
People Connection (Lobby)	chat, people connection, pc, people, talk
PC Studio	pcstudio
Romance Connection chat room	dating, romance
Quantum Que	que
Teen Scene	teen, teens, teen scene
Tammy's Tips	tips
Trivia Club	trivia, trivia club
Wine & Dine Online	wine, restaurant, beer

Travel & Shopping Keywords

Forum	Keyword
American Airlines	eaasy sabre, sabre, easy sabre
Autovantage	auto
Comp-U-Store Online	compustore
Computer Express	computer express
Eaasy Sabre	sabre, american airlines, eaasy sabre

(continues)

Travel & Shopping Keywords (Continued)

Forum	Keyword
Entertainment	entertainment, games&entertainment
Flower Shop	flower shop
Home Shopping	shopping, the mall, stores
Kim Komando's Komputer Tutor	komando, komputer tutor, commando
The Mall/Shopping	mall, store, stores, shopping&travel
Travel	travel
Independent Traveler	traveler

Computing & Software Keywords

Online Area	Keyword
Computing Forums	forums
File Searcher	quickfinder, file search
Hardware	hardware
Programming (developing)	programming
Software Center	software

Computing News and Reference Area Keywords

Online Area	Keyword
Crossman's Computer America	crossman
Cyberlaw/Cyberlex	cyberlaw
Dictionary of Computer Terms	computing (then go to News and Reference)
Inside Technology	inside technology
IYM Software Review	iym
Local Newspapers	newspapers

Online Area	Keyword
Microsoft Knowledge Base	microsoft
New Product Information	new product
NewsBytes	newsbytes
PC Catalog	pc catalog

Mutual Interest Area Keywords

Forum	Keyword

General Forums

BBS Corner	bbs, bbs corners
Beginners	abf, beginners, newlinks
Downloading Hall of Fame	hall of fame
Forum Auditorium	rotundas
Mac Bible/Peachpit	mac bibles
Mac Shareware 500	mac 500
PC AO	pcforums (then select PC Forums)
Personal Digital Assistant Forum	pda, newton, palmtop
Rotunda	rotunda
Software Center	computing, software center
User Group Forum	ugc, ugf, user groups
Windows Shareware 500	windows 500

PC Forums

Applications	pap, pc applications
DOS	dos
DTP Resource Center	desktop publishing, DTP
DeskMate	des, deskmate

(continues)

Mutual Interest Area Keywords (Continued)	
Forum	**Keyword**
PC Forums	
Flight Simulator Resource	flight simulations, flight sims, FSRC, flight
Games	pgm, pc games
Graphics	pgr, pc graphics
Hardware	phw, pc hardware
Music/Sound	pmu, pc music
PC World Magazine	pc world
Programming	pdv, pc development
Telecom	ptc, pc telecom
Windows	win, windows
Macintosh Forums	
Business	mbs, macbusiness
Communications	mcm, maccommunication
Desktop Publishing/WP	mdp, macdesktop
Development	mdv, macdevelopment
Education	med, maceducation
Games & Entertainment	mgm, macgame
Graphic Art & CAD	mgr, macgraphics
Hardware	mhw, machardware
HyperCard	mhc, machypercard
Mac Bible/Peachpit	mac bible, forums
Macworld Expo Center	macworld expo
Macworld Magazine	macworld, forums
Multimedia Forum	mmm
Music & Sound	mms, macmusic

Forum	Keyword
NAQP	naqp, quick printers
Operating Systems	mos, system 7
PDA Forum	pda, palmtop, newton
User Groups	user groups
Utilities	mut, macutilities

Other Areas of Interest in Computing & Software

Forum	Keyword
Craig Crossman's Computer America	computer america
CyberLaw, Cyberlex	cyberlaw
Kim Komando's Komputer Tutor	komando, commando, komputer tutor
Mac Shareware 500	mac500
MacWorld Magazine	macworld
PC World Magazine	pcworld

Note

You can access the areas in the following table by clicking on the Company Support or Special Interest items of the forums to which these keywords take you.

Company Support & Special Interest Groups Keywords

Forum	Keyword
Adult Literacy	aed, med
Applescript SIG	applescript
Architects, Engineers and Construction SIG	AECSIG

(continues)

Company Support & Special Interest Groups Keywords (Continued)	
Forum	**Keyword**
APDA	mdv
Advertising	mdp
Apple Classrooms of Tomorrow	med
Apple Professional Exchange (APX)	mcm
AppleNet BBS	acm
The Awakened Eye	mcm
BBS SysOps Club	acm
Bering Bridge Project	aed, med
Berkeley Macintosh User Group	ugf
Boston Computer Society	bcs
CP/M & MS-DOS SIG	adv
Education Connection	aed, med
Electronic Frontier Foundation	eff
Game Designers SIG	adv, mdv, agm
Groupware	mcm, mdv
HyperStudio Network	aed, apr, ams, apr
Industrial Computing Society	mbs
Legal SIG	acm, mcm, mdp
MacApp Developers Association	mada
MacSciTech	mbs
Music Programmers SIG	mms, mdv
National Home & School MUG	med
Nomadic Computing Discussion	mcm
PhotoShop	mgr

Appendixes

Forum	Keyword
PowerDraw	mgr
Powershift	mms
Programmer U	adv, mdv, pdv
Psion	psion
Science and Engineering Service Bureau	mdp
Small Business	mbs
Supercard	mhc
TeleFinder	telefinder
Video SIG	video sig, mgr, mhw, mmm
Virus Information Center	virus, mut
XCMD Developers	mdv, mhc
XNet SIG	mhc

Industry Connection Keywords

Forum	Keyword
Aatrix Software, Inc.	aatrix
Abbatte Video	abbattevideo, videotoolkit
Access Software	access software, links
Acer America Corporation	acer
Activision	activision
Advanced Gravis	gravis, advancedgravis
Advanced Software, Inc.	advanced
Auto*des*sys, Inc.	ads, formz
Affinity Microsystems	affinity

(continues)

Industry Connection Keywords (Continued)	
Forum	**Keyword**
Aladdin Systems, Inc.	aladdin
Aldus Corporation	aldus
Alpha Software Corporation	alphatech, asctech, ascts
Altsys Corporation	altsys
Alysis Software	alysis
Akimbo Systems	fullwrite
Ambrosia Software	ambrosia
Animated Software	animatedsoftware
Another Company	anotherco
Apple Professional Developer's Association	APDA
Apogee Software	apogee
Ares Microdevelopment, Inc.	ares
Argosy	argosy
Ariel Publishing	ariel
Artifice, Inc.	artifice
Articulate Systems	asi, articulate
Asymetrix Corporation	asymetrix
Atticus Software	atticus
Avid DTV Group	avid, avidtv
Avocat Systems	avocat
Baseline Publishing	baseline
Baseview Products, Inc.	baseview
Bentley Systems, Inc.	mstation
Berkeley Systems	berksys, berksyswin
Bethesda Softwares	bethesda, bethesdasoftworks

Forum	Keyword
Beyond, Inc.	beyond
Bit Jugglers	bitjugglers
Bowers Development (AppMaker)	bowers, appmaker
Broderbund	broderbund
Bungie Software	bungie
Business Sense	businesssense
ByteWorks	byte, byteworks
Byte By Byte Corporation	bytebybyte
Caere Corporation	caere, caerecorporation
Callisto Corporation	callisto
Cardinal Technologies, Inc.	cardinal
Casa Blanca Works	casablanca
Casady & Greene	casady
CE Software	cesoftware
Central Point Software	centralpoint, cps
Claris	claris
Coda Music Tech	coda, cmt, codamusic
Compaq	compaq
Connectix	connectix
JLCooper Electronics	cooper, jlcooper
Company of Science and Art	cosa
Computer Peripherals, Inc.	cpi, computerperipherals
CoStar	costar
DacEasy, Inc.	daceasy
Dancing Rabbit Creations	dancingrabbit
DataPak Software	datapak

(continues)

Industry Connection Keywords (Continued)	
Forum	**Keyword**
Datawatch	datawatch
Davidson & Associates	davidson
Dayna Communications	dayna
DayStar Digital	daystar
Dell Computer Corporation	dell
Delrina Corporation	delrina
Delta Point	deltapoint
Delta Tao	deltatao
Deneba	deneba
Diamond Computer Systems	diamond
Digital Eclipse	digitaleclipse
Digital F/X	dfx, digitalf/x
Digital Tech	digitaltech
Digital Vision	digital
Direct Software	direct
Disney/Buena Vista Software	disneysoftware
Dreamworld	dreamworld
Dynaware USA	dynaware, dynawareusa
Dubl-Click Software, Inc.	dublclick
EBBS	ebbs
Edmark Technologies	edmark, kiddesk, penpal
Electric Image	electric
Electronic Courseware	ecs, electroniccourseware
Emigre Fonts	emigre
Expert Software, Inc.	expert
Farallon	farallon

Forum	Keyword
Fifth Generation	fifth
Focus Enhancements	focus, focusenhancements
FontBank	fontbank
Fractal Design	fractal, fractaldesign
Franklin Quest	franklin
FullWrite	fullwrite
Future Labs, Inc.	futurelabs, talkshow
Gateway 2000, Inc.	gateway, gateway2000, moo
GCC Technologies	gcc
General Magic	general magic
GeoWorks	geoworks
GIFConverter	gifconverter
Global Village Communication	global village, global, teleport
Graphisoft	graphisoft
Gryphon Software	gryphon, gryphonsoftware, moph
Global Software Support	gss
hDC Corporation	hdc, hdccorporation
Helios USA	helios, heliosusa
HSC Software	hscsoftware, kpt
IBVA Technologies	ibva, psychiclabs
Inline Design	inline
Insignia Solutions	insignia
Intel Corporation	intel, pentium
Intellimation	intellimation
InterCon Systems Corporation	intercon
Interplay	interplay

(continues)

Industry Connection Keywords (Continued)	
Forum	**Keyword**
Iomega Corporation	iomega
ISIS International	isis, isisinternational
Island Graphics Corporation	islandgraphics
IYM Software Review	iym, iymsoftwarereview
JPEGview	jpegview
Kensington Microware, Ltd.	kensington
Kent*Marsh	kentmarsh
Kiwi Software	kiwi
Koala: Featuring MacVision	macvision, koala
Language Systems	language sys
Leader Technologies	leader, leadertech, leadertechnologies
Leading Edge	leading edge
Letraset	letraset
LinksWare, Inc.	linksware
LucasArts Games	lucasarts
The Macintosh Bible/Peachpit Forum	macbible, peachpit, macintoshbible
MacroMedia, Inc.	macromedia, macromind
Mainstay	mainstay
Mallard Software	mallard
Manhattan Graphics	manhattangraphics, rsg
Market Master	market
Marketfield Software	marketfield
Martinsens Software	martinsen
Maxis	maxis
MECC	mecc
Meridian Data	meridian

Forum	Keyword
Metrowerks	metrowerks
Metz	metz
Micro Dynamics, Ltd.	micro dynamics
MicroFrontier, Ltd.	microfrontier
Micrografx, Inc.	mgx, micrografx
Micro J Systems, Inc.	micro j
MicroMat Computer Systems	micromat
MicroProse	microprose
Microseeds Publishing, Inc.	microseeds
Microsoft Knowledge Base	knowledgebase, microsoft
Mirror Technologies	mirror
MoraffWare	moraffware
Management Science Associates	msa
Mustang Software	mustang software, mustang
NeoLogic	neologic
New Era, Inc.	new era
New World Computing	newworld
Nikon Electronic Imaging	nikon
Niels and Associates	Niels, endnote
No Hands Software	nohands
Novell Desktop Systems	novell, digitalresearch, digitalresearchinc, dri
Now Software	now
Object Factory	object factory
Olduvai Software, Inc.	olduvai
ON Technology	on
Onyx Technology	onyx

(continues)

Industry Connection Keywords (Continued)	
Forum	**Keyword**
Opcode Systems, Inc.	opcode, opcodesystems
OptImage Interactive Services	optimage
Origin Systems	origin
Otter Solution	otter, ottersolution
PaceMark Technologies, Inc.	pacemark
Packer Software	packer
Palm Computing	palm, palm computing
Papyrus	papyrus
Passport Designs	passport
PC Catalog	pccatalog
Peachtree Software	peachtree
Personal Computer Peripherals	pcpc
Pixar	pixar
Pixel Resources	pixel, pixelresources
Playmation	playmation
Portfolio Systems, Inc.	dyno
Power Up Software	power up
Practical Peripherals, Inc.	ppi, practicalperipherals
PrairieSoft, Inc.	prairiesoft
Prograph International, Inc.	prograph, tghs
ProVUE Development	provue
Psion	psion
Qualitas	qualitas
Quark, Inc.	quark
Radius, Inc.	radius
Ray Dream	raydream, ray

Appendixes

Forum	Keyword
ResNova Software	resnova, resnovasoftware
Rockland Software	rockland, rocklandsoftware
Roger Wagner Publishing	rogerwagner
Salient Software	salient
Serius	serius
Shareware Solutions	sharewaresolutions
Shiva Corporation	shiva
Sierra On-Line	sierra
SoftArc	softarc
Softdisk Superscore	softdisk (PC platform only)
Softsync, Inc.	softsync
Software Creations	swc, softwarecreations
Software Toolworks	toolworks, softwaretoolworks
Sophisticated Circuits	sophcir
Spectrum HoloByte	spectrum
Specular International	specular
SSSi	sssi
Stac Electronics	stac
STF Technologies	stf, stftechnologies
Strata, Inc.	strata
Strategic Simulations	ssi, strategic
SuperMac	supermac
Synex	synex
Survivor Software	survivor, survivorsoftware
Symantec	symantec
Tactic Software	tactic, newera

(continues)

Industry Connection Keywords (Continued)	
Forum	**Keyword**
Technology Works	techworks
Teknosys Works	teknosys
Texas Instruments	ti, texasinstruments
Three-Sixty Software	threesixty
Thrustmaster	thrustmaster
Thunderware	thunderware
Tiger Direct, Inc.	tiger, tigerdirect
True Image Audio	tia, trueimageaudio, macspeakerz
T/Maker	tmaker
Tseng	tseng
Unlimited Adventures	ua, unlimitedadventures
Userland	userland
Videodiscovery	vdisc, videodisc, videodiscovery
Vertisoft	vertisoft
Viacom New Media	viacom, icom, icomsimulations
VIDI	vidi
Viewpoint DataLabs	viewpoint
Virtus Corporation	virtus, walkthrough
Visionary Software	visionary
The Voyager Company	voyager
Virtual Reality Labs, Inc.	vrli
Weigand Report	weigand
Westwood Studios	westwood
Wired Magazine	wired
WordPerfect Magazine	wpmag
WordPerfect Support Center	wordperfect

Forum	Keyword
Working Software	working
Wilson Windowware	www, windowware
Xceed Technology	xceed, micron
Xaos Tools	xaos, xaostools
Zedcor, Inc.	zedcor

Appendixes

Appendix B

Glossary

abbreviations   Abbreviations are often used while chatting in the People Connection and other chat rooms and when exchanging instant messages and E-mail. Examples include LOL (*laughing out loud*) and BRB (*be right back*). See also *shorthand* and *emoticons*.

access number   Usually a local telephone number that your modem calls to gain access to America Online's main computer. Use the keyword *Access* while online to locate numbers near your current or future calling location. See also *SprintNet, Tymnet,* and *DataPac.*

Address Book   This feature of your AOL software, accessible by double-clicking on its icon when addressing E-mail or by choosing it under your Mail menu, allows you to store screen names for easy access while composing mail. See also *E-mail* and *screen name.*

AFK   Abbreviation for *away from keyboard.* Used in chat/conference rooms and in instant messages to tell people that you are not going to be in front of your computer for awhile and that queries may not be answered during that time. Upon return, you use BAK to indicate that you are *back at keyboard.* See also *abbreviations* and *BAK.*

Alt key   The Alt key is a special function key on the PC keyboard. It is the key with the letters *Alt* on it and is usually located near the space bar. It is used for accessing menu functions and may be used for special-purpose functions within some applications.

America Online, Inc.   Formerly Quantum Computer Services, this parent company runs three online services—America Online, PC-Link, and Q-Link. America Online's stock exchange symbol is *AMER* on NASDAQ. Compare with *CompuServe Information Service, PC-Link,* and *Prodigy.*

AOL   *AOL* is the most common abbreviation for America Online, Inc. See also *America Online, Inc.*

ARC   An older compression utility that was the PC standard prior to ZIP. This utility compresses one or more files into a smaller file—called an *archive*—that has the extension ARC. The smaller the file, the faster you can download it. See also *archive, download, file compression, PKZip,* and *StuffIt.*

archive   (1) A file or files compressed into a smaller, single file using compression software. (2) A file, usually available in Computing Forum software libraries, consisting of compilations of message board postings that (usually) have been removed from a message board due to inactivity or lack of message board space. See also *file compression, ARC, PKZip,* and *StuffIt.*

attached file/attachment   A file from your computer, or another's, sent in conjunction with E-mail. The file is separate from the actual message contained within the E-mail item and is downloadable to your computer. An attached file is uploaded or downloaded, but it is a separate entity from files contained within AOL's software libraries. See also *E-mail* and *FlashMail.*

auditoriums   Auditoriums are online *chat rooms* designed to allow large groups of AOL members (up to 300) to meet in a highly organized setting. Auditoriums are divided into two parts: the stage, where the host and the guests are located, and the chat rows, where the audience is located. Communication between the audience and people "on stage" is accomplished through the use of special tools. Unless specifically enabled, audience chat is seen only by members in the same chat row. See also *chat rooms.*

BAK   Abbreviation for *back at keyboard.* Used in chat/conference rooms and in instant messages to tell people that you are back in front of your computer after a break and that you are available for queries. When you leave your computer, you use AFK to indicate *away from keyboard.* See also *abbreviations* and *AFK.*

Banner   See *Network News.*

baud   A unit for measuring the speed of serial (as opposed to parallel) data transmission. Not the same as bps, but often used as a conceptual equivalent. See also *bits per second.*

BBS   See *bulletin board system.*

bcc   See *blind carbon copy.*

bits per second (bps)   A method of measuring data transmission speed. Currently, 300, 1200, 2400, 9600, and 14,400 bps are supported on AOL. See also *baud.*

blind carbon copy (bcc)   A blind carbon copy used in E-mail directs a duplicate of the E-mail to a third party and specifically excludes the recipient's name from the list of people included in the body of the received E-mail form. The recipient who is *bcc'd* is said to be blind to other recipients. See also *E-mail* and *carbon copy.*

board   See *message board.*

bps   See *bits per second.*

BRB   Abbreviation for *be right back.* Used in chats, instant messages, and other areas where live interaction occurs online. See also *abbreviations, chat rooms,* and *shorthand.*

browse   Casual examination of messages or file lists, rather than a specific examination of the messages or file descriptions.

bulletin board system (BBS)   A central system accessed using a computer, a modem, and phone lines, or a network connection, where data is placed by users for dissemination to one or more other users. America Online is considered a BBS, but most BBSs are much smaller than AOL and are often run on a single microcomputer with a single phone line in a hobbyist environment. See also *message board* and *message center.*

carbon copy (cc)   The act of sending E-mail to a third party who may have only a secondary or casual interest in the content of said E-mail. A person who is *cc'd* is also usually not expected to participate or provide a reactive position to the E-mail. See also *E-mail* and *blind carbon copy.*

cc   See *carbon copy.*

Center Stage   Center Stage is the People Connection's primary auditorium, located in the People Connection department or by using the keyword *Center Stage.* See also *auditoriums.*

chat protocol   See *protocol.*

chat rooms   Online "rooms"—that is, special windows—where America Online members congregate and interact by typing messages to one another in real time. See also *auditoriums, conference room, Guide,* and *host.*

CIS (CI$)   See *CompuServe Information Service.*

Command key   A special function key on the Macintosh keyboard, the Command key is located near the space bar and contains the and ⌘ symbols. This key is also called the *Open-Apple key.* See also *Control key* and *Option key.*

Comment to Staff   This button is available in file libraries while viewing the File Descriptions. Clicking on this button brings up a form in which you may compose and send a note to the AOL staff responsible for that library. On the PC platform it is labeled *Ask The Staff.* This form is not transmitted to the uploaders of the files. See also *library, download,* and *upload.*

compression   See *file compression.*

CompuServe Information Service (CIS or CI$)   One of the first commercial online services, similar to America Online but with more databases available and less emphasis on community and graphical interface. CompuServe Information Service is owned by H&R Block. It may be referred to as *CIS* or *CI$* in shorthand during chat. (The latter designation is a humorous reference to the view that CompuServe is a costlier service than America Online). Compare with *America Online, PC-Link,* and *Prodigy.*

conference room   A special chat room designed to hold 48 people rather than the 23 of People Connection rooms. While chats are usually spontaneous and ongoing affairs, conferences are usually held periodically, and are more structured. Examples of conference rooms can be found in any of the Computing & Software forums, such as the Macintosh Multimedia Forum or the PC Applications Forum. See also *chat rooms* and *protocol.*

Control key   The Control key is a special function key on the PC and Macintosh. It is the one with the letters *Ctrl* or *Control* on it. On the PC, the Ctrl key is equivalent to the Macintosh's Command key (⌘) in the America Online environment. See also *Command key, Option key,* and *Alt key.*

CS Live   See *Tech Live.*

Customer Relations   America Online's Customer Relations Hotline is open Monday through Friday from 9 AM to 2 AM Eastern time, and noon to 9 PM on weekends. Call 1-800-827-6364 during these hours. See also *Tech Live.*

cyberspace   A virtual world created by our computers. No physical entities are present in cyberspace, but intellectual interaction is accomplished through the collective connections of many people. See also *Online community.*

database   A database is an organized collection of information, usually maintained by a computer and often searchable. An example of this is the Online Encyclopedia found by using the keyword *Encyclopedia.*

DataPac   A packet-switching network operated by Bell Canada that provides local access numbers for Canadian members at an extra fee. Canadians living near the U.S. border can usually dial a U.S. access number to avoid the extra charge and pay less in toll charges than the Datapac surcharge. See also *access number, node, SprintNet,* and *Tymnet.*

demoware   Software that can be downloaded and used for evaluation, but that is functionally disabled in some areas and/or ceases to operate after a certain length of use. See also *shareware, freeware,* and *public domain.*

department   This is the broadest category of information into which America Online divides its material. The Departments window can be brought up from anywhere online by pressing ⌘-D from a Macintosh, Ctrl+D from a PC, or by selecting Departments from the Go To menu in your menu bar.

Directory of Services   A searchable database that allows AOL members to quickly locate AOL's available services. This database is available at the keyword *Dir. of Services* or by selecting Directory of Services from the Go To menu.

download   The movement of information or files located on a remote host computer to a storage device of your choosing on your computer. Most commonly used to describe the act of transferring files from AOL's libraries to your hard drive for use after disconnecting from AOL. Compare with *upload.* See also *file compression.*

download count   The download count is the number of times a file has been downloaded from AOL and is often used to measure a file's popularity. (In other words, 50,000 AOL members can't be wrong!)

Download Manager   A function in the AOL software that allows you to create and manage a list of files for later downloading. See also *download* and *FlashMail.*

E-mail   Short for *electronic mail,* E-mail is one or more private messages sent from one computer user to another or to a group of users. Using America Online's E-mail, you can send messages to other members or to people who can receive mail through the Internet.

emoticons   A combination of keyboard characters, mostly consisting of punctuation, that convey information about the emotional state of the user. They usually appear sideways; for example, you can type **:)** to indicate a smile. This emoticon might be the original one and also is probably the source of the term *smileys,* which refers to all emoticons. A short list of emoticons is available in Chapter 6 and at the keyword *Shorthand.* See also *shorthand* and *chat rooms.*

FAQ   Abbreviation for *frequently asked questions,* usually in the form of a question-and-answer text file. FAQs are posted to help newcomers find answers to common concerns.

file compression   A technique by which many computer files can be reduced to half (or even less) of their original size. Though they must be decompressed to be used, compressed files take up much less storage space than their uncompressed counterparts, and require far less time to transfer via the AOL system or any modem. File compression comes in many flavors, the most common of which are StuffIt, DiskDoubler, and Compact Pro for the Macintosh. PC users have PKZip, ARC, and others. See also *download.*

FlashMail   This America Online feature allows you to automate the sending and receiving of E-mail and attachments, as well as retrieve files listed for later download in your Download Manager. See also *attached file/ attachment, download, Download Manager,* and *E-mail.*

forum   AOL's forums are areas where people with similar interests visit to share their ideas, opinions, and comments, and to download or upload software. Most forums offer message boards, articles, chat rooms, and libraries organized in a forum format accessible by an AOL keyword. Forums are overseen by Hosts or Forum Leaders; for example, in the

Macintosh Computing & Software department, each forum has a Forum Leader (denoted by *AFL* at the beginning of the screen name), who is assisted by Forum Assistants (AFA), Forum Consultants (AFC), and Technical Assistants (AFT). See also *Forum Leader/Assistant/Consultant/ Technical Assistant*.

Forum Leader/Assistant/Consultant/Technical Assistant   These folks are considered staff members of AOL's forums, but are not usually employees of America Online. They moderate the various Computing & Software forums and maintain the file libraries and message boards of each. See also *forum*.

freeware   Software offered for distribution through general channels, including, but not limited to, online services such as AOL. Freeware is specifically copyrighted software for which no monetary charge is made by the author or developer, but to which the author or developer retains rights in accordance with U.S. copyright laws. See also *demoware* and *public domain*.

GA   Abbreviation for *go ahead,* often used during conferences with protocol. See also *protocol*.

gateway   A link to other types of telecommunications services, usually E-mail and other host computing environments. The Eaasy Sabre travel reservations service, for example, is an entirely separate system that is accessed by AOL users through a gateway. See also *Internet*.

Get a Member's Profile   Commonly called *Get Info,* a feature of America Online that allows you to easily retrieve and view a specific member's online profile, if he or she has provided one, by selecting Get a Member's Info from the Member menu, or by pressing ⌘-G (Ctrl+G for PC users) and typing a screen name. See also *member, Member Directory,* and *Member Profile*.

Get Info   See *Get a Member's Profile*.

GIF   See *Graphic Interchange Format*.

Graphic Interchange Format (GIF)   A type of graphic file that most computer platforms can read—the electronic version of photographic images. The GIF standard was developed by CompuServe as a standard for sharing graphical information across platforms.

Guide   Guides are AOL members who specialize in helping other members in the various chat rooms of People Connection.

Guide Pager   An AOL feature allowing you to page a Guide when there is a problem in a chat or conference room. See also *Guide* and *TOS*.

Help room   Online "rooms" where members can go to get interactive help with using their AOL software or service, as well as assistance in finding files and areas of special interest online. Help rooms are located in the People Connection area and in the Members' Online Support area. See also *Guide, Members Helping Members,* and *Tech Live*.

host   (1) The main computer system of a BBS, such as America Online. AOL's host consists of a high-speed computer network, containing both mini- and microcomputers, as described in this book's Introduction. (2) An AOL member who facilitates discussion in chat rooms.

icon   A pictographic representation of a command or request. When you click on an icon with your mouse, the computer usually takes some form of action.

Ignore   (1) The feature that allows a member to stop another member's chat room text from appearing on their screen. (2) The ability to designate specific users from whom you wish to not receive E-mail.

IM   See *instant message*.

Information Provider (IP)   A person who provides time and effort to, and is responsible for, the content of specific areas on America Online. An AFL (AOL Forum Leader), for example, is also referred to as an *IP*. See also *Remote Staff*.

instant message (IM)   Instant messaging is a way to have a private interactive "meeting" with another AOL member online. By choosing Send Instant Message from the Member menu, you can have a one-on-one mini-chat with another AOL member. IMs may also be thought of as private rooms for two—and only two—people at a time, although multiple IM windows can be open on your screen at any given time. See also *E-mail* and *chat rooms*.

Internet   The Internet can be thought of as a meganetwork of computer networks, which are interconnected at all times. The Internet began in 1969 as a Defense Department computer network and today spans the globe, connecting more than 100,000 machines, many of which serve as hubs for local networks that each serve numerous users. The Internet is maintained by the National Science Foundation. AOL offers Internet E-mail, the USENET Newsgroup information service, and other Internet services.

IP   See *Information Provider.*

keyboard shortcuts   The AOL software provides keyboard command equivalents for menu selections. For example, rather than using your mouse to select Send Instant Message from your menu, you can press ⌘-I on a Mac or Ctrl+I on a PC.

keyword   (1) Keywords are shortcuts to specific destinations within America Online; they allow you to move instantaneously to a different area. You can jump directly to Time Online, for instance, by using the keyword *Time*. To use a keyword, press ⌘-K (Ctrl+K if you use a PC), type the keyword, and then press Return (or Enter on a PC). (2) A word or words you feel are likely to match one or more entries in a database or file collection. You would use the keyword or combination of keywords in the search form to look for entries matching your needs.

library   An area containing files that you can download or to which you can upload files. The files can be of any type—text, graphics, software, or sounds—and are intended to be transferred to a storage device on your own computer.

line noise   Spurious noise on telephone lines that is often heard as clicks or static and that tends to interfere with computer communications via modem. Line noise on your telephone line can sometimes abruptly terminate an online connection.

Lobby   The Lobby is AOL's primary public chat room. Members can stop by the Lobby at any time to chat with other members or to see a list of other public rooms. It's also the gateway to America Online's *People Connection.*

LOL   Common shorthand for *laughing out loud,* often used in chat rooms and instant message conversations. See also *abbreviations, emoticons,* and *shorthand.*

lurk   To sit in a chat or conference room and say nothing or very little.

member   A customer of America Online.

Member Directory   A listing of AOL member screen names that have profiles. To be included in this database, you simply need to create your own Member Profile. You can get to the Member Directory by using the keyword *Members*. See also *member, Member Profile,* and *Get a Member's Info.*

Member Profile An optional online information document that provides a brief description of the AOL member. In addition to your name, you can provide (for others to see) such information as your city, birthday, gender, marital status, hobbies, computers you use, occupation, and favorite quotation. This feature can be explored in the area located at the keyword *Members* or *Profile*. See also *member* and *Member Directory*.

Members Helping Members (MHM) A message board in the Members' Online Support area where America Online members can assist and get assistance from other members. The keyword is *MHM*. See also *Help room*.

menu A text- or graphical-based window containing a list of options or commands you can use to initiate an action or select an item. Menus can be located anywhere on the computer screen, but most frequently they are in a menu bar at the top of the screen or window.

message board An area where members can post messages, typically to solicit a reply or to comment on a prior message. See also *bulletin board system*.

message center A collection of message boards in one convenient area. See also *message board*.

MHM See *Members Helping Members*.

modem The word *modem* is short for *modulator/demodulator*. This peripheral device enables a computer to transfer data across telephone lines. Your computer interacts with America Online through a modem.

Network News An announcement that appears intermittently on members' screens promoting one of AOL's services/events, broadcasting AOL maintenance information, and/or providing member feedback. Also known as a *Banner*.

newbie Affectionate term for a new member (a member for less than six months). Newbies are often found in the Beginners' Forum, for which the keyword is *ABF*.

node The geographical point at which you first connect to the communications network after your modem dials its local access number when connecting to America Online. See also *SprintNet, Tymnet,* and *Datapac*.

online Refers to the state of your America Online connection when you are actually connected to the AOL service through your modem.

Online community A group of people bound together by their shared interest or characteristic of interacting with other computer users through online services, BBSs, or networks. See also *cyberspace*.

Online Host The pseudo-screen name of AOL's host computer. Online Host will, at your choosing, inform you when a member enters or leaves a chat room if you are on a PC platform system. On all platforms except PC-Link, the Online Host will also show you the result of your rolling the AOL dice. See also *chat room, conference room, auditoriums,* and *//roll*.

Online Profile See *Member Profile*.

Open-Apple key See *Command key*.

Option key A special modifier key commonly found on Macintosh keyboards and used for typing special characters. See also *Command key*.

P* Shorthand for *Prodigy Service*. See also *Prodigy*.

Parental Chat Controls Parental Control enables the master account holder to restrict access to certain areas and features on AOL, such as blocking instant messages and rooms. It can be set for one or all screen names on the account. Once Parental Control is set for a particular screen name, it is active each time that screen name signs on. Changes can be made by the master account holder at any time. To access controls, use the keyword *Parental Control*.

PC-Link (PCL) America Online Inc.'s service for PC users, which uses a DeskMate-style interface with special support areas provided by the Tandy Corporation (Tandy Headquarters in PC-Link Basic, for example). Compare with *CompuServe* and *Prodigy*. See also *America Online, Inc.*

People Connection (PC) The AOL department dedicated to real-time chat. Many different rooms can be found here: Lobbies, officially sanctioned rooms, member-created rooms, private rooms, the Center Stage Auditorium, and PC Studio. You can access this area with the keyword *People*.

PKZip A compression utility for PCs to compress one or more files into a smaller file (called an *archive*), which makes for shorter up/downloading. See also *archive, download, file compression, ARC,* and *StuffIt*.

post (1) The act of putting something online, usually into a message board. (2) A message in a message board.

private room   A chat room created by a member via an option in People Connection where the name is not public knowledge. To enter this room, a member must first know the exact name used to originally create it. This arrangement provides an area where people may converse without fear of interruption by other uninvited members.

Prodigy   This online service, founded as a joint venture between IBM and Sears, is currently one of the larger competitors faced by America Online. Prodigy's interface (with its continuous online advertising, screening of messages before they're allowed to be posted, and other quirks that make it seem like attending a chaperoned high school dance) differs from that of America Online. For all its drawbacks, Prodigy still has an enormous subscriber base. If you are among the astute members who defected from Prodigy to AOL, check out the Prodigy Refugees Forum, which you can get to by using the keyword *Prodigy*. Compare with *America Online, Inc.* and *CompuServe*.

Profile   See *Member Profile*.

protocol   The procedure used in conference rooms to keep order and ensure orderly discussion. When you have a question, you type a question mark (?); when you have a comment, you type an exclamation mark (!); and when you are finished, you type *ga*. A queue of those waiting with questions and answers is displayed at regular points throughout the conference, and members are invited to speak by the moderator or host. It is considered impolite and a breach of protocol to speak out of turn. See also *conference room*.

public domain   Public domain software is completely free software and not copyrighted, so you can use it any way you wish. See also *demoware*, *freeware*, and *shareware*.

punt   The process of being knocked offline (disconnected), usually as a result of a problem with telephone line noise, your local access number, or the AOL host computer.

Q-Link   America Online's service for Commodore 64 and 128 users. See also *America Online, Inc.*

Remote Staff   These are members who staff the various forums and areas but are not employees of AOL; they work from their homes. Usually these are Guides, Hosts, Forum Leaders, Assistants, Consultants, or Technical Assistants.

return receipt   Somewhat like its post office counterpart, it is a message you receive indicating that the E-mail you've sent has been read by a particular recipient.

revolving door   A chat or conference room has a *revolving door* when members are quickly moving in and out of the room.

//roll   A unique command used in any People Connection or other chat room to roll the AOL Dice. Its default is to produce two random numbers imitating the roll of two six-sided dice; for example, you might see

```
OnlineHost: JLR63 rolled 2 6-sided dice: 6 4
```

You can also roll other combinations of dice by varying the number of dice and the number of sides on each die. The proper use of this command is //roll-dicenn-sidesnnn, where *nn* is 1–15 and *nnn* is 1–999.

It is outside the rules of etiquette to roll dice in public chat rooms without explicit invitation by a host or by previously set ground rules, such as when role-playing in the Red Dragon Inn. Invitations to roll dice are sometimes issued in chats where prizes are offered to the winners by the host. Rolling the AOL Dice is an online form of *drawing straws*.

Rotunda   An auditorium that features conferences with companies or renowned guests in the Computing & Software department. The keyword is *Rotunda*. See also *auditoriums*.

screen name   Screen names are the pseudonyms used by America Online members to identify themselves online. See also *Member* and *Member Profile*.

scroll   (1) In a chat or conference, the act of repeatedly typing similar words on-screen, spacing out the letters of a word, or sending multiple lines of chat in rapid sequence in such a fashion as to be disruptive. (2) Refers to the movement of incoming text and other information on-screen.

self-extracting archive   Most compressed files must be decompressed using the same software that compressed them originally. A self-extracting file, on the other hand, contains not only the compressed data, but also the program information necessary to decompress itself.

shareware   Shareware is software provided for evaluation by the author or developer for a set period of time before payment is required. Most shareware is distributed through BBSs and online services and almost always contains the necessary disclaimers and conditions that the downloader must legally adhere to, including the payment of fees. See also *demoware, freeware,* and *public domain.*

shorthand   Used during chats and in message boards, E-mail, and instant messages. A brief list of these is available at the keyword *Shorthand.* See also *abbreviations* and *emoticons.*

smileys   See *shorthand* and *emoticons.*

snail mail   Mail sent via the U.S. Postal Service. Not E-mail. Derogatory in origin, this term refers to the legendary slowness of conventional mail delivery methods.

SprintNet   Formerly known as Telenet, SprintNet is a data network providing AOL members 1200, 2400, 9600, and 14,400 bps local access numbers to America Online. SprintNet networks are owned and operated by US Sprint. To find SprintNet local access numbers, use the keyword Numbers. See also *Tymnet* and *Datapac.*

Stratus   The name of the computer system on which America Online runs its service. Actually, the AOL system includes a distributed network that consists not only of Stratus computers, but computers from other manufacturers as well.

StuffIt   StuffIt is the trade name of a specific type of Macintosh file-compression software published by Aladdin Systems. Various versions of StuffIt are distributed, in both shareware and commercial forms, on almost every online service, including AOL. See also *file compression, download,* and *upload.*

SYSOP   Acronym for *system operator,* a person who runs a bulletin board system. See *Forum Leader/Assistant/Consultant/Technical Assistant* and *Information Provider.*

Tech Live   Also known as *CS Live.* A free area for members to interactively ask questions and obtain assistance from AOL's Tech Support staff. The Tech Live Auditorium is open from 9 AM to 2 AM Eastern time, Monday through Friday, and from 12 PM to 9 PM Saturday and Sunday. This service is available by using the keyword *CS Live.*

TOS   An abbreviation for *terms of service*—it amounts to your contract with America Online. When you join the service, you agree to abide by these terms, which apply to all America Online accounts. The areas covered by AOL's terms of service include General Information, Payment

Information, Third-Party Sales and Service, Termination Information, Disclaimer and Liability Notices, Online Conduct, America Online Software License, Copyright Notices, Information Supplied By Members, Electronic Mail, and Other Provisions. You can read these terms at the keyword *TOS*. Also included are avenues of reporting TOS violations to America Online.

Tymnet   A computer data network providing AOL members with 1200 and 2400 bps local access numbers to America Online. Tymnet networks are owned and operated by MCI/BT Tymnet. To find Tymnet local access numbers, use the keyword *Numbers* or call 1-800-336-0149. See also *Datapac, SprintNet,* and *access number.*

Uniform   As used on America Online, a screen name preceded by a prefix of 2–8 letters, and a personal name or initials indicating the title of a Remote Staff person. These special prefixes and their definitions include the following:

Prefix	Definition
Advisor	AOL staffer
AFL	Apple/Mac Forum Leader
AFA	Apple/Mac Forum Assistant
AFC	Apple/Mac Forum Consultant
AFT	Apple/Mac Forum Technical Assistant
CNR	CNN News Room staff
CSS	Company Support Staff
Guide	General system guide
GWRep	GeoWorks Representative
IC	Industry Connection
NPR	National Public Radio Outreach staff
OMNI	OMNI Magazine Online staff
PC	PC Forum Leader
PCA	PC Forum Assistant
PCC	PC Forum Consultant

(continues)

Appendixes

Prefix	Definition
PCW	PC World Online
PG	AOL Portrait Gallery staff
PS1	PS1 Connection staff
Teacher	IES Teacher
TECHLive	Tech Live representative
VGS	Video Game Systems staff
WCC	Chicago Online/Windy City chat staff

See also *Guide, Forum Leader/Assistant/Consultant,* and *Remote Staff.*

upload   The transfer of files from your computer to AOL's host computer. Uploaded files may be attached to E-mail (these files are more frequently referred to as *attached files*), or they may be uploaded for inclusion in a library. Attached files are typically intended for a single recipient, whereas library files are for all to see and use once the file has been reviewed and released by the library staff. Generally, to make the transfer faster and therefore save money, you should compress any file over 16K (with the exception of text files) before uploading it. Approved compression formats are ZIP, ARC, SIT, and SEAs. Compare with *download.* See also *file compression* and *library.*

virus   Computer software that can attach itself to other software or files without the permission or knowledge of the user. Viruses are generally designed with one intent: to propagate themselves. They might be intentionally destructive; however, not all virus damage is intentional. Some benign viruses suffer from having been poorly written and have been known to cause damage as well. Virus-prevention software and information may be found by using the keyword *Virus* on the Mac or *McAfee* on the PC.

zip   See *PKZip.*

Index

Symbols